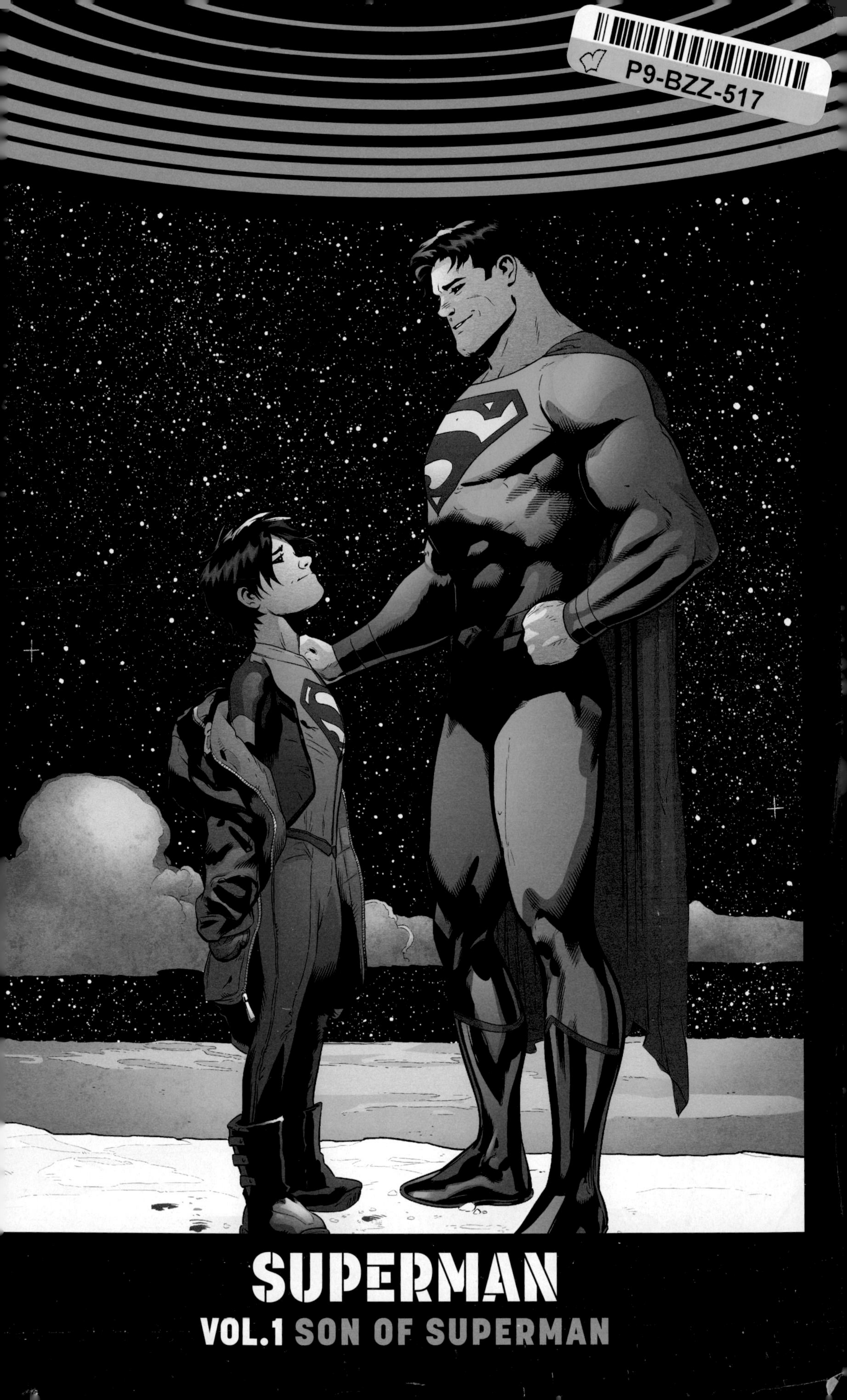

SUPERMAN

VOL.1 SON OF SUPERMAN

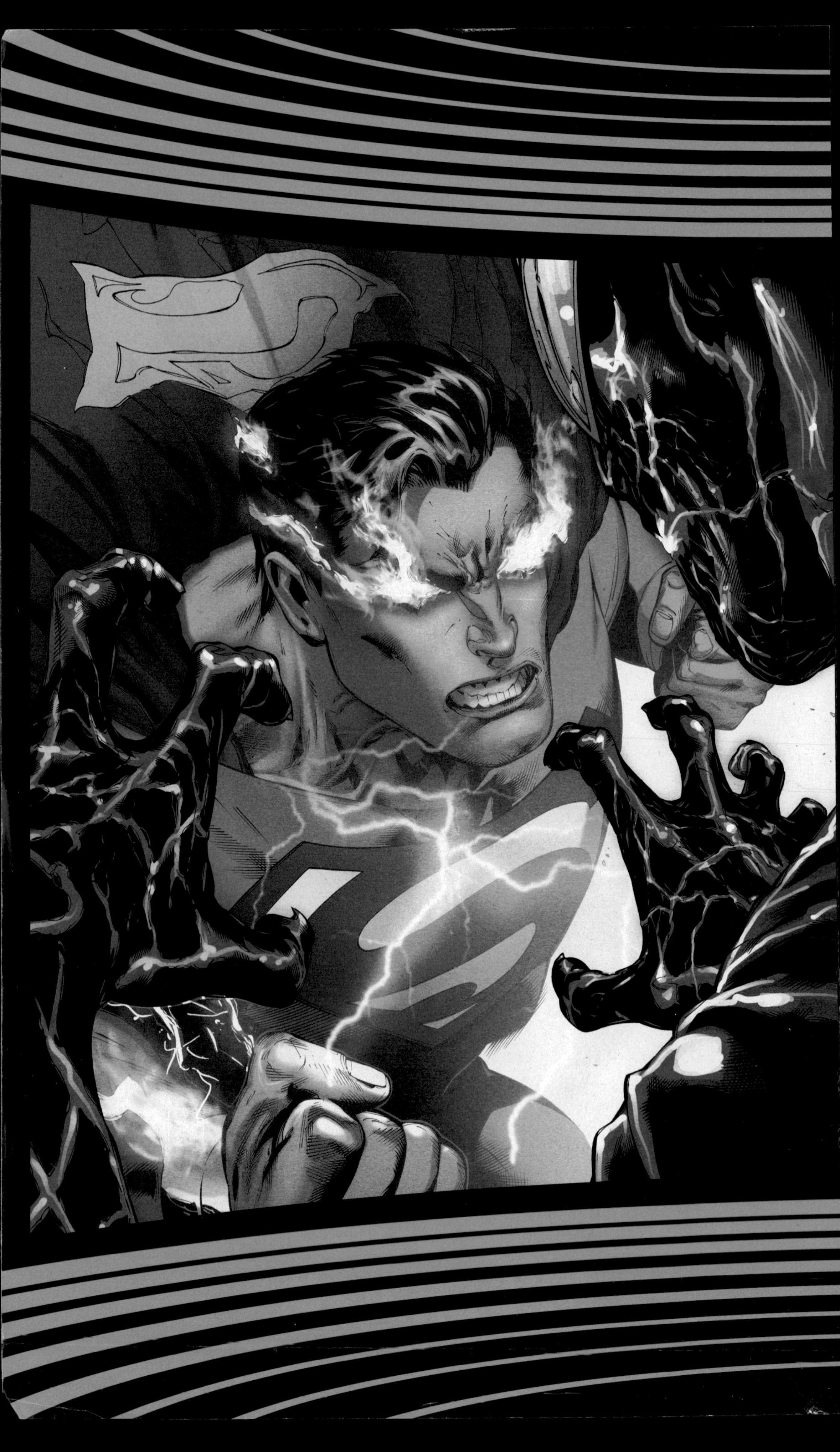

SUPERMAN
VOL.1 SON OF SUPERMAN

PETER J. TOMASI and **PATRICK GLEASON**
writers

PATRICK GLEASON * **DOUG MAHNKE**
JORGE JIMENEZ * **MICK GRAY**
JAIME MENDOZA
artists

JOHN KALISZ * **WIL QUINTANA**
ALEJANDRO SANCHEZ
colorists

ROB LEIGH
letterer

DOUG MAHNKE, JAIME MENDOZA and **WIL QUINTANA**
collection cover artists

PATRICK GLEASON, MICK GRAY & JOHN KALISZ
DOUG MAHNKE, JAIME MENDOZA & WIL QUINTANA
DOUG MAHNKE & WIL QUINTANA
original series cover artists

SUPERMAN created by **JERRY SIEGEL** and **JOE SHUSTER**
By special arrangement with the Jerry Siegel family

EDDIE BERGANZA Editor - Original Series ◆ ANDREW MARINO Assistant Editor - Original Series
JEB WOODARD Group Editor - Collected Editions ◆ SCOTT NYBAKKEN Editor - Collected Edition
STEVE COOK Design Director - Books ◆ AMIE BROCKWAY-METCALF Publication Design

BOB HARRAS Senior VP - Editor-in-Chief, DC Comics

DIANE NELSON President ◆ DAN DiDIO Publisher ◆ JIM LEE Publisher ◆ GEOFF JOHNS President & Chief Creative Officer
AMIT DESAI Executive VP - Business & Marketing Strategy, Direct to Consumer & Global Franchise Management
SAM ADES Senior VP - Direct to Consumer ◆ BOBBIE CHASE VP - Talent Development
MARK CHIARELLO Senior VP - Art, Design & Collected Editions ◆ JOHN CUNNINGHAM Senior VP - Sales & Trade Marketing
ANNE DePIES Senior VP - Business Strategy, Finance & Administration ◆ DON FALLETTI VP - Manufacturing Operations
LAWRENCE GANEM VP - Editorial Administration & Talent Relations ◆ ALISON GILL Senior VP - Manufacturing & Operations
HANK KANALZ Senior VP - Editorial Strategy & Administration ◆ JAY KOGAN VP - Legal Affairs
THOMAS LOFTUS VP - Business Affairs ◆ JACK MAHAN VP - Business Affairs
NICK J. NAPOLITANO VP - Manufacturing Administration ◆ EDDIE SCANNELL VP - Consumer Marketing
COURTNEY SIMMONS Senior VP - Publicity & Communications
JIM (SKI) SOKOLOWSKI VP - Comic Book Specialty Sales & Trade Marketing
NANCY SPEARS VP - Mass, Book, Digital Sales & Trade Marketing

SUPERMAN VOL. 1: SON OF SUPERMAN

DC Comics 2900 West Alameda Ave. Burbank, CA 91505
Printed by LSC Communications, Salem, VA, USA. 12/2/16.
First Printing.
ISBN: 978-1-4012-6776-6
Library of Congress Cataloging-in-Publication Data is available.

PEFC Certified

Printed on paper from
sustainably managed
forests, controlled
sources

PEFC/29-31-337   www.pefc.org

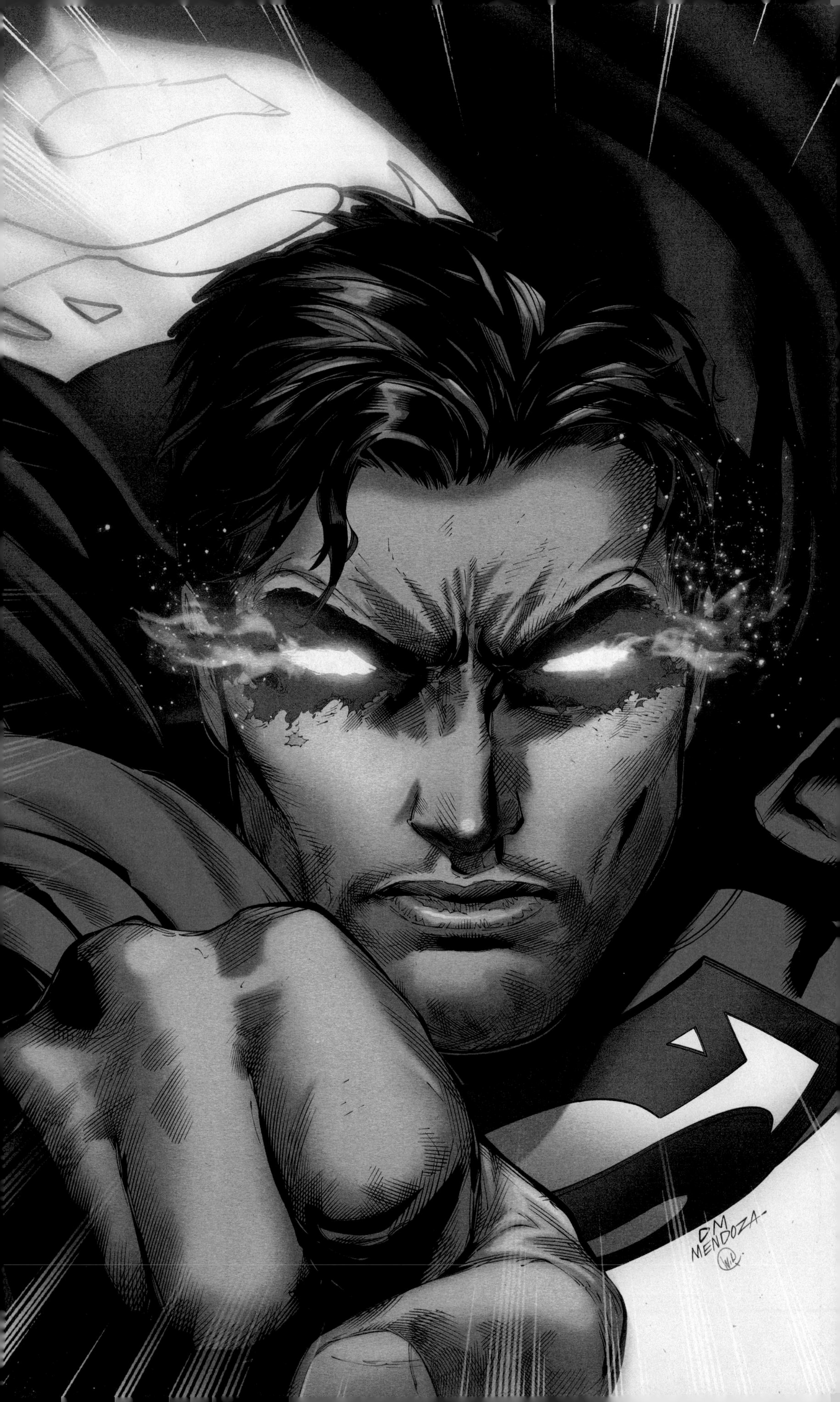
DM
MENDOZA

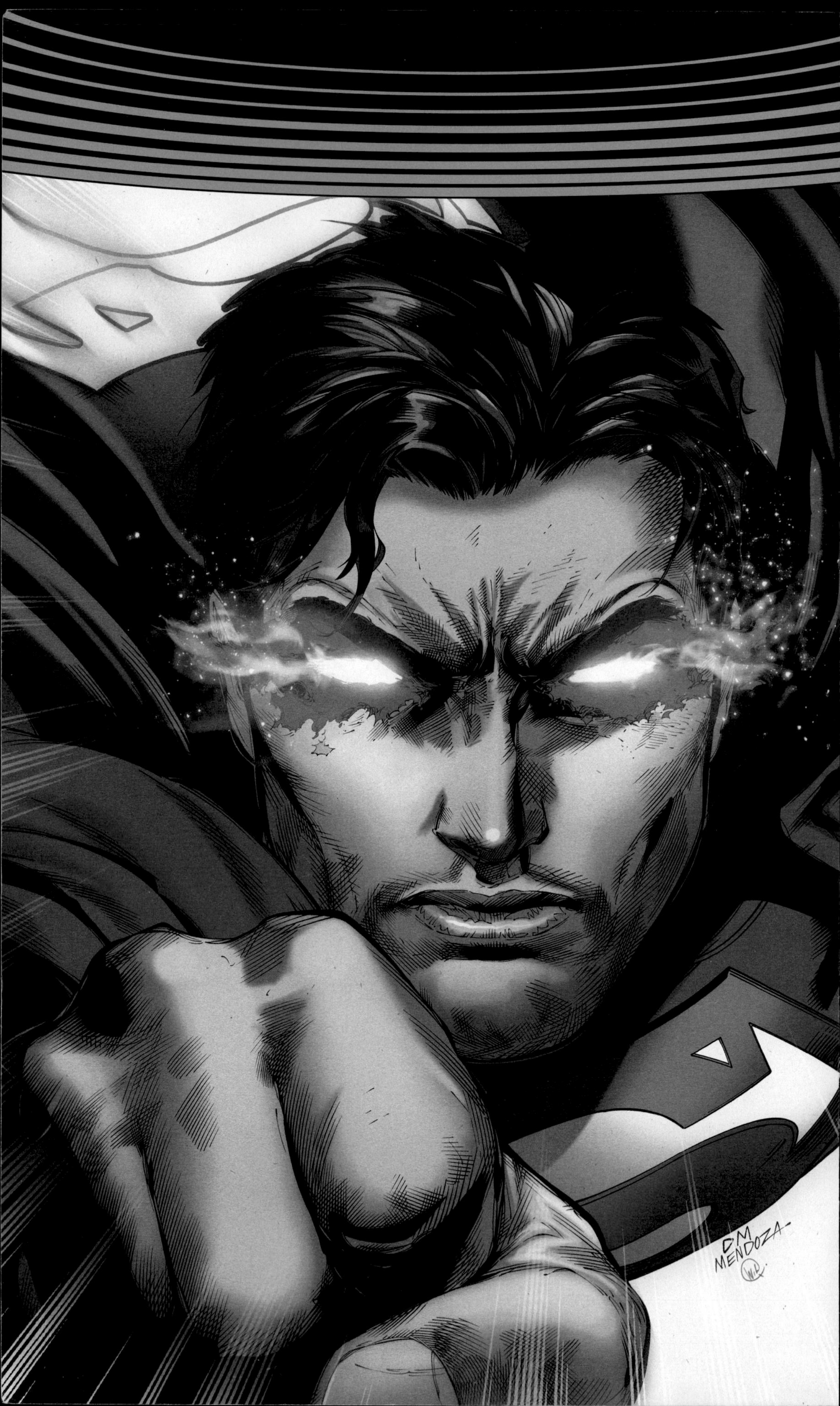
DM
MENDOZA

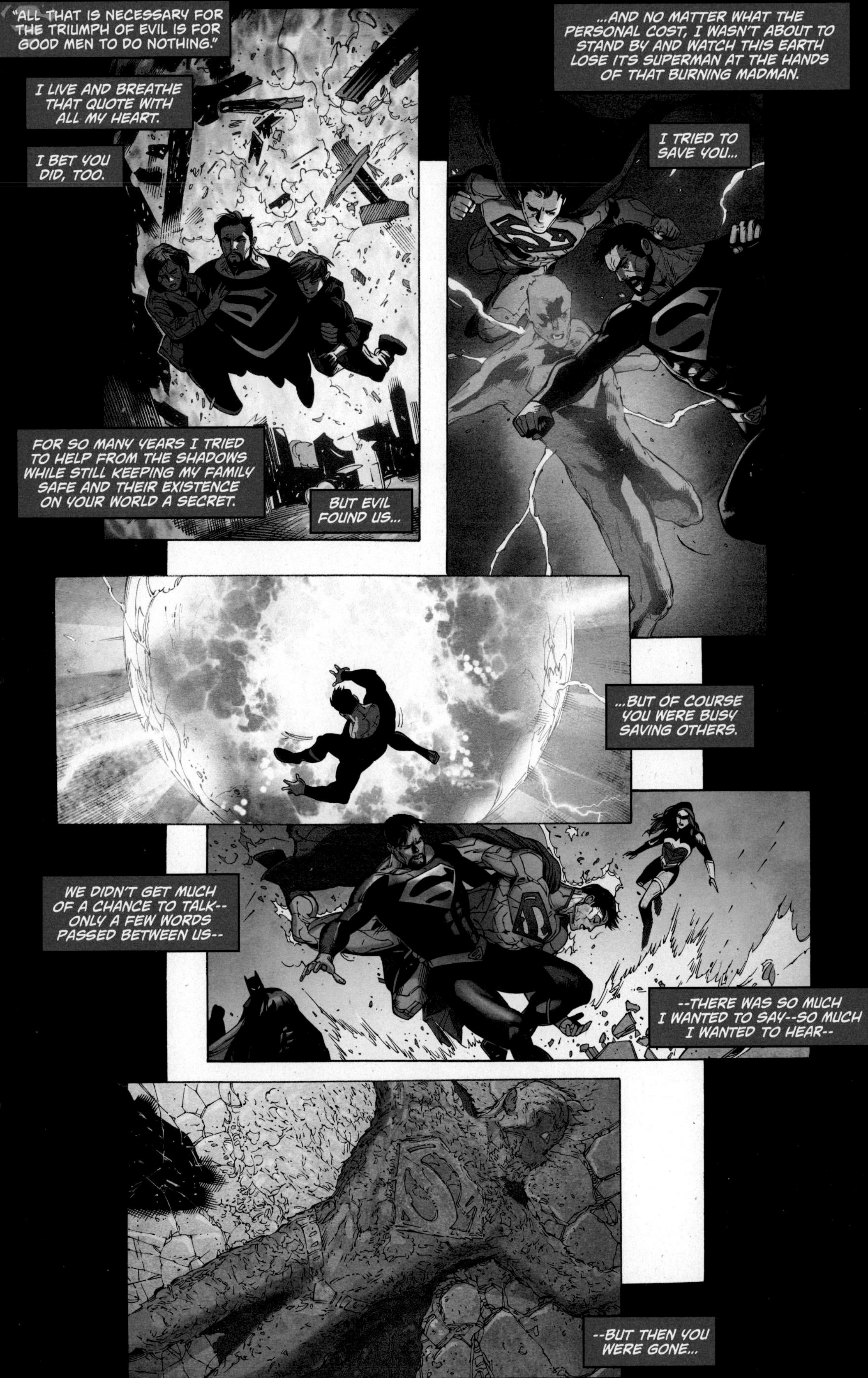
"ALL THAT IS NECESSARY FOR THE TRIUMPH OF EVIL IS FOR GOOD MEN TO DO NOTHING."
I LIVE AND BREATHE THAT QUOTE WITH ALL MY HEART.
I BET YOU DID, TOO.
FOR SO MANY YEARS I TRIED TO HELP FROM THE SHADOWS WHILE STILL KEEPING MY FAMILY SAFE AND THEIR EXISTENCE ON YOUR WORLD A SECRET.
BUT EVIL FOUND US...
...AND NO MATTER WHAT THE PERSONAL COST, I WASN'T ABOUT TO STAND BY AND WATCH THIS EARTH LOSE ITS SUPERMAN AT THE HANDS OF THAT BURNING MADMAN.
I TRIED TO SAVE YOU...
...BUT OF COURSE YOU WERE BUSY SAVING OTHERS.
WE DIDN'T GET MUCH OF A CHANCE TO TALK-- ONLY A FEW WORDS PASSED BETWEEN US--
--THERE WAS SO MUCH I WANTED TO SAY--SO MUCH I WANTED TO HEAR--
--BUT THEN YOU WERE GONE...

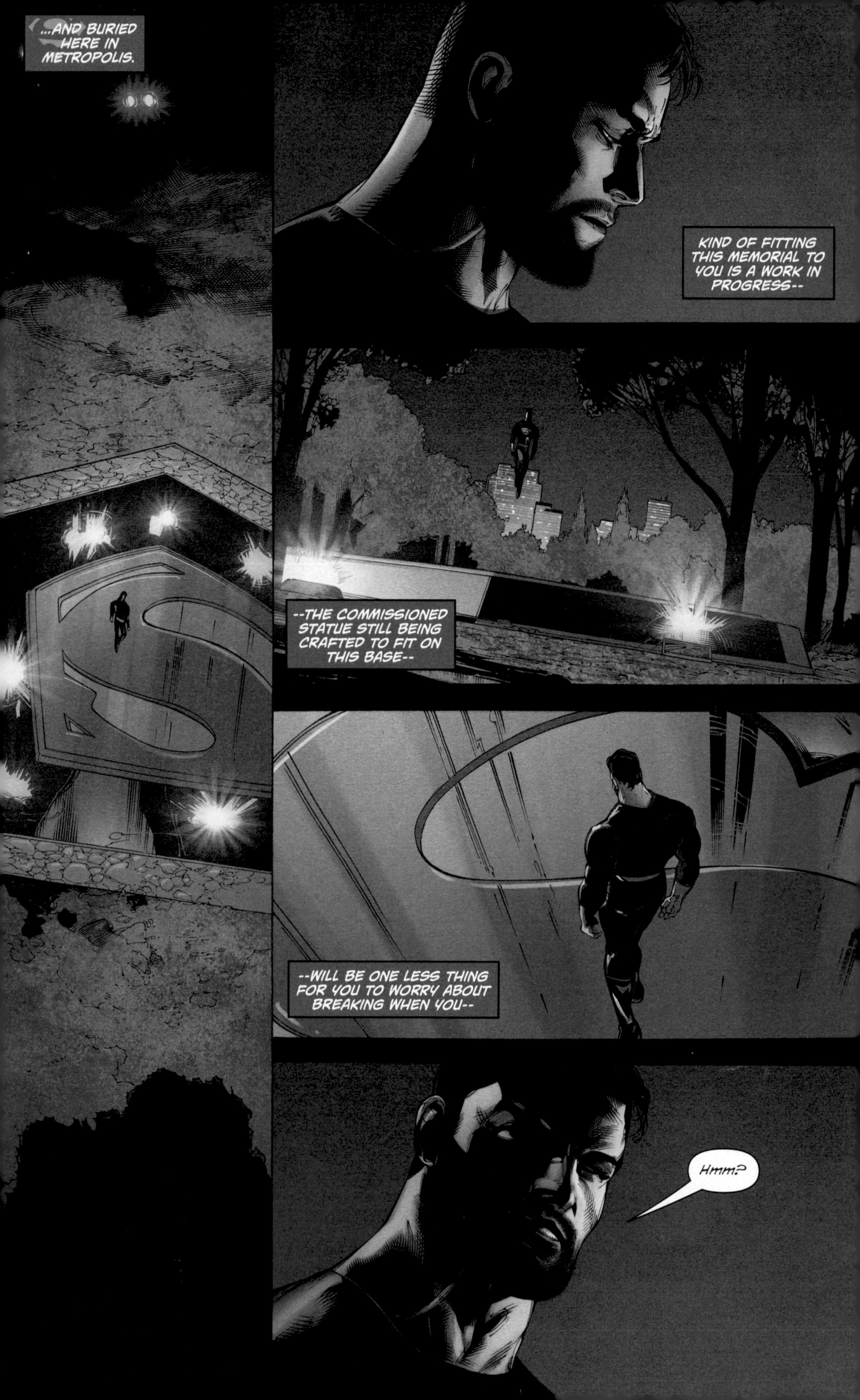
...AND BURIED HERE IN METROPOLIS.
KIND OF FITTING THIS MEMORIAL TO YOU IS A WORK IN PROGRESS--
--THE COMMISSIONED STATUE STILL BEING CRAFTED TO FIT ON THIS BASE--
--WILL BE ONE LESS THING FOR YOU TO WORRY ABOUT BREAKING WHEN YOU--
Hmm?

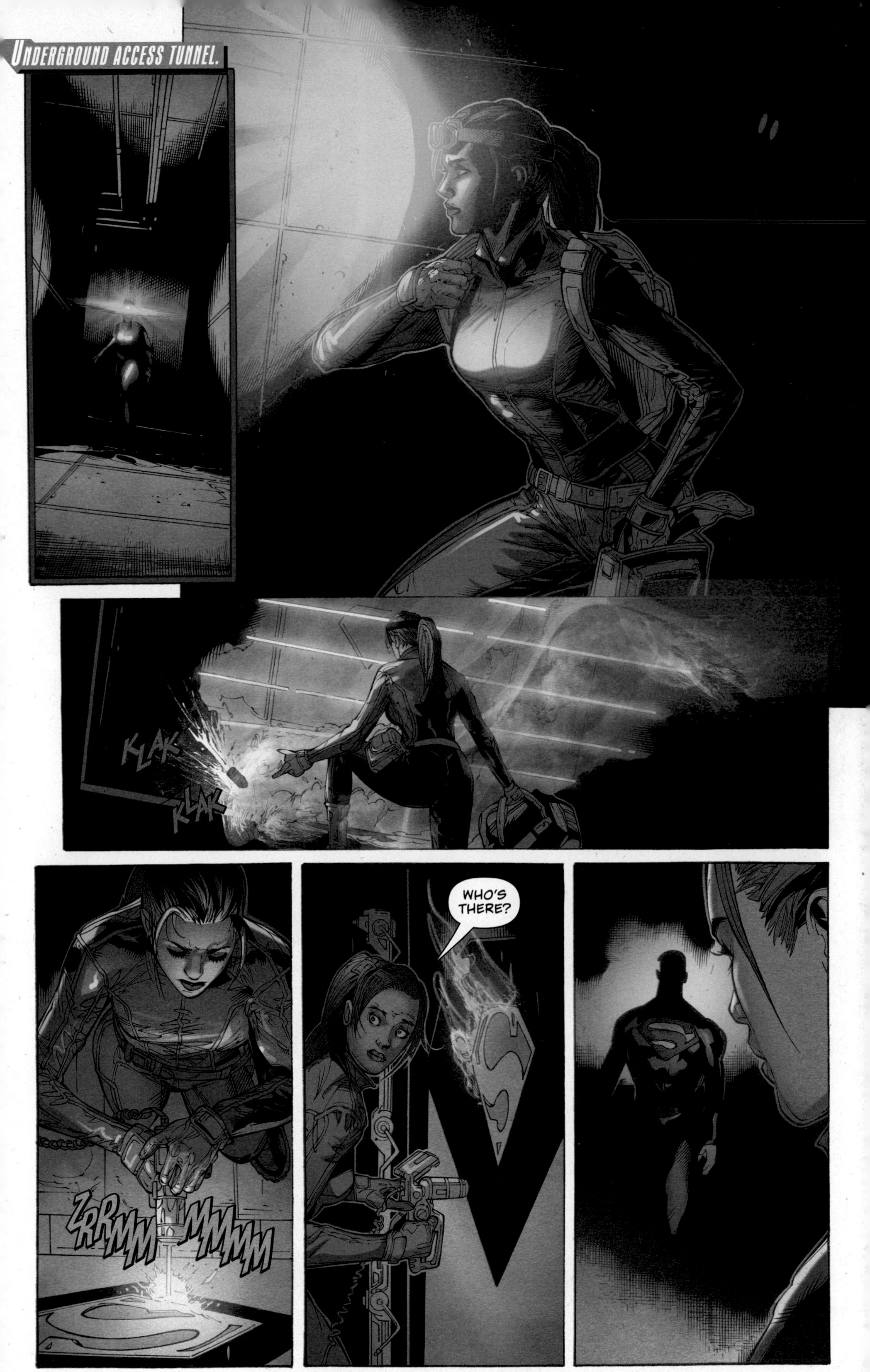

Underground access tunnel.
KLAK
KLAK
ZRRMM MMMM
WHO'S THERE?

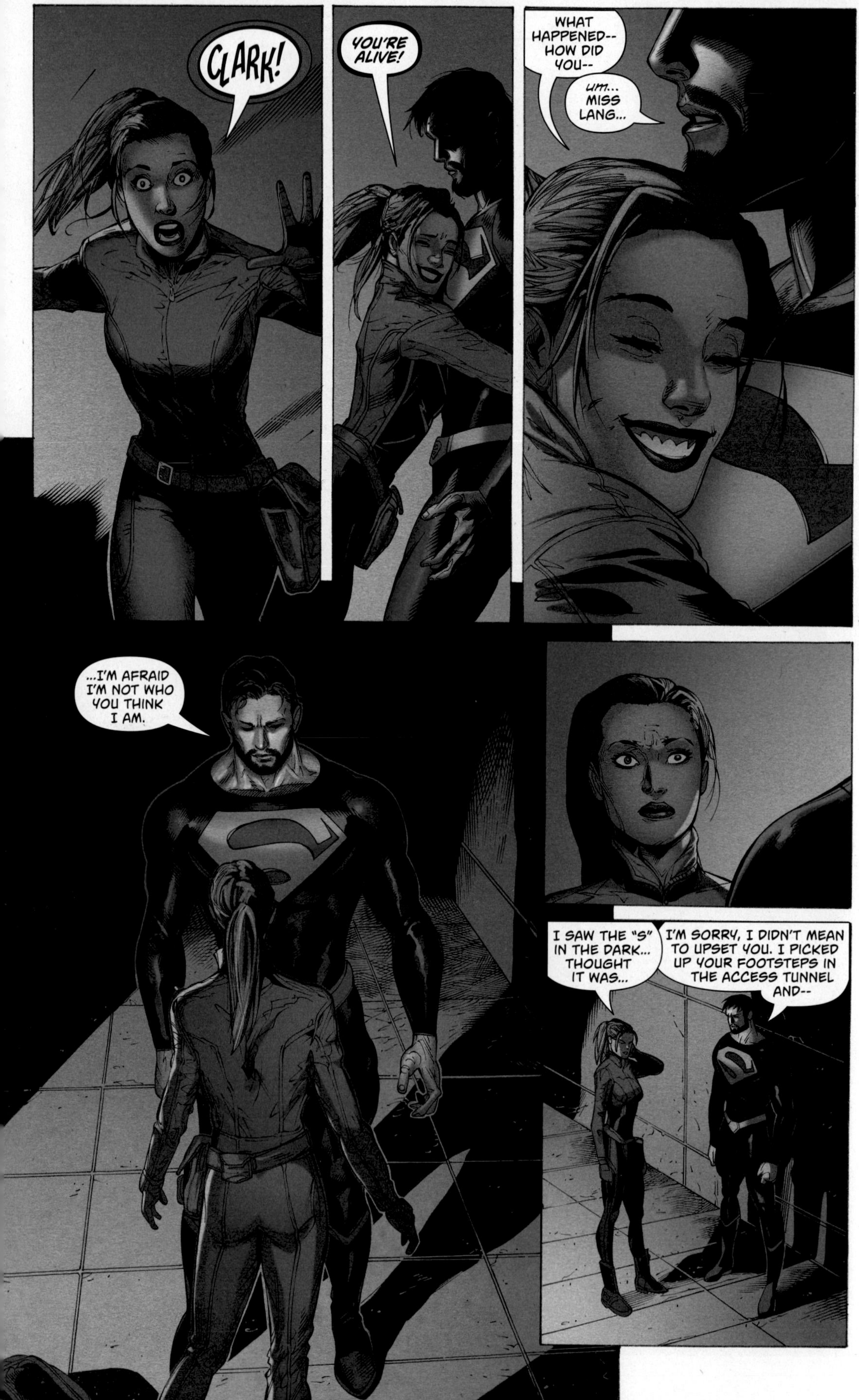
CLARK!
YOU'RE ALIVE!
WHAT HAPPENED-- HOW DID YOU--
UM... MISS LANG...
...I'M AFRAID I'M NOT WHO YOU THINK I AM.
I SAW THE "S" IN THE DARK... THOUGHT IT WAS...
I'M SORRY, I DIDN'T MEAN TO UPSET YOU. I PICKED UP YOUR FOOTSTEPS IN THE ACCESS TUNNEL AND--

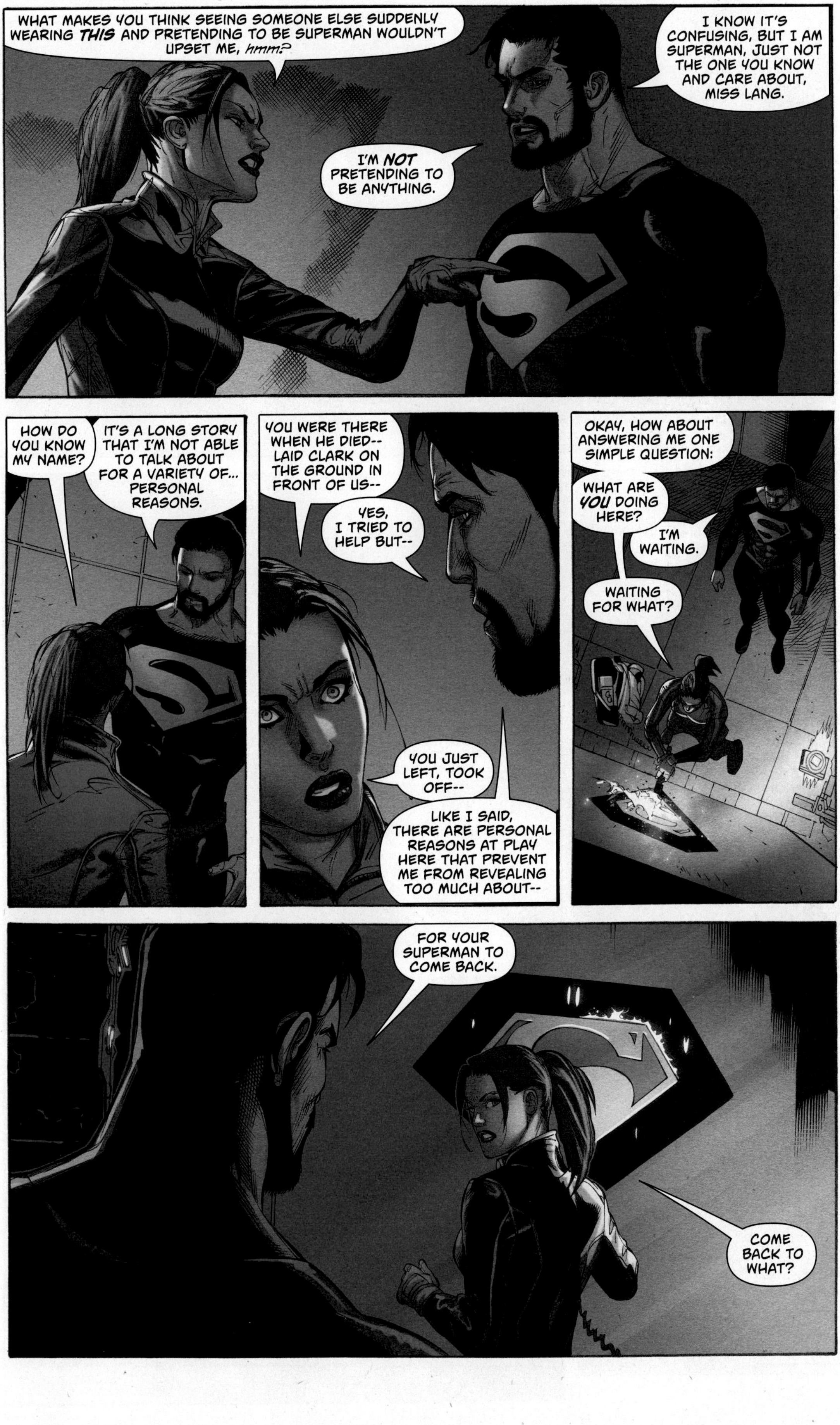
WHAT MAKES YOU THINK SEEING SOMEONE ELSE SUDDENLY WEARING *THIS* AND PRETENDING TO BE SUPERMAN WOULDN'T UPSET ME, *hmm?*
I'M *NOT* PRETENDING TO BE ANYTHING.
I KNOW IT'S CONFUSING, BUT I AM SUPERMAN, JUST NOT THE ONE YOU KNOW AND CARE ABOUT, MISS LANG.
HOW DO YOU KNOW MY NAME?
IT'S A LONG STORY THAT I'M NOT ABLE TO TALK ABOUT FOR A VARIETY OF... PERSONAL REASONS.
YOU WERE THERE WHEN HE DIED-- LAID CLARK ON THE GROUND IN FRONT OF US--
YES, I TRIED TO HELP BUT--
YOU JUST LEFT, TOOK OFF--
LIKE I SAID, THERE ARE PERSONAL REASONS AT PLAY HERE THAT PREVENT ME FROM REVEALING TOO MUCH ABOUT--
OKAY, HOW ABOUT ANSWERING ME ONE SIMPLE QUESTION:
WHAT ARE *YOU* DOING HERE?
I'M WAITING.
WAITING FOR WHAT?
FOR YOUR SUPERMAN TO COME BACK.
COME BACK TO WHAT?

TO LIFE.

CLARK'S NOT COMING BACK!

YOU SAW WHAT HAPPENED TO HIM-- WHAT WAS LEFT OF HIS BODY!

LET'S JUST SAY I HAVE FAITH.

WELL, I DON'T. I KNOW WHAT I SAW WITH MY OWN EYES.

CLARK IS DEAD.

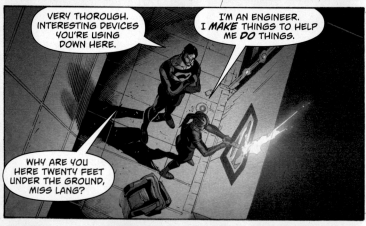

VERY THOROUGH. INTERESTING DEVICES YOU'RE USING DOWN HERE.

I'M AN ENGINEER. I MAKE THINGS TO HELP ME DO THINGS.

WHY ARE YOU HERE TWENTY FEET UNDER THE GROUND, MISS LANG?

TO KEEP A PROMISE.

WHICH IS?

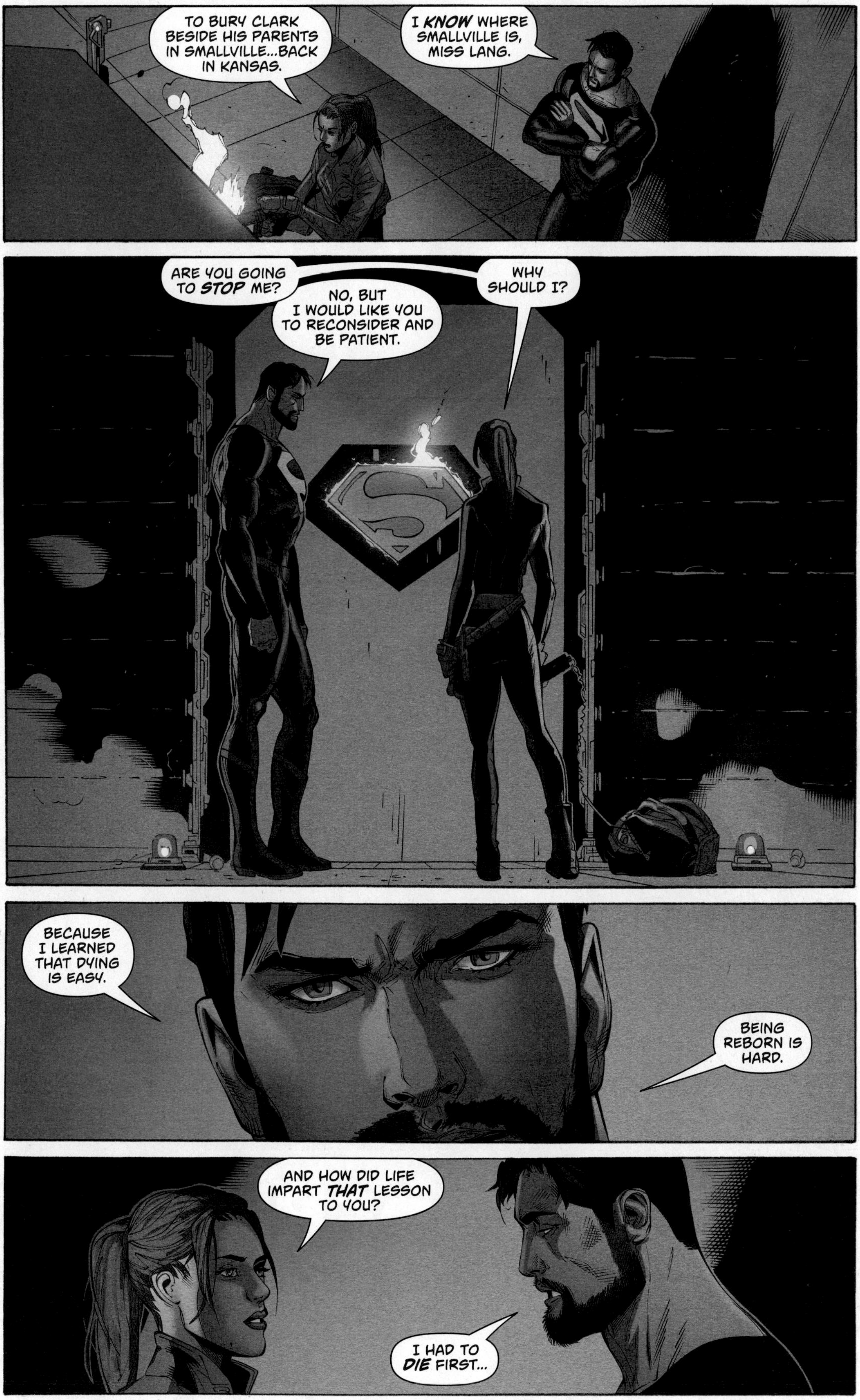
TO BURY CLARK BESIDE HIS PARENTS IN SMALLVILLE...BACK IN KANSAS.
I KNOW WHERE SMALLVILLE IS, MISS LANG.
ARE YOU GOING TO STOP ME?
NO, BUT I WOULD LIKE YOU TO RECONSIDER AND BE PATIENT.
WHY SHOULD I?
BECAUSE I LEARNED THAT DYING IS EASY.
BEING REBORN IS HARD.
AND HOW DID LIFE IMPART THAT LESSON TO YOU?
I HAD TO DIE FIRST...

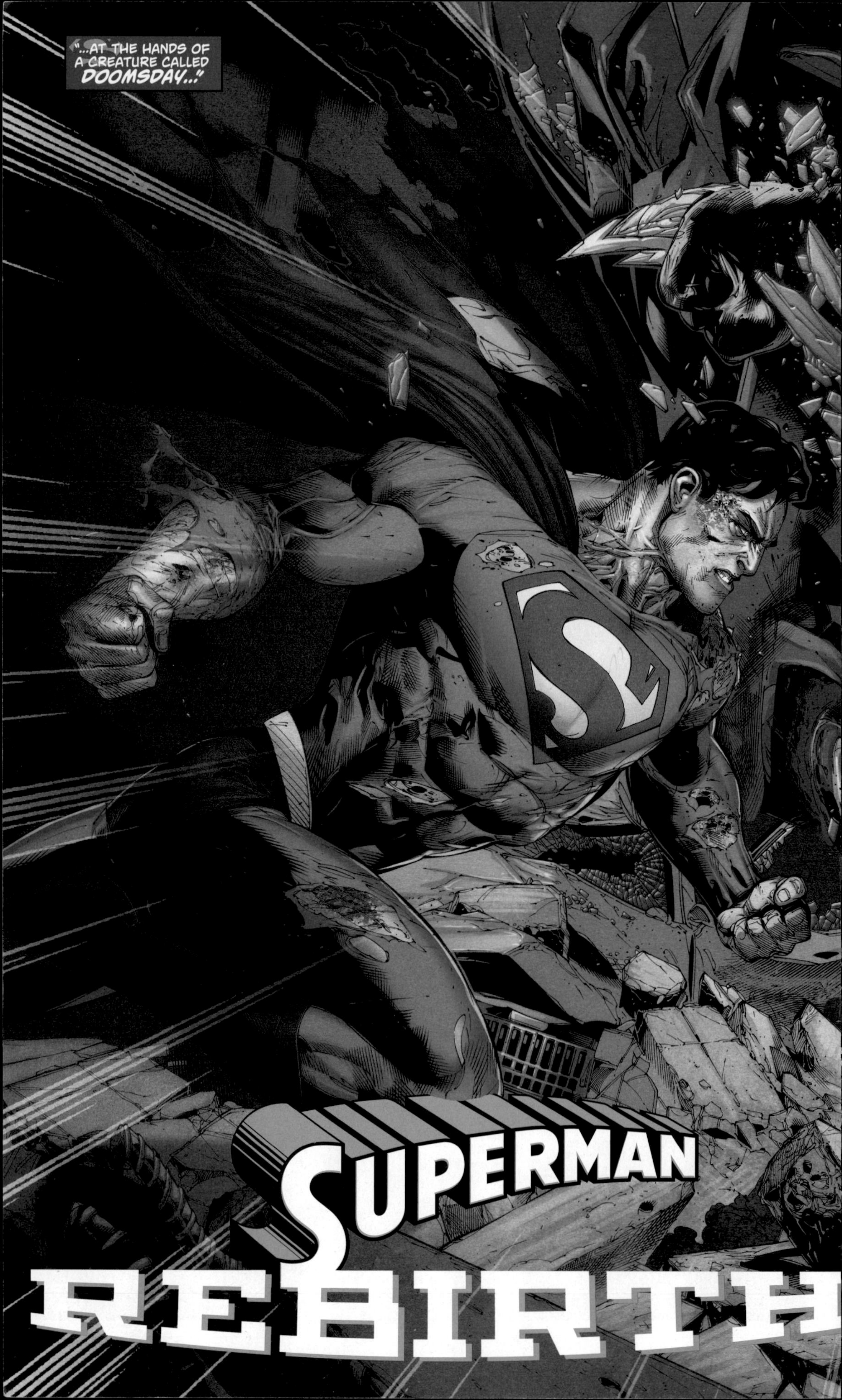
"...AT THE HANDS OF A CREATURE CALLED DOOMSDAY..."
SUPERMAN
REBIRTH

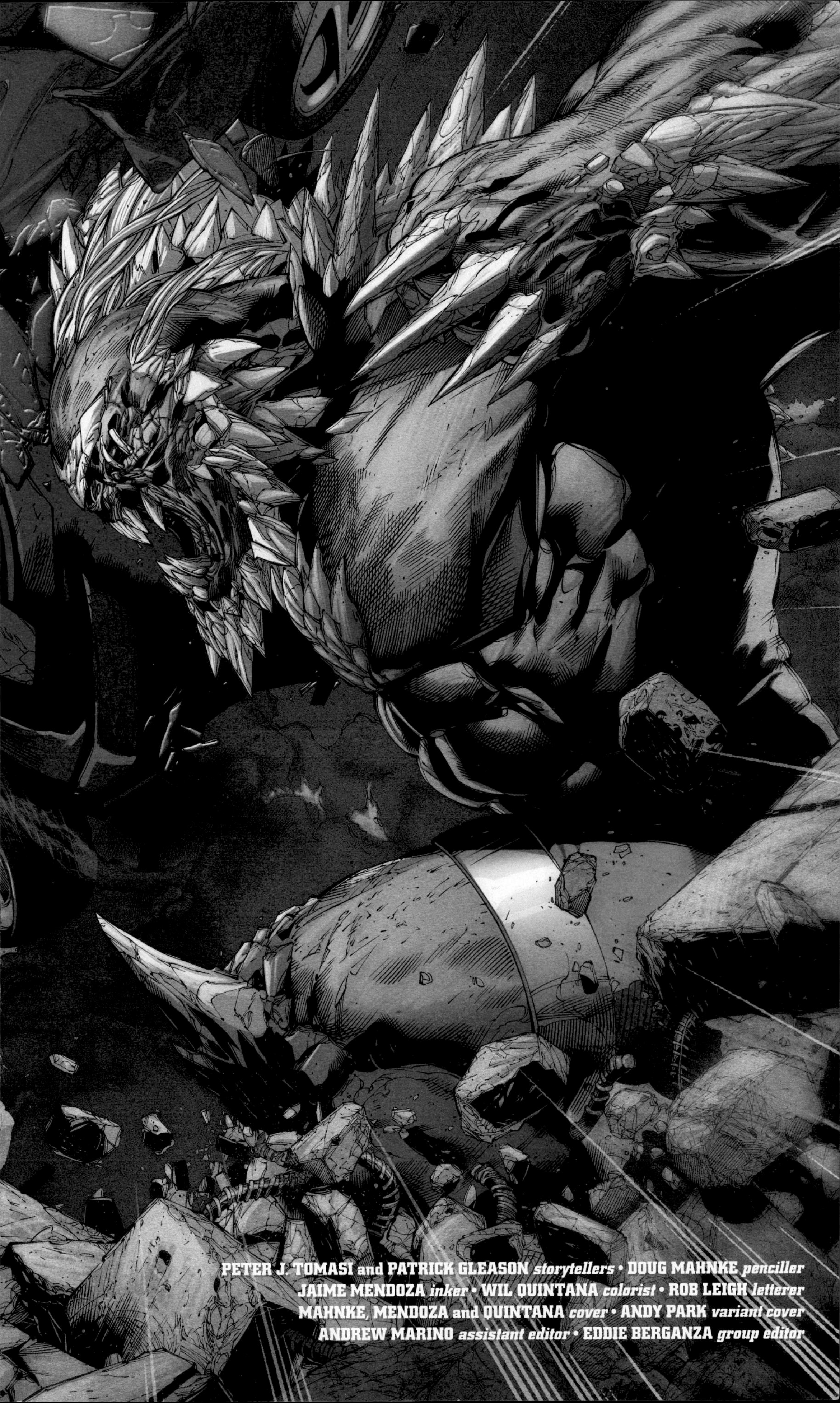
PETER J. TOMASI and PATRICK GLEASON storytellers • DOUG MAHNKE penciller
JAIME MENDOZA inker • WIL QUINTANA colorist • ROB LEIGH letterer
MAHNKE, MENDOZA and QUINTANA cover • ANDY PARK variant cover
ANDREW MARINO assistant editor • EDDIE BERGANZA group editor

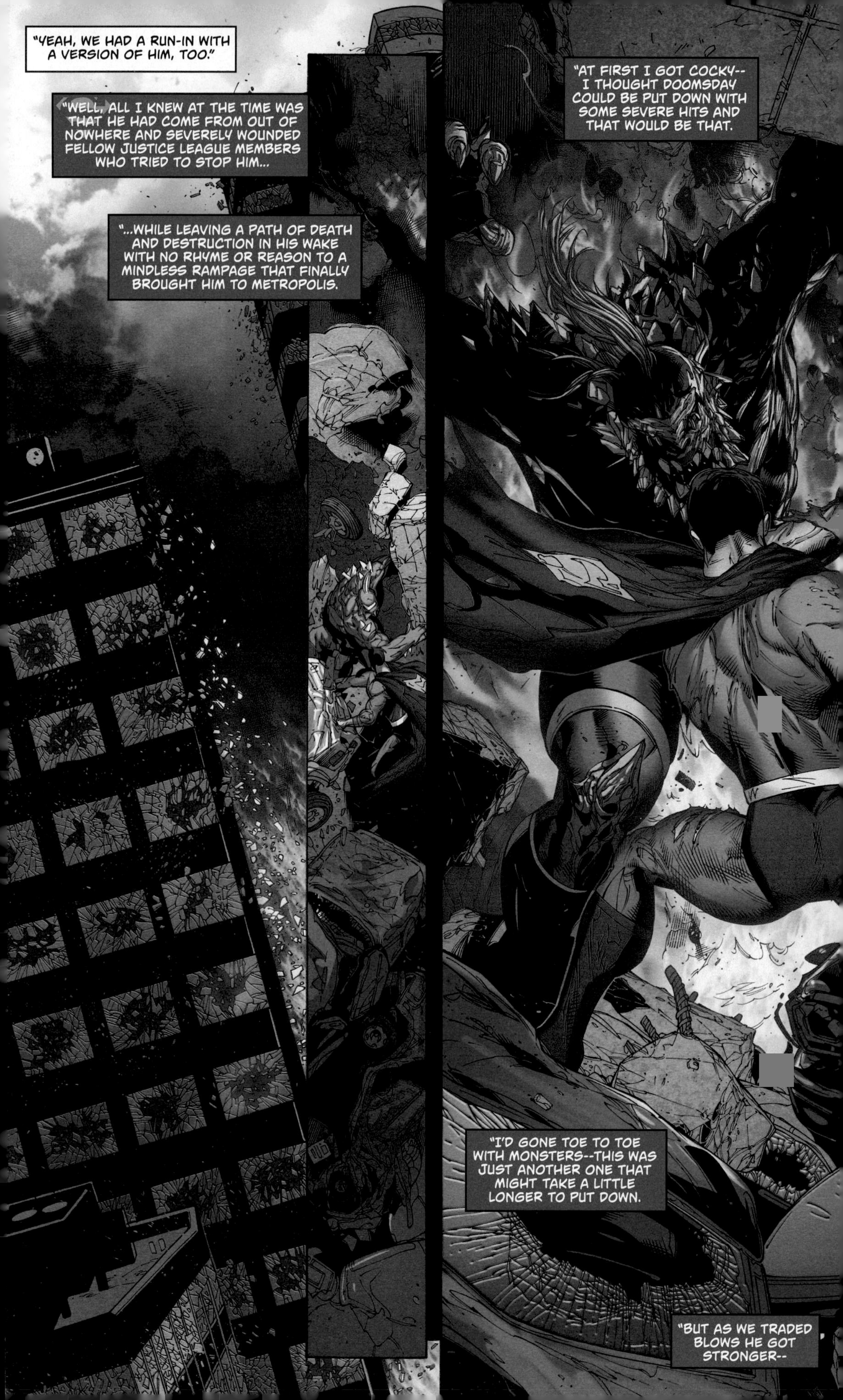
"YEAH, WE HAD A RUN-IN WITH A VERSION OF HIM, TOO."
"WELL, ALL I KNEW AT THE TIME WAS THAT HE HAD COME FROM OUT OF NOWHERE AND SEVERELY WOUNDED FELLOW JUSTICE LEAGUE MEMBERS WHO TRIED TO STOP HIM...
"...WHILE LEAVING A PATH OF DEATH AND DESTRUCTION IN HIS WAKE WITH NO RHYME OR REASON TO A MINDLESS RAMPAGE THAT FINALLY BROUGHT HIM TO METROPOLIS.
"AT FIRST I GOT COCKY-- I THOUGHT DOOMSDAY COULD BE PUT DOWN WITH SOME SEVERE HITS AND THAT WOULD BE THAT.
"I'D GONE TOE TO TOE WITH MONSTERS--THIS WAS JUST ANOTHER ONE THAT MIGHT TAKE A LITTLE LONGER TO PUT DOWN.
"BUT AS WE TRADED BLOWS HE GOT STRONGER--

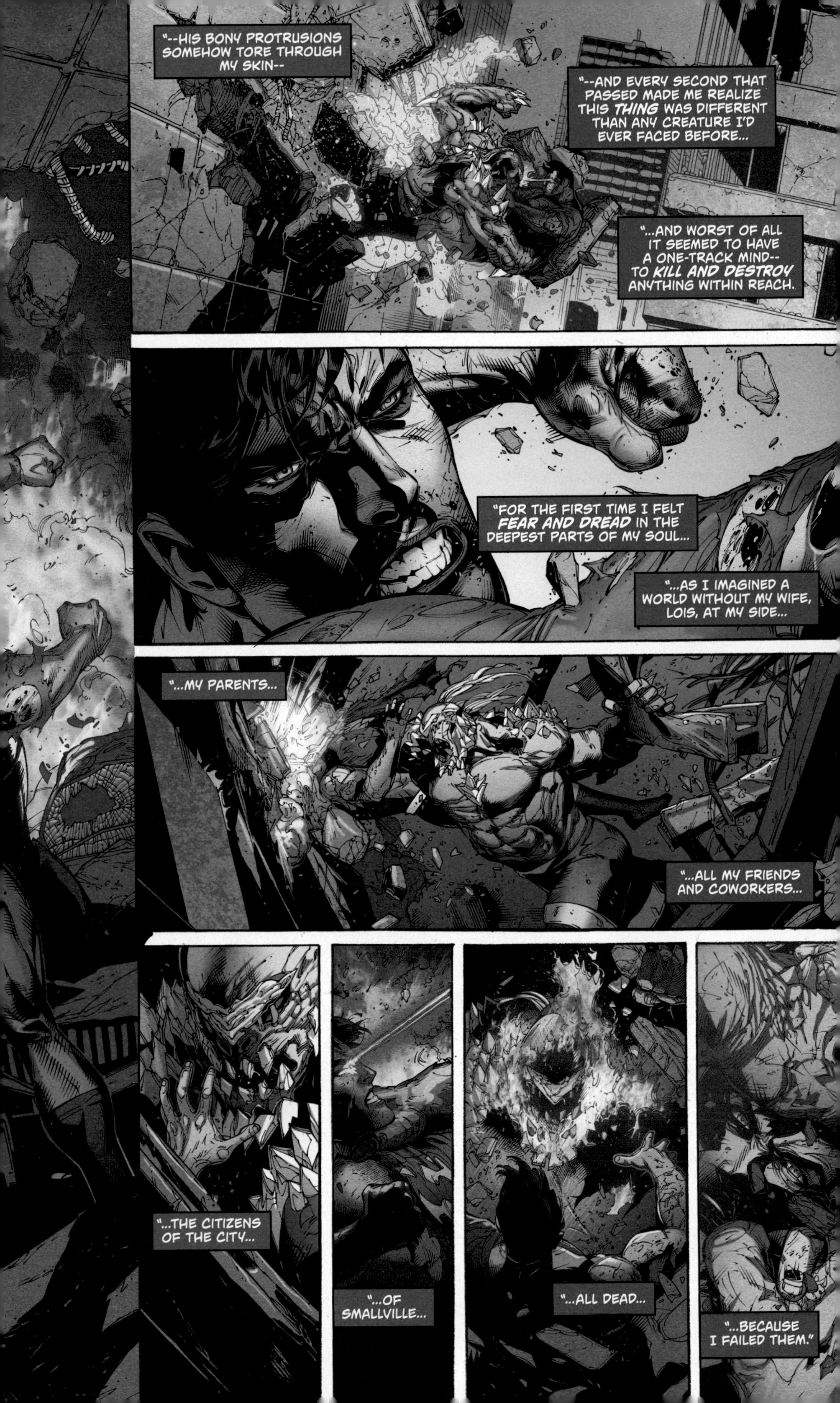
"--HIS BONY PROTRUSIONS SOMEHOW TORE THROUGH MY SKIN--
"--AND EVERY SECOND THAT PASSED MADE ME REALIZE THIS THING WAS DIFFERENT THAN ANY CREATURE I'D EVER FACED BEFORE...
"...AND WORST OF ALL IT SEEMED TO HAVE A ONE-TRACK MIND--TO KILL AND DESTROY ANYTHING WITHIN REACH.
"FOR THE FIRST TIME I FELT FEAR AND DREAD IN THE DEEPEST PARTS OF MY SOUL...
"...AS I IMAGINED A WORLD WITHOUT MY WIFE, LOIS, AT MY SIDE...
"...MY PARENTS...
"...ALL MY FRIENDS AND COWORKERS...
"...THE CITIZENS OF THE CITY...
"...OF SMALLVILLE...
"...ALL DEAD...
"...BECAUSE I FAILED THEM."

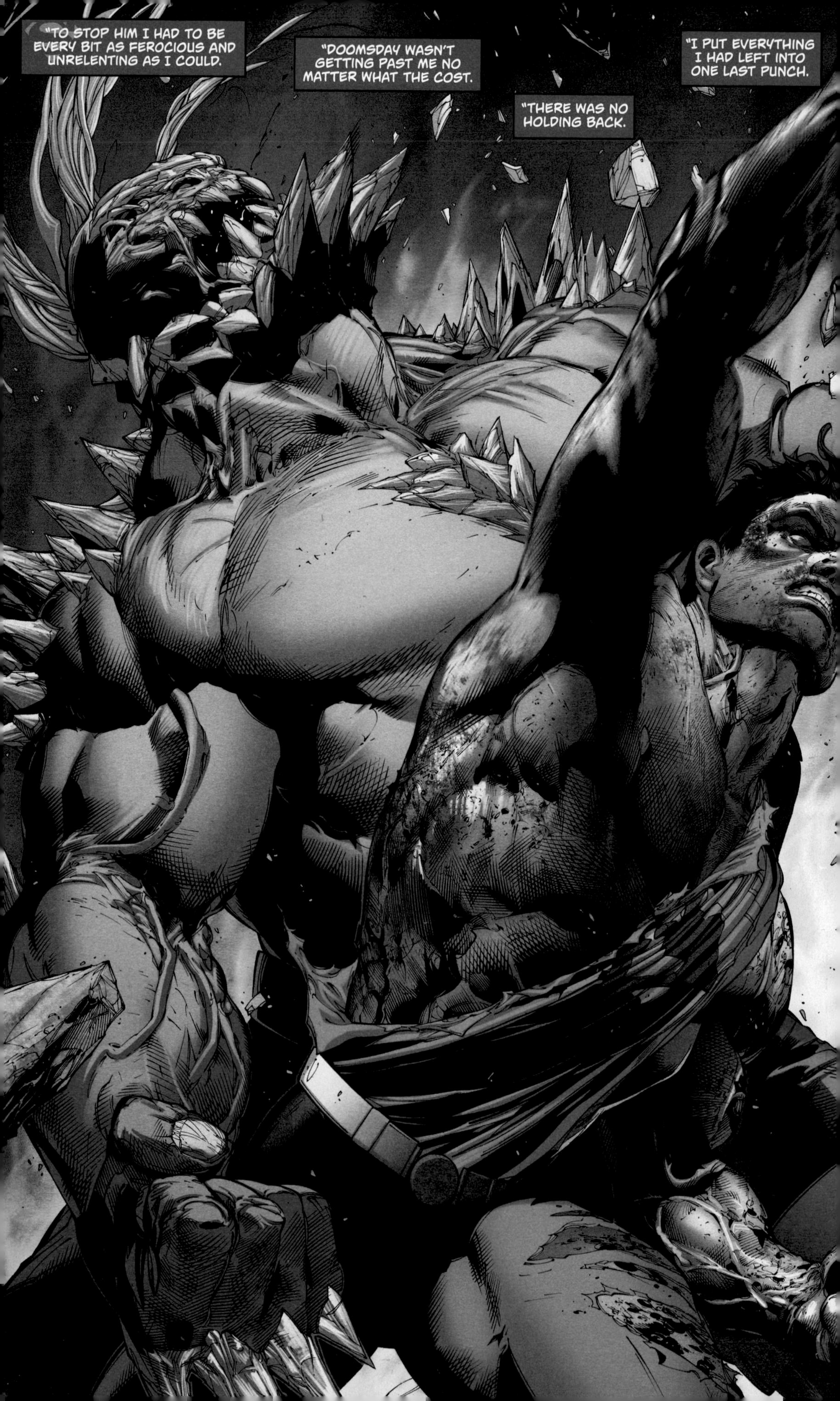
"TO STOP HIM I HAD TO BE EVERY BIT AS FEROCIOUS AND UNRELENTING AS I COULD.
"DOOMSDAY WASN'T GETTING PAST ME NO MATTER WHAT THE COST.
"THERE WAS NO HOLDING BACK.
"I PUT EVERYTHING I HAD LEFT INTO ONE LAST PUNCH.

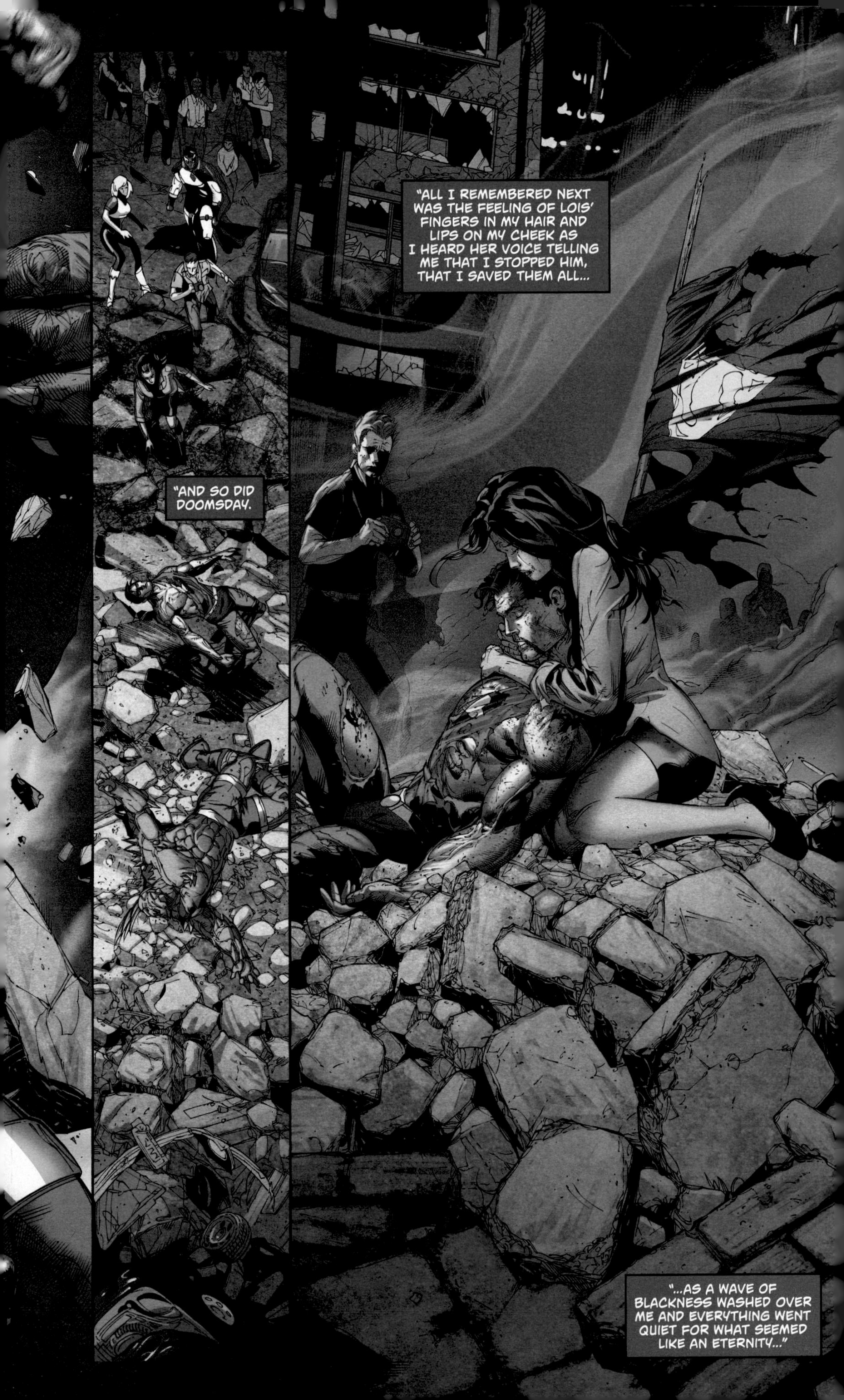
"AND SO DID DOOMSDAY.
"ALL I REMEMBERED NEXT WAS THE FEELING OF LOIS' FINGERS IN MY HAIR AND LIPS ON MY CHEEK AS I HEARD HER VOICE TELLING ME THAT I STOPPED HIM, THAT I SAVED THEM ALL...
"...AS A WAVE OF BLACKNESS WASHED OVER ME AND EVERYTHING WENT QUIET FOR WHAT SEEMED LIKE AN ETERNITY..."

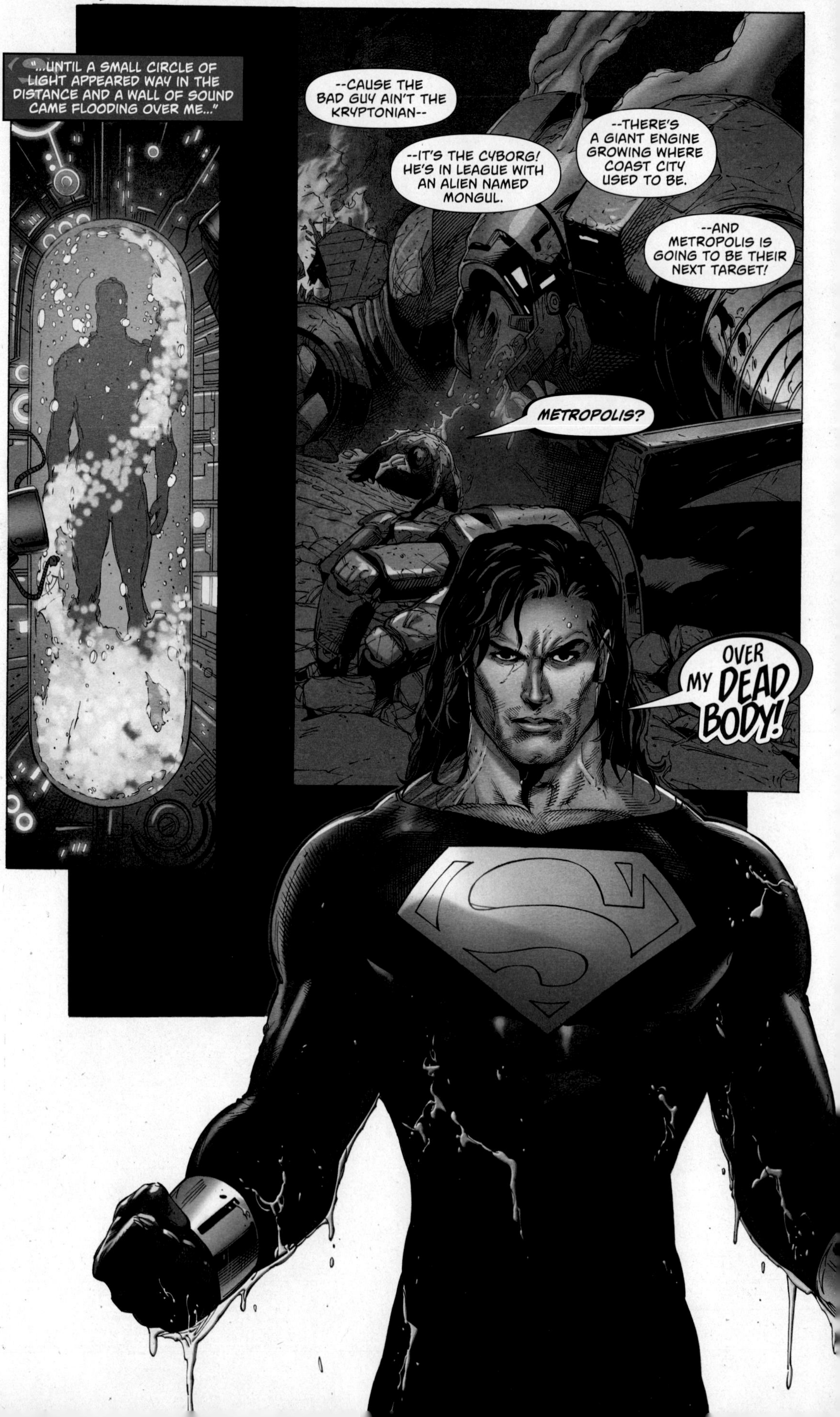
"...UNTIL A SMALL CIRCLE OF LIGHT APPEARED WAY IN THE DISTANCE AND A WALL OF SOUND CAME FLOODING OVER ME..."
--CAUSE THE BAD GUY AIN'T THE KRYPTONIAN--
--IT'S THE CYBORG! HE'S IN LEAGUE WITH AN ALIEN NAMED MONGUL.
--THERE'S A GIANT ENGINE GROWING WHERE COAST CITY USED TO BE.
--AND METROPOLIS IS GOING TO BE THEIR NEXT TARGET!
METROPOLIS?
OVER MY DEAD BODY!

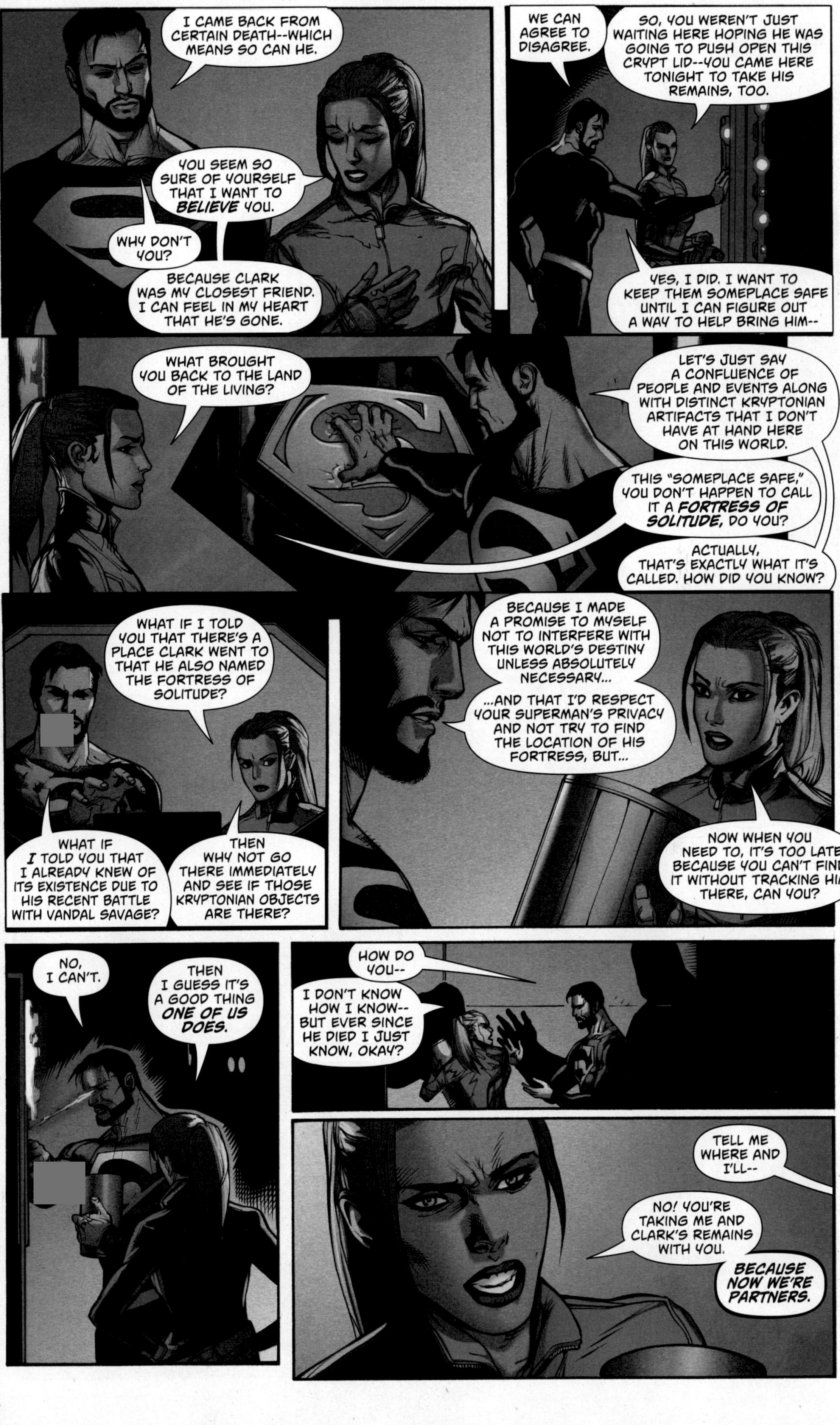
I CAME BACK FROM CERTAIN DEATH--WHICH MEANS SO CAN HE.
YOU SEEM SO SURE OF YOURSELF THAT I WANT TO *BELIEVE* YOU.
WHY DON'T YOU?
BECAUSE CLARK WAS MY CLOSEST FRIEND. I CAN FEEL IN MY HEART THAT HE'S GONE.
WE CAN AGREE TO DISAGREE.
SO, YOU WEREN'T JUST WAITING HERE HOPING HE WAS GOING TO PUSH OPEN THIS CRYPT LID--YOU CAME HERE TONIGHT TO TAKE HIS REMAINS, TOO.
YES, I DID. I WANT TO KEEP THEM SOMEPLACE SAFE UNTIL I CAN FIGURE OUT A WAY TO HELP BRING HIM--
WHAT BROUGHT YOU BACK TO THE LAND OF THE LIVING?
LET'S JUST SAY A CONFLUENCE OF PEOPLE AND EVENTS ALONG WITH DISTINCT KRYPTONIAN ARTIFACTS THAT I DON'T HAVE AT HAND HERE ON THIS WORLD.
THIS "SOMEPLACE SAFE," YOU DON'T HAPPEN TO CALL IT A *FORTRESS OF SOLITUDE,* DO YOU?
ACTUALLY, THAT'S EXACTLY WHAT IT'S CALLED. HOW DID YOU KNOW?
WHAT IF I TOLD YOU THAT THERE'S A PLACE CLARK WENT TO THAT HE ALSO NAMED THE FORTRESS OF SOLITUDE?
WHAT IF *I* TOLD YOU THAT I ALREADY KNEW OF ITS EXISTENCE DUE TO HIS RECENT BATTLE WITH VANDAL SAVAGE?
THEN WHY NOT GO THERE IMMEDIATELY AND SEE IF THOSE KRYPTONIAN OBJECTS ARE THERE?
BECAUSE I MADE A PROMISE TO MYSELF NOT TO INTERFERE WITH THIS WORLD'S DESTINY UNLESS ABSOLUTELY NECESSARY...
...AND THAT I'D RESPECT YOUR SUPERMAN'S PRIVACY AND NOT TRY TO FIND THE LOCATION OF HIS FORTRESS, BUT...
NOW WHEN YOU NEED TO, IT'S TOO LATE BECAUSE YOU CAN'T FIND IT WITHOUT TRACKING HIM THERE, CAN YOU?
NO, I CAN'T.
THEN I GUESS IT'S A GOOD THING *ONE OF US DOES.*
HOW DO YOU--
I DON'T KNOW HOW I KNOW--BUT EVER SINCE HE DIED I JUST KNOW, OKAY?
TELL ME WHERE AND I'LL--
NO! YOU'RE TAKING ME AND CLARK'S REMAINS WITH YOU.
BECAUSE NOW WE'RE PARTNERS.

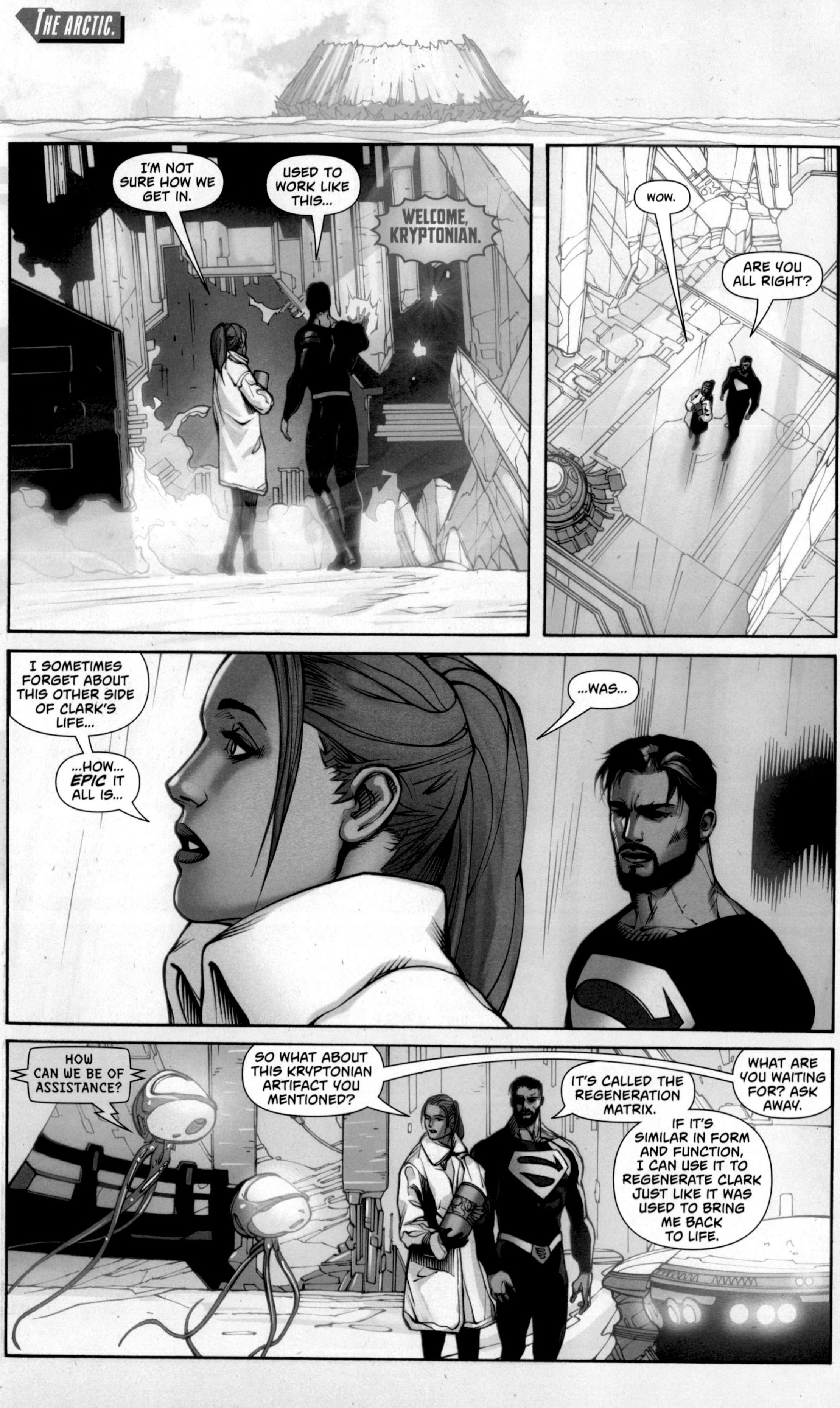
THE ARCTIC.
I'M NOT SURE HOW WE GET IN.
USED TO WORK LIKE THIS...
WELCOME, KRYPTONIAN.
WOW.
ARE YOU ALL RIGHT?
I SOMETIMES FORGET ABOUT THIS OTHER SIDE OF CLARK'S LIFE...
...HOW... EPIC IT ALL IS...
...WAS...
HOW CAN WE BE OF ASSISTANCE?
SO WHAT ABOUT THIS KRYPTONIAN ARTIFACT YOU MENTIONED?
WHAT ARE YOU WAITING FOR? ASK AWAY.
IT'S CALLED THE REGENERATION MATRIX.
IF IT'S SIMILAR IN FORM AND FUNCTION, I CAN USE IT TO REGENERATE CLARK JUST LIKE IT WAS USED TO BRING ME BACK TO LIFE.

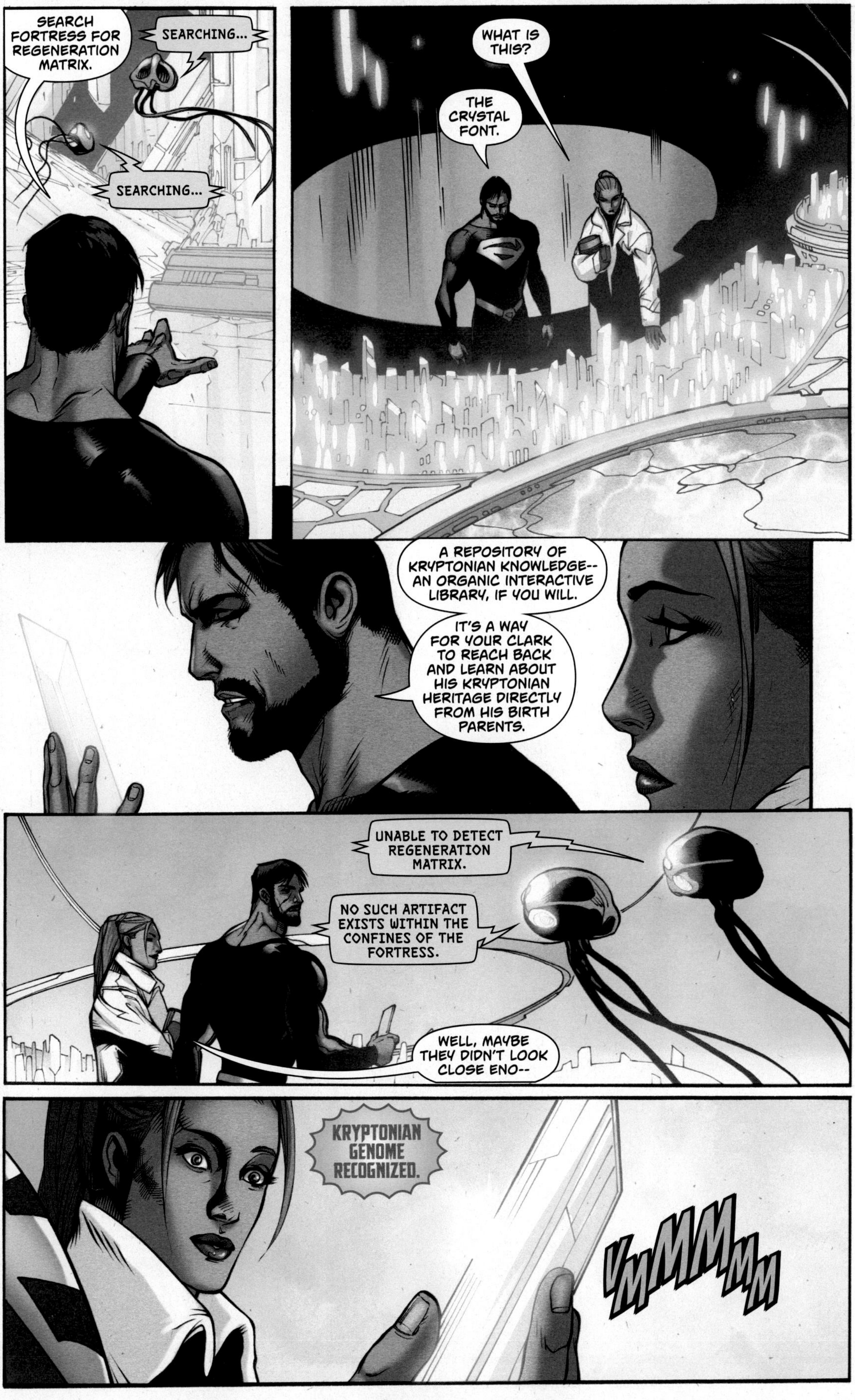
SEARCH FORTRESS FOR REGENERATION MATRIX.
SEARCHING...
SEARCHING...
WHAT IS THIS?
THE CRYSTAL FONT.
A REPOSITORY OF KRYPTONIAN KNOWLEDGE-- AN ORGANIC INTERACTIVE LIBRARY, IF YOU WILL.
IT'S A WAY FOR YOUR CLARK TO REACH BACK AND LEARN ABOUT HIS KRYPTONIAN HERITAGE DIRECTLY FROM HIS BIRTH PARENTS.
UNABLE TO DETECT REGENERATION MATRIX.
NO SUCH ARTIFACT EXISTS WITHIN THE CONFINES OF THE FORTRESS.
WELL, MAYBE THEY DIDN'T LOOK CLOSE ENO--
KRYPTONIAN GENOME RECOGNIZED.
VMMMMMM

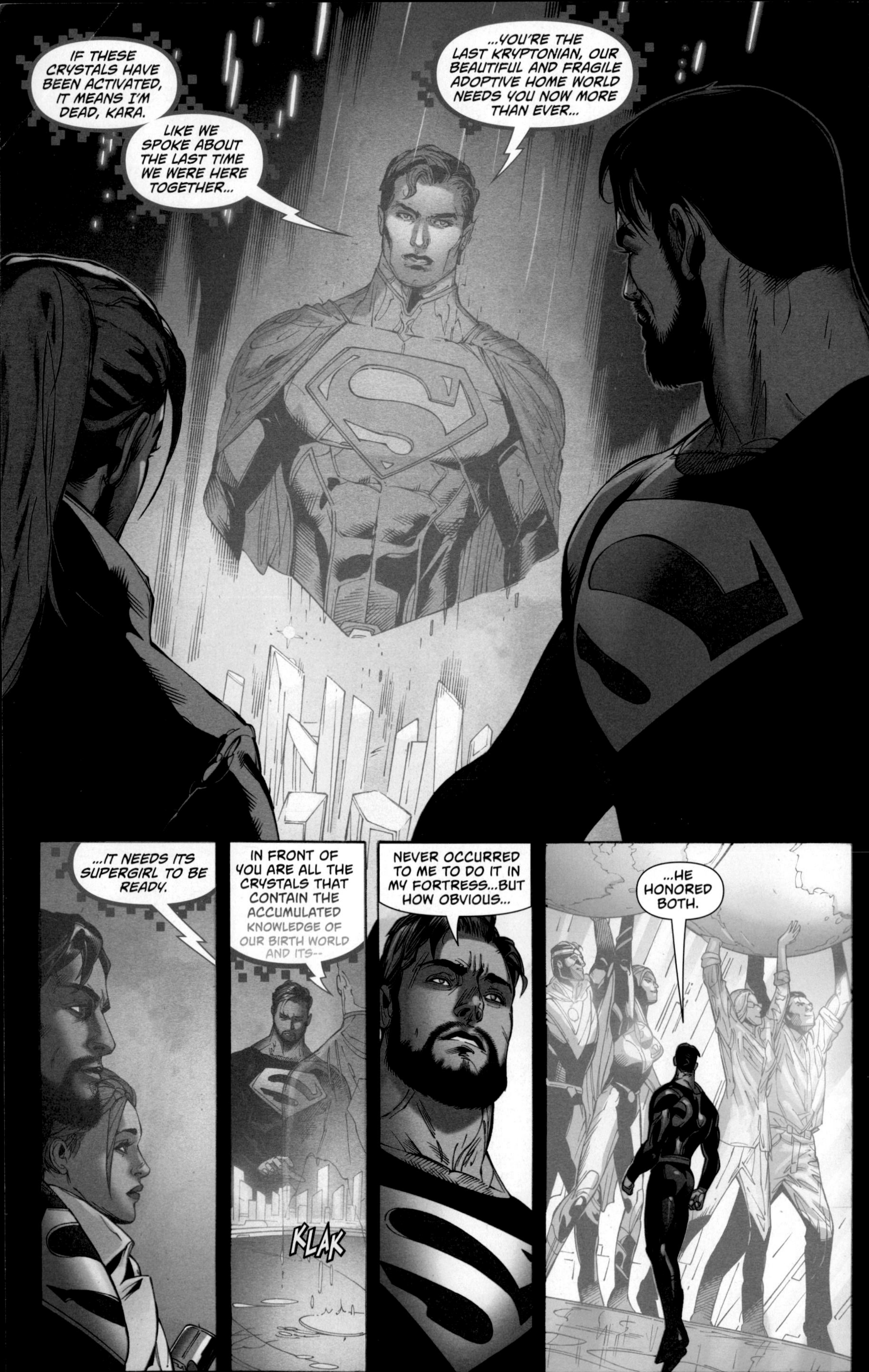
IF THESE CRYSTALS HAVE BEEN ACTIVATED, IT MEANS I'M DEAD, KARA.
LIKE WE SPOKE ABOUT THE LAST TIME WE WERE HERE TOGETHER...
...YOU'RE THE LAST KRYPTONIAN, OUR BEAUTIFUL AND FRAGILE ADOPTIVE HOME WORLD NEEDS YOU NOW MORE THAN EVER...
...IT NEEDS ITS SUPERGIRL TO BE READY.
IN FRONT OF YOU ARE ALL THE CRYSTALS THAT CONTAIN THE ACCUMULATED KNOWLEDGE OF OUR BIRTH WORLD AND ITS--
KLAK
NEVER OCCURRED TO ME TO DO IT IN MY FORTRESS...BUT HOW OBVIOUS...
...HE HONORED BOTH.

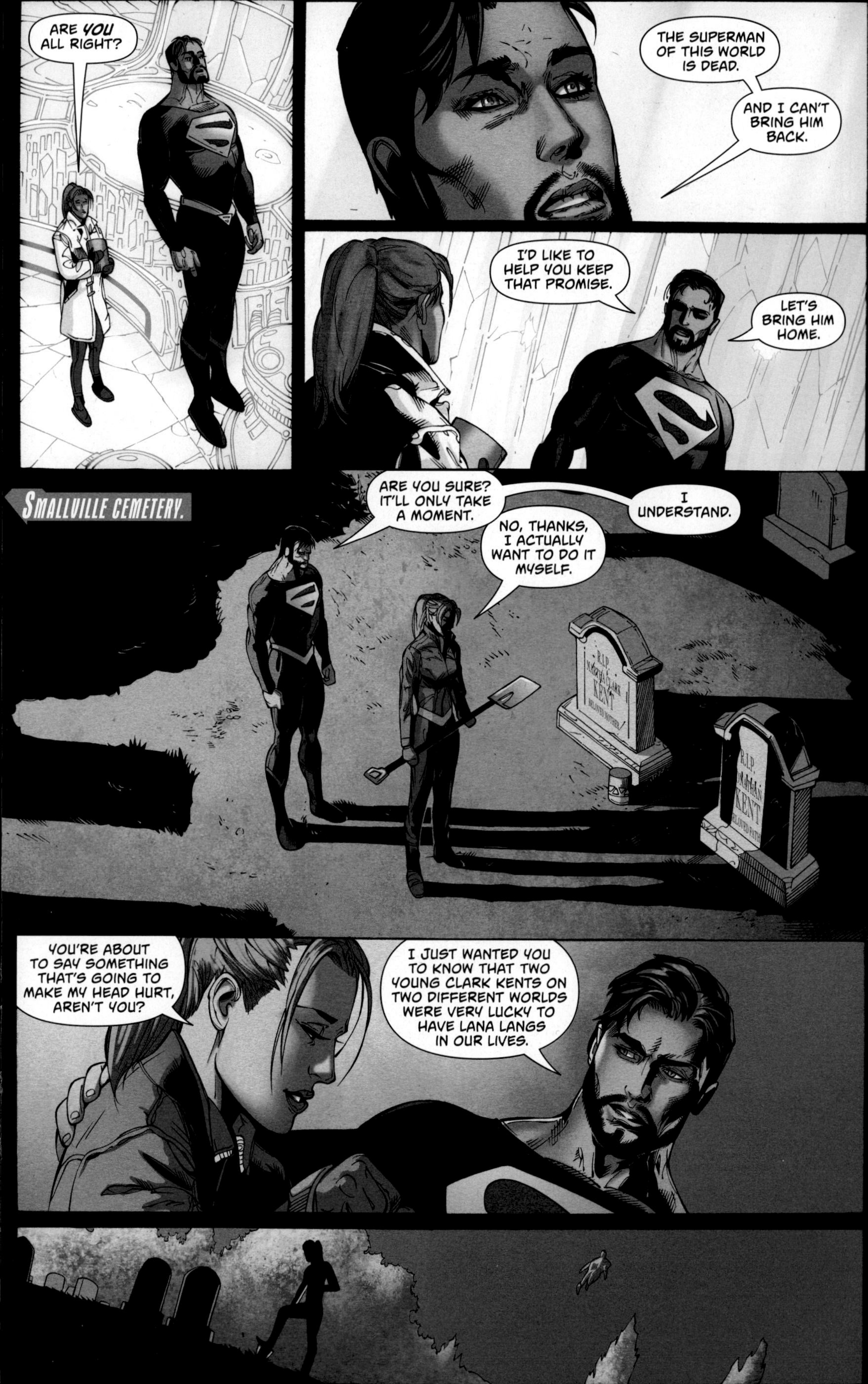
ARE *YOU* ALL RIGHT?
THE SUPERMAN OF THIS WORLD IS DEAD.
AND I CAN'T BRING HIM BACK.
I'D LIKE TO HELP YOU KEEP THAT PROMISE.
LET'S BRING HIM HOME.
SMALLVILLE CEMETERY.
ARE YOU SURE? IT'LL ONLY TAKE A MOMENT.
NO, THANKS, I ACTUALLY WANT TO DO IT MYSELF.
I UNDERSTAND.
R.I.P. MARTHA CLARK KENT BELOVED MOTHER
YOU'RE ABOUT TO SAY SOMETHING THAT'S GOING TO MAKE MY HEAD HURT, AREN'T YOU?
I JUST WANTED YOU TO KNOW THAT TWO YOUNG CLARK KENTS ON TWO DIFFERENT WORLDS WERE VERY LUCKY TO HAVE LANA LANGS IN OUR LIVES.

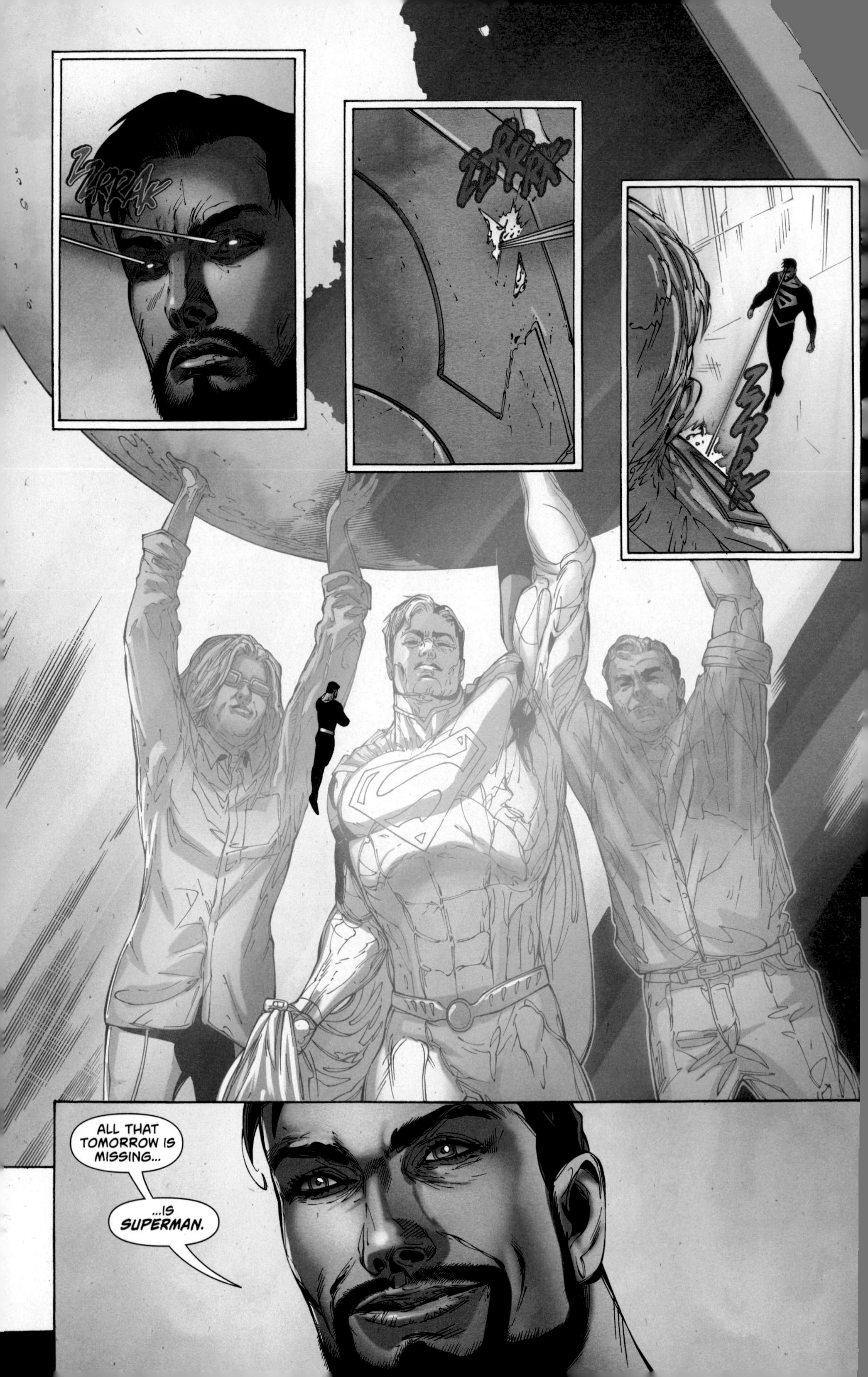

ZZRRAK
ZZRRRK
ZZRRRK
ALL THAT TOMORROW IS MISSING...
...IS SUPERMAN.

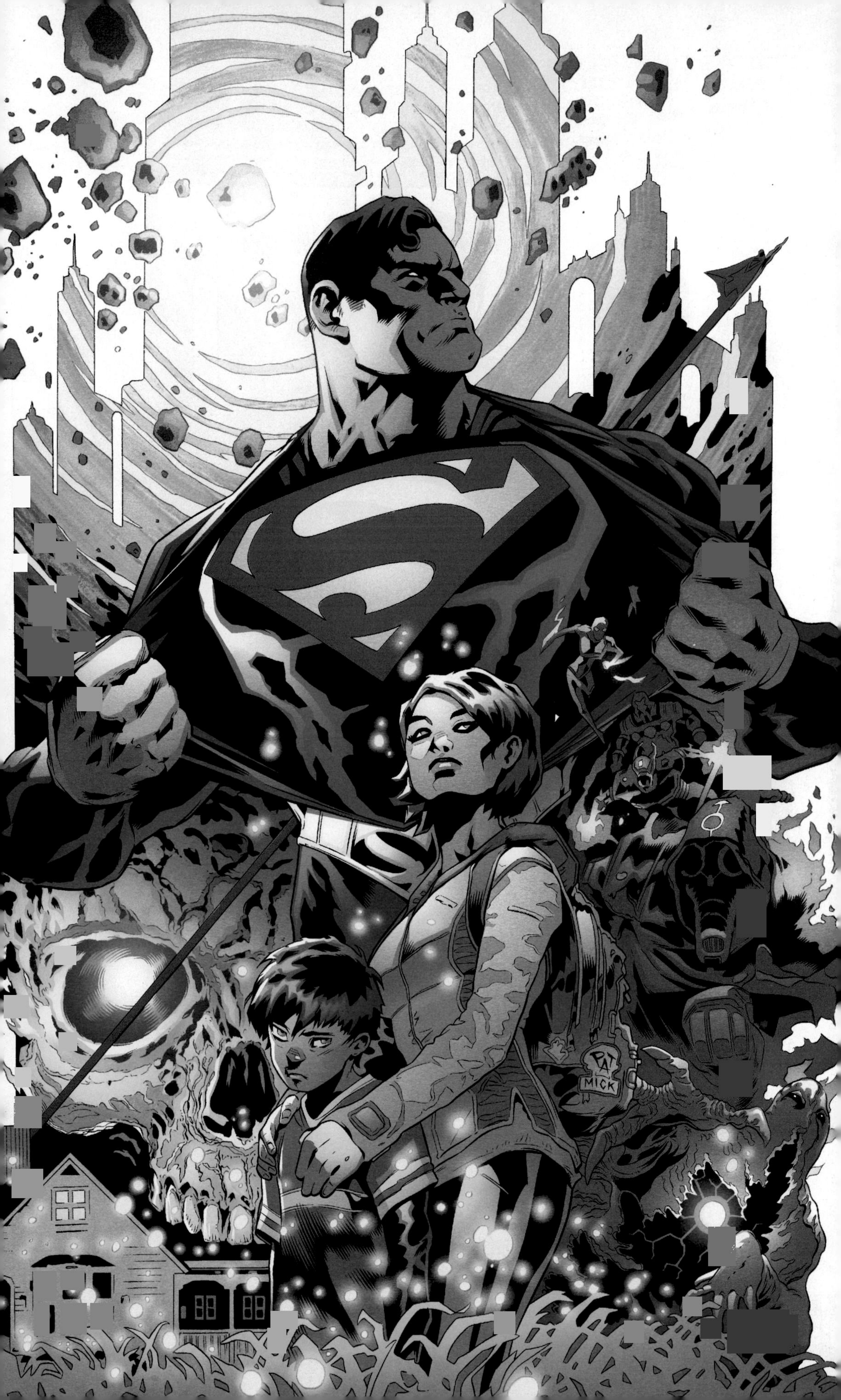
PAT
MICK

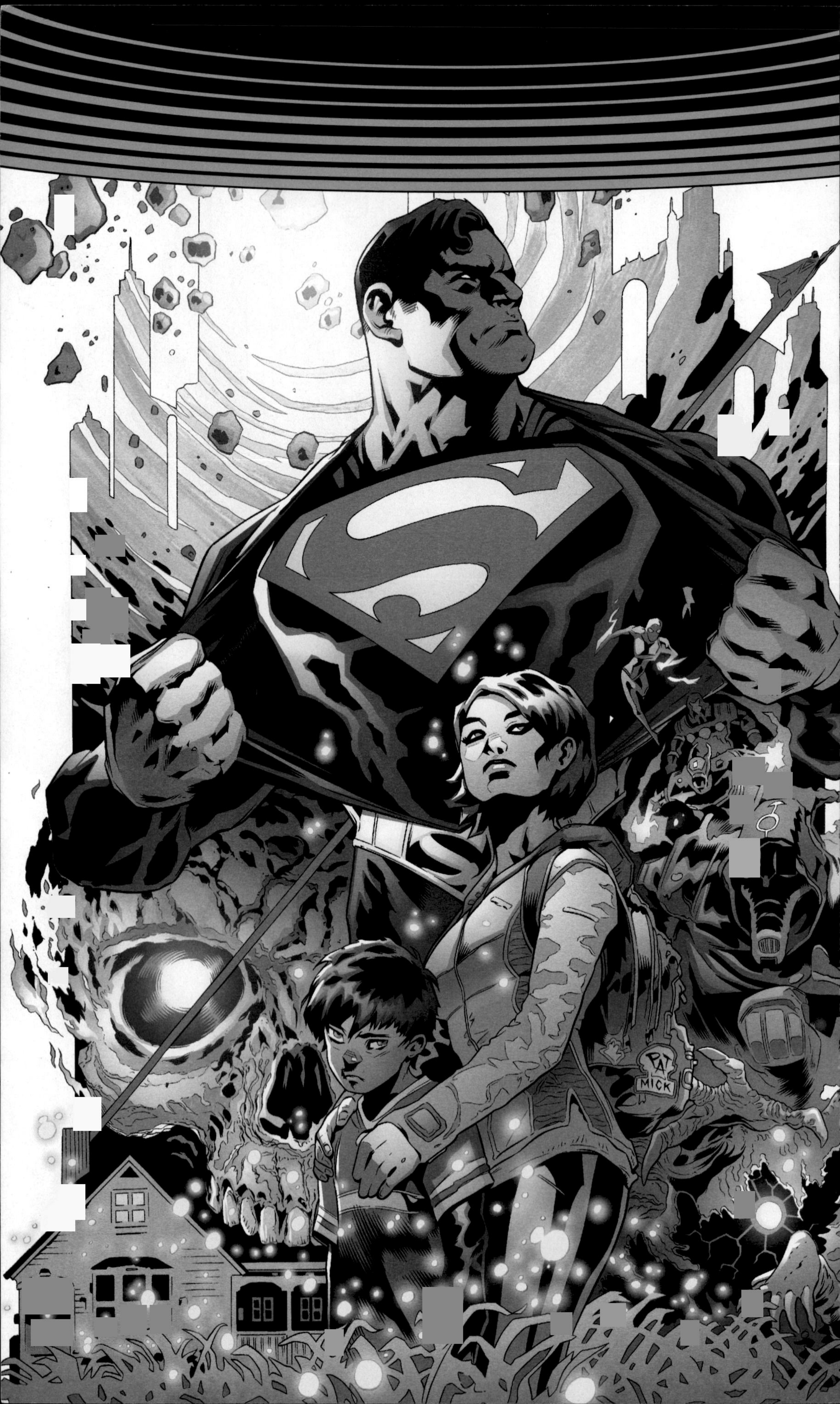
PAT
MICK

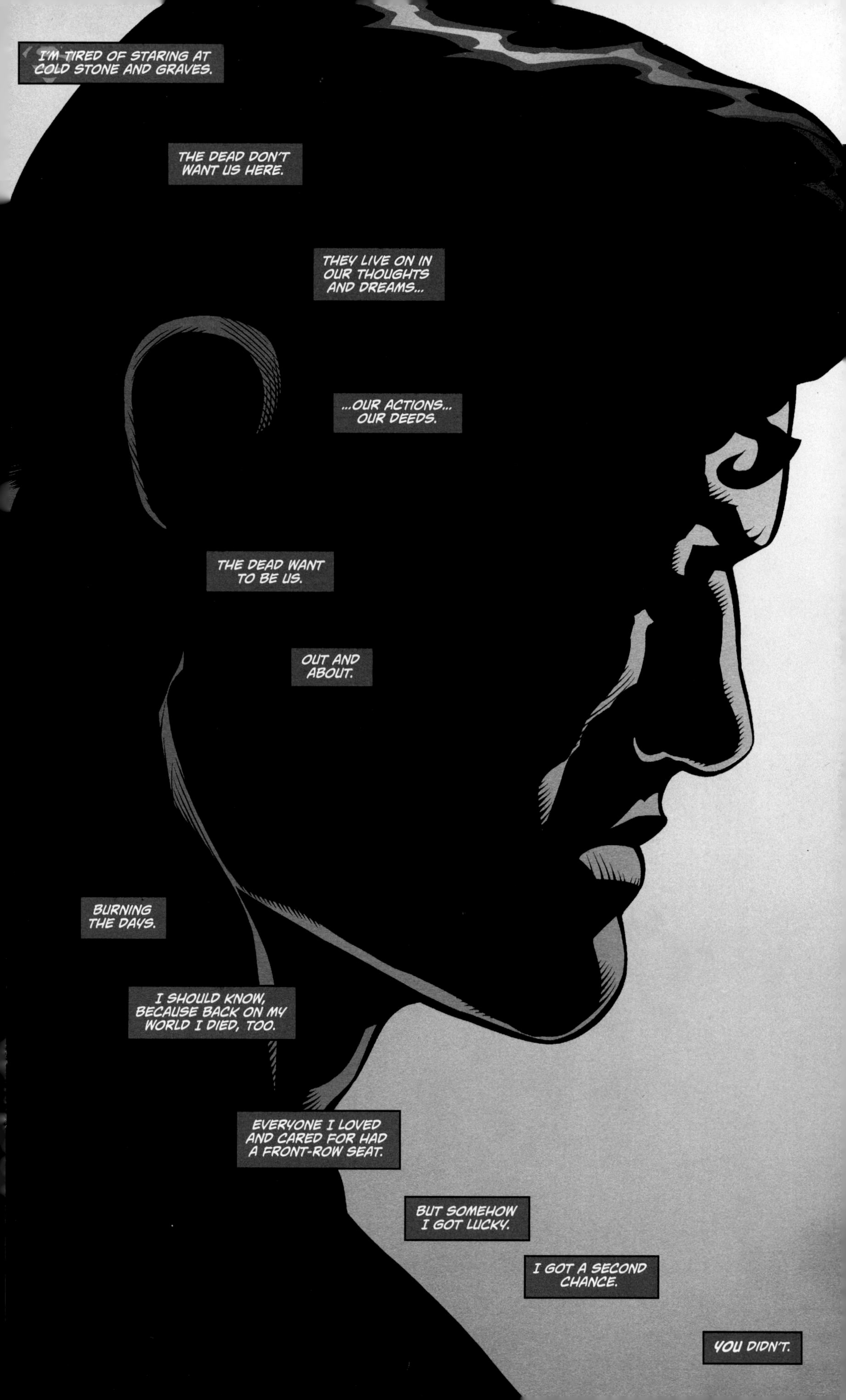
I'M TIRED OF STARING AT COLD STONE AND GRAVES.
THE DEAD DON'T WANT US HERE.
THEY LIVE ON IN OUR THOUGHTS AND DREAMS...
...OUR ACTIONS... OUR DEEDS.
THE DEAD WANT TO BE US.
OUT AND ABOUT.
BURNING THE DAYS.
I SHOULD KNOW, BECAUSE BACK ON MY WORLD I DIED, TOO.
EVERYONE I LOVED AND CARED FOR HAD A FRONT-ROW SEAT.
BUT SOMEHOW I GOT LUCKY.
I GOT A SECOND CHANCE.
YOU DIDN'T.

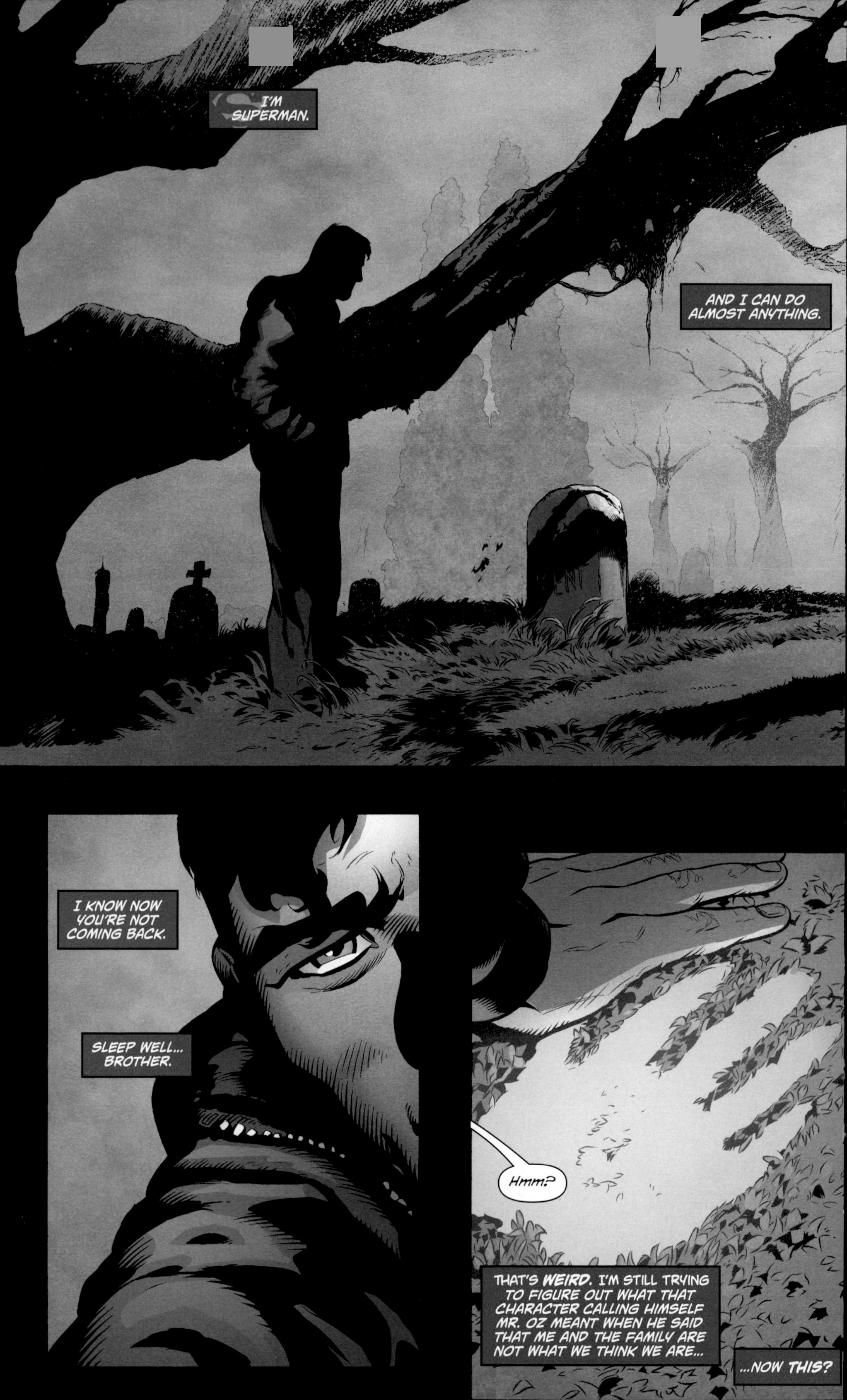
I'M SUPERMAN.
AND I CAN DO ALMOST ANYTHING.
I KNOW NOW YOU'RE NOT COMING BACK.
SLEEP WELL... BROTHER.
Hmm?
THAT'S WEIRD. I'M STILL TRYING TO FIGURE OUT WHAT THAT CHARACTER CALLING HIMSELF MR. OZ MEANT WHEN HE SAID THAT ME AND THE FAMILY ARE NOT WHAT WE THINK WE ARE...
...NOW THIS?

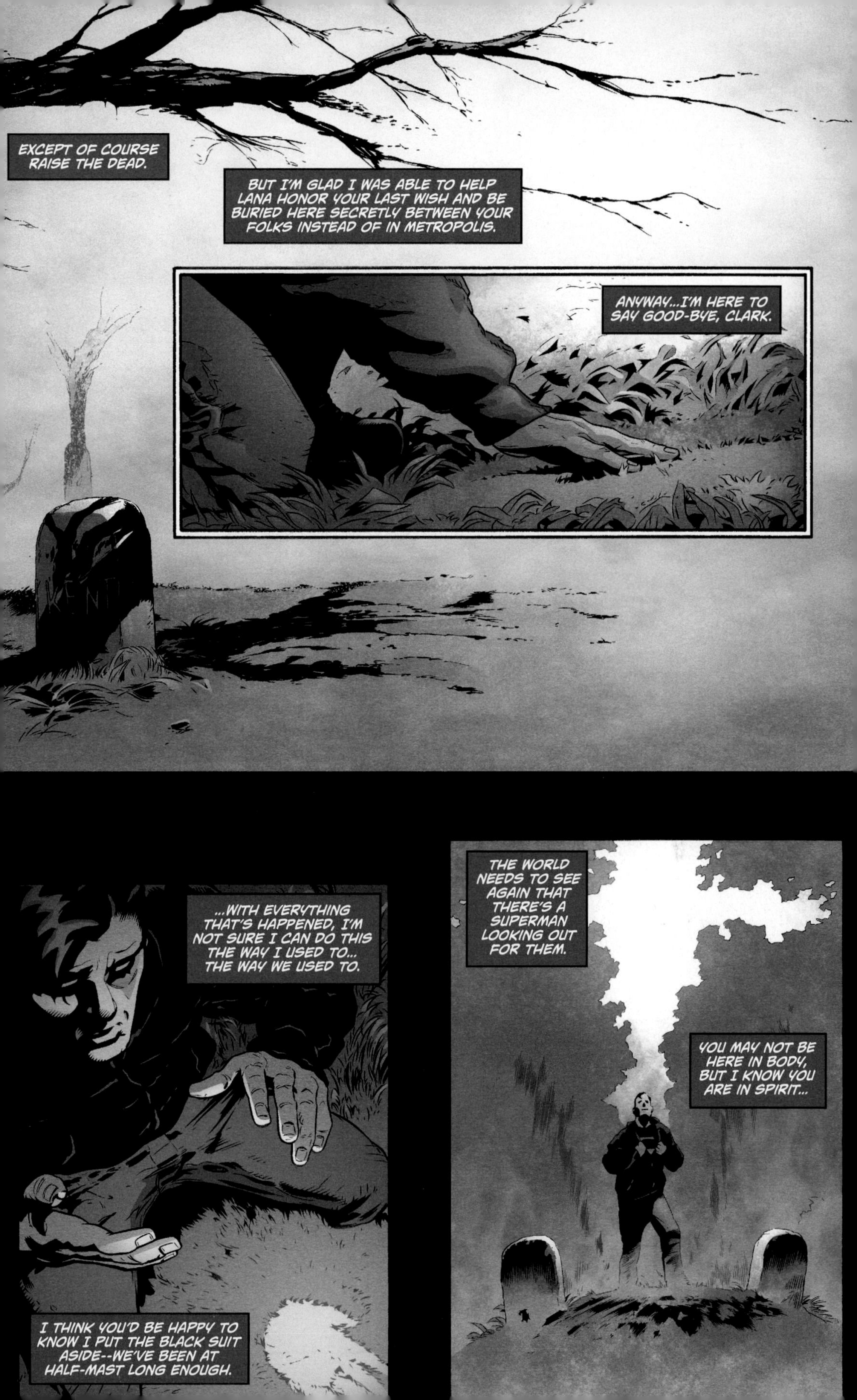
EXCEPT OF COURSE RAISE THE DEAD.
BUT I'M GLAD I WAS ABLE TO HELP LANA HONOR YOUR LAST WISH AND BE BURIED HERE SECRETLY BETWEEN YOUR FOLKS INSTEAD OF IN METROPOLIS.
ANYWAY...I'M HERE TO SAY GOOD-BYE, CLARK.
KENT
...WITH EVERYTHING THAT'S HAPPENED, I'M NOT SURE I CAN DO THIS THE WAY I USED TO... THE WAY WE USED TO.
I THINK YOU'D BE HAPPY TO KNOW I PUT THE BLACK SUIT ASIDE--WE'VE BEEN AT HALF-MAST LONG ENOUGH.
THE WORLD NEEDS TO SEE AGAIN THAT THERE'S A SUPERMAN LOOKING OUT FOR THEM.
YOU MAY NOT BE HERE IN BODY, BUT I KNOW YOU ARE IN SPIRIT...

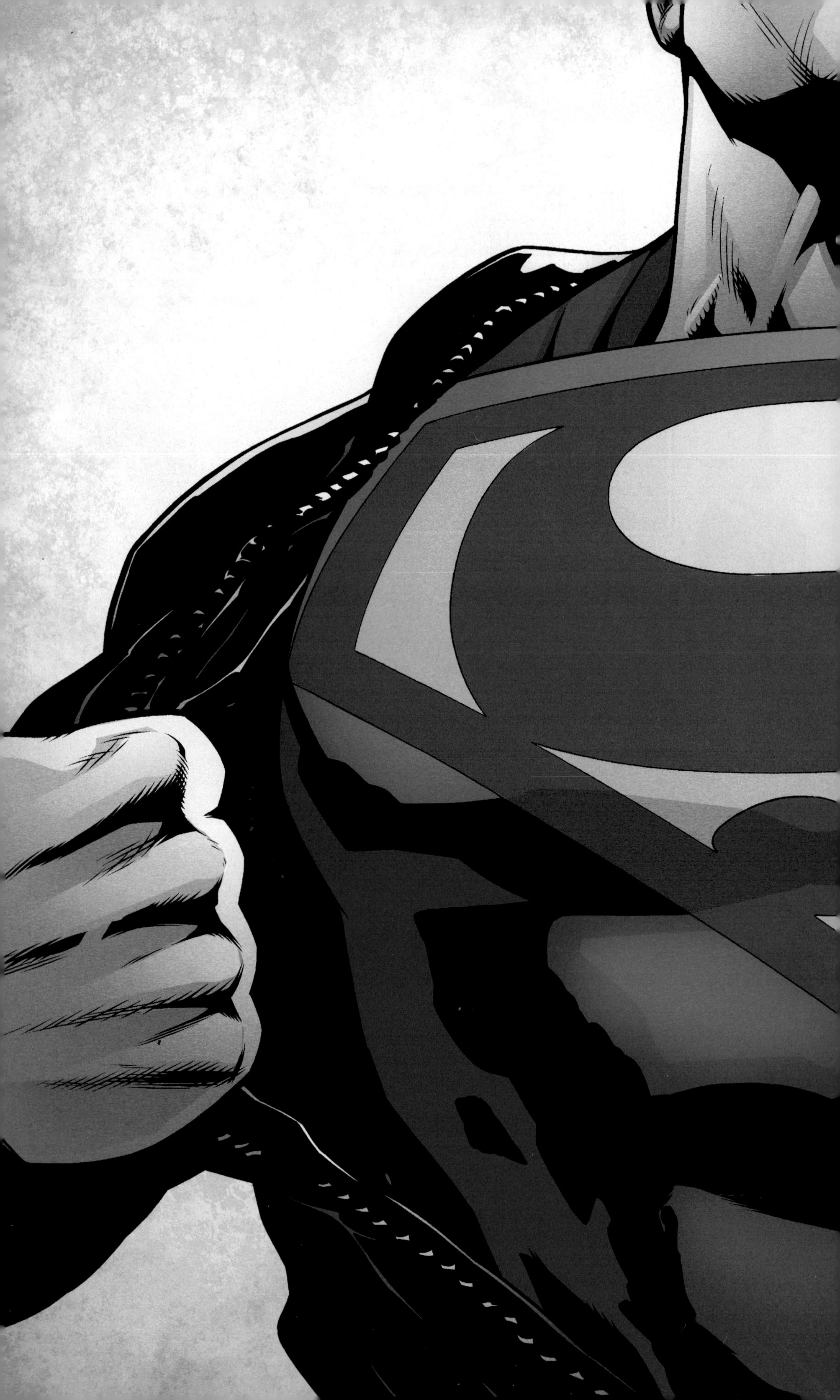

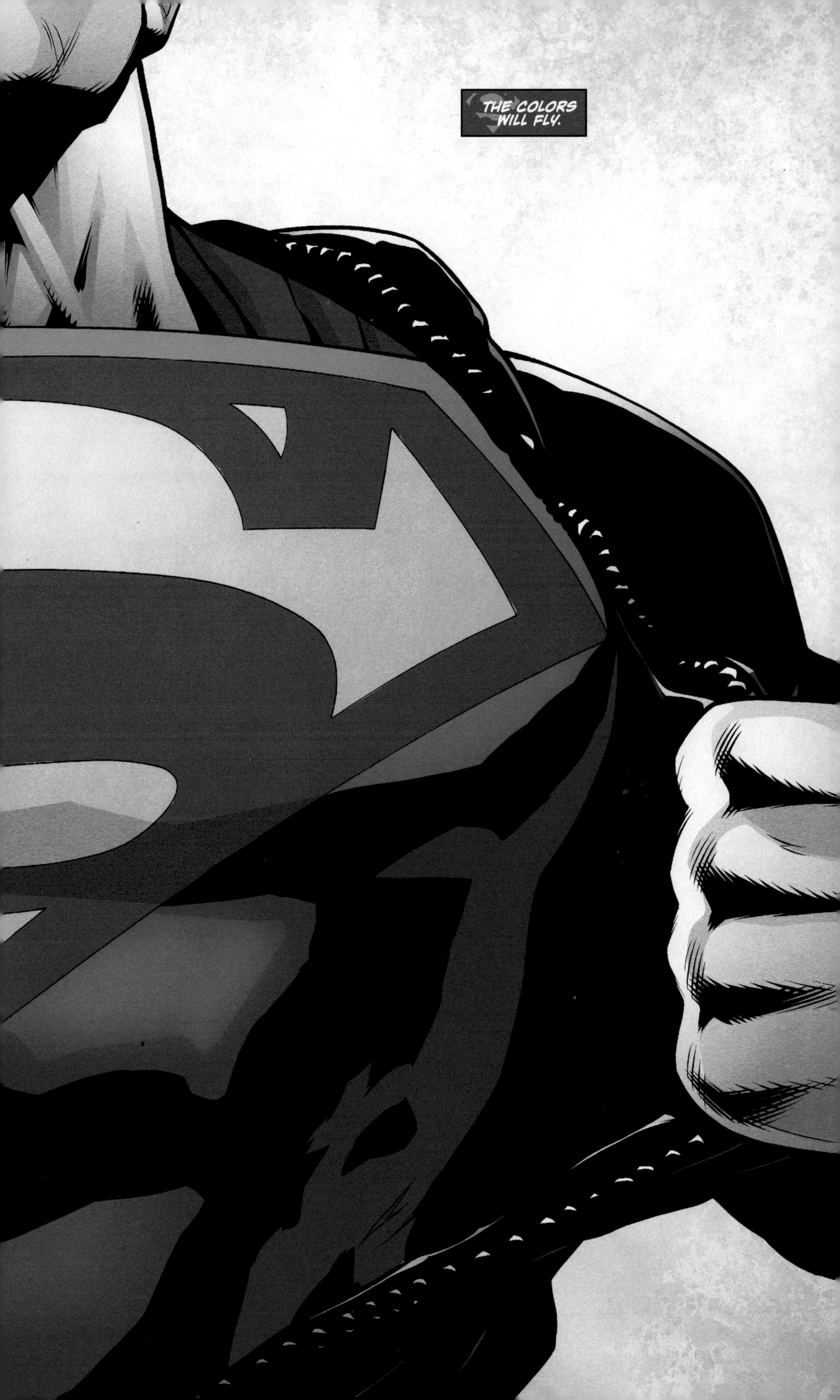
THE COLORS WILL FLY.

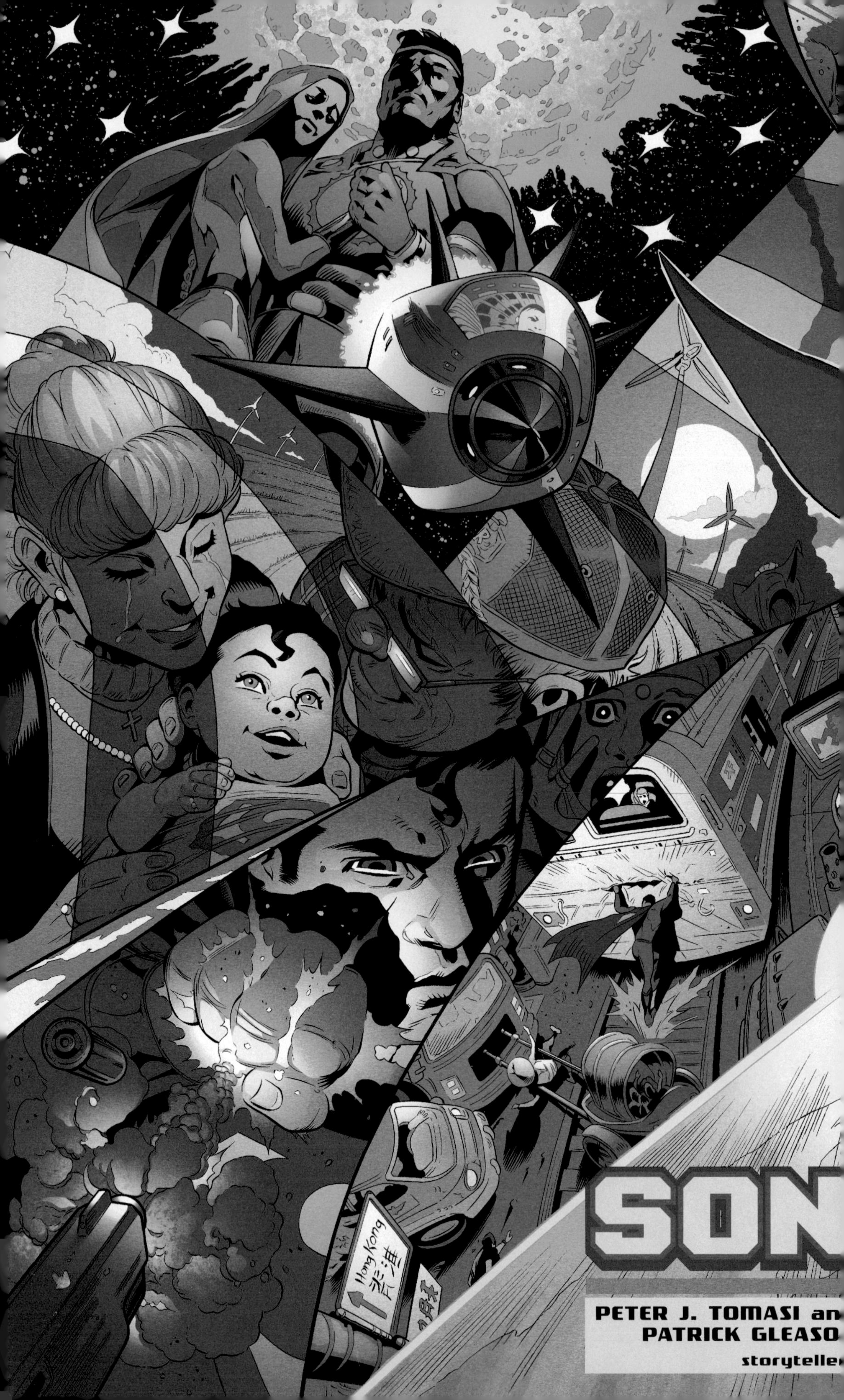
Hong Kong
香港
SON
PETER J. TOMASI an
PATRICK GLEASO
storytelle

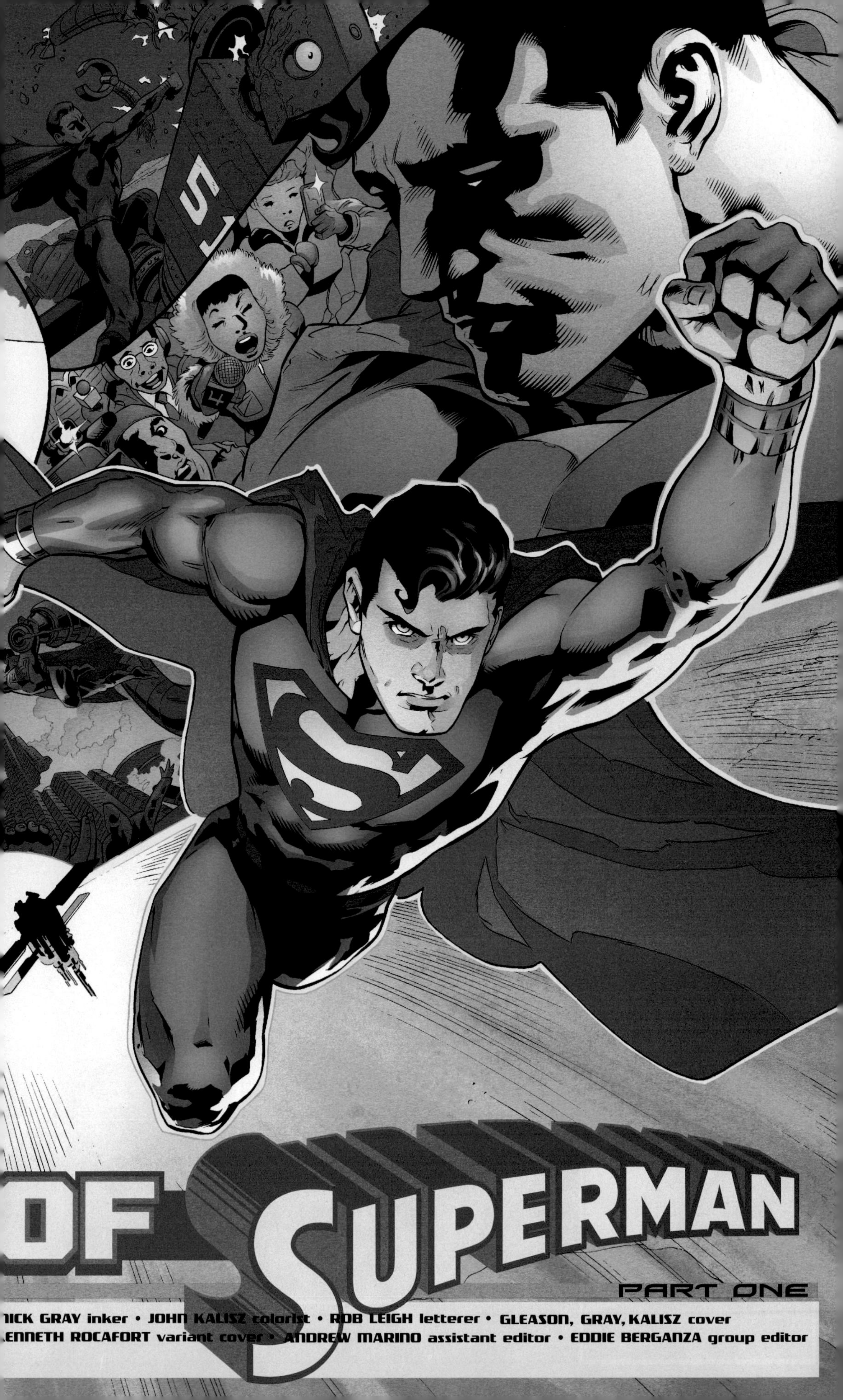
OF SUPERMAN
PART ONE
NICK GRAY inker • JOHN KALISZ colorist • ROB LEIGH letterer • GLEASON, GRAY, KALISZ cover
KENNETH ROCAFORT variant cover • ANDREW MARINO assistant editor • EDDIE BERGANZA group editor

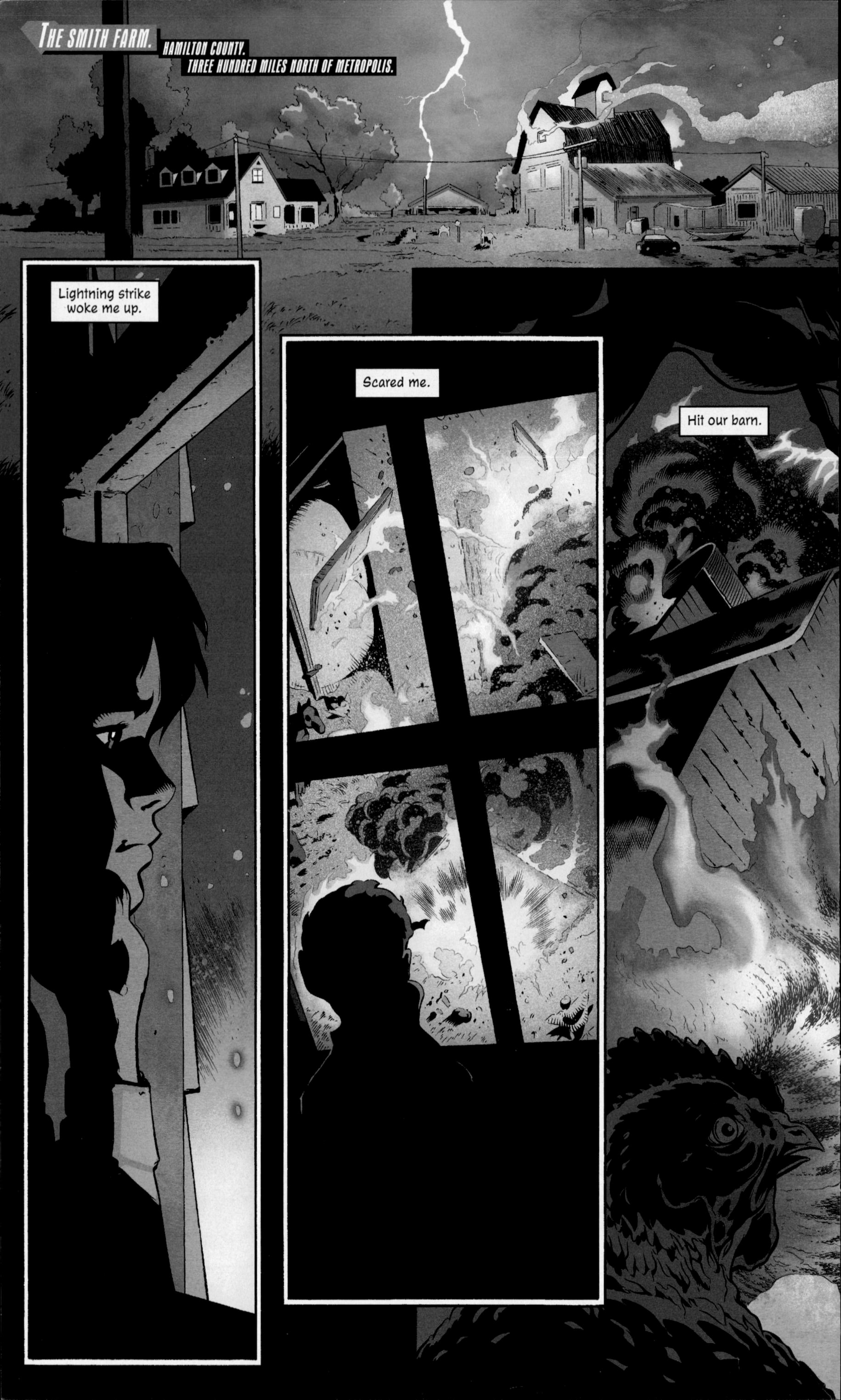

THE SMITH FARM.
HAMILTON COUNTY.
THREE HUNDRED MILES NORTH OF METROPOLIS.
Lightning strike woke me up.
Scared me.
Hit our barn.

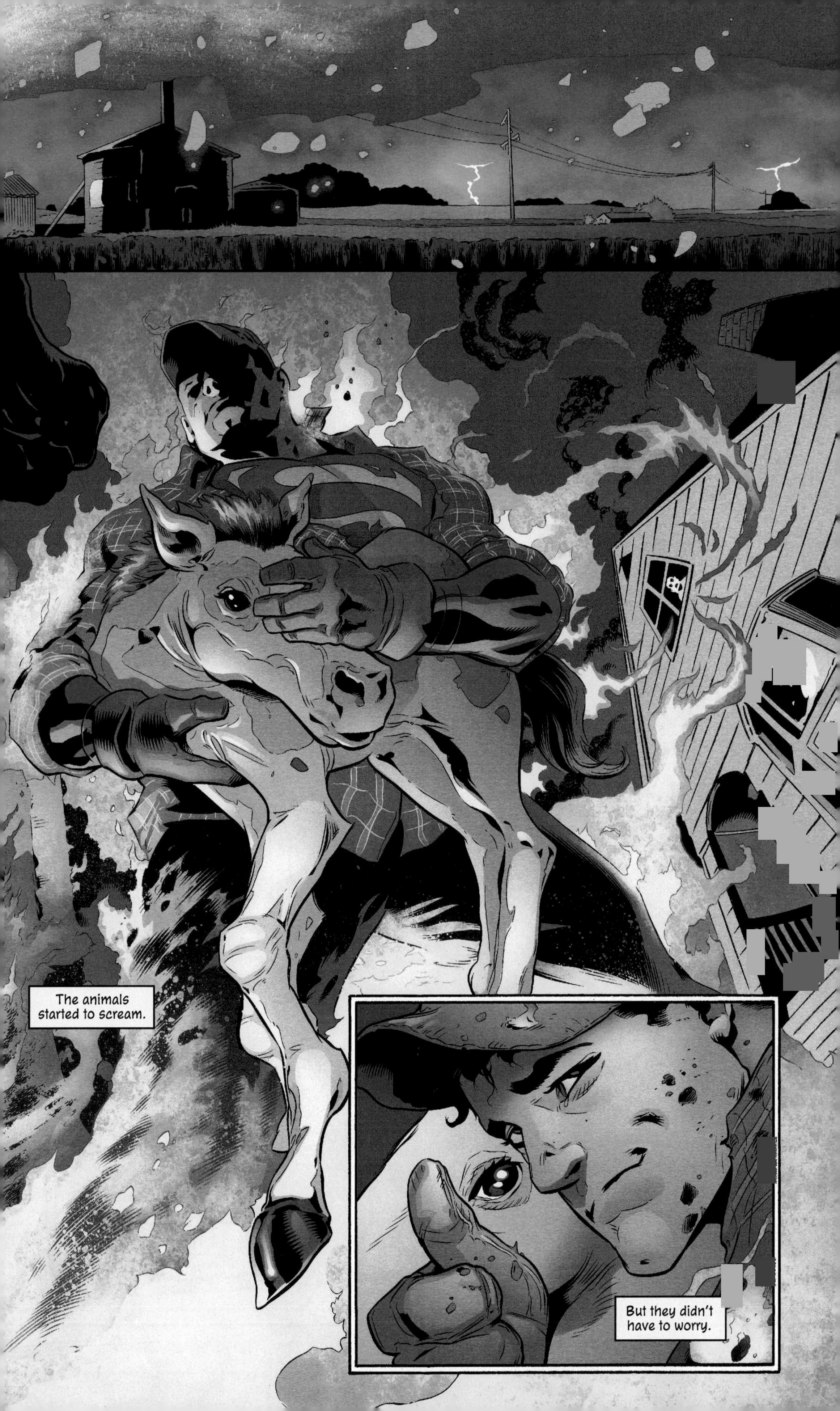
The animals started to scream.
But they didn't have to worry.

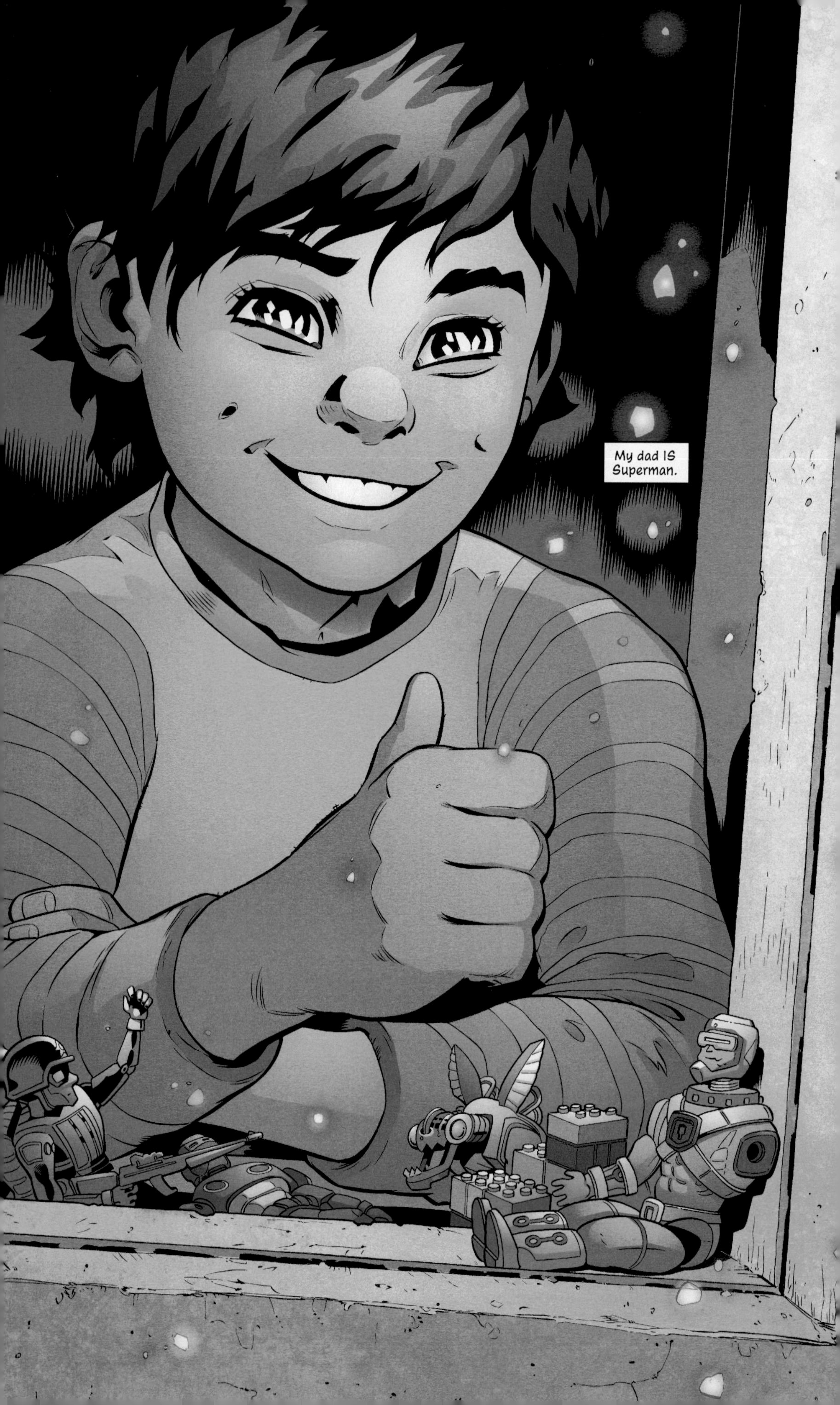
My dad IS Superman.

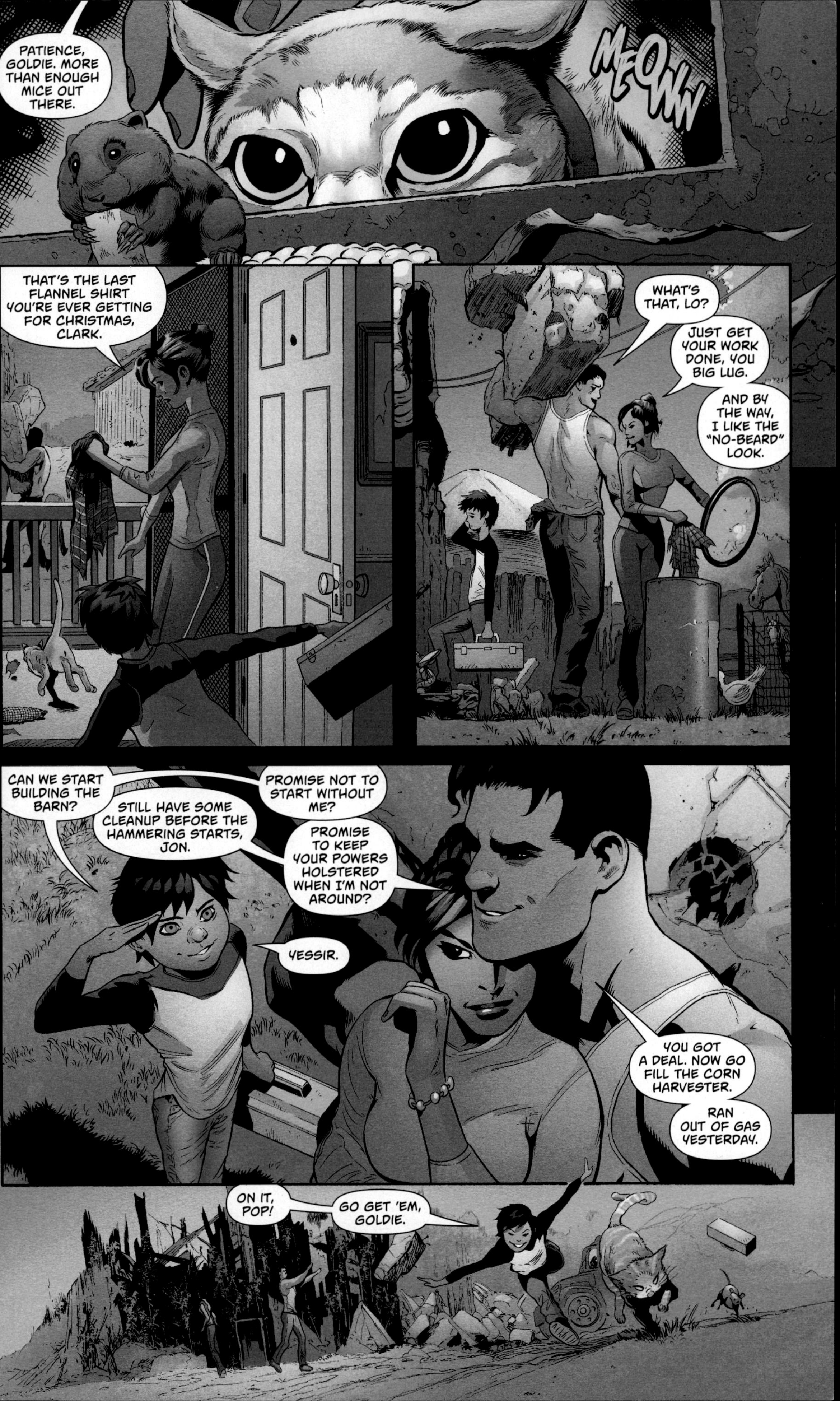
PATIENCE, GOLDIE. MORE THAN ENOUGH MICE OUT THERE.
MEOWW
THAT'S THE LAST FLANNEL SHIRT YOU'RE EVER GETTING FOR CHRISTMAS, CLARK.
WHAT'S THAT, LO?
JUST GET YOUR WORK DONE, YOU BIG LUG.
AND BY THE WAY, I LIKE THE "NO-BEARD" LOOK.
CAN WE START BUILDING THE BARN?
STILL HAVE SOME CLEANUP BEFORE THE HAMMERING STARTS, JON.
PROMISE NOT TO START WITHOUT ME?
PROMISE TO KEEP YOUR POWERS HOLSTERED WHEN I'M NOT AROUND?
YESSIR.
YOU GOT A DEAL. NOW GO FILL THE CORN HARVESTER.
RAN OUT OF GAS YESTERDAY.
ON IT, POP!
GO GET 'EM, GOLDIE.

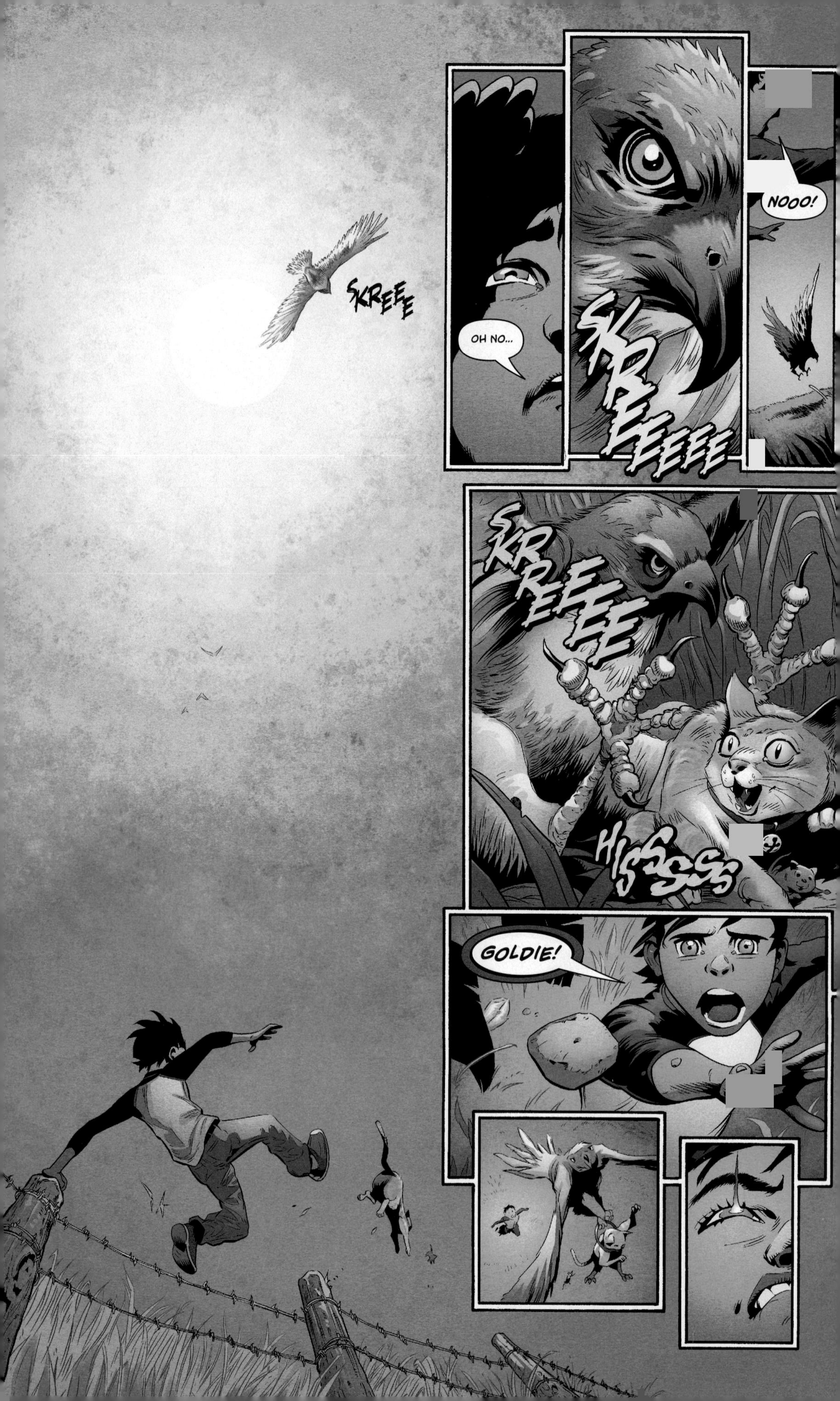
SKREEE
OH NO...
SKREEEEEE
NOOO!
SKREEEEEE
HISSSSS
GOLDIE!

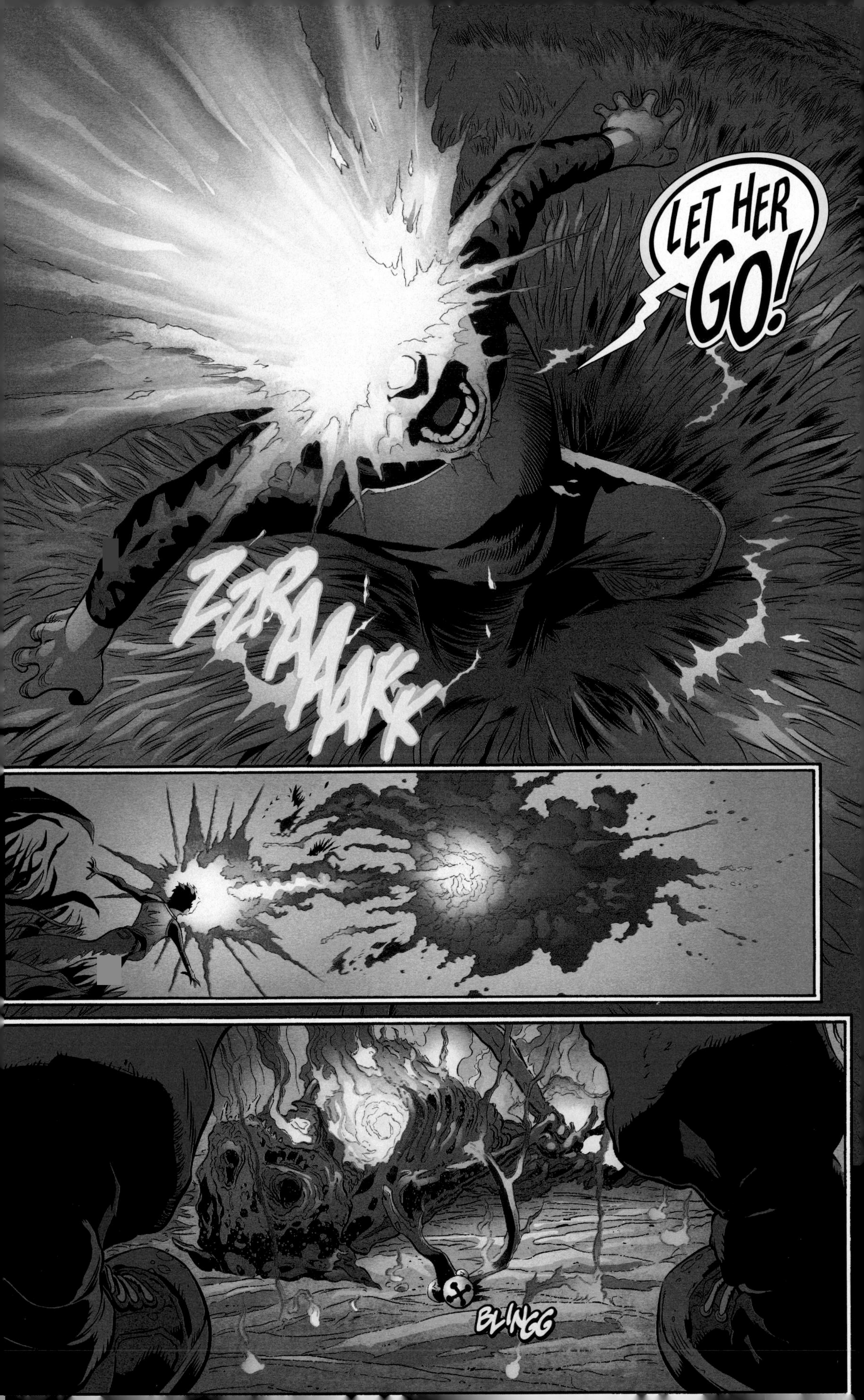
LET HER GO!
ZZRAAAKK
BLINGG

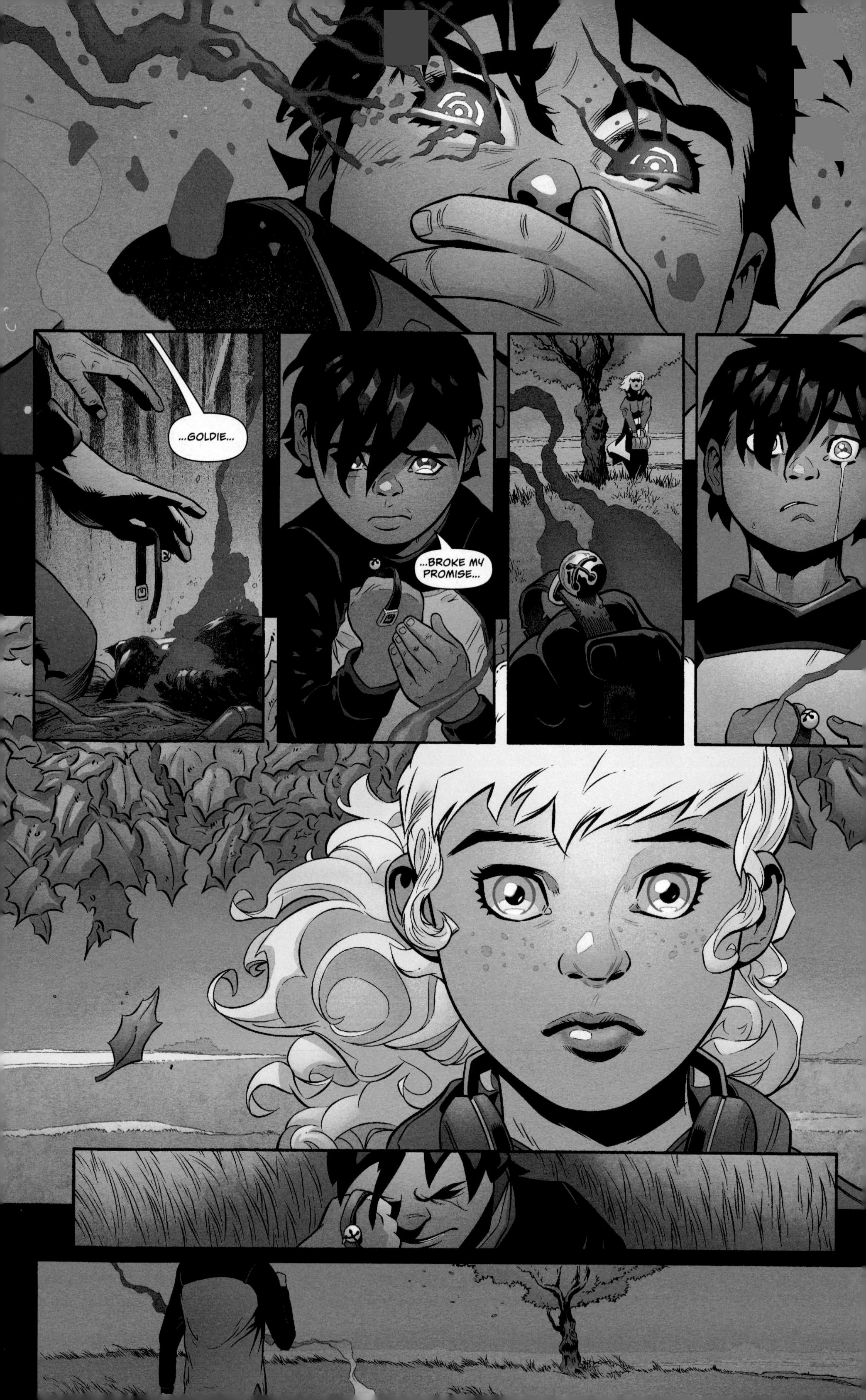
...GOLDIE...
...BROKE MY PROMISE...

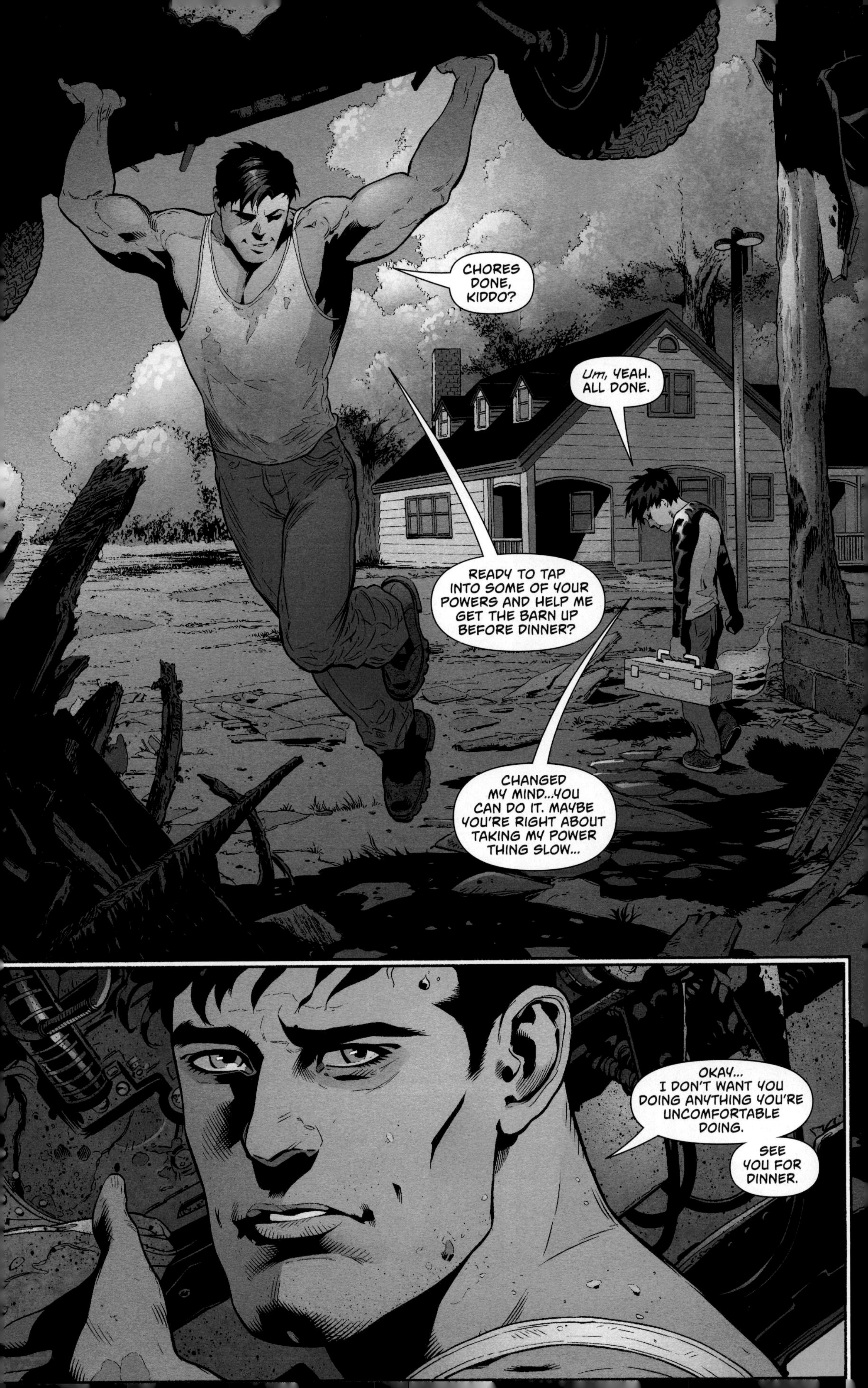
CHORES DONE, KIDDO?
Um, YEAH. ALL DONE.
READY TO TAP INTO SOME OF YOUR POWERS AND HELP ME GET THE BARN UP BEFORE DINNER?
CHANGED MY MIND...YOU CAN DO IT. MAYBE YOU'RE RIGHT ABOUT TAKING MY POWER THING SLOW...
OKAY... I DON'T WANT YOU DOING ANYTHING YOU'RE UNCOMFORTABLE DOING.
SEE YOU FOR DINNER.

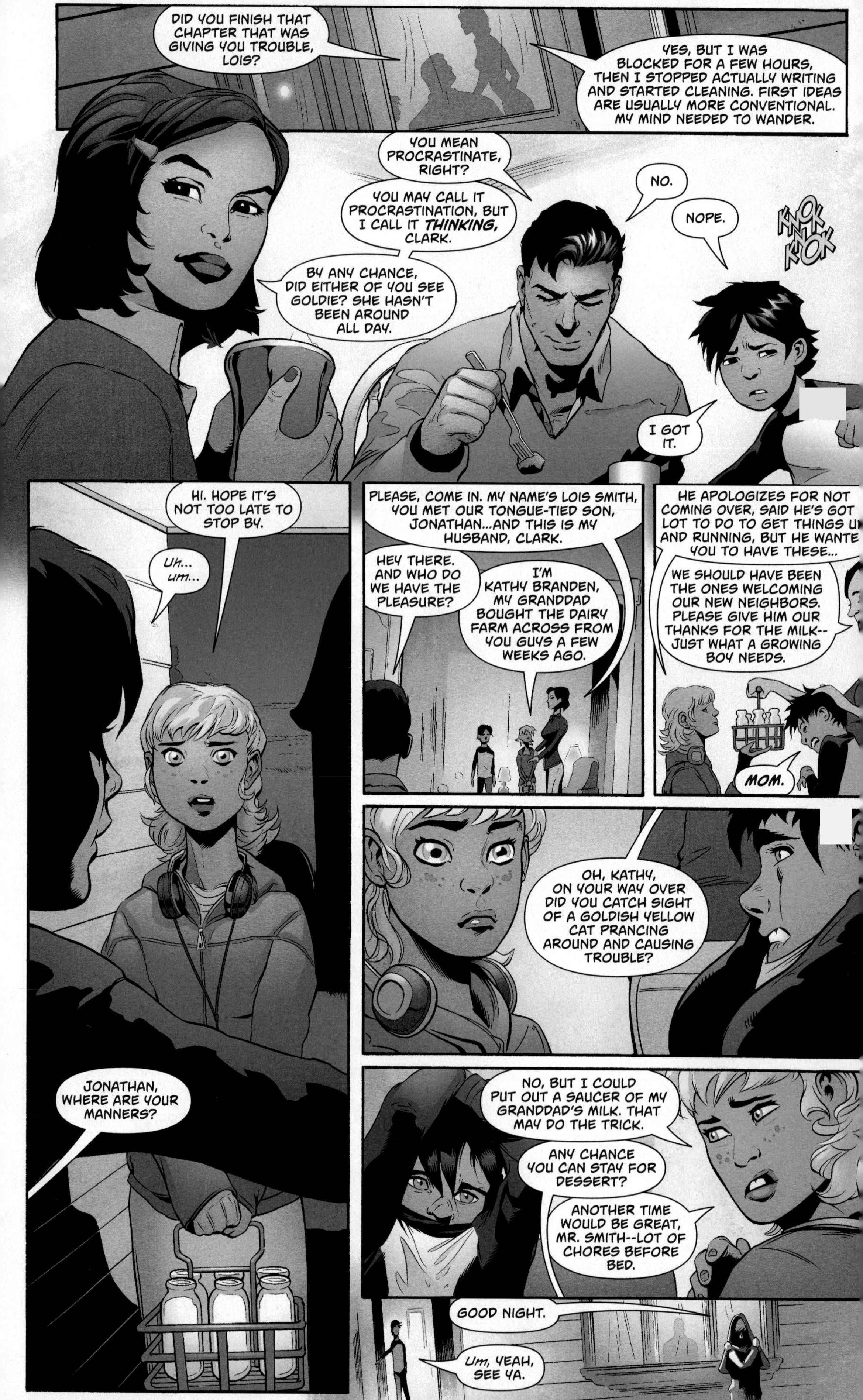

DID YOU FINISH THAT CHAPTER THAT WAS GIVING YOU TROUBLE, LOIS?
YES, BUT I WAS BLOCKED FOR A FEW HOURS, THEN I STOPPED ACTUALLY WRITING AND STARTED CLEANING. FIRST IDEAS ARE USUALLY MORE CONVENTIONAL. MY MIND NEEDED TO WANDER.
YOU MEAN PROCRASTINATE, RIGHT?
YOU MAY CALL IT PROCRASTINATION, BUT I CALL IT THINKING, CLARK.
BY ANY CHANCE, DID EITHER OF YOU SEE GOLDIE? SHE HASN'T BEEN AROUND ALL DAY.
NO.
NOPE.
KNOK KNOK
I GOT IT.
HI. HOPE IT'S NOT TOO LATE TO STOP BY.
Uh... um...
JONATHAN, WHERE ARE YOUR MANNERS?
PLEASE, COME IN. MY NAME'S LOIS SMITH, YOU MET OUR TONGUE-TIED SON, JONATHAN...AND THIS IS MY HUSBAND, CLARK.
HEY THERE. AND WHO DO WE HAVE THE PLEASURE?
I'M KATHY BRANDEN, MY GRANDDAD BOUGHT THE DAIRY FARM ACROSS FROM YOU GUYS A FEW WEEKS AGO.
HE APOLOGIZES FOR NOT COMING OVER, SAID HE'S GOT LOT TO DO TO GET THINGS U AND RUNNING, BUT HE WANTE YOU TO HAVE THESE...
WE SHOULD HAVE BEEN THE ONES WELCOMING OUR NEW NEIGHBORS. PLEASE GIVE HIM OUR THANKS FOR THE MILK-- JUST WHAT A GROWING BOY NEEDS.
MOM.
OH, KATHY, ON YOUR WAY OVER DID YOU CATCH SIGHT OF A GOLDISH YELLOW CAT PRANCING AROUND AND CAUSING TROUBLE?
NO, BUT I COULD PUT OUT A SAUCER OF MY GRANDDAD'S MILK. THAT MAY DO THE TRICK.
ANY CHANCE YOU CAN STAY FOR DESSERT?
ANOTHER TIME WOULD BE GREAT, MR. SMITH--LOT OF CHORES BEFORE BED.
GOOD NIGHT.
Um, YEAH, SEE YA.

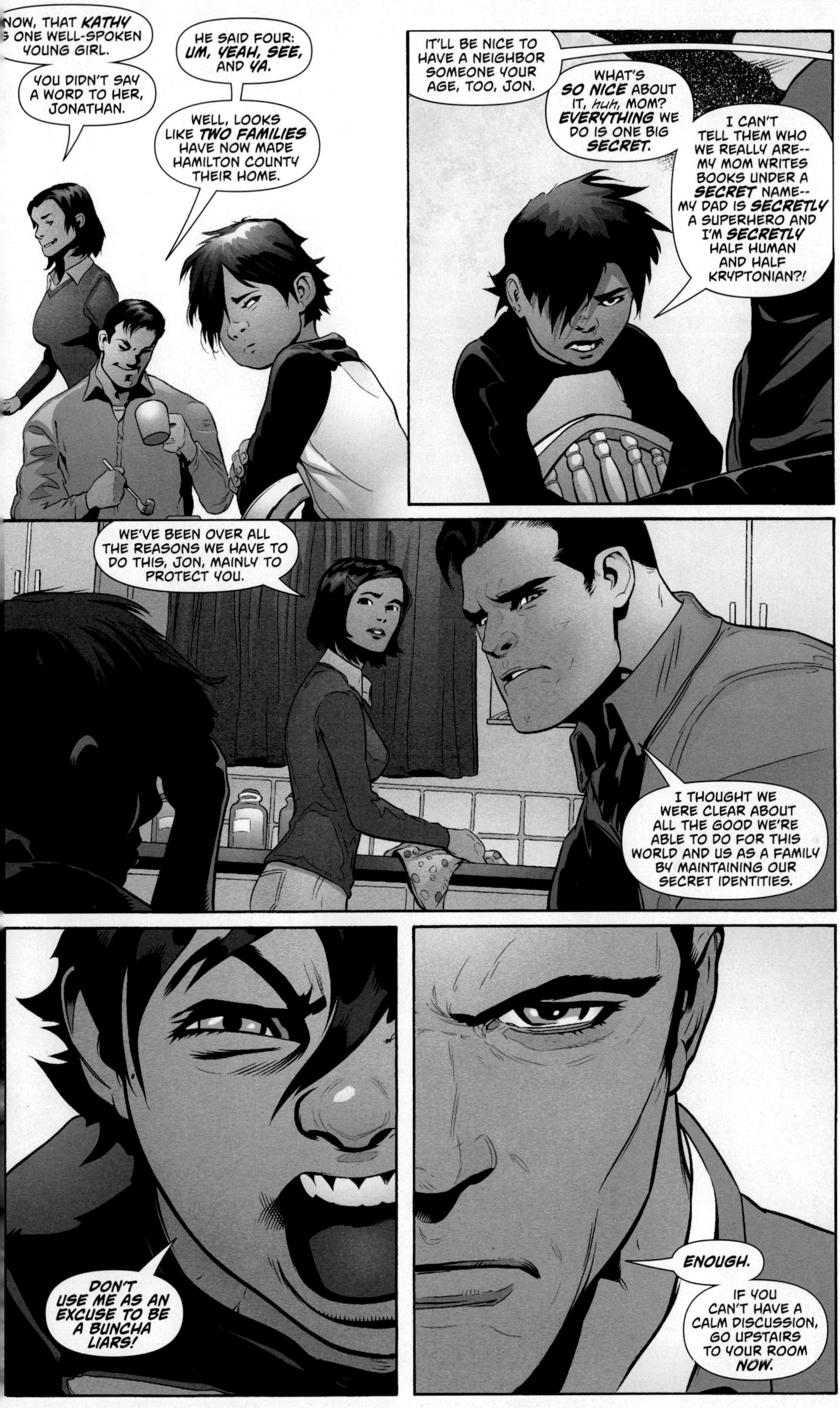
NOW, THAT KATHY 'S ONE WELL-SPOKEN YOUNG GIRL.
YOU DIDN'T SAY A WORD TO HER, JONATHAN.
HE SAID FOUR: UM, YEAH, SEE, AND YA.
WELL, LOOKS LIKE TWO FAMILIES HAVE NOW MADE HAMILTON COUNTY THEIR HOME.
IT'LL BE NICE TO HAVE A NEIGHBOR SOMEONE YOUR AGE, TOO, JON.
WHAT'S SO NICE ABOUT IT, huh, MOM? EVERYTHING WE DO IS ONE BIG SECRET.
I CAN'T TELL THEM WHO WE REALLY ARE-- MY MOM WRITES BOOKS UNDER A SECRET NAME-- MY DAD IS SECRETLY A SUPERHERO AND I'M SECRETLY HALF HUMAN AND HALF KRYPTONIAN?!
WE'VE BEEN OVER ALL THE REASONS WE HAVE TO DO THIS, JON, MAINLY TO PROTECT YOU.
I THOUGHT WE WERE CLEAR ABOUT ALL THE GOOD WE'RE ABLE TO DO FOR THIS WORLD AND US AS A FAMILY BY MAINTAINING OUR SECRET IDENTITIES.
DON'T USE ME AS AN EXCUSE TO BE A BUNCHA LIARS!
ENOUGH.
IF YOU CAN'T HAVE A CALM DISCUSSION, GO UPSTAIRS TO YOUR ROOM NOW.

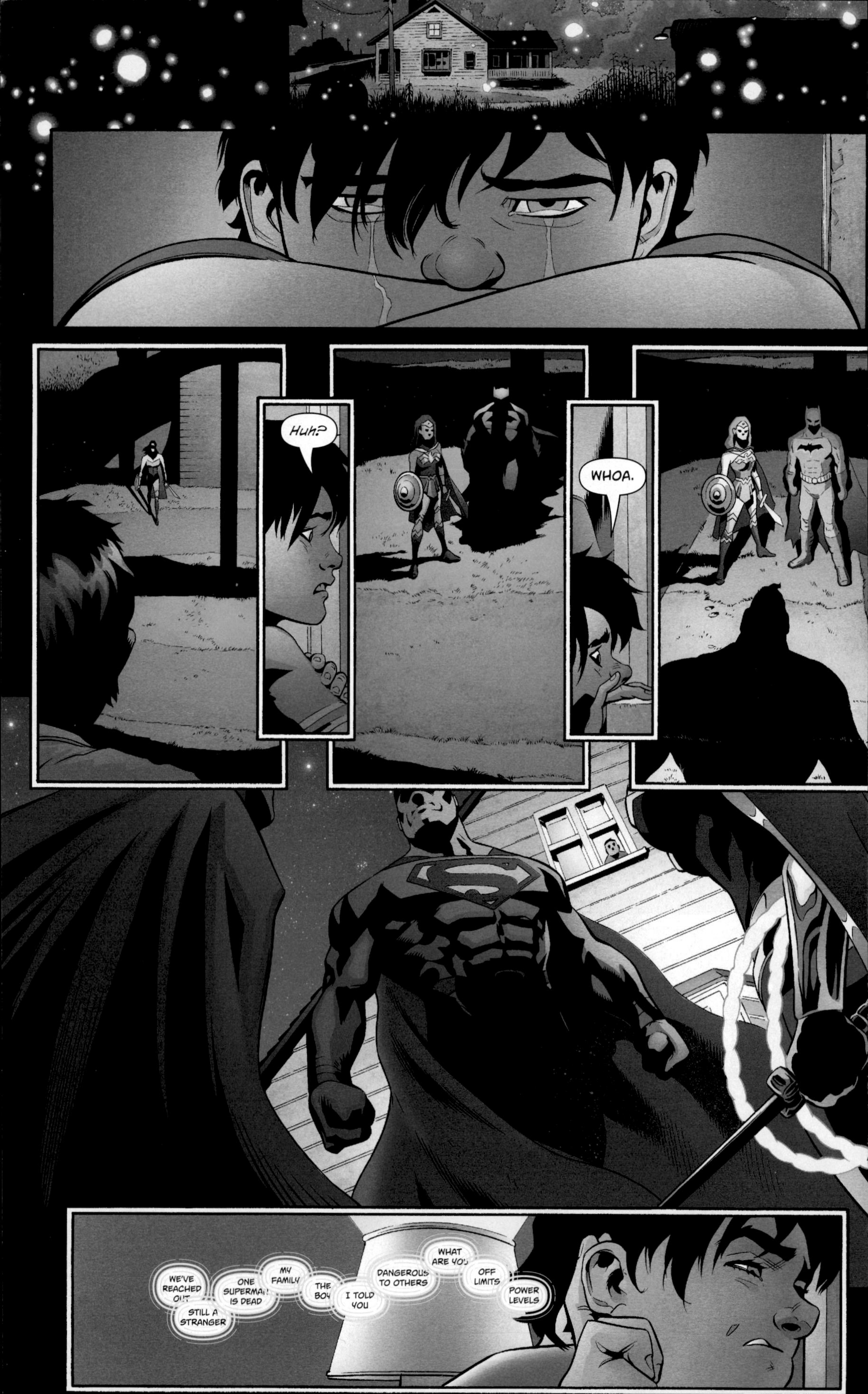
Huh?
WHOA.
WE'VE REACHED OUT
STILL A STRANGER
ONE SUPERMAN IS DEAD
MY FAMILY
THE BOY
I TOLD YOU
DANGEROUS TO OTHERS
WHAT ARE YOU
OFF LIMITS
POWER LEVELS

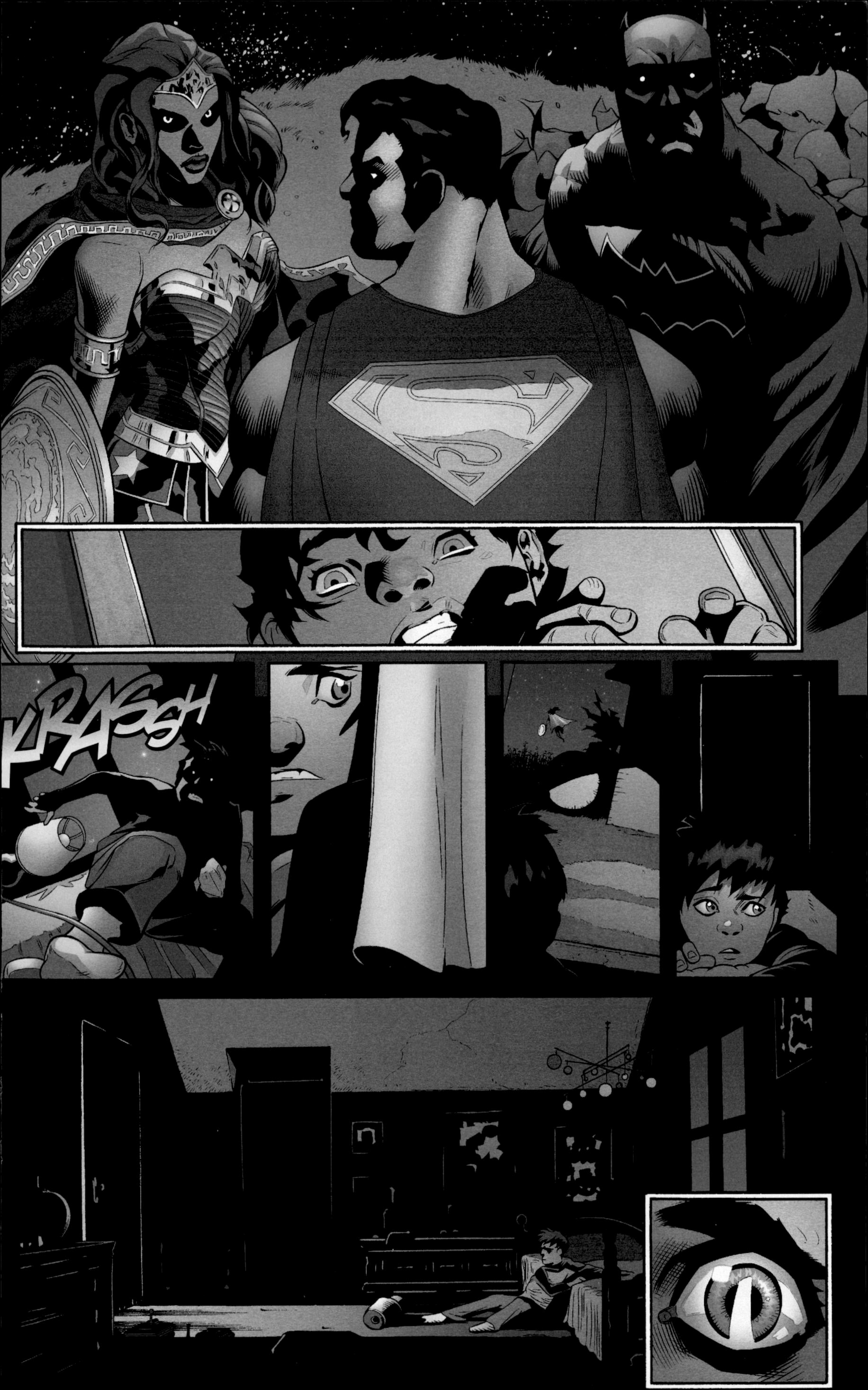
KRASSH

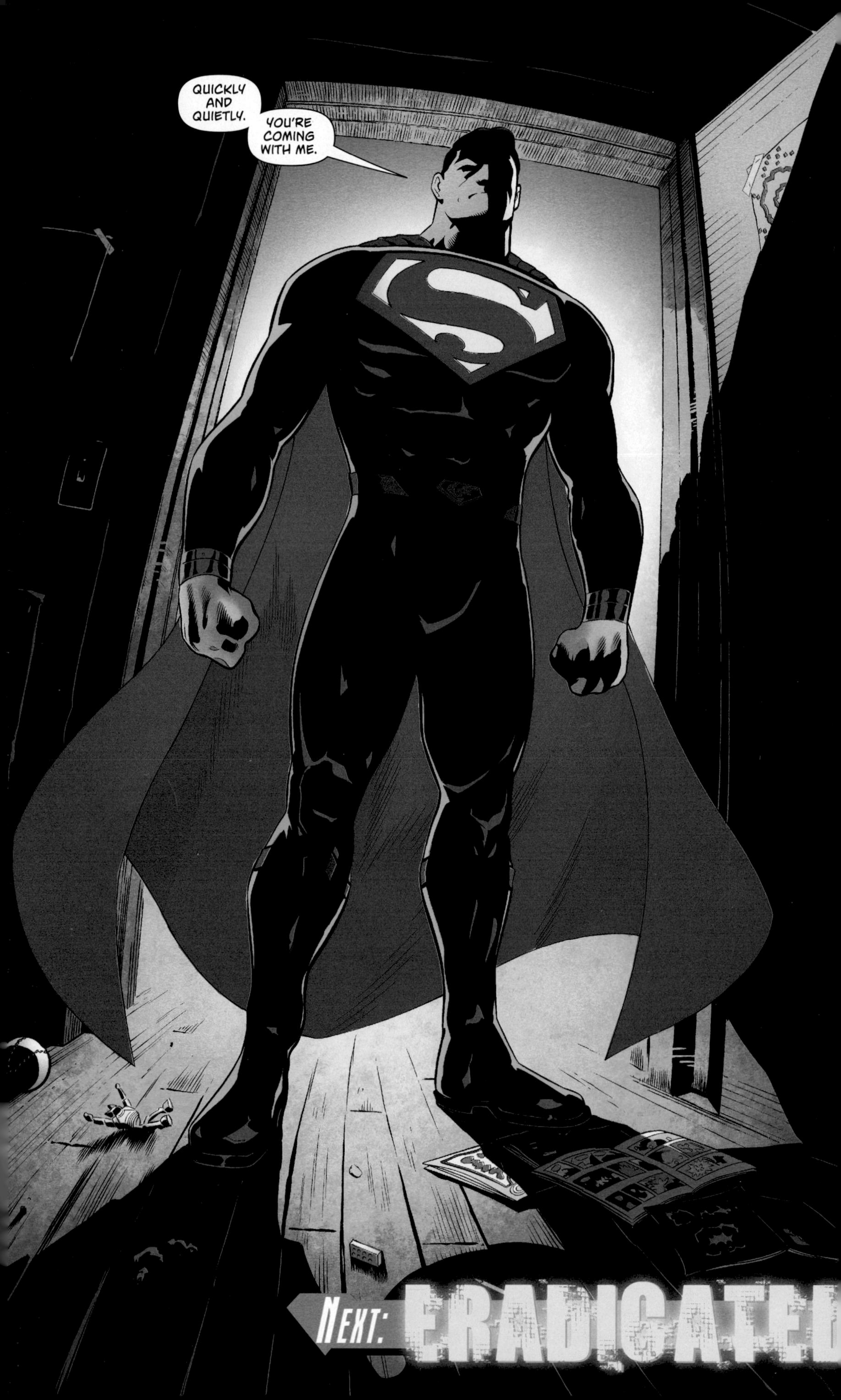
QUICKLY AND QUIETLY.
YOU'RE COMING WITH ME.
NEXT: ERADICATED

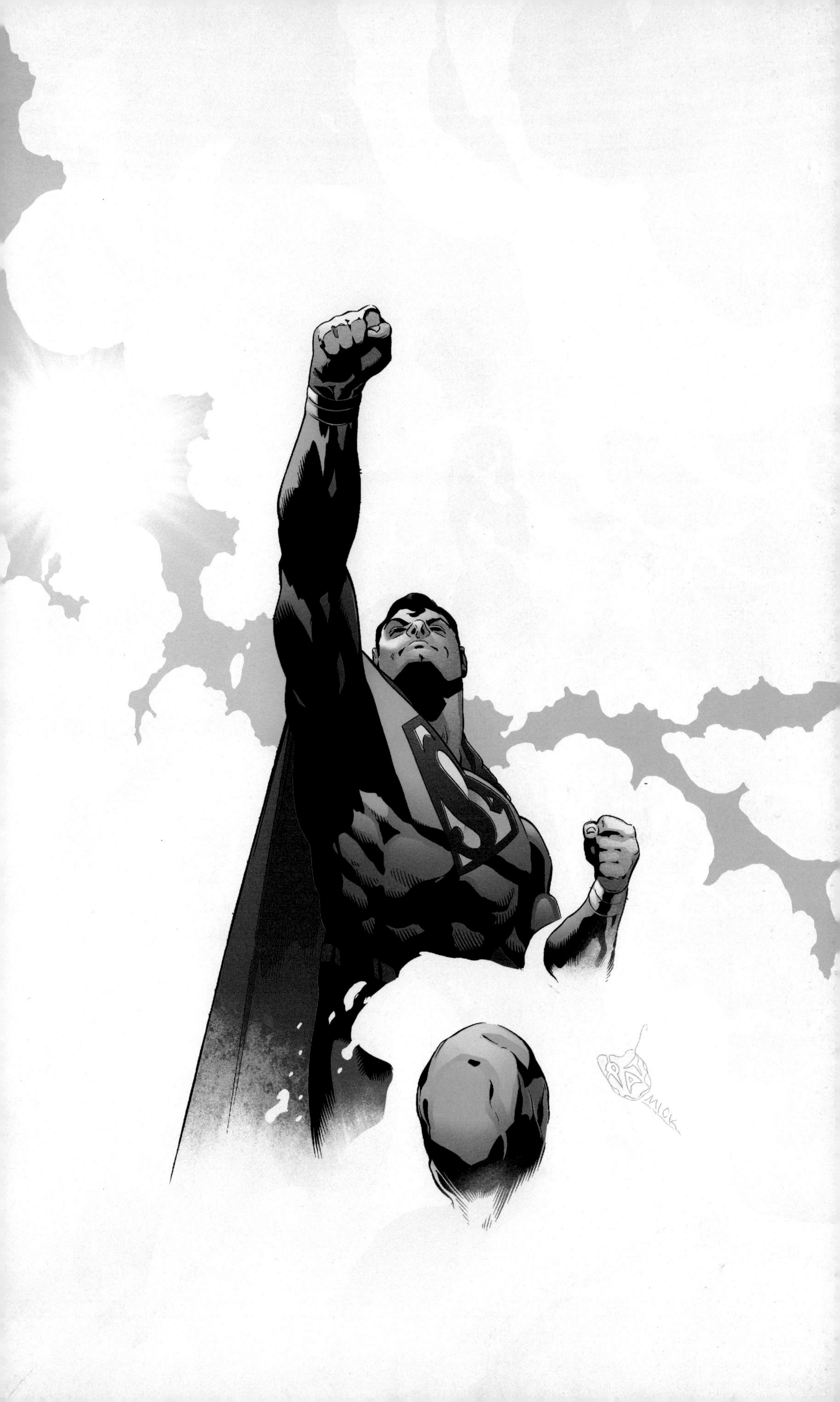

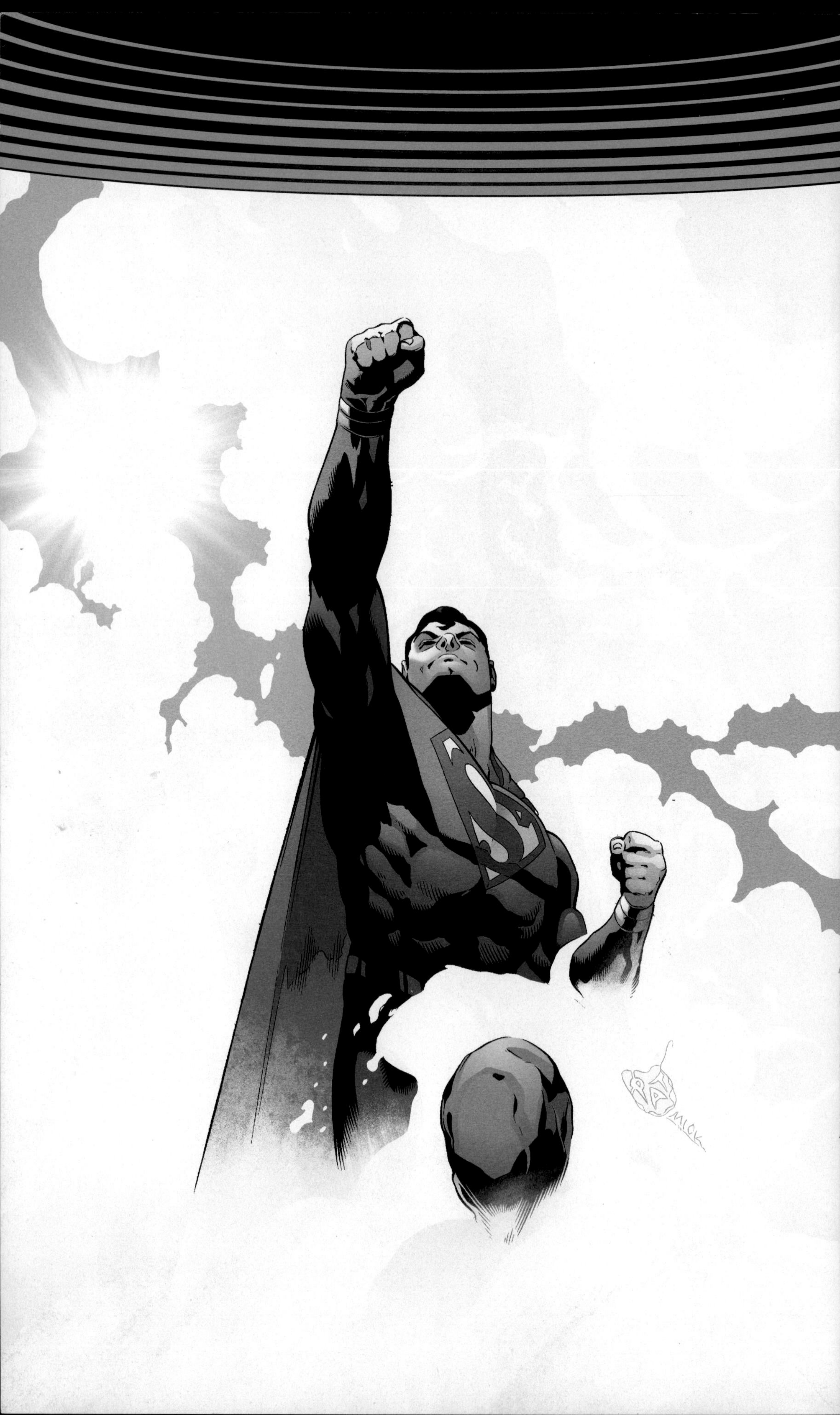

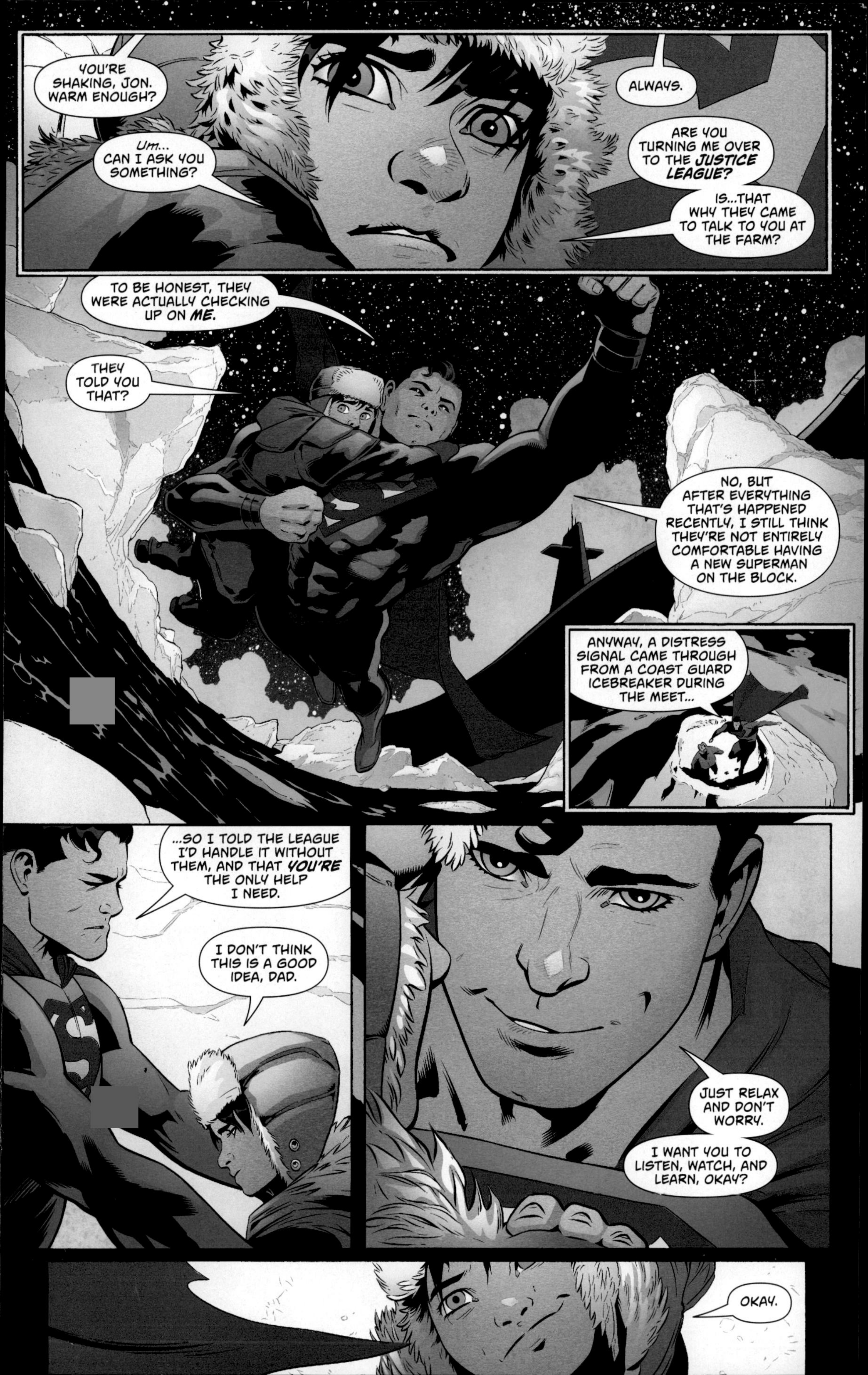

YOU'RE SHAKING, JON. WARM ENOUGH?
ALWAYS.
UM... CAN I ASK YOU SOMETHING?
ARE YOU TURNING ME OVER TO THE JUSTICE LEAGUE?
IS...THAT WHY THEY CAME TO TALK TO YOU AT THE FARM?
TO BE HONEST, THEY WERE ACTUALLY CHECKING UP ON ME.
THEY TOLD YOU THAT?
NO, BUT AFTER EVERYTHING THAT'S HAPPENED RECENTLY, I STILL THINK THEY'RE NOT ENTIRELY COMFORTABLE HAVING A NEW SUPERMAN ON THE BLOCK.
ANYWAY, A DISTRESS SIGNAL CAME THROUGH FROM A COAST GUARD ICEBREAKER DURING THE MEET...
...SO I TOLD THE LEAGUE I'D HANDLE IT WITHOUT THEM, AND THAT YOU'RE THE ONLY HELP I NEED.
I DON'T THINK THIS IS A GOOD IDEA, DAD.
JUST RELAX AND DON'T WORRY.
I WANT YOU TO LISTEN, WATCH, AND LEARN, OKAY?
OKAY.

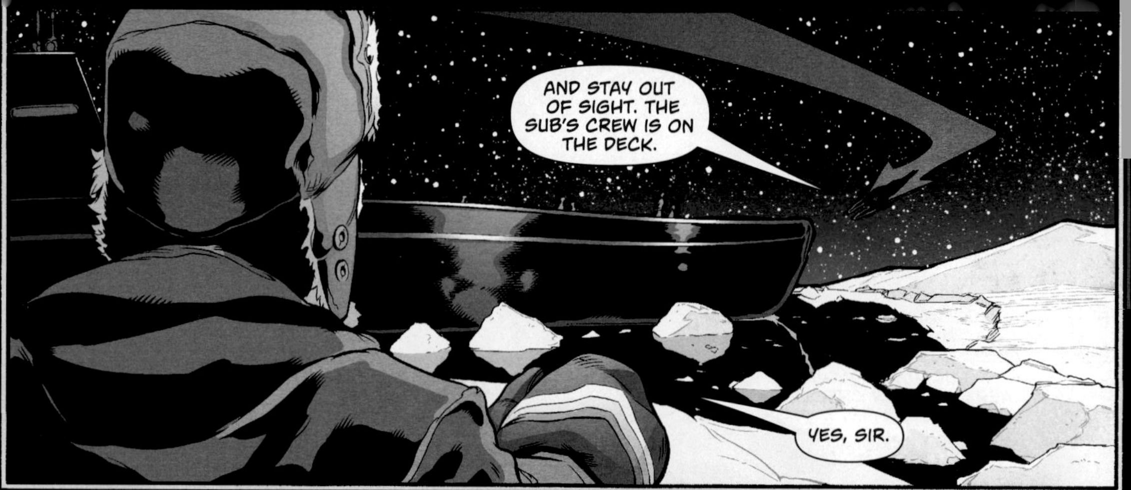
AND STAY OUT OF SIGHT. THE SUB'S CREW IS ON THE DECK.
YES, SIR.

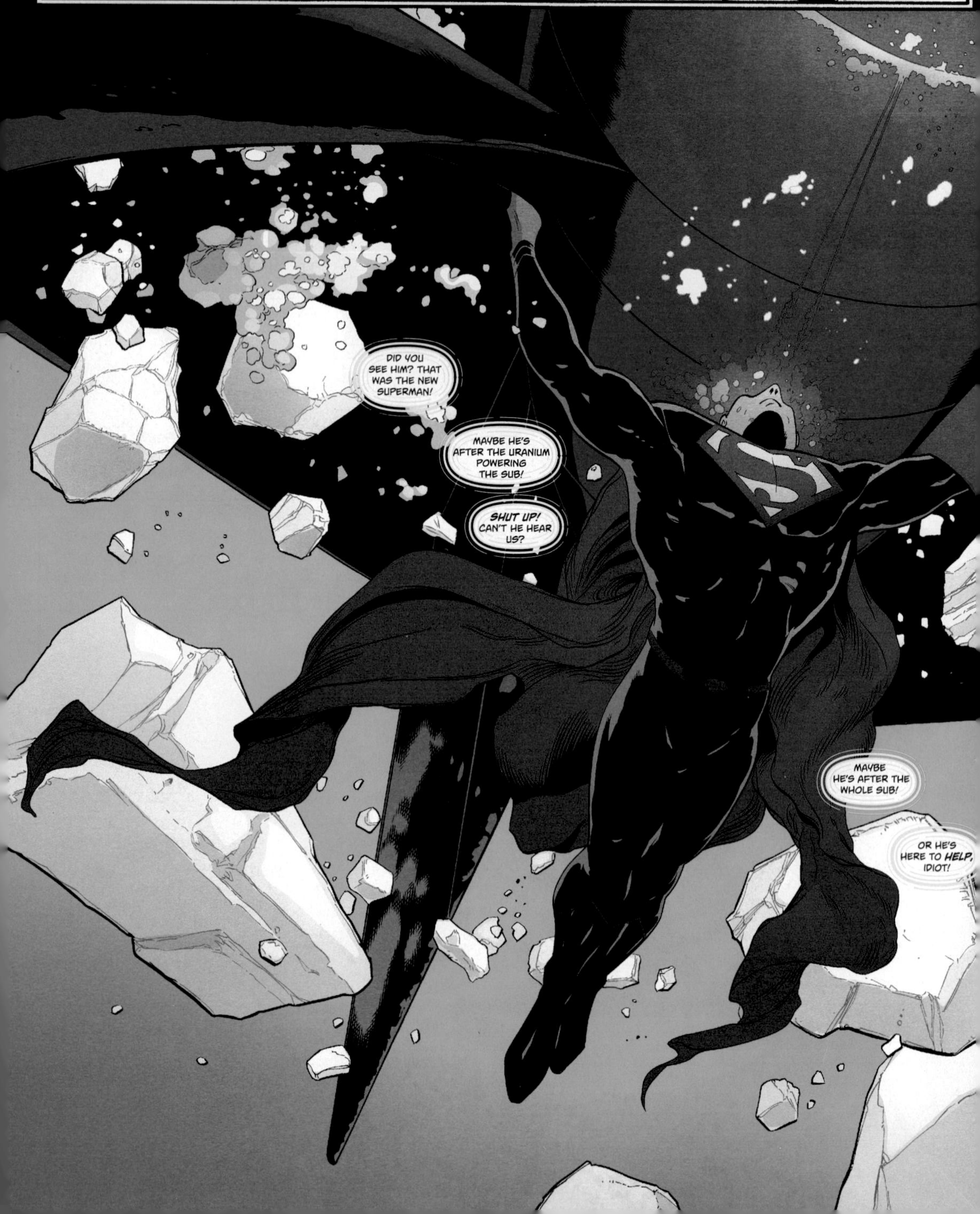
DID YOU SEE HIM? THAT WAS THE NEW SUPERMAN!
MAYBE HE'S AFTER THE URANIUM POWERING THE SUB!
SHUT UP! CAN'T HE HEAR US?
MAYBE HE'S AFTER THE WHOLE SUB!
OR HE'S HERE TO HELP, IDIOT!

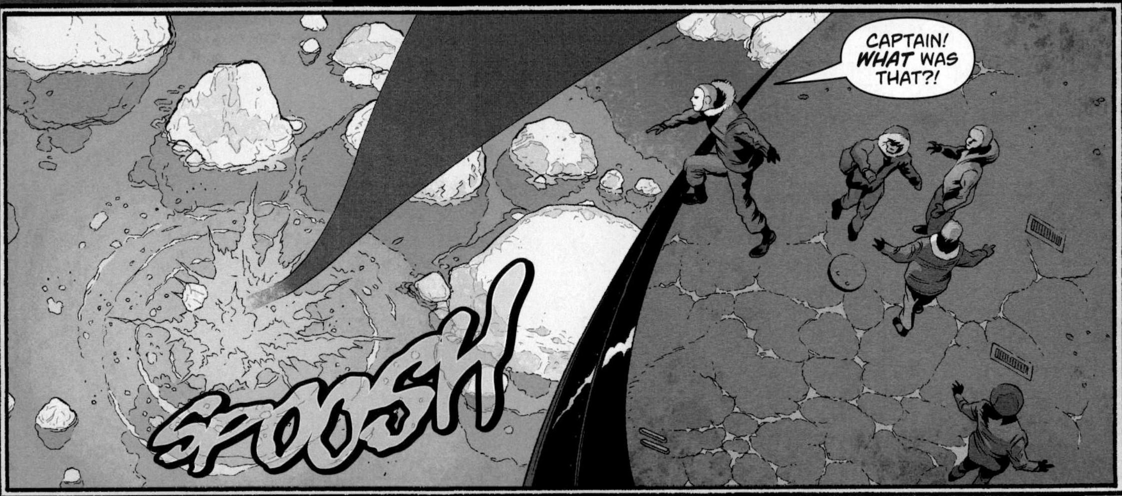
CAPTAIN! WHAT WAS THAT?!
SPOOSH

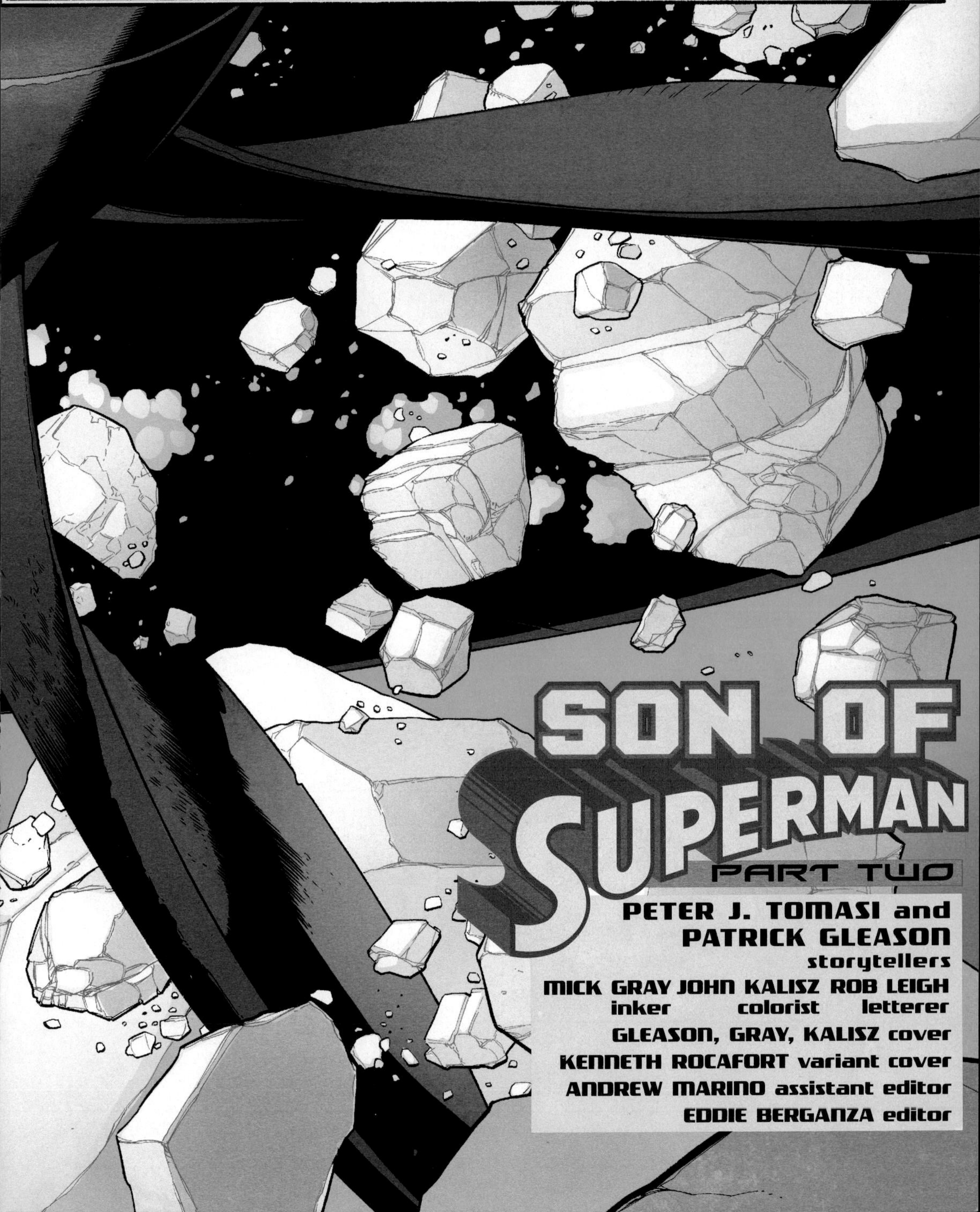
SON OF SUPERMAN
PART TWO
PETER J. TOMASI and PATRICK GLEASON storytellers
MICK GRAY inker
JOHN KALISZ colorist
ROB LEIGH letterer
GLEASON, GRAY, KALISZ cover
KENNETH ROCAFORT variant cover
ANDREW MARINO assistant editor
EDDIE BERGANZA editor

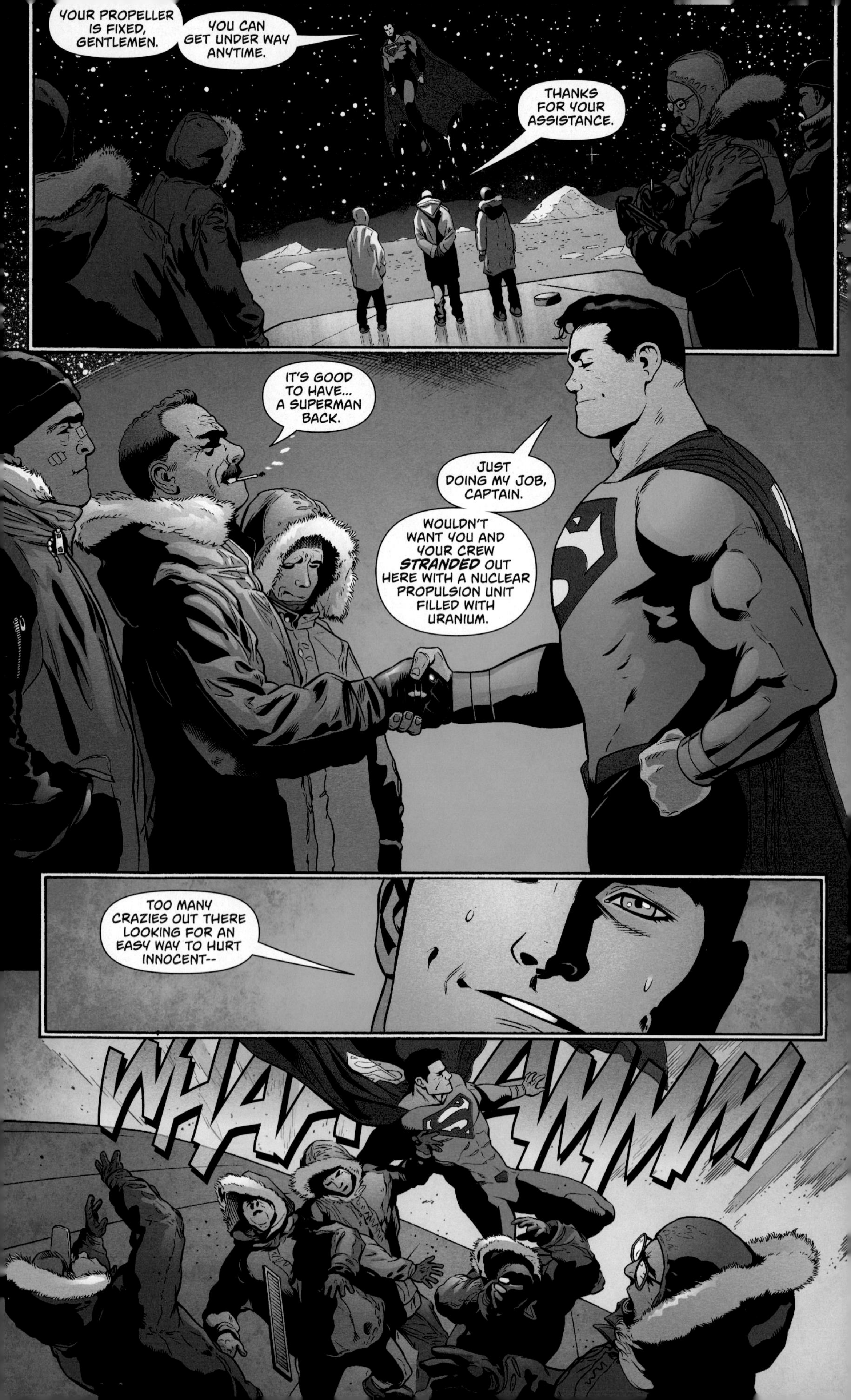
YOUR PROPELLER IS FIXED, GENTLEMEN.
YOU CAN GET UNDER WAY ANYTIME.
THANKS FOR YOUR ASSISTANCE.
IT'S GOOD TO HAVE... A SUPERMAN BACK.
JUST DOING MY JOB, CAPTAIN.
WOULDN'T WANT YOU AND YOUR CREW STRANDED OUT HERE WITH A NUCLEAR PROPULSION UNIT FILLED WITH URANIUM.
TOO MANY CRAZIES OUT THERE LOOKING FOR AN EASY WAY TO HURT INNOCENT--

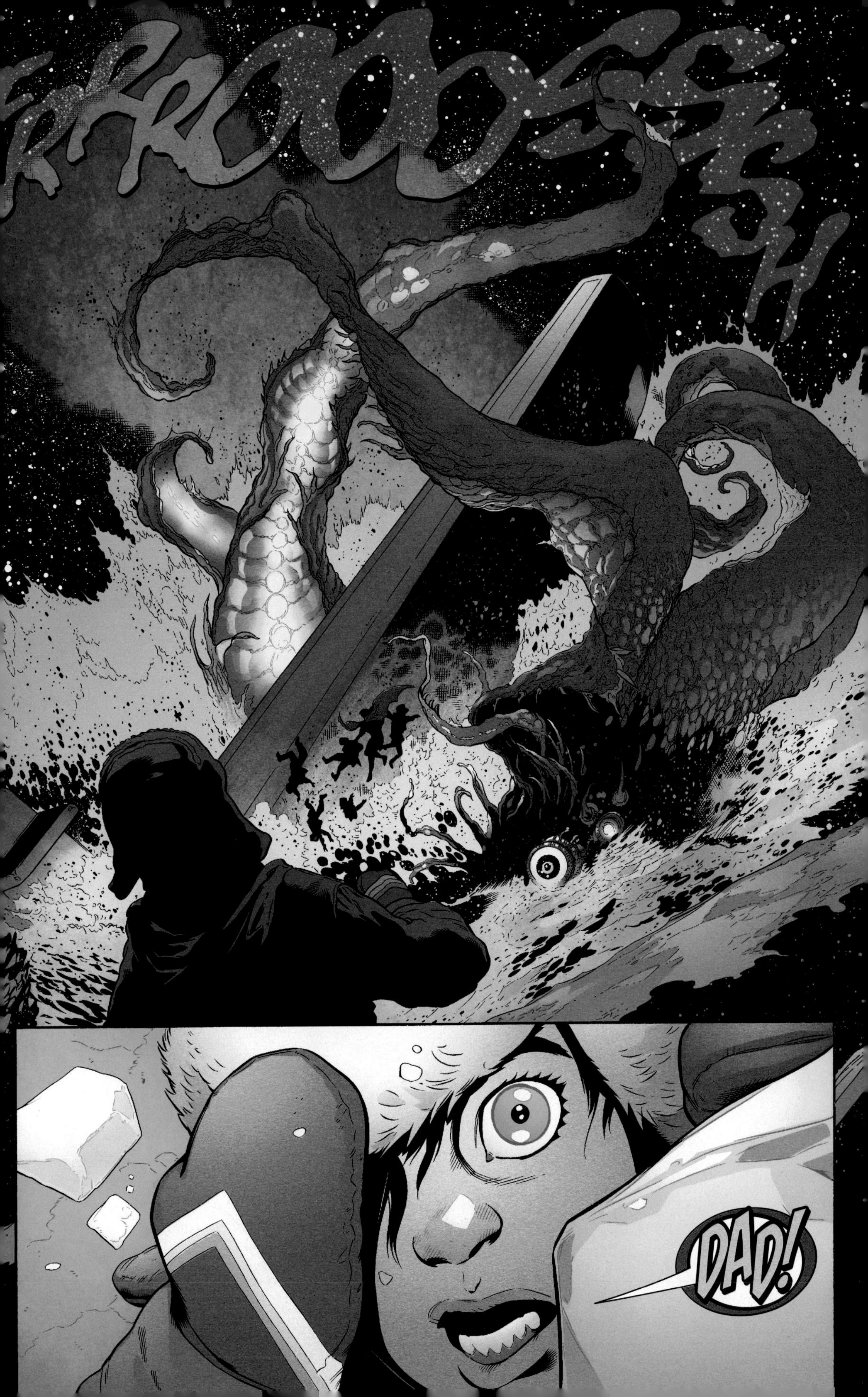
DAD!

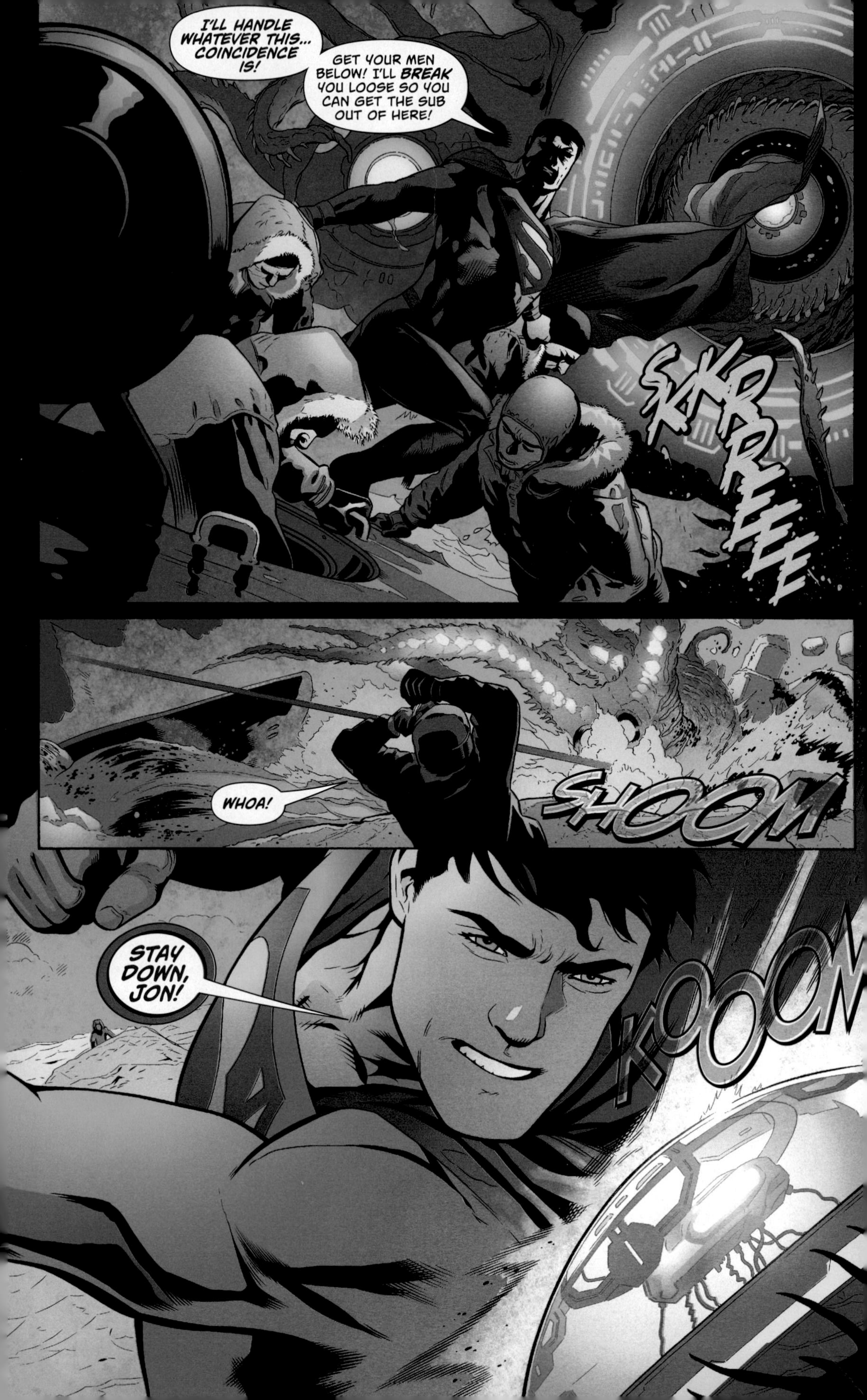
I'LL HANDLE WHATEVER THIS... COINCIDENCE IS!
GET YOUR MEN BELOW! I'LL BREAK YOU LOOSE SO YOU CAN GET THE SUB OUT OF HERE!
SKKRREEEE
WHOA!
SHOOM
STAY DOWN, JON!
KOOOOM

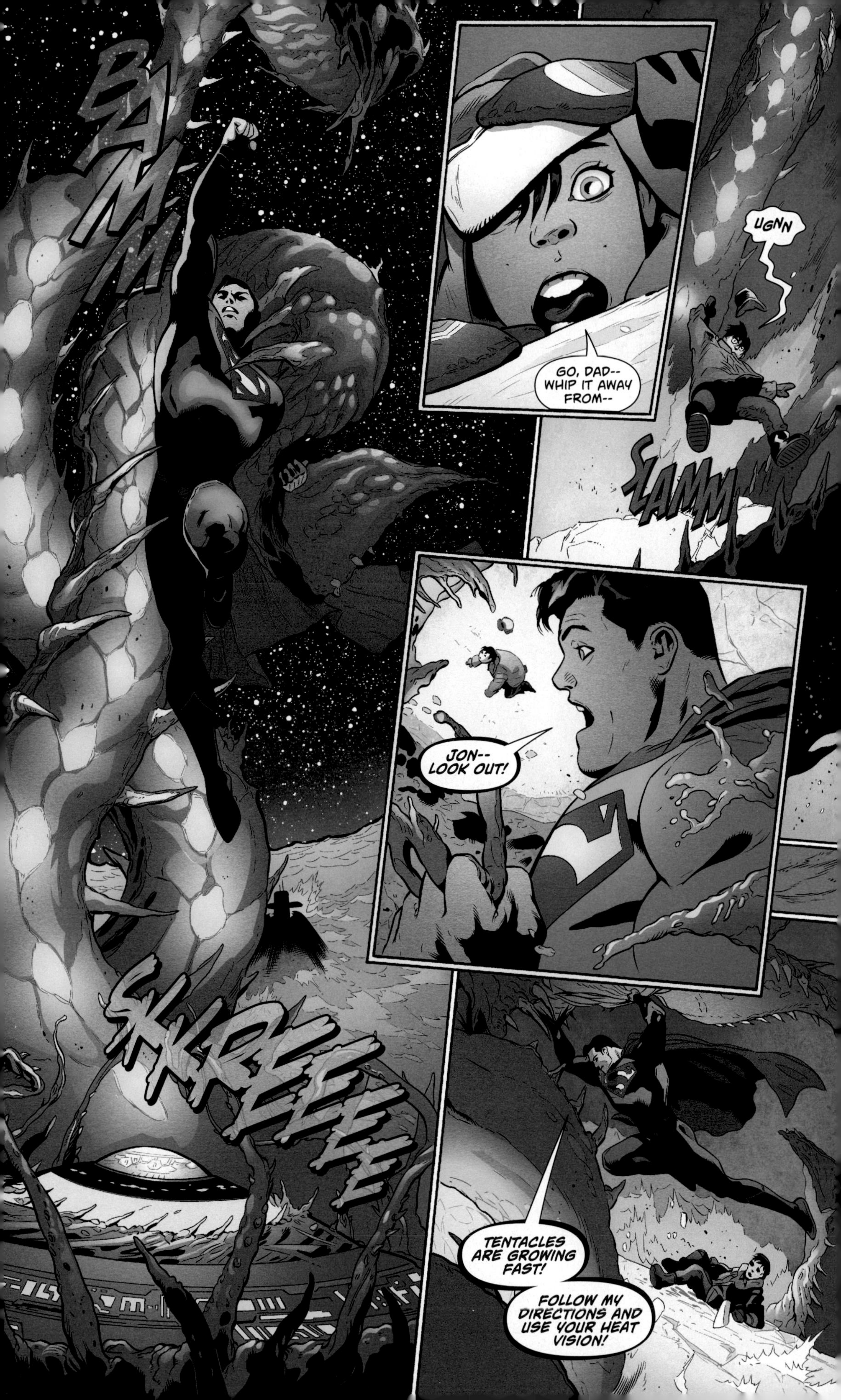
BAMM
GO, DAD--
WHIP IT AWAY
FROM--
UGNN
SLAMM
JON--
LOOK OUT!
SKREEEE
TENTACLES
ARE GROWING
FAST!
FOLLOW MY
DIRECTIONS AND
USE YOUR HEAT
VISION!

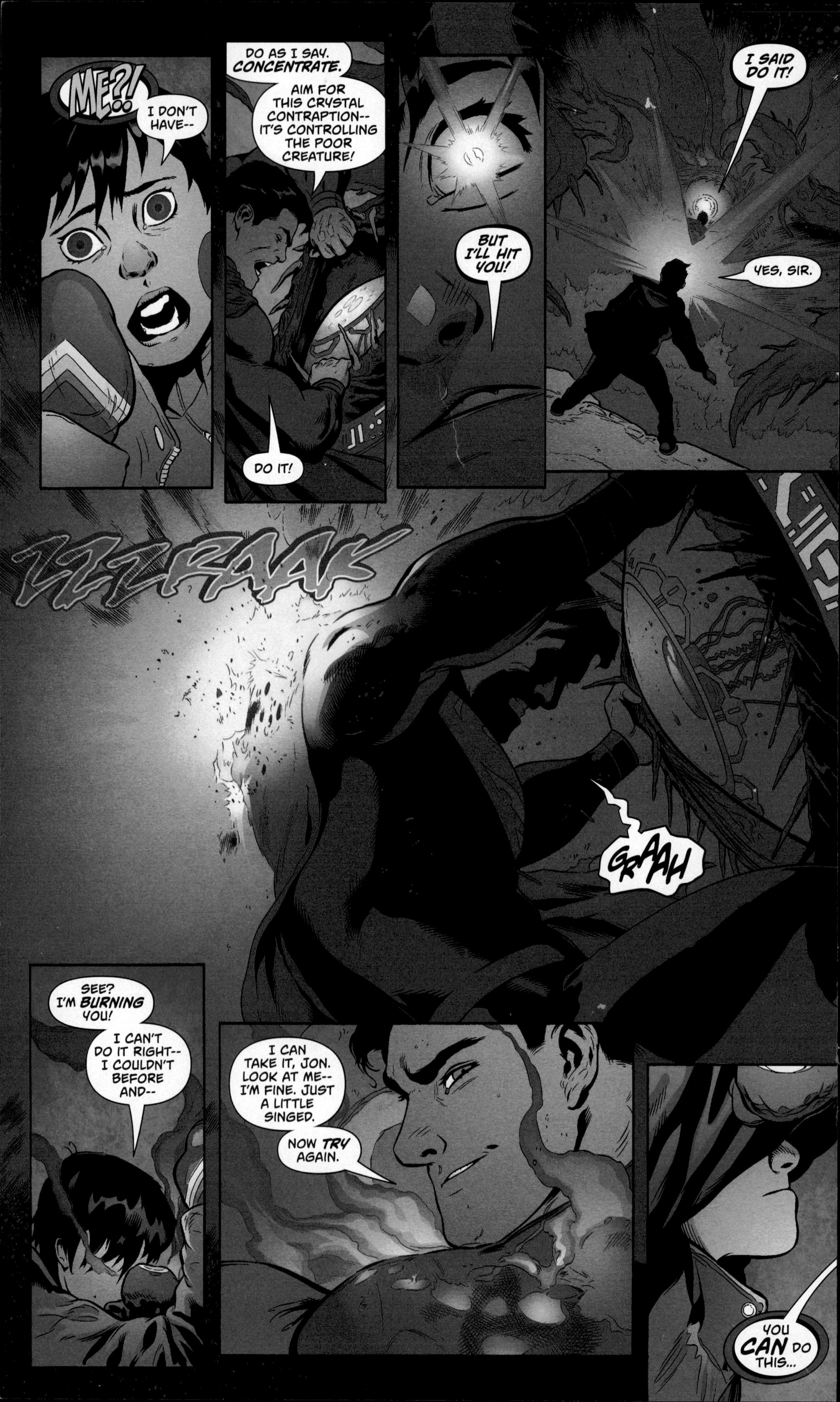

ME?!
I DON'T HAVE--
DO AS I SAY. CONCENTRATE.
AIM FOR THIS CRYSTAL CONTRAPTION-- IT'S CONTROLLING THE POOR CREATURE!
DO IT!
BUT I'LL HIT YOU!
I SAID DO IT!
YES, SIR.
ZZZRAAAK
GRAAAH
SEE? I'M BURNING YOU!
I CAN'T DO IT RIGHT-- I COULDN'T BEFORE AND--
I CAN TAKE IT, JON. LOOK AT ME-- I'M FINE. JUST A LITTLE SINGED.
NOW TRY AGAIN.
YOU CAN DO THIS...

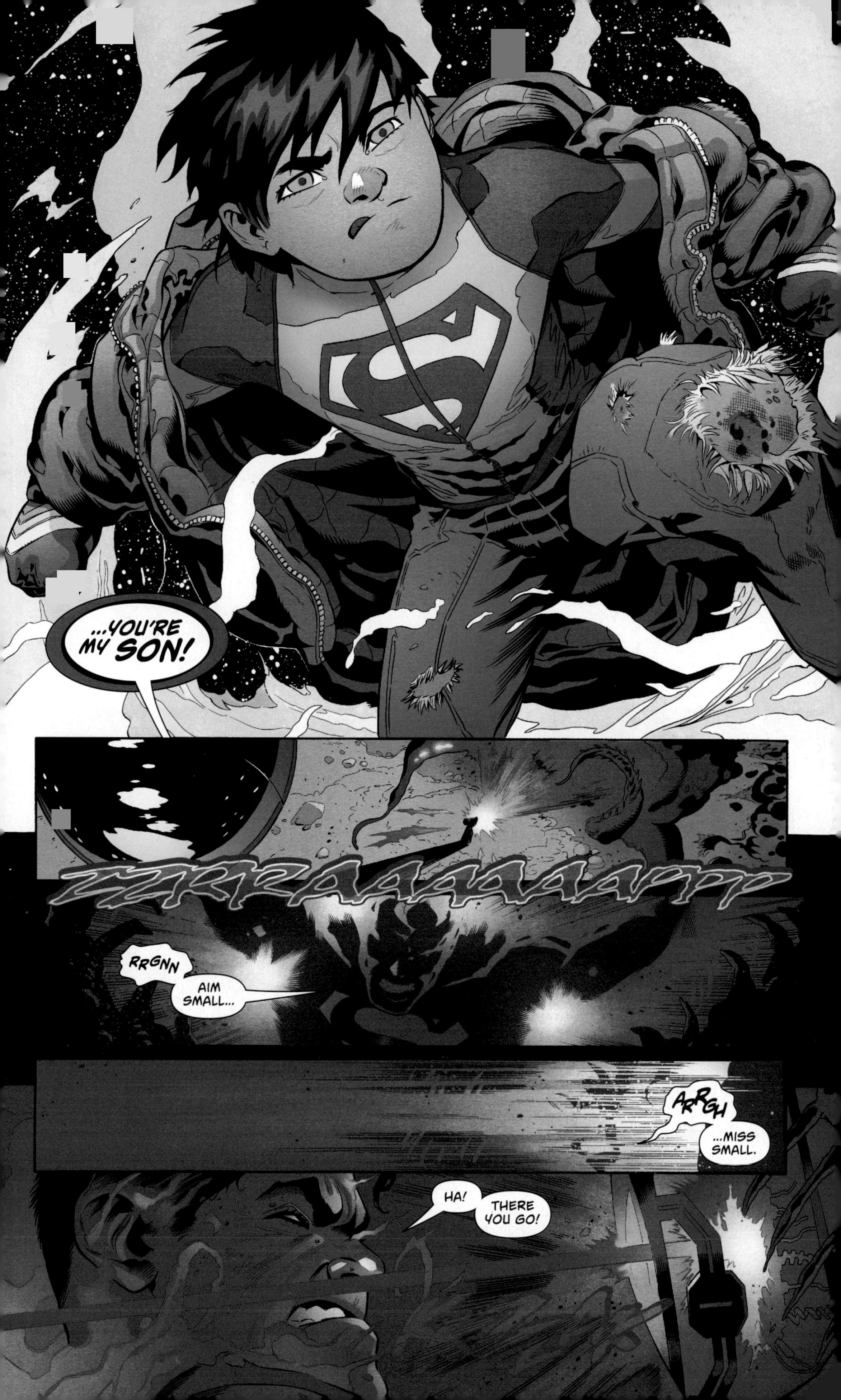
...YOU'RE MY SON!
TZZRAAAAAAAPP
RRGNN
AIM SMALL...
ARRGH
...MISS SMALL.
HA!
THERE YOU GO!

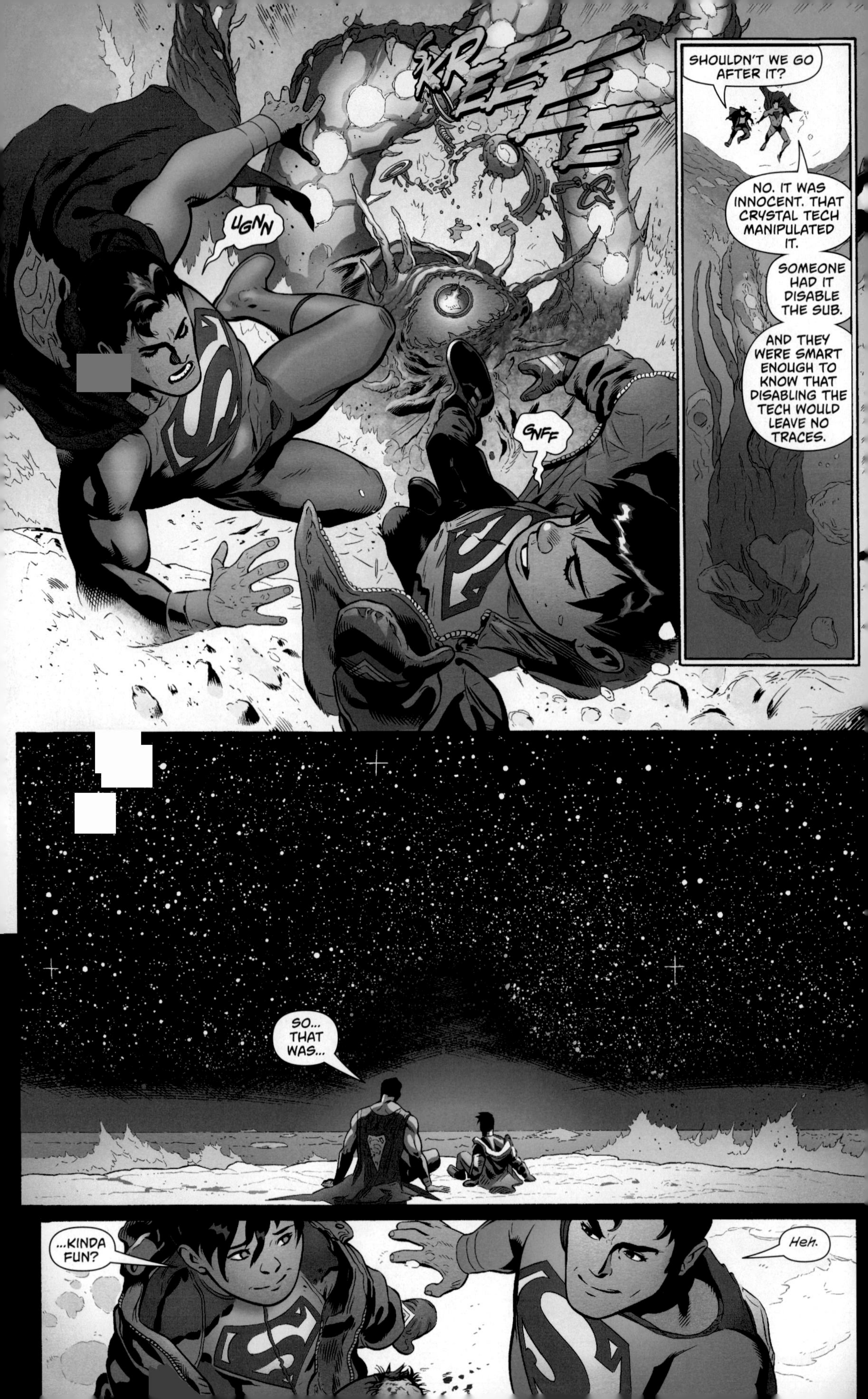
SKREEEEE
UGNN
GNFF
SHOULDN'T WE GO AFTER IT?
NO. IT WAS INNOCENT. THAT CRYSTAL TECH MANIPULATED IT.
SOMEONE HAD IT DISABLE THE SUB.
AND THEY WERE SMART ENOUGH TO KNOW THAT DISABLING THE TECH WOULD LEAVE NO TRACES.
SO... THAT WAS...
...KINDA FUN?
Heh.

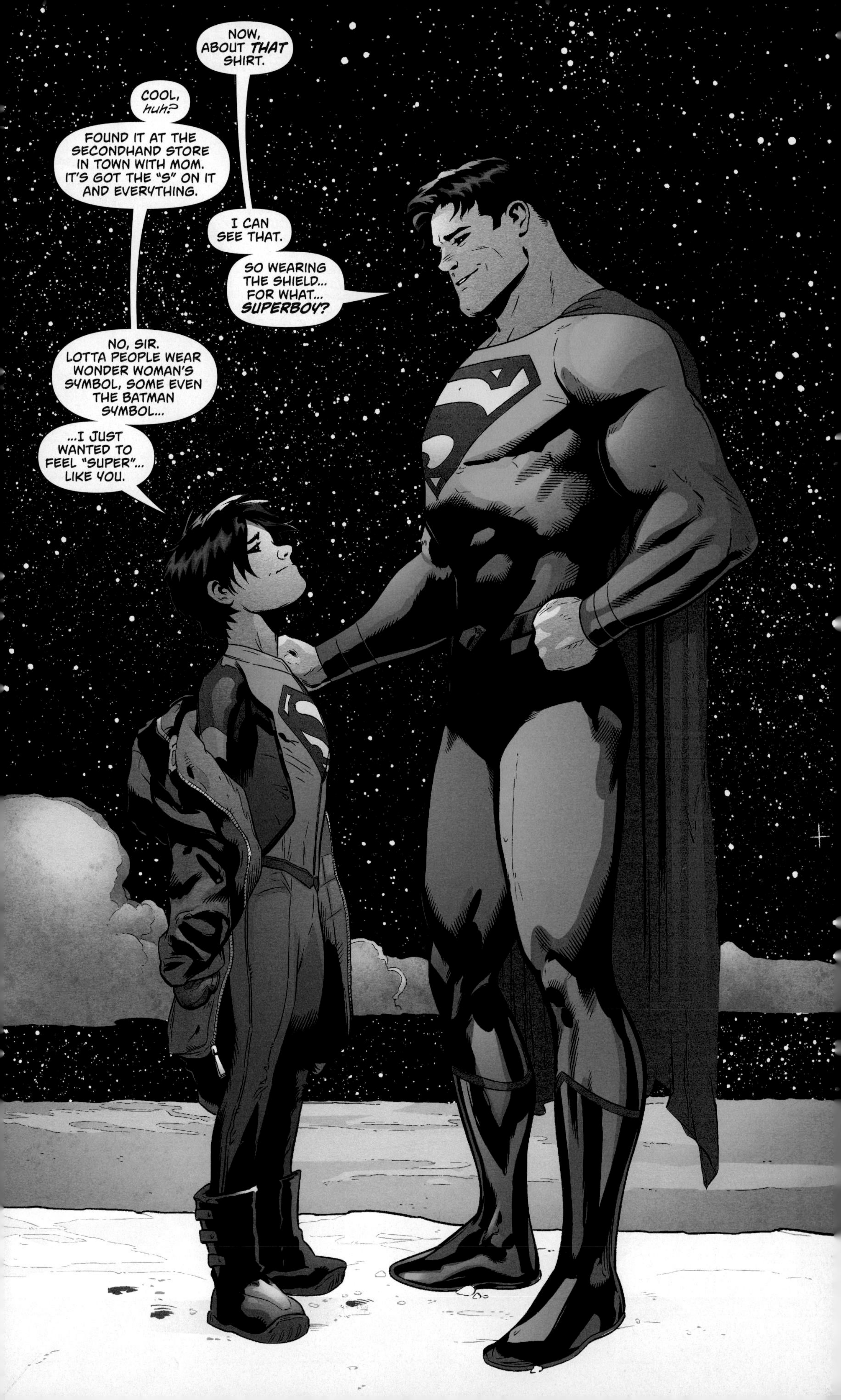
COOL, huh?
FOUND IT AT THE SECONDHAND STORE IN TOWN WITH MOM. IT'S GOT THE "S" ON IT AND EVERYTHING.
NOW, ABOUT THAT SHIRT.
I CAN SEE THAT.
SO WEARING THE SHIELD... FOR WHAT... SUPERBOY?
NO, SIR. LOTTA PEOPLE WEAR WONDER WOMAN'S SYMBOL, SOME EVEN THE BATMAN SYMBOL...
...I JUST WANTED TO FEEL "SUPER"... LIKE YOU.

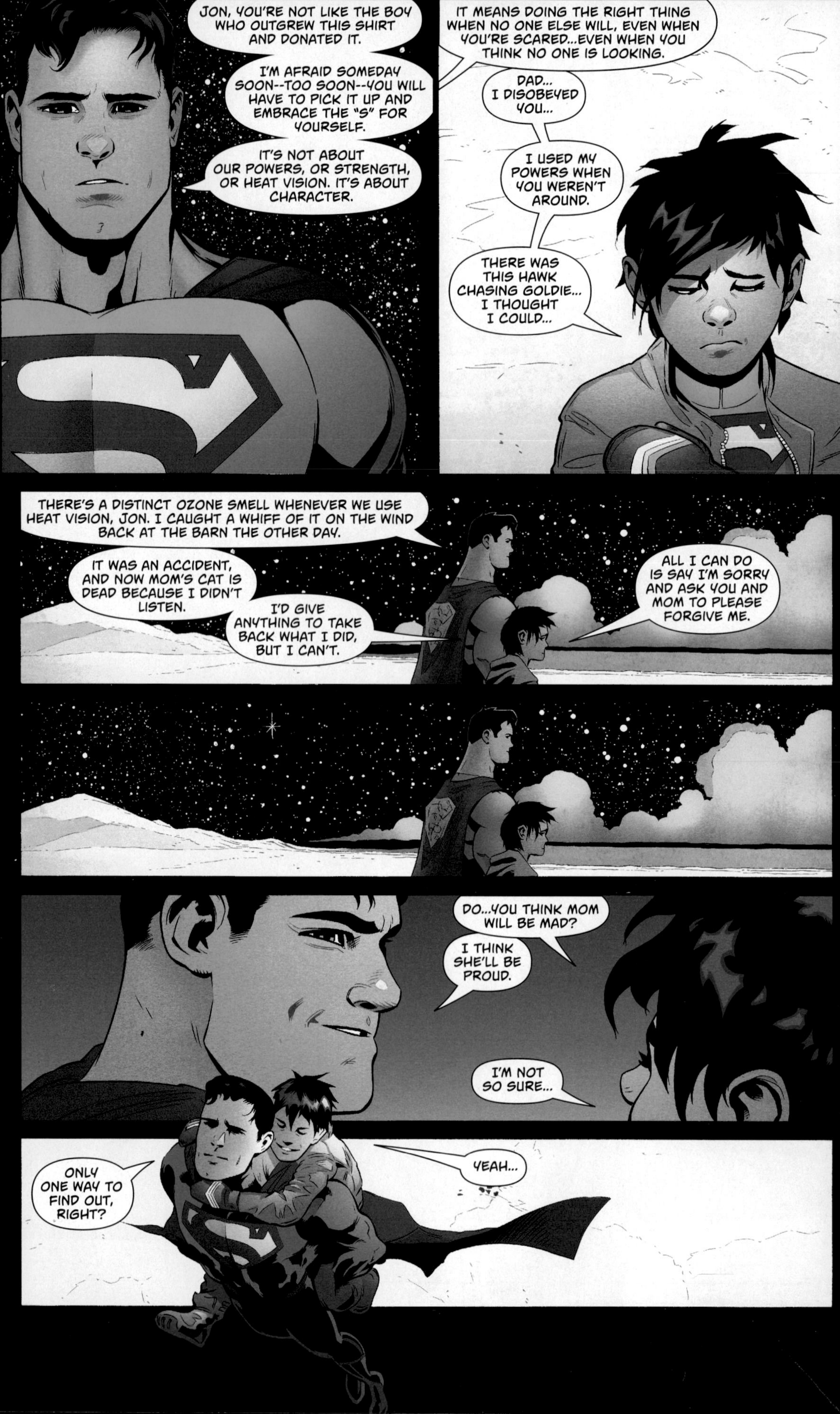
JON, YOU'RE NOT LIKE THE BOY WHO OUTGREW THIS SHIRT AND DONATED IT.
I'M AFRAID SOMEDAY SOON--TOO SOON--YOU WILL HAVE TO PICK IT UP AND EMBRACE THE "S" FOR YOURSELF.
IT'S NOT ABOUT OUR POWERS, OR STRENGTH, OR HEAT VISION. IT'S ABOUT CHARACTER.
IT MEANS DOING THE RIGHT THING WHEN NO ONE ELSE WILL, EVEN WHEN YOU'RE SCARED...EVEN WHEN YOU THINK NO ONE IS LOOKING.
DAD... I DISOBEYED YOU...
I USED MY POWERS WHEN YOU WEREN'T AROUND.
THERE WAS THIS HAWK CHASING GOLDIE... I THOUGHT I COULD...
THERE'S A DISTINCT OZONE SMELL WHENEVER WE USE HEAT VISION, JON. I CAUGHT A WHIFF OF IT ON THE WIND BACK AT THE BARN THE OTHER DAY.
IT WAS AN ACCIDENT, AND NOW MOM'S CAT IS DEAD BECAUSE I DIDN'T LISTEN.
I'D GIVE ANYTHING TO TAKE BACK WHAT I DID, BUT I CAN'T.
ALL I CAN DO IS SAY I'M SORRY AND ASK YOU AND MOM TO PLEASE FORGIVE ME.
DO...YOU THINK MOM WILL BE MAD?
I THINK SHE'LL BE PROUD.
I'M NOT SO SURE...
ONLY ONE WAY TO FIND OUT, RIGHT?
YEAH...

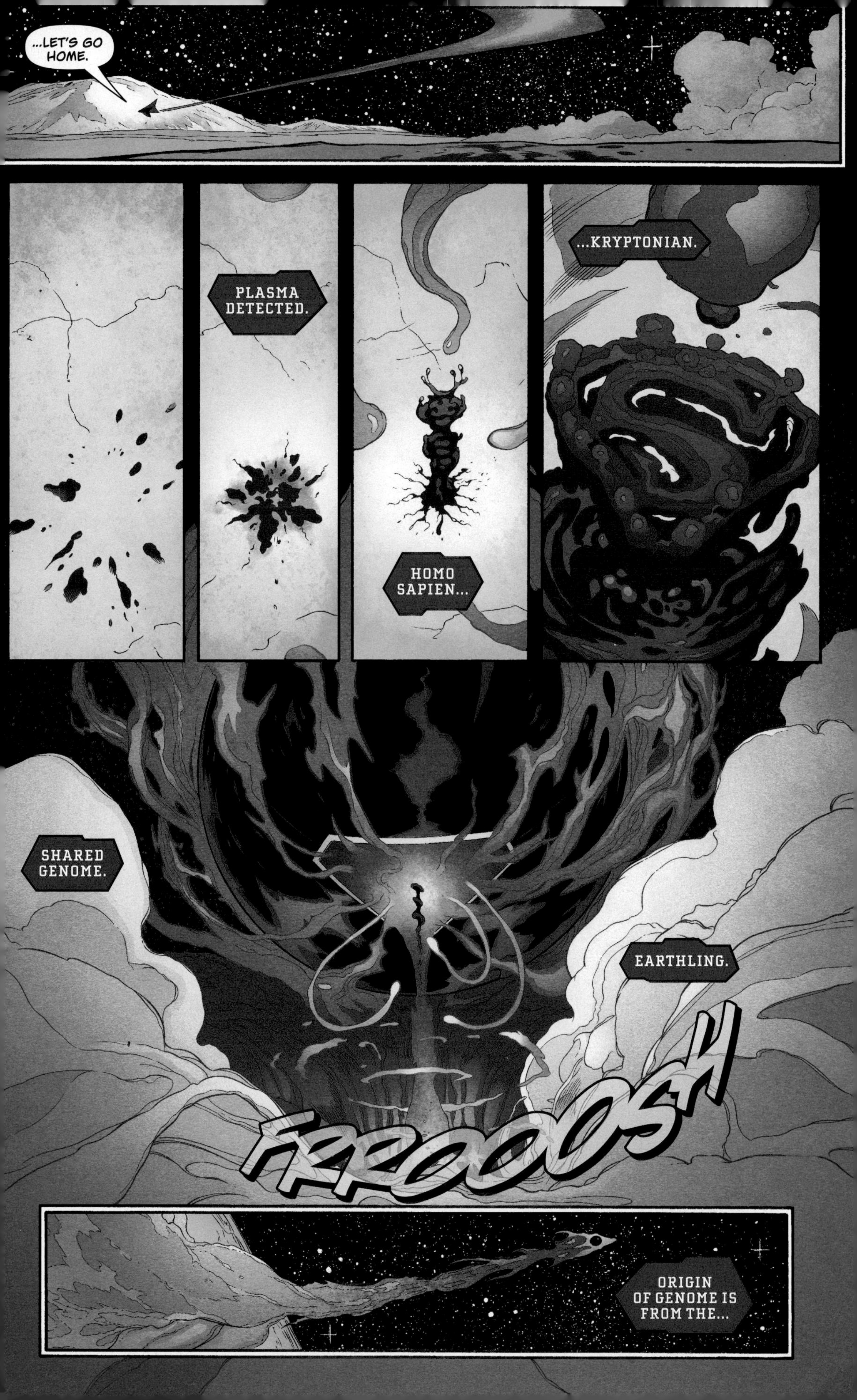

...LET'S GO HOME.

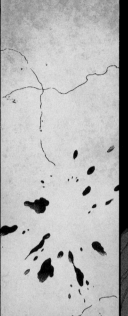

PLASMA DETECTED.

HOMO SAPIEN...

...KRYPTONIAN.

SHARED GENOME.

EARTHLING.

FRROOOSH

ORIGIN OF GENOME IS FROM THE...

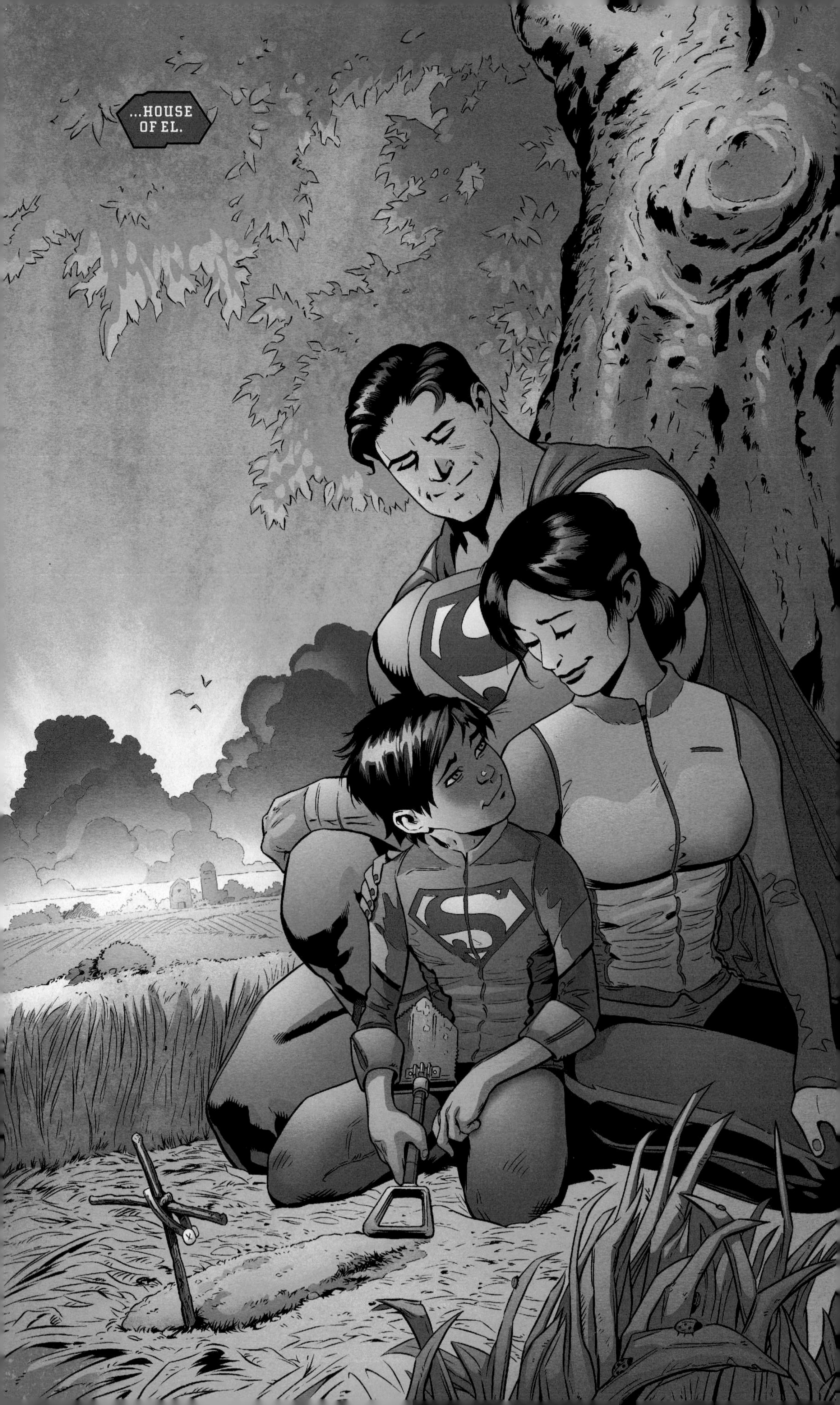
...HOUSE OF EL.

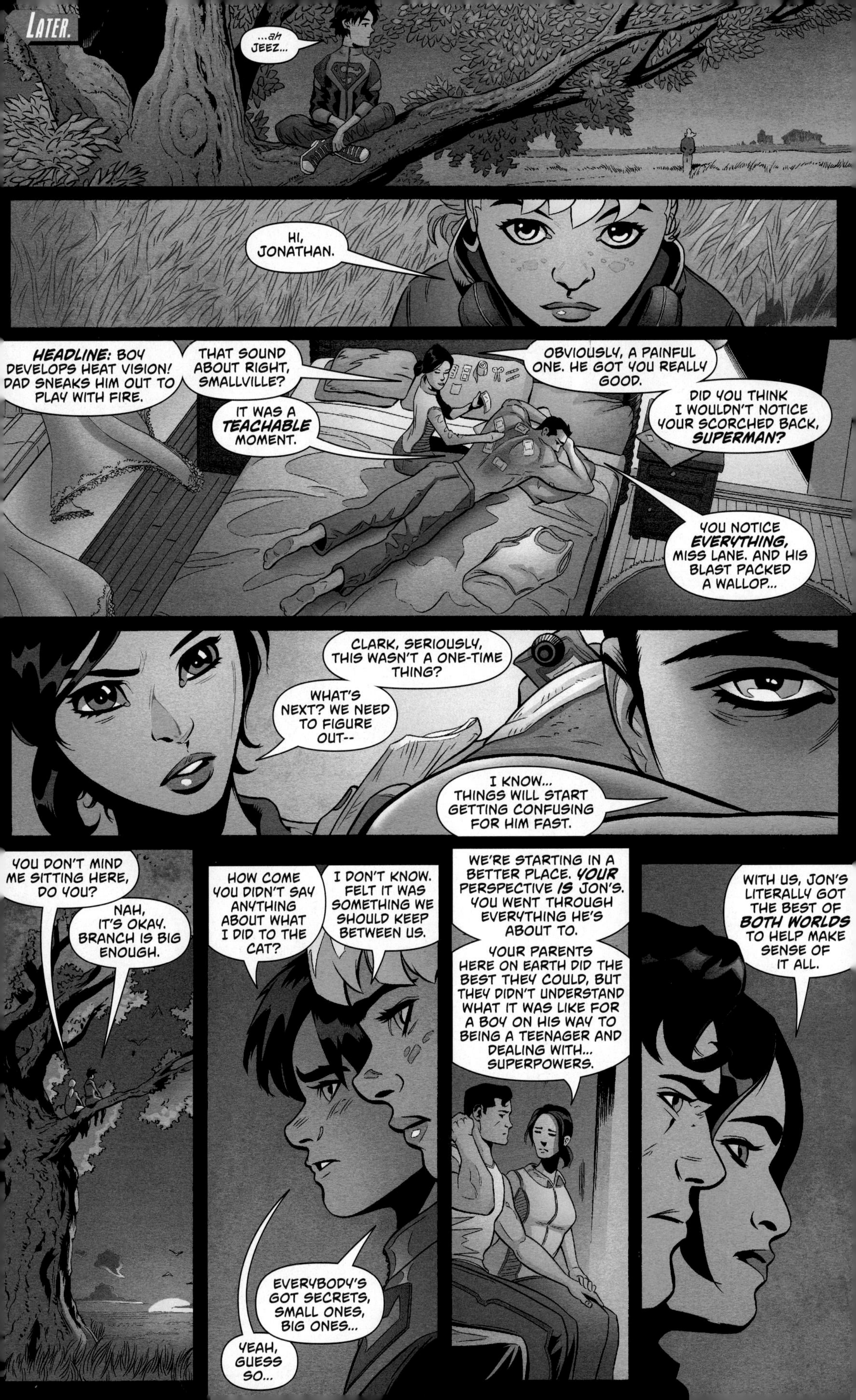
LATER.
...ah JEEZ...
HI, JONATHAN.
HEADLINE: BOY DEVELOPS HEAT VISION! DAD SNEAKS HIM OUT TO PLAY WITH FIRE.
THAT SOUND ABOUT RIGHT, SMALLVILLE?
IT WAS A TEACHABLE MOMENT.
OBVIOUSLY, A PAINFUL ONE. HE GOT YOU REALLY GOOD.
DID YOU THINK I WOULDN'T NOTICE YOUR SCORCHED BACK, SUPERMAN?
YOU NOTICE EVERYTHING, MISS LANE. AND HIS BLAST PACKED A WALLOP...
CLARK, SERIOUSLY, THIS WASN'T A ONE-TIME THING?
WHAT'S NEXT? WE NEED TO FIGURE OUT--
I KNOW... THINGS WILL START GETTING CONFUSING FOR HIM FAST.
YOU DON'T MIND ME SITTING HERE, DO YOU?
NAH, IT'S OKAY. BRANCH IS BIG ENOUGH.
HOW COME YOU DIDN'T SAY ANYTHING ABOUT WHAT I DID TO THE CAT?
I DON'T KNOW. FELT IT WAS SOMETHING WE SHOULD KEEP BETWEEN US.
EVERYBODY'S GOT SECRETS, SMALL ONES, BIG ONES...
YEAH, GUESS SO...
WE'RE STARTING IN A BETTER PLACE. YOUR PERSPECTIVE IS JON'S. YOU WENT THROUGH EVERYTHING HE'S ABOUT TO.
YOUR PARENTS HERE ON EARTH DID THE BEST THEY COULD, BUT THEY DIDN'T UNDERSTAND WHAT IT WAS LIKE FOR A BOY ON HIS WAY TO BEING A TEENAGER AND DEALING WITH... SUPERPOWERS.
WITH US, JON'S LITERALLY GOT THE BEST OF BOTH WORLDS TO HELP MAKE SENSE OF IT ALL.

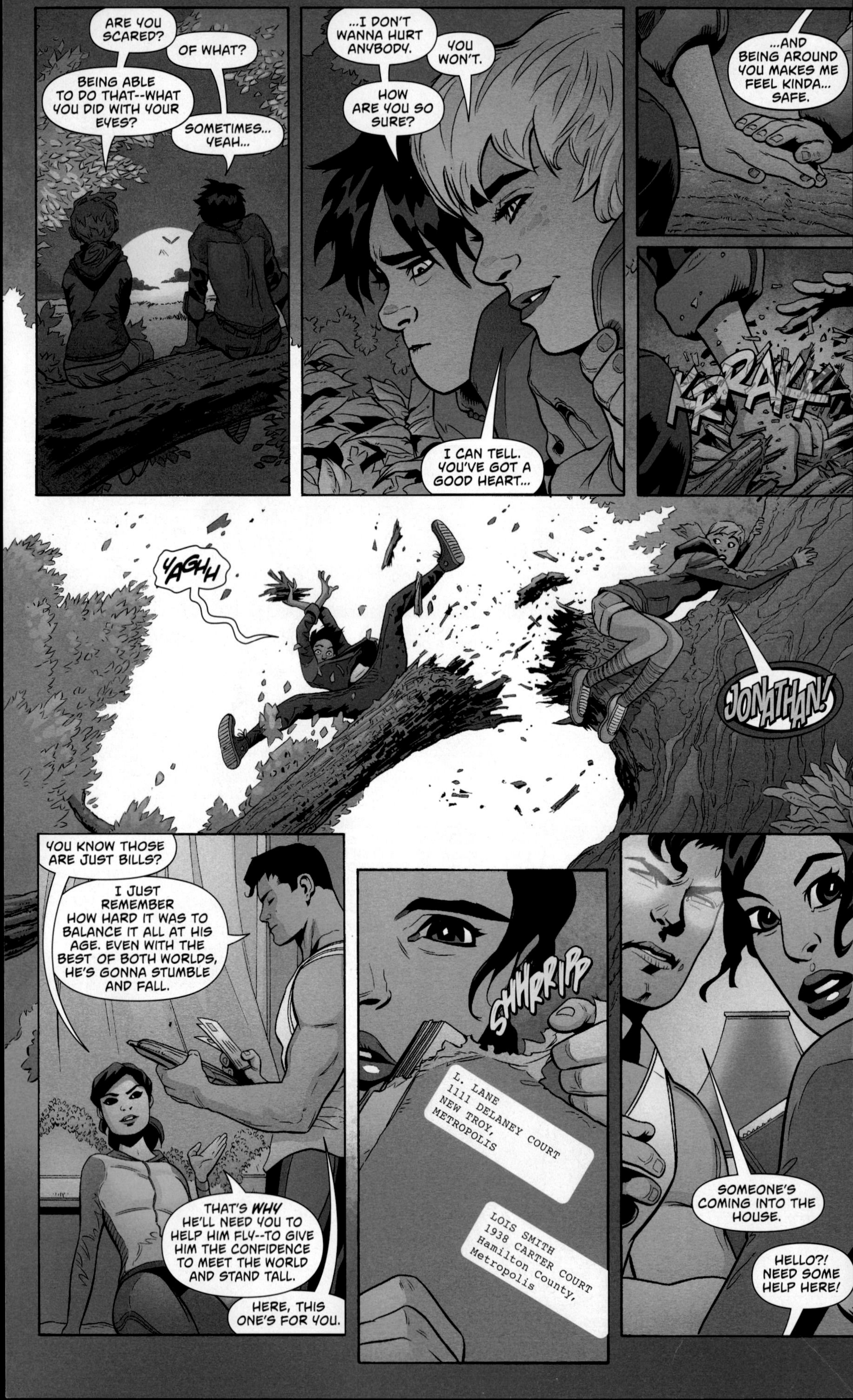
ARE YOU SCARED?
OF WHAT?
BEING ABLE TO DO THAT--WHAT YOU DID WITH YOUR EYES?
SOMETIMES... YEAH...
...I DON'T WANNA HURT ANYBODY.
YOU WON'T.
HOW ARE YOU SO SURE?
I CAN TELL. YOU'VE GOT A GOOD HEART...
...AND BEING AROUND YOU MAKES ME FEEL KINDA... SAFE.
KRAKK
YAGHH
JONATHAN!
YOU KNOW THOSE ARE JUST BILLS?
I JUST REMEMBER HOW HARD IT WAS TO BALANCE IT ALL AT HIS AGE. EVEN WITH THE BEST OF BOTH WORLDS, HE'S GONNA STUMBLE AND FALL.
THAT'S WHY HE'LL NEED YOU TO HELP HIM FLY--TO GIVE HIM THE CONFIDENCE TO MEET THE WORLD AND STAND TALL.
HERE, THIS ONE'S FOR YOU.
SHHRRIPP
L. LANE
1111 DELANEY COURT
NEW TROY,
METROPOLIS
LOIS SMITH
1938 CARTER COURT
Hamilton County,
Metropolis
SOMEONE'S COMING INTO THE HOUSE.
HELLO?! NEED SOME HELP HERE!

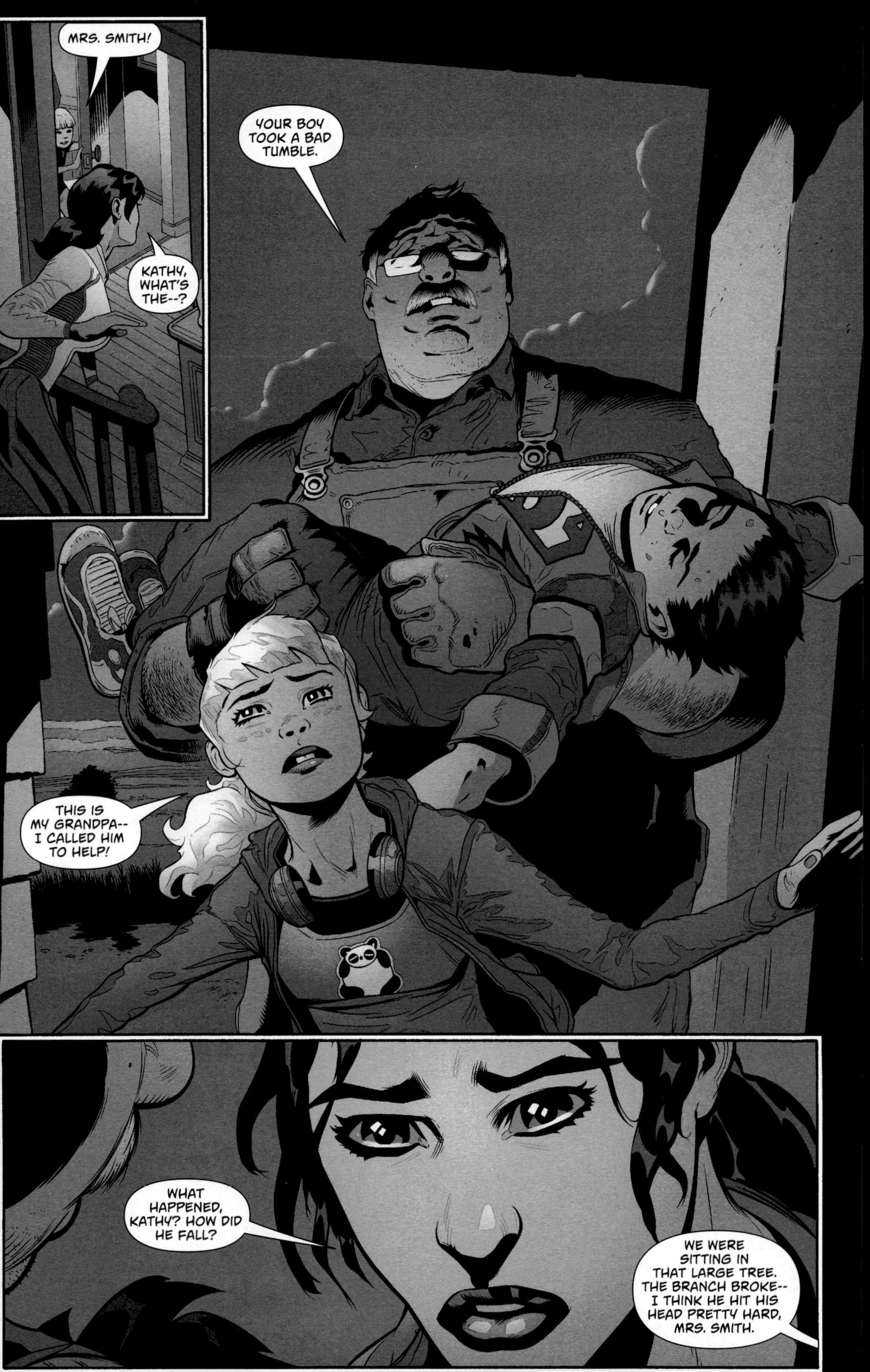
MRS. SMITH!
KATHY, WHAT'S THE--?
YOUR BOY TOOK A BAD TUMBLE.
THIS IS MY GRANDPA-- I CALLED HIM TO HELP!
WHAT HAPPENED, KATHY? HOW DID HE FALL?
WE WERE SITTING IN THAT LARGE TREE. THE BRANCH BROKE-- I THINK HE HIT HIS HEAD PRETTY HARD, MRS. SMITH.

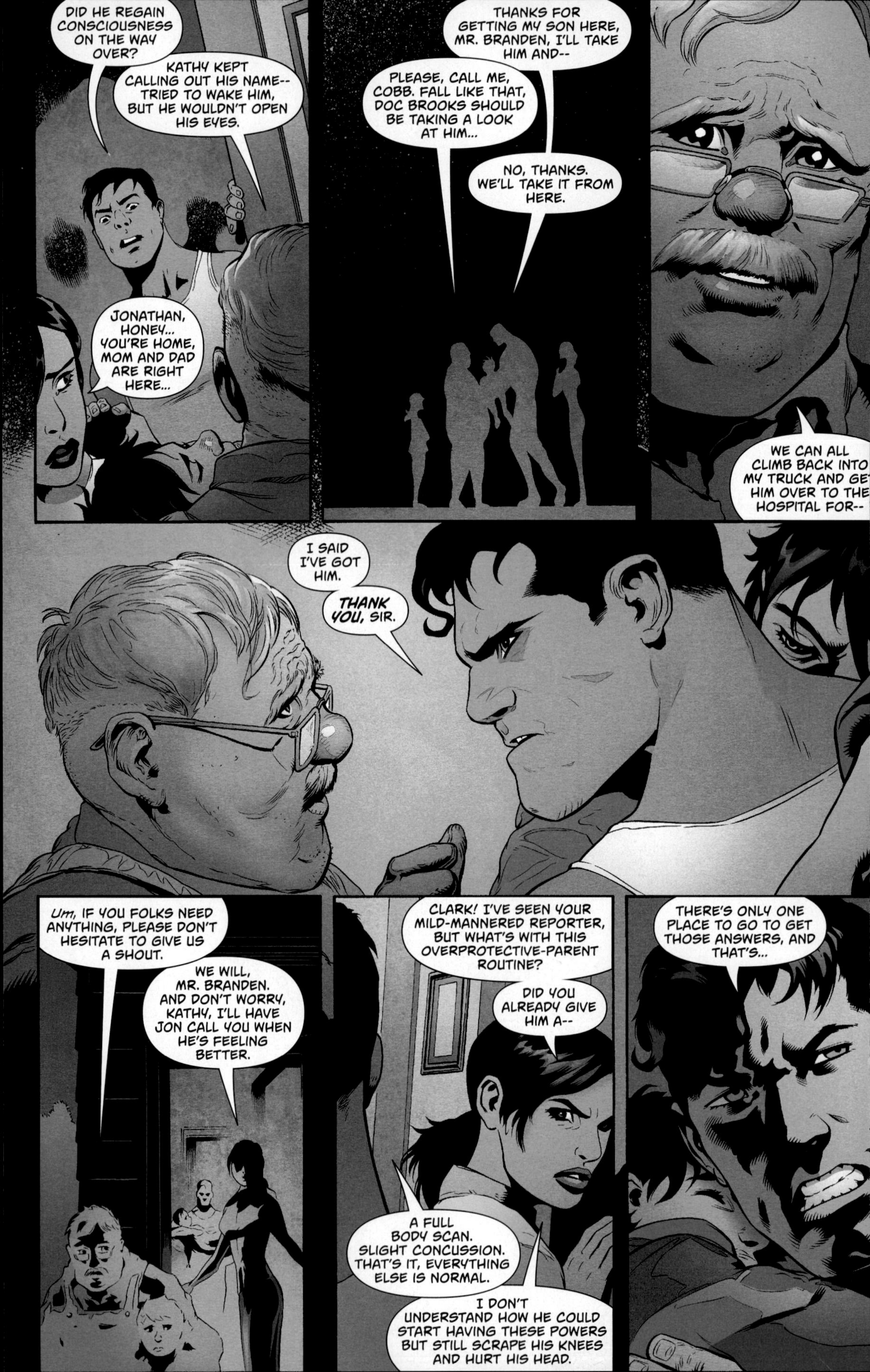
DID HE REGAIN CONSCIOUSNESS ON THE WAY OVER?
KATHY KEPT CALLING OUT HIS NAME-- TRIED TO WAKE HIM, BUT HE WOULDN'T OPEN HIS EYES.
JONATHAN, HONEY... YOU'RE HOME, MOM AND DAD ARE RIGHT HERE...
THANKS FOR GETTING MY SON HERE, MR. BRANDEN, I'LL TAKE HIM AND--
PLEASE, CALL ME, COBB. FALL LIKE THAT, DOC BROOKS SHOULD BE TAKING A LOOK AT HIM...
NO, THANKS. WE'LL TAKE IT FROM HERE.
WE CAN ALL CLIMB BACK INTO MY TRUCK AND GET HIM OVER TO THE HOSPITAL FOR--
I SAID I'VE GOT HIM.
THANK YOU, SIR.
UM, IF YOU FOLKS NEED ANYTHING, PLEASE DON'T HESITATE TO GIVE US A SHOUT.
WE WILL, MR. BRANDEN. AND DON'T WORRY, KATHY, I'LL HAVE JON CALL YOU WHEN HE'S FEELING BETTER.
CLARK! I'VE SEEN YOUR MILD-MANNERED REPORTER, BUT WHAT'S WITH THIS OVERPROTECTIVE-PARENT ROUTINE?
DID YOU ALREADY GIVE HIM A--
A FULL BODY SCAN. SLIGHT CONCUSSION. THAT'S IT, EVERYTHING ELSE IS NORMAL.
I DON'T UNDERSTAND HOW HE COULD START HAVING THESE POWERS BUT STILL SCRAPE HIS KNEES AND HURT HIS HEAD.
THERE'S ONLY ONE PLACE TO GO TO GET THOSE ANSWERS, AND THAT'S...

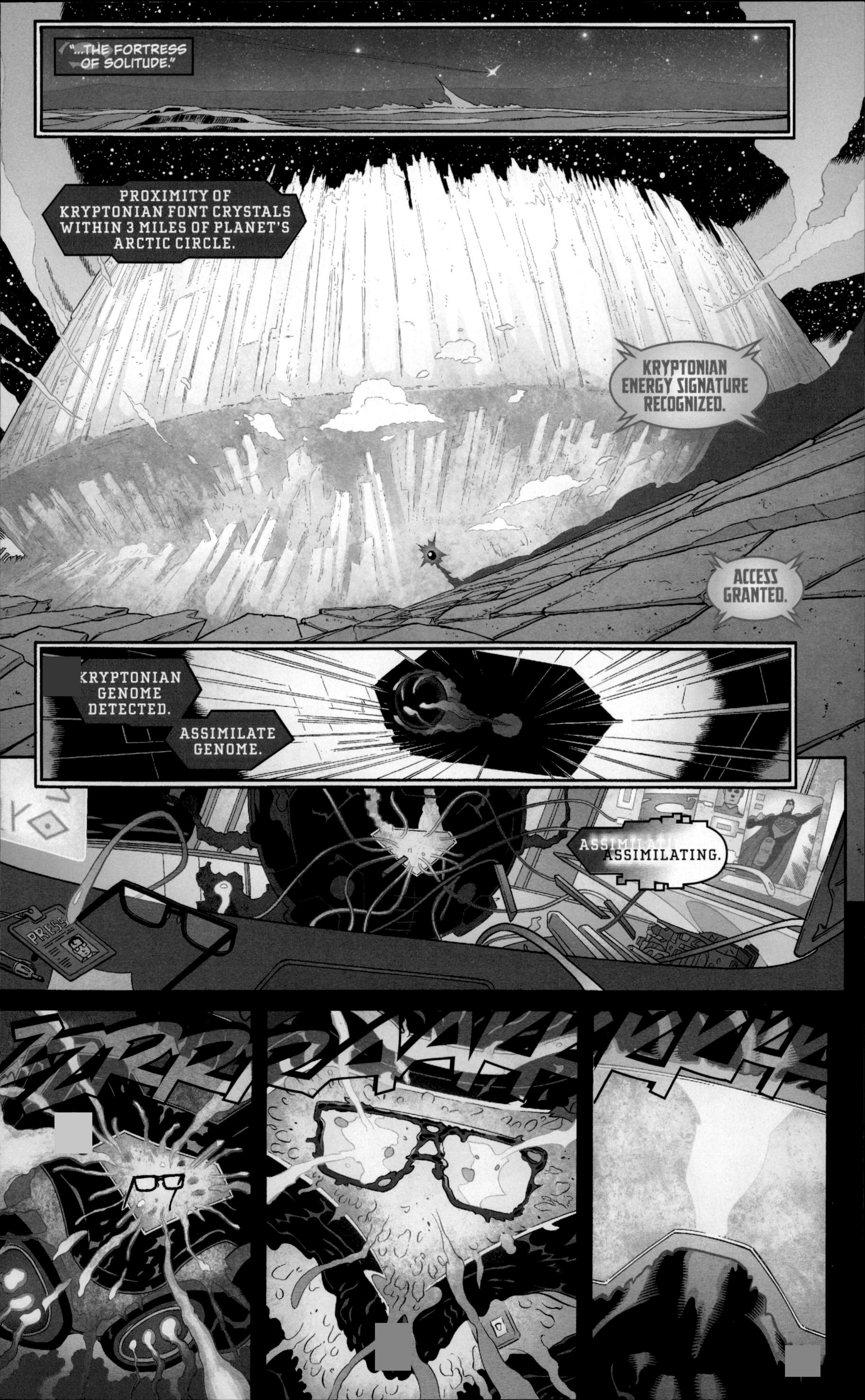
"...THE FORTRESS OF SOLITUDE."
PROXIMITY OF KRYPTONIAN FONT CRYSTALS WITHIN 3 MILES OF PLANET'S ARCTIC CIRCLE.
KRYPTONIAN ENERGY SIGNATURE RECOGNIZED.
ACCESS GRANTED.
KRYPTONIAN GENOME DETECTED.
ASSIMILATE GENOME.
ASSIMILATING.
PRESS

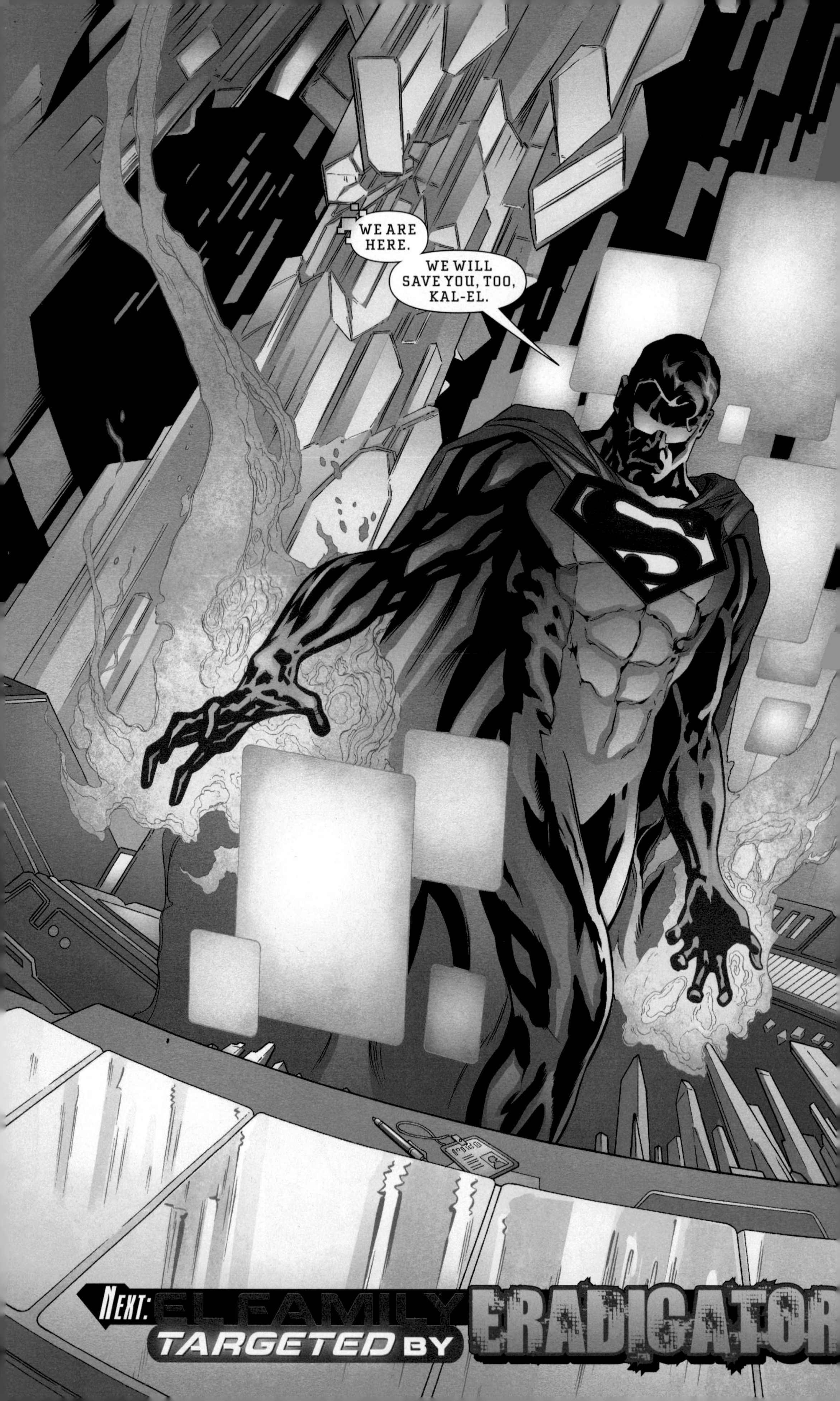

WE ARE HERE.
WE WILL SAVE YOU, TOO, KAL-EL.
NEXT: EL FAMILY TARGETED BY ERADICATOR

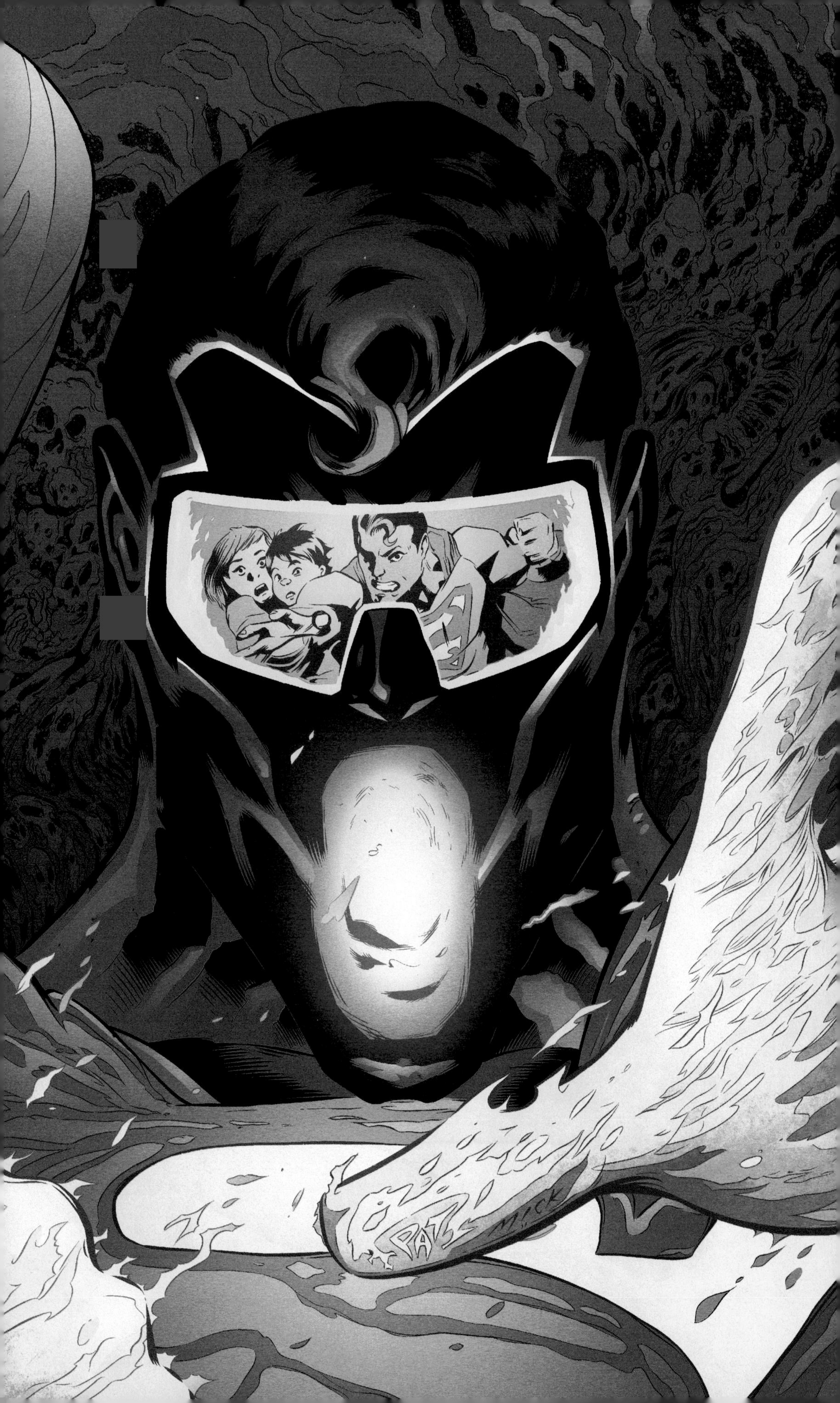
PAT
MICK

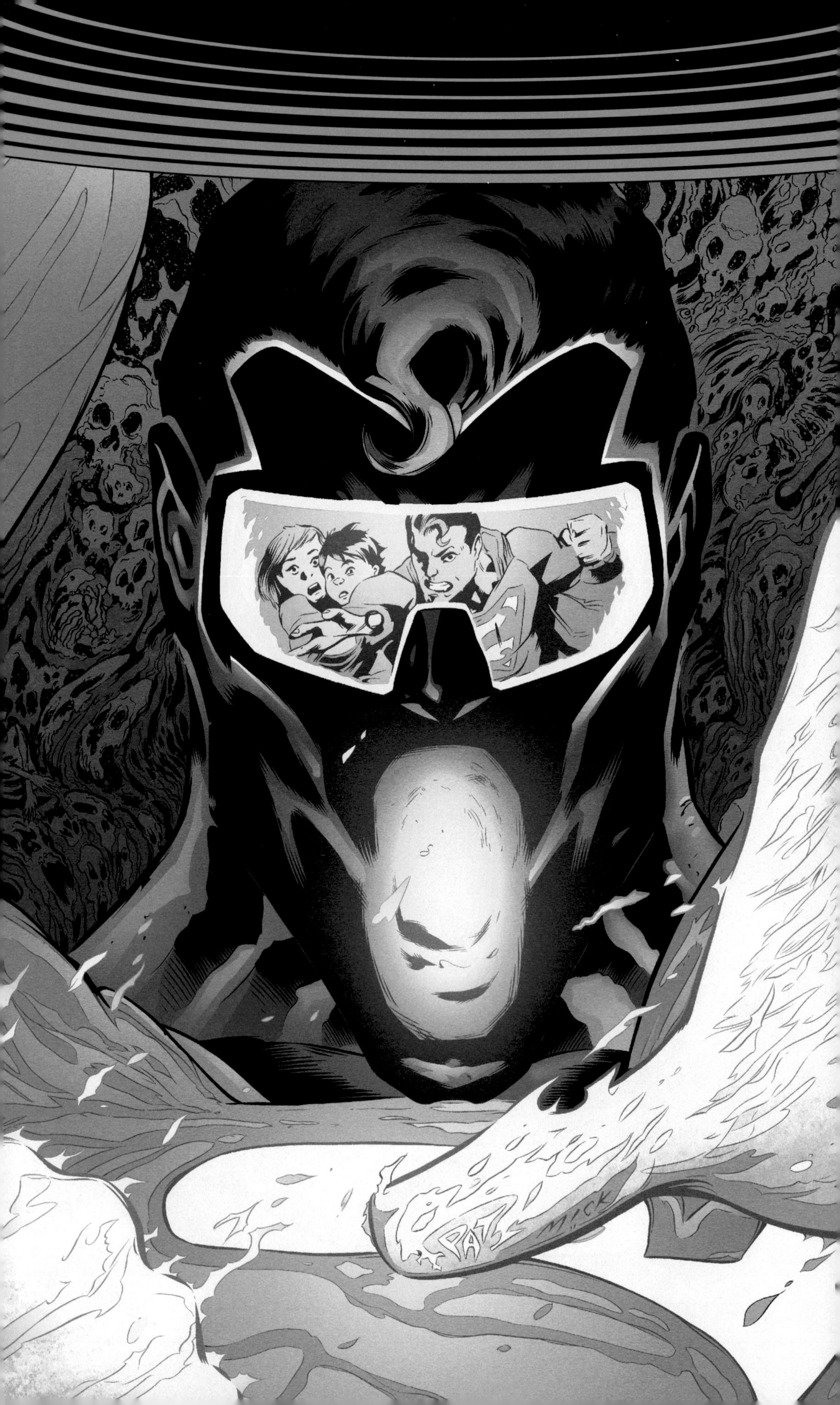
PAT
MICK

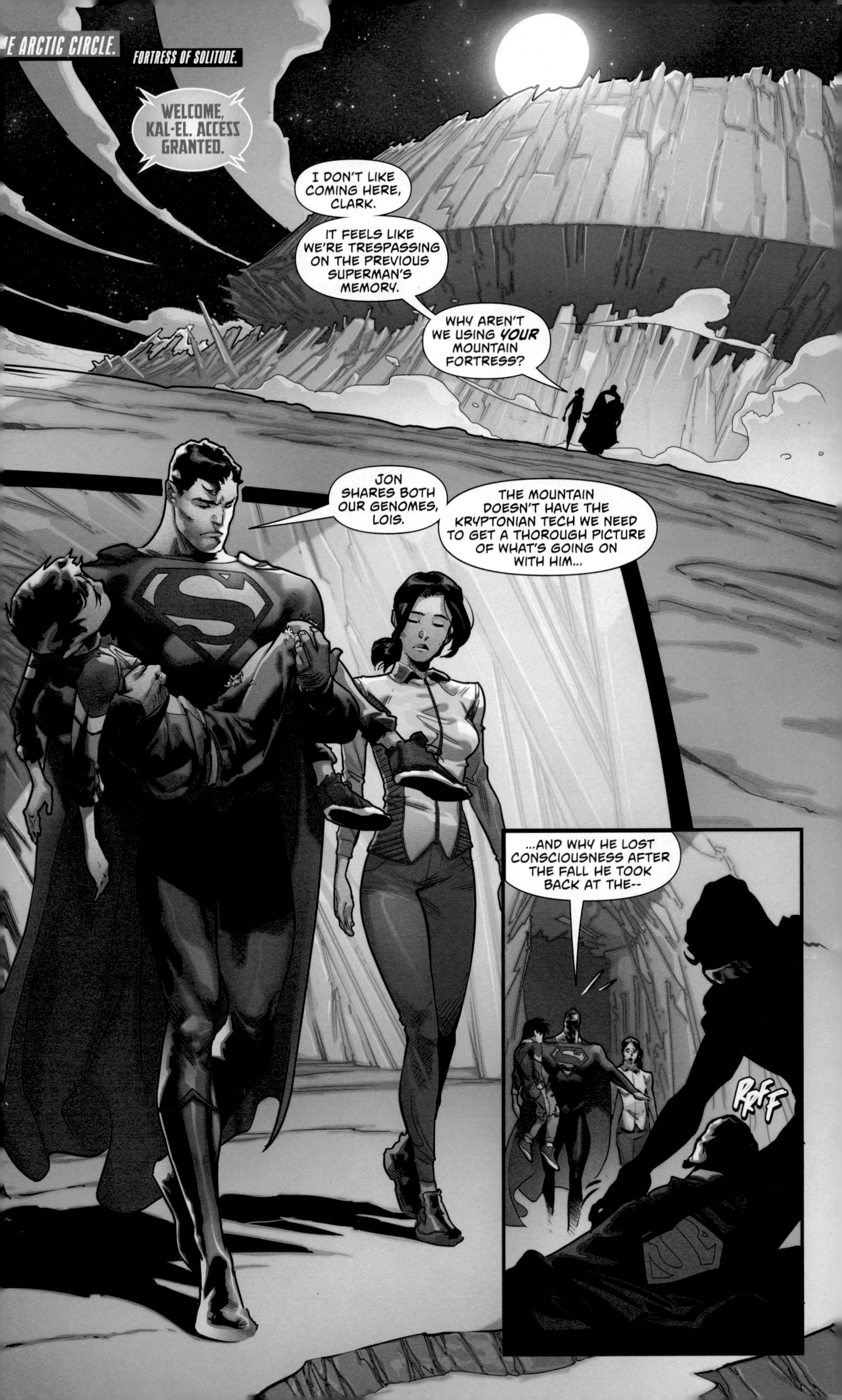
E ARCTIC CIRCLE.
FORTRESS OF SOLITUDE.
WELCOME, KAL-EL. ACCESS GRANTED.
I DON'T LIKE COMING HERE, CLARK.
IT FEELS LIKE WE'RE TRESPASSING ON THE PREVIOUS SUPERMAN'S MEMORY.
WHY AREN'T WE USING YOUR MOUNTAIN FORTRESS?
JON SHARES BOTH OUR GENOMES, LOIS.
THE MOUNTAIN DOESN'T HAVE THE KRYPTONIAN TECH WE NEED TO GET A THOROUGH PICTURE OF WHAT'S GOING ON WITH HIM...
...AND WHY HE LOST CONSCIOUSNESS AFTER THE FALL HE TOOK BACK AT THE--
RRFF

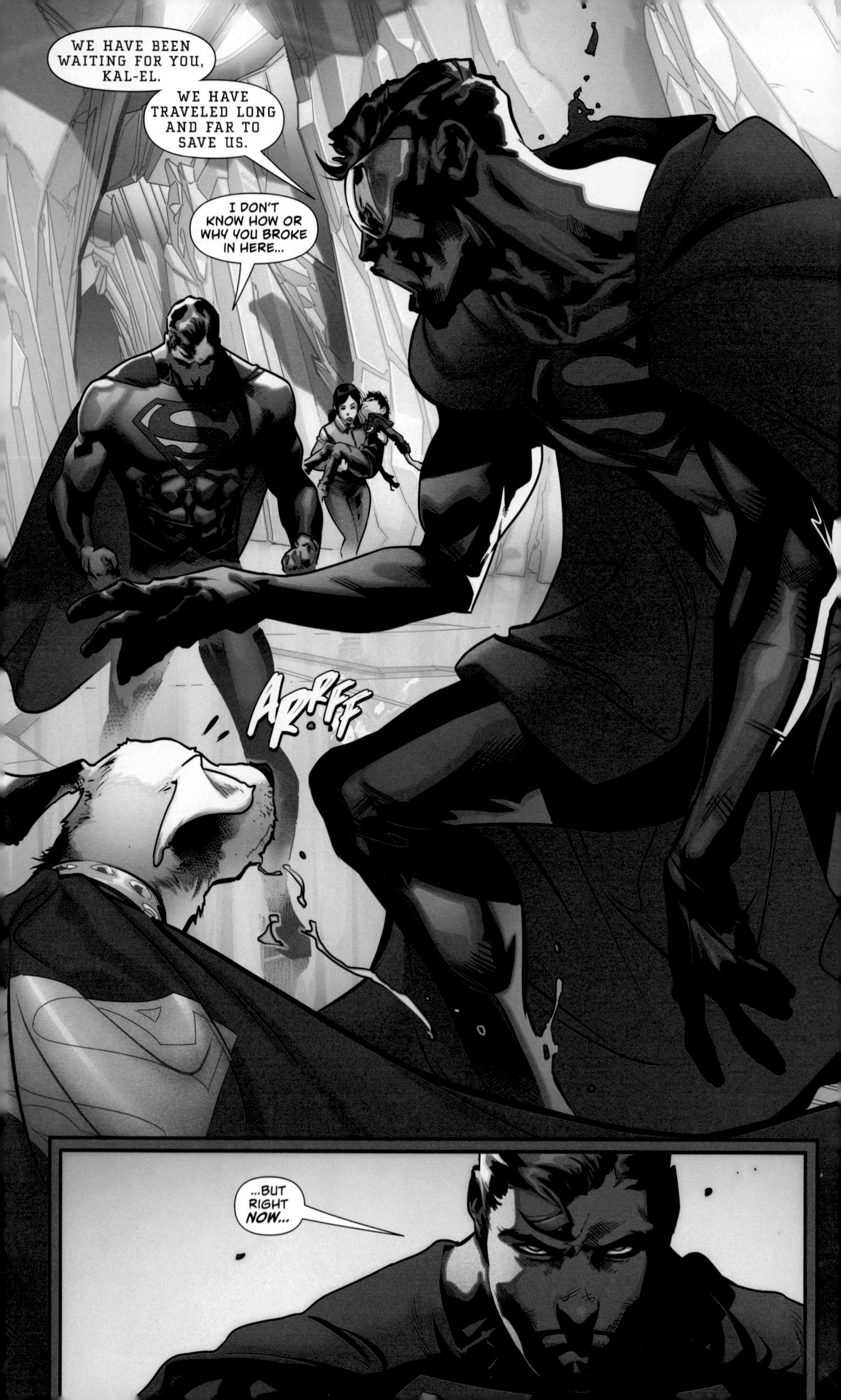

WE HAVE BEEN WAITING FOR YOU, KAL-EL.
WE HAVE TRAVELED LONG AND FAR TO SAVE US.
I DON'T KNOW HOW OR WHY YOU BROKE IN HERE...
ARFFF
...BUT RIGHT NOW...

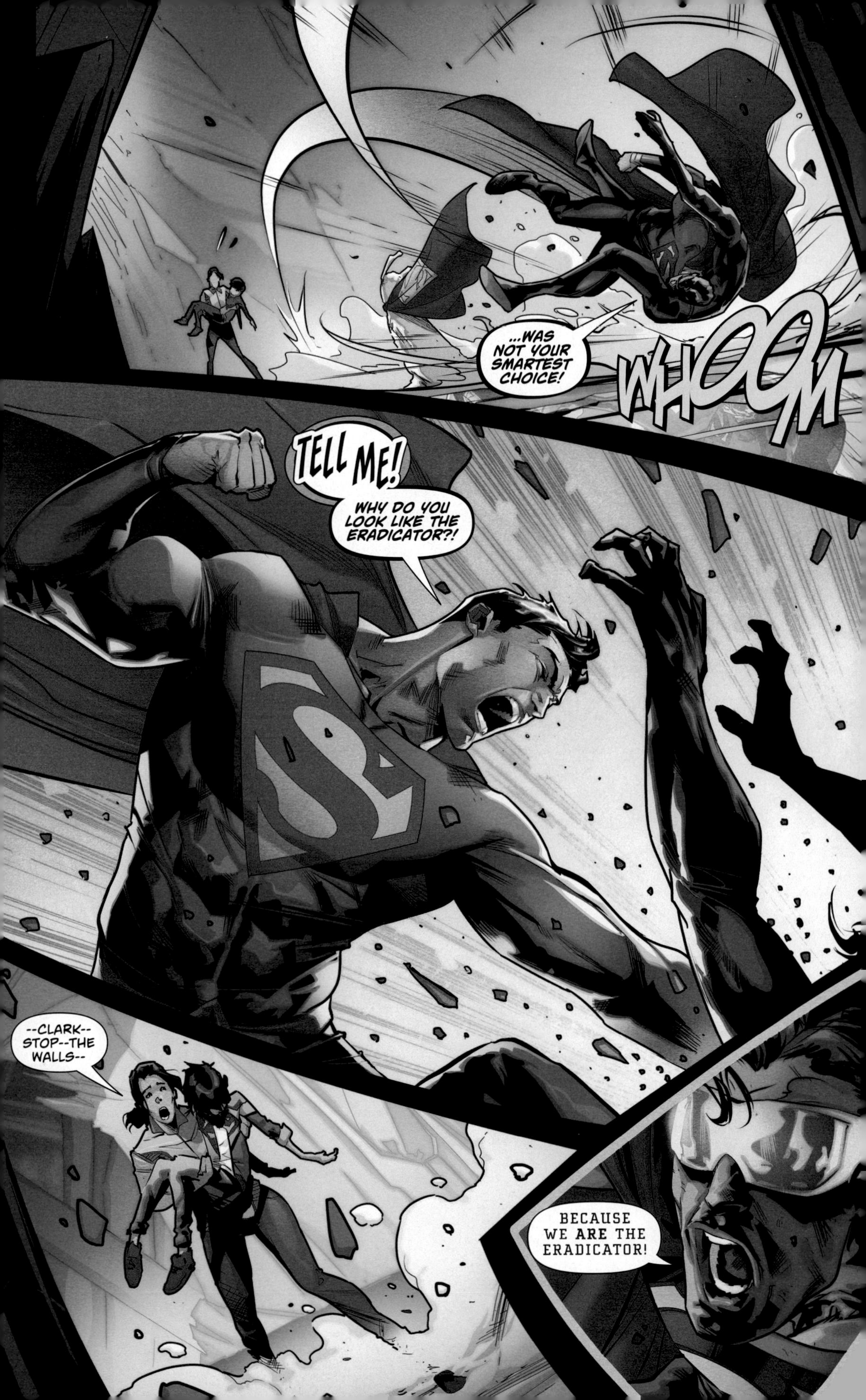
...WAS NOT YOUR SMARTEST CHOICE!
WHOOM
TELL ME!
WHY DO YOU LOOK LIKE THE ERADICATOR?!
--CLARK-- STOP--THE WALLS--
BECAUSE WE ARE THE ERADICATOR!

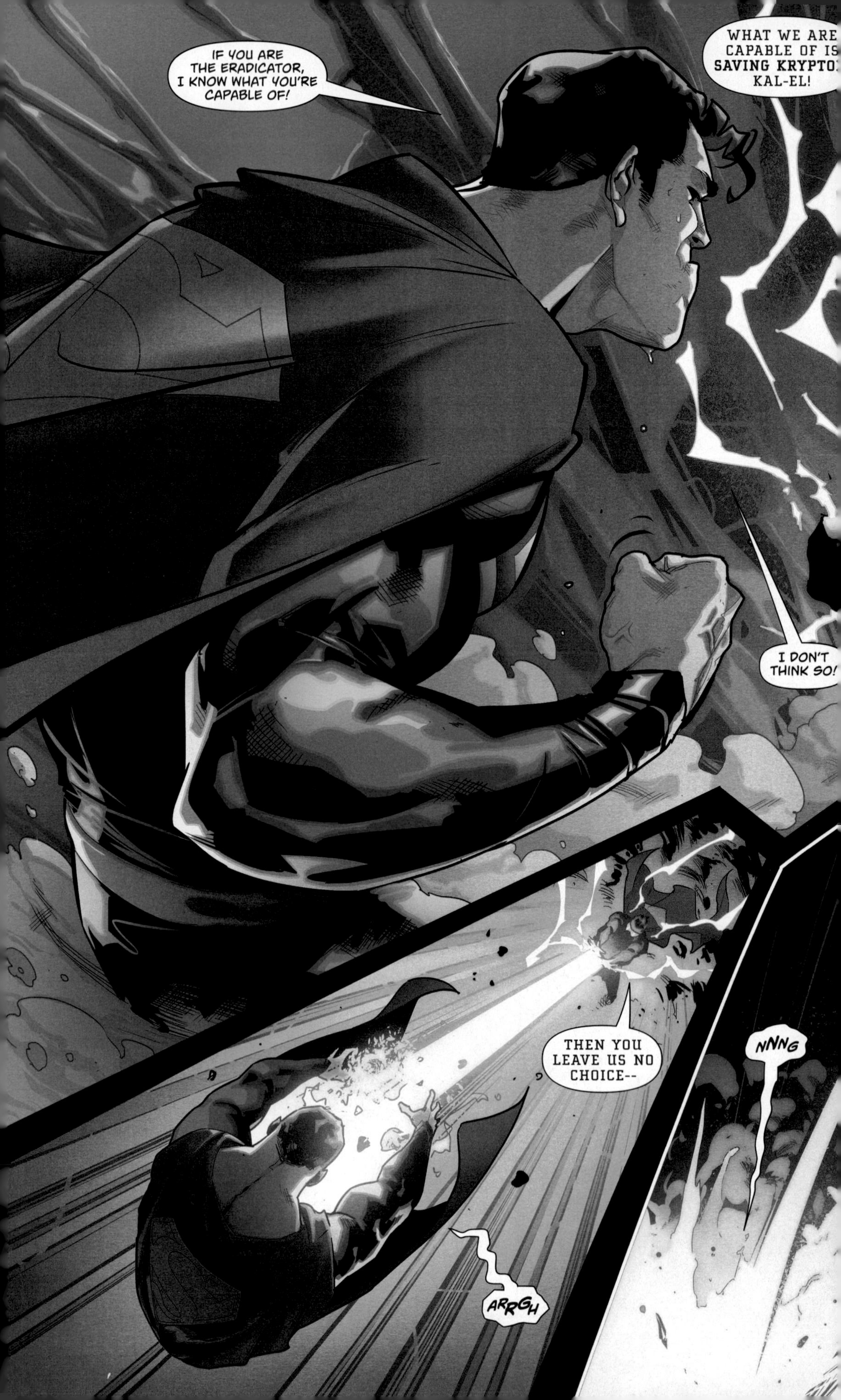
IF YOU ARE THE ERADICATOR, I KNOW WHAT YOU'RE CAPABLE OF!
WHAT WE ARE CAPABLE OF IS SAVING KRYPTO KAL-EL!
I DON'T THINK SO!
THEN YOU LEAVE US NO CHOICE--
NNNG
ARRGH

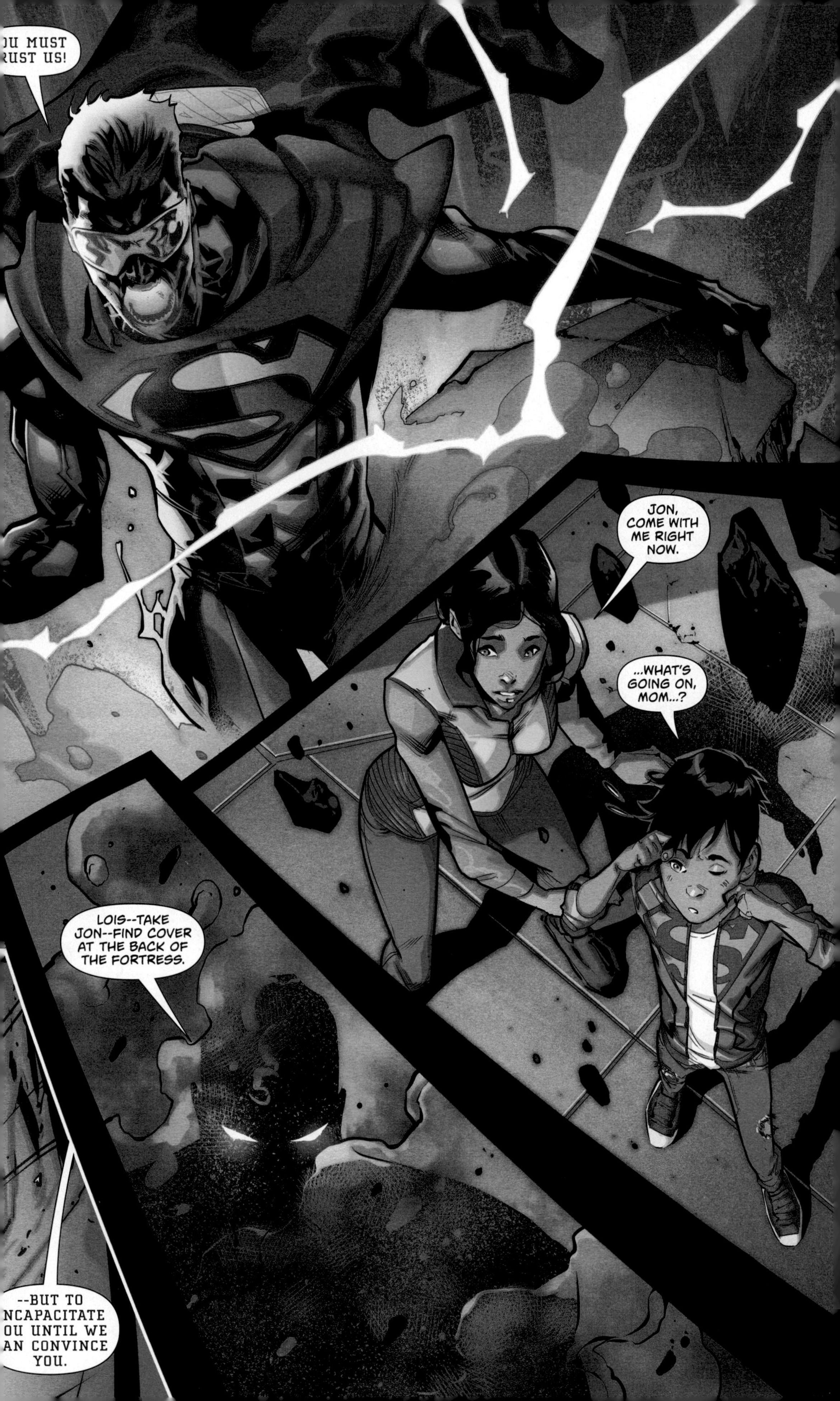

OU MUST RUST US!
JON, COME WITH ME RIGHT NOW.
...WHAT'S GOING ON, MOM...?
LOIS--TAKE JON--FIND COVER AT THE BACK OF THE FORTRESS.
--BUT TO NCAPACITATE OU UNTIL WE AN CONVINCE YOU.

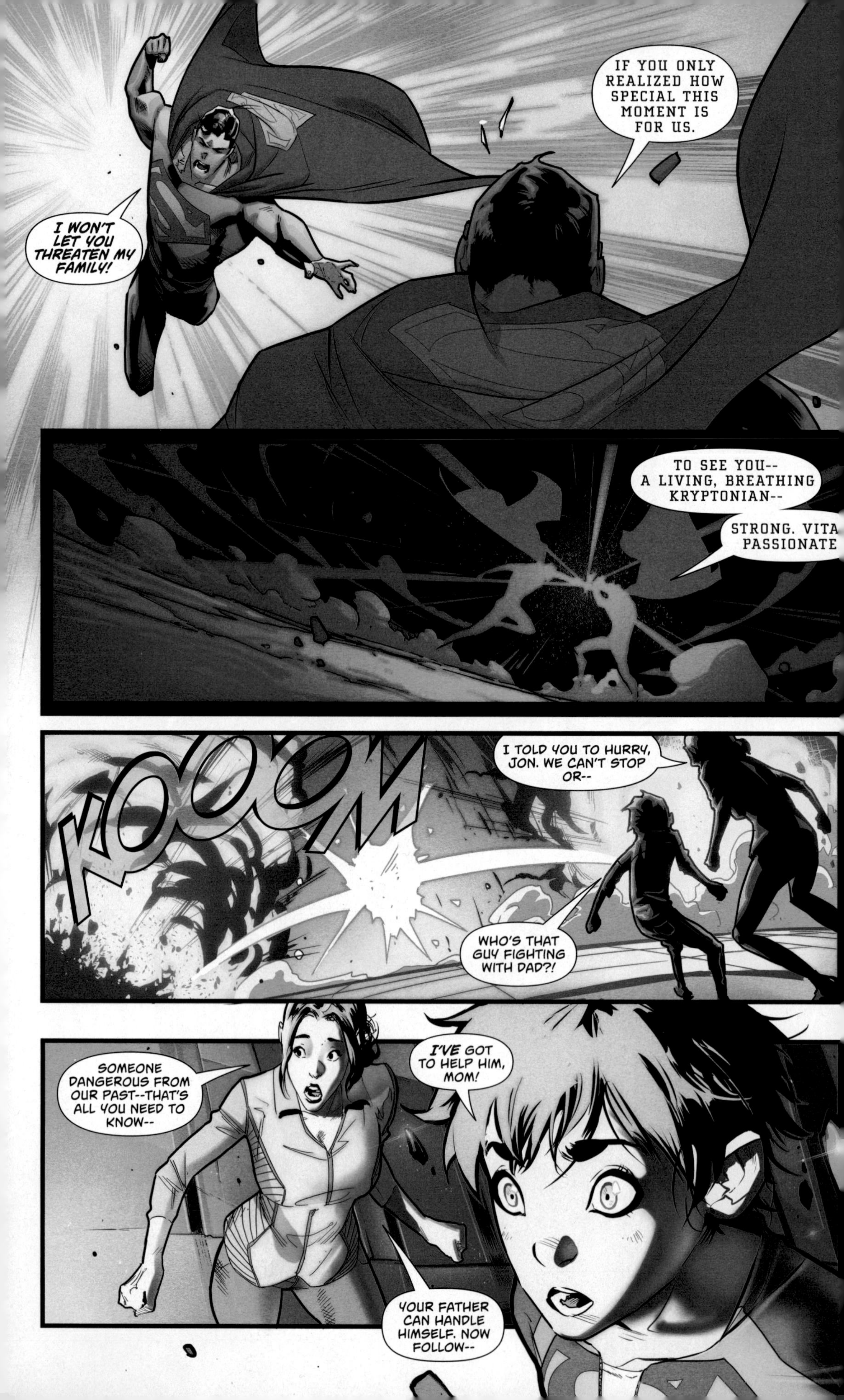
IF YOU ONLY REALIZED HOW SPECIAL THIS MOMENT IS FOR US.
I WON'T LET YOU THREATEN MY FAMILY!
TO SEE YOU-- A LIVING, BREATHING KRYPTONIAN--
STRONG. VITA PASSIONATE
KOOOM
I TOLD YOU TO HURRY, JON. WE CAN'T STOP OR--
WHO'S THAT GUY FIGHTING WITH DAD?!
SOMEONE DANGEROUS FROM OUR PAST--THAT'S ALL YOU NEED TO KNOW--
I'VE GOT TO HELP HIM, MOM!
YOUR FATHER CAN HANDLE HIMSELF. NOW FOLLOW--

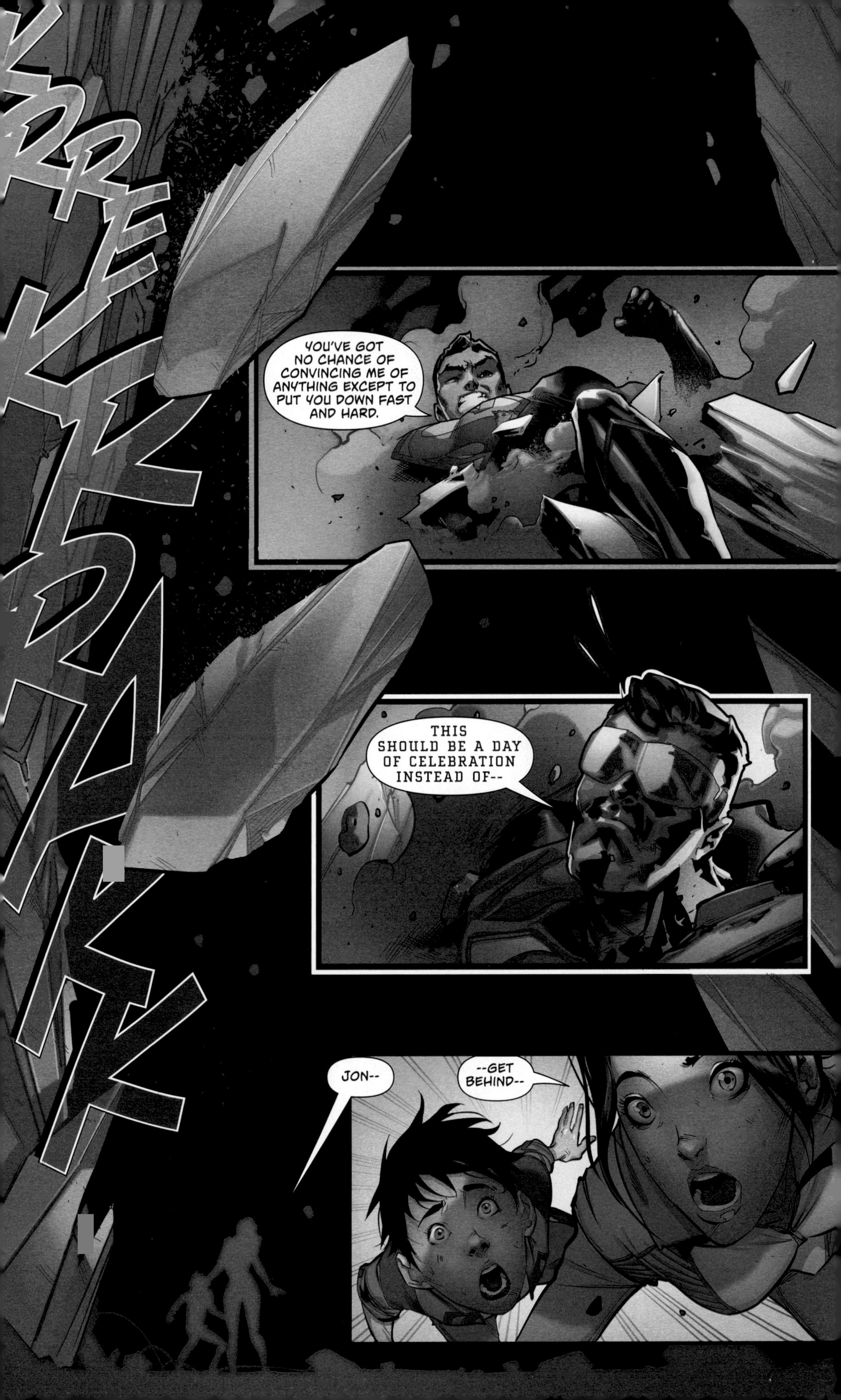
YOU'VE GOT NO CHANCE OF CONVINCING ME OF ANYTHING EXCEPT TO PUT YOU DOWN FAST AND HARD.
THIS SHOULD BE A DAY OF CELEBRATION INSTEAD OF--
JON--
--GET BEHIND--

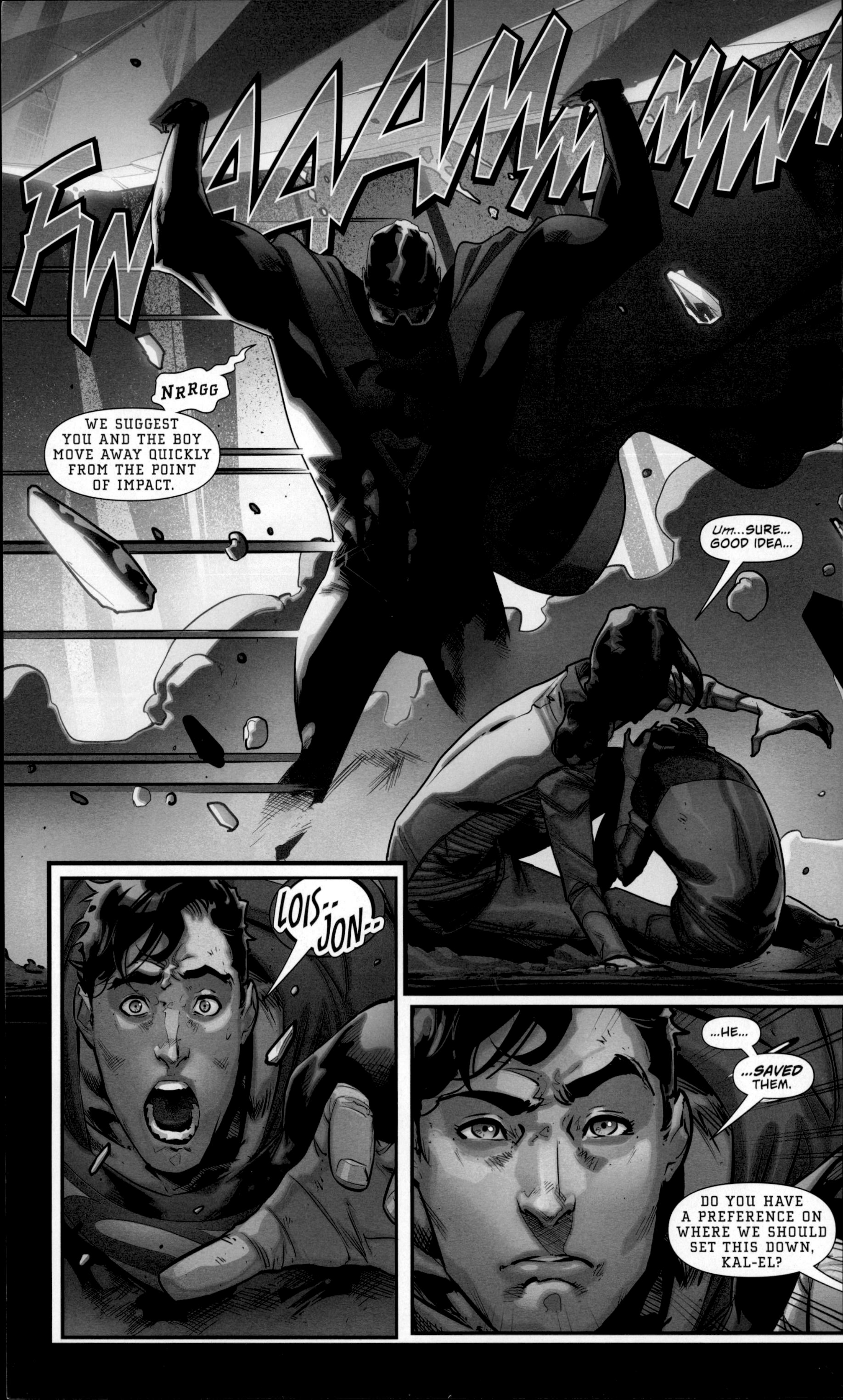
FWAAAMMMMM
NRRGG
WE SUGGEST YOU AND THE BOY MOVE AWAY QUICKLY FROM THE POINT OF IMPACT.
UM...SURE... GOOD IDEA...
LOIS-- JON--
...HE...
...SAVED THEM.
DO YOU HAVE A PREFERENCE ON WHERE WE SHOULD SET THIS DOWN, KAL-EL?

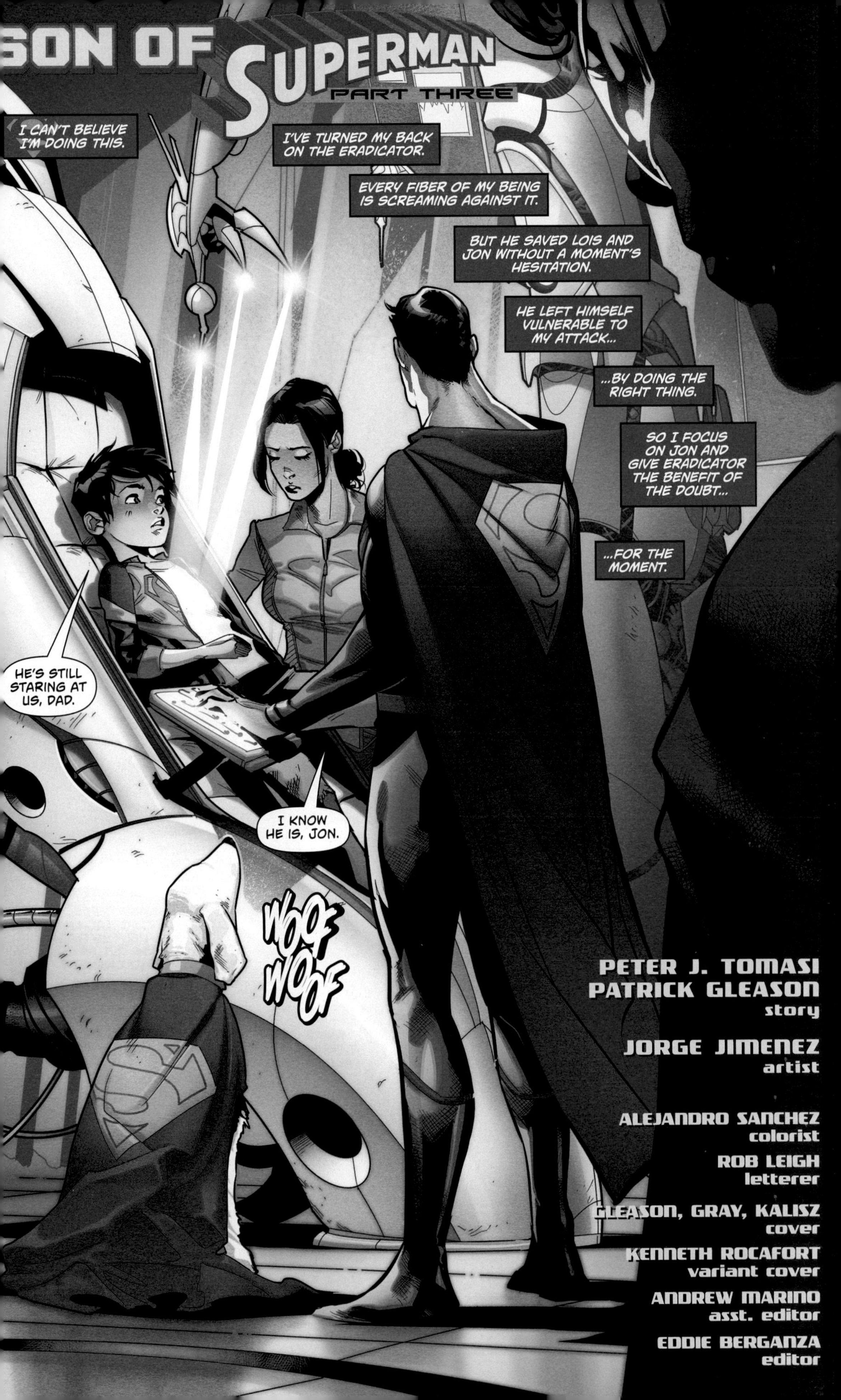

SON OF SUPERMAN
PART THREE
I CAN'T BELIEVE I'M DOING THIS.
I'VE TURNED MY BACK ON THE ERADICATOR.
EVERY FIBER OF MY BEING IS SCREAMING AGAINST IT.
BUT HE SAVED LOIS AND JON WITHOUT A MOMENT'S HESITATION.
HE LEFT HIMSELF VULNERABLE TO MY ATTACK...
...BY DOING THE RIGHT THING.
SO I FOCUS ON JON AND GIVE ERADICATOR THE BENEFIT OF THE DOUBT...
...FOR THE MOMENT.
HE'S STILL STARING AT US, DAD.
I KNOW HE IS, JON.
WOOF WOOF
PETER J. TOMASI
PATRICK GLEASON
story
JORGE JIMENEZ
artist
ALEJANDRO SANCHEZ
colorist
ROB LEIGH
letterer
GLEASON, GRAY, KALISZ
cover
KENNETH ROCAFORT
variant cover
ANDREW MARINO
asst. editor
EDDIE BERGANZA
editor

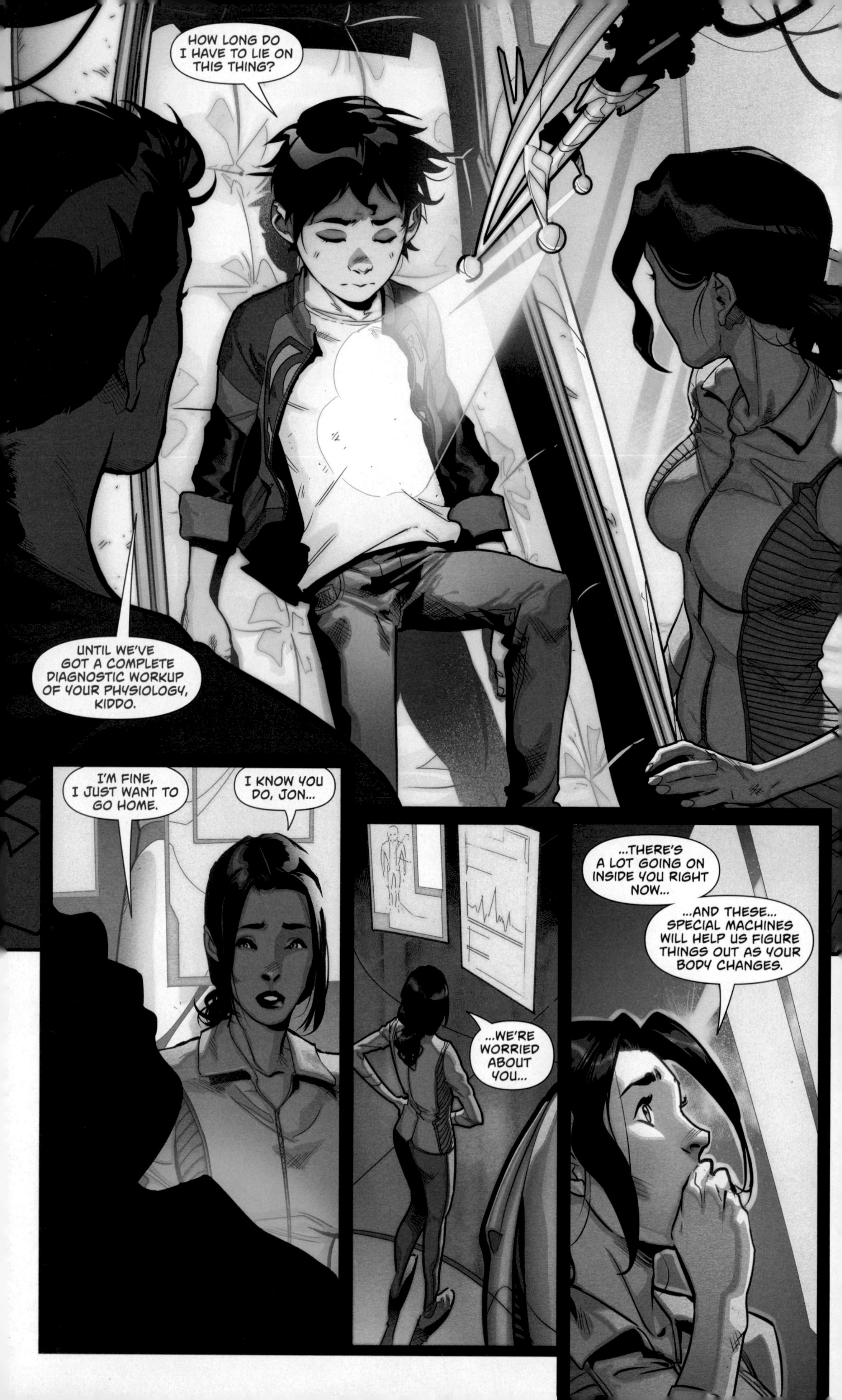
HOW LONG DO I HAVE TO LIE ON THIS THING?
UNTIL WE'VE GOT A COMPLETE DIAGNOSTIC WORKUP OF YOUR PHYSIOLOGY, KIDDO.
I'M FINE, I JUST WANT TO GO HOME.
I KNOW YOU DO, JON...
...WE'RE WORRIED ABOUT YOU...
...THERE'S A LOT GOING ON INSIDE YOU RIGHT NOW...
...AND THESE... SPECIAL MACHINES WILL HELP US FIGURE THINGS OUT AS YOUR BODY CHANGES.

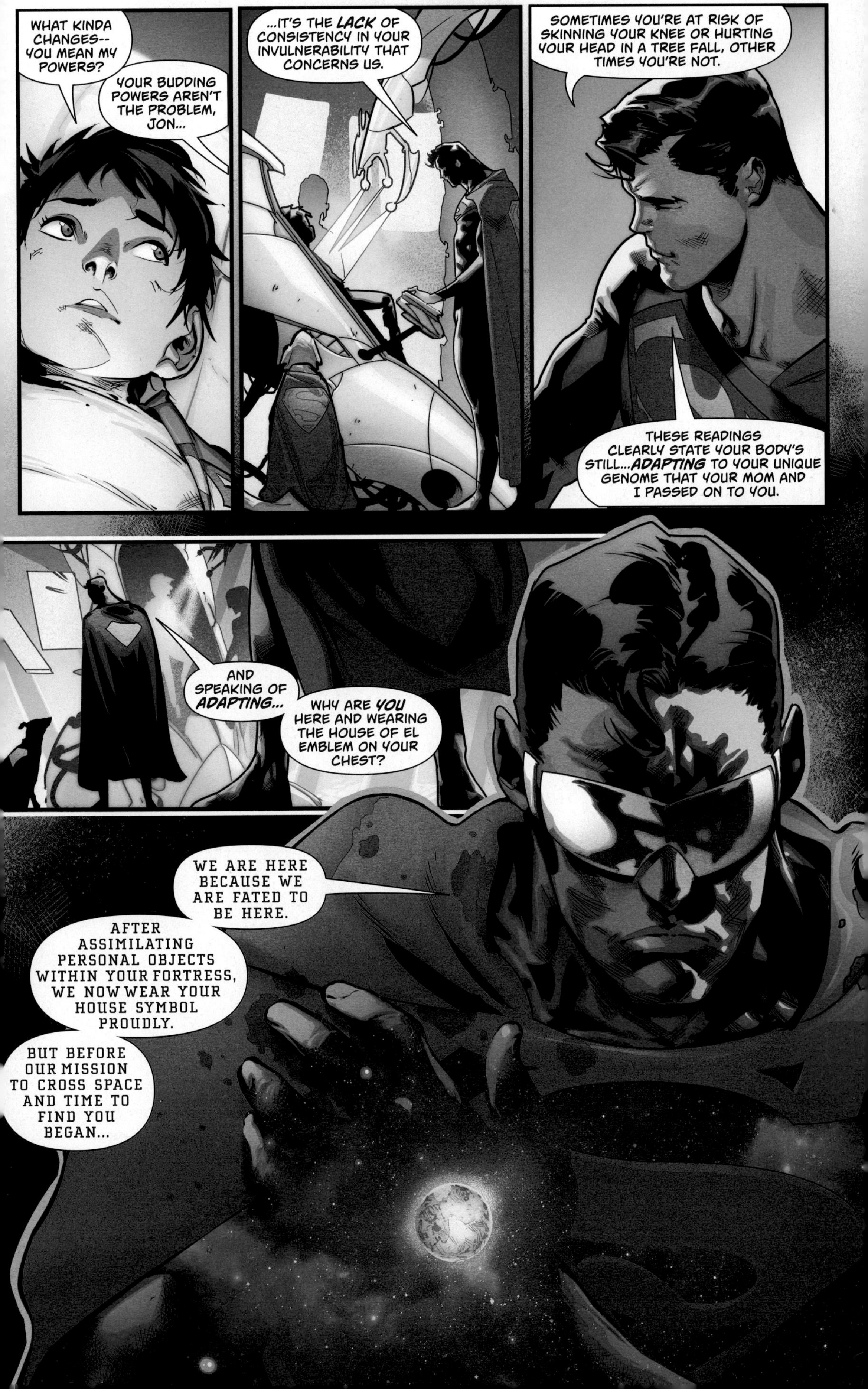
WHAT KINDA CHANGES-- YOU MEAN MY POWERS?
YOUR BUDDING POWERS AREN'T THE PROBLEM, JON...
...IT'S THE LACK OF CONSISTENCY IN YOUR INVULNERABILITY THAT CONCERNS US.
SOMETIMES YOU'RE AT RISK OF SKINNING YOUR KNEE OR HURTING YOUR HEAD IN A TREE FALL, OTHER TIMES YOU'RE NOT.
THESE READINGS CLEARLY STATE YOUR BODY'S STILL...ADAPTING TO YOUR UNIQUE GENOME THAT YOUR MOM AND I PASSED ON TO YOU.
AND SPEAKING OF ADAPTING...
WHY ARE YOU HERE AND WEARING THE HOUSE OF EL EMBLEM ON YOUR CHEST?
WE ARE HERE BECAUSE WE ARE FATED TO BE HERE.
AFTER ASSIMILATING PERSONAL OBJECTS WITHIN YOUR FORTRESS, WE NOW WEAR YOUR HOUSE SYMBOL PROUDLY.
BUT BEFORE OUR MISSION TO CROSS SPACE AND TIME TO FIND YOU BEGAN...

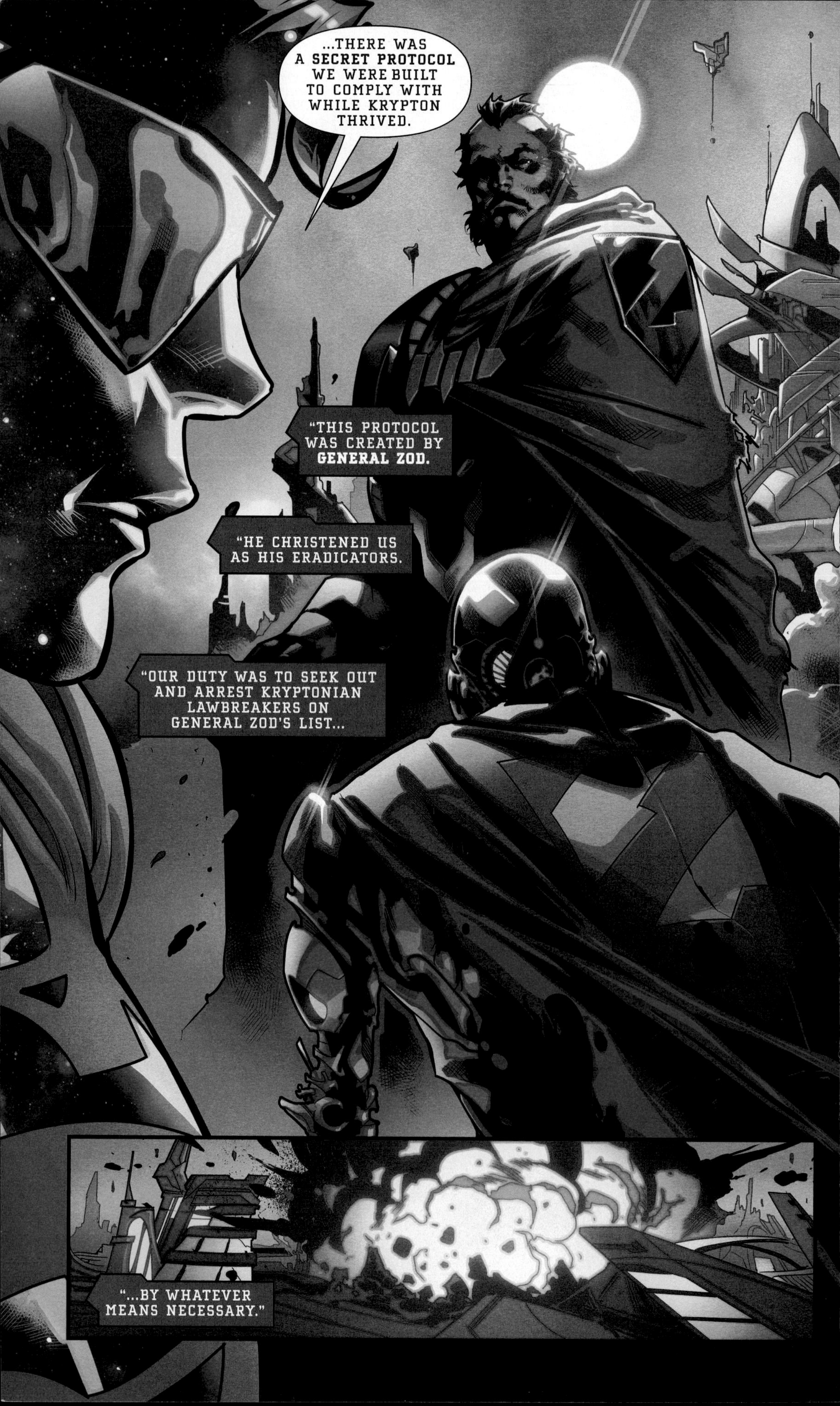
...THERE WAS A **SECRET PROTOCOL** WE WERE BUILT TO COMPLY WITH WHILE KRYPTON THRIVED.
"THIS PROTOCOL WAS CREATED BY **GENERAL ZOD.**
"HE CHRISTENED US AS HIS ERADICATORS.
"OUR DUTY WAS TO SEEK OUT AND ARREST KRYPTONIAN LAWBREAKERS ON GENERAL ZOD'S LIST...
"...BY WHATEVER MEANS NECESSARY."

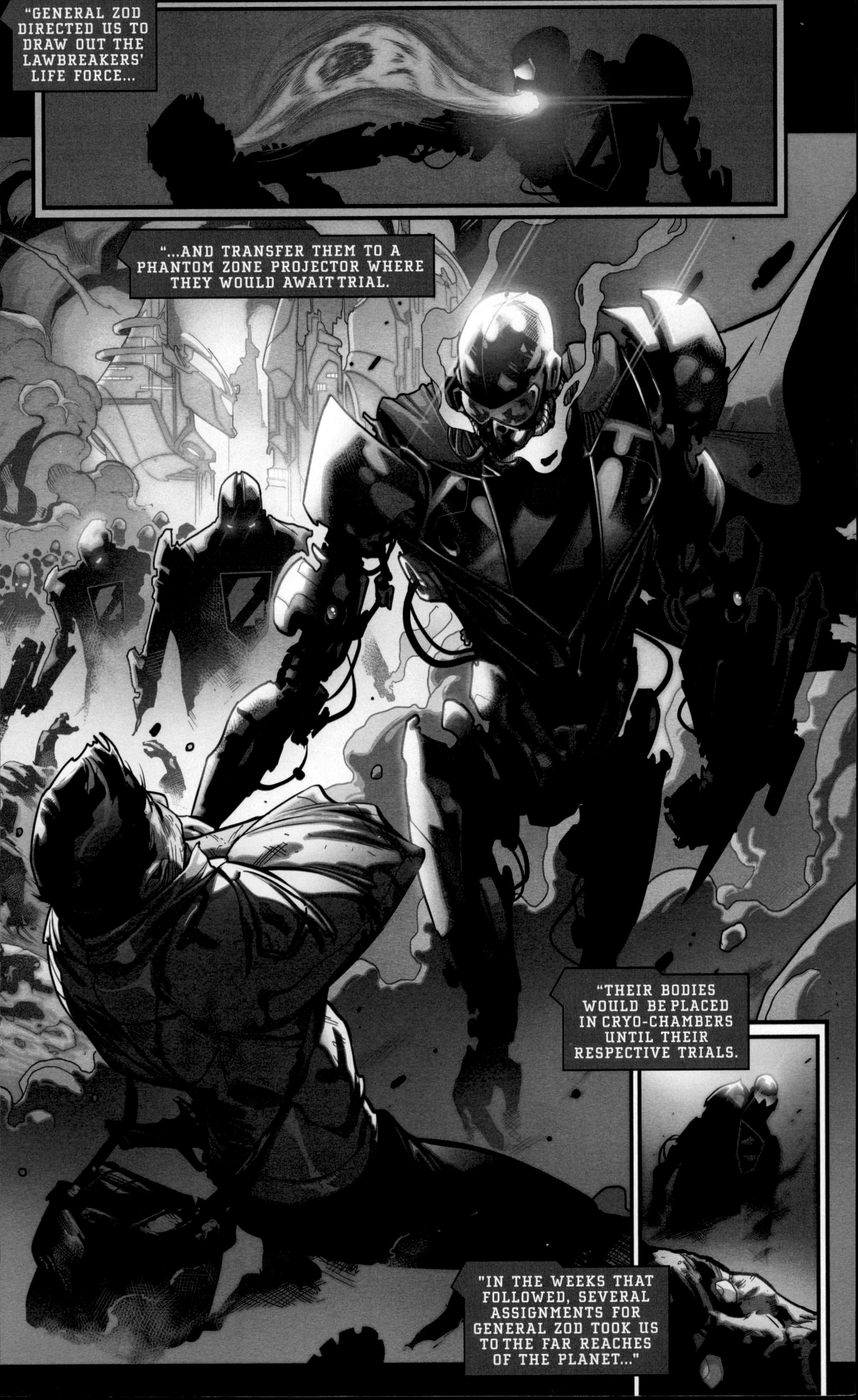
"GENERAL ZOD DIRECTED US TO DRAW OUT THE LAWBREAKERS' LIFE FORCE...
"...AND TRANSFER THEM TO A PHANTOM ZONE PROJECTOR WHERE THEY WOULD AWAIT TRIAL.
"THEIR BODIES WOULD BE PLACED IN CRYO-CHAMBERS UNTIL THEIR RESPECTIVE TRIALS.
"IN THE WEEKS THAT FOLLOWED, SEVERAL ASSIGNMENTS FOR GENERAL ZOD TOOK US TO THE FAR REACHES OF THE PLANET..."

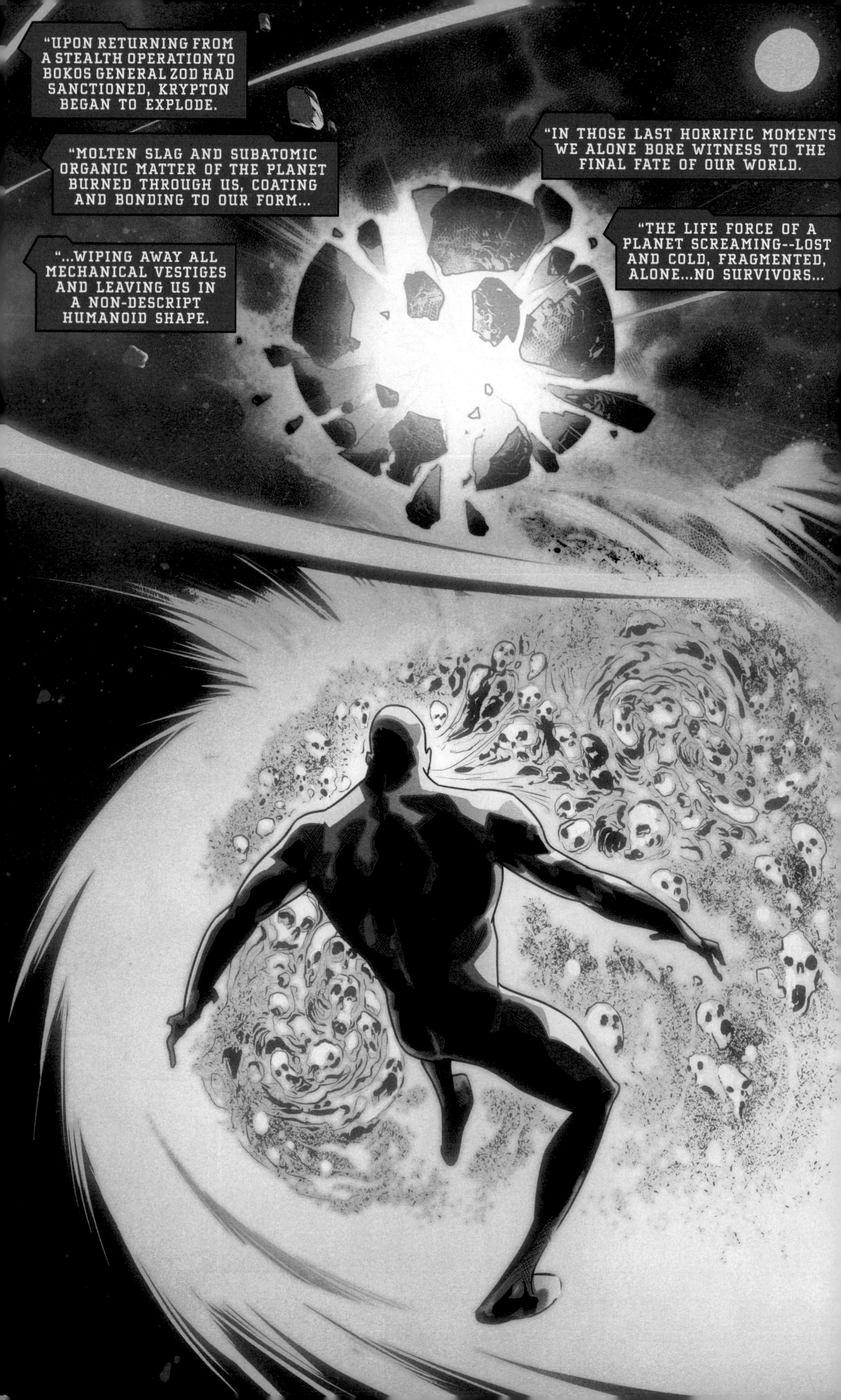
"UPON RETURNING FROM A STEALTH OPERATION TO BOKOS GENERAL ZOD HAD SANCTIONED, KRYPTON BEGAN TO EXPLODE.
"MOLTEN SLAG AND SUBATOMIC ORGANIC MATTER OF THE PLANET BURNED THROUGH US, COATING AND BONDING TO OUR FORM...
"...WIPING AWAY ALL MECHANICAL VESTIGES AND LEAVING US IN A NON-DESCRIPT HUMANOID SHAPE.
"IN THOSE LAST HORRIFIC MOMENTS WE ALONE BORE WITNESS TO THE FINAL FATE OF OUR WORLD.
"THE LIFE FORCE OF A PLANET SCREAMING--LOST AND COLD, FRAGMENTED, ALONE...NO SURVIVORS...

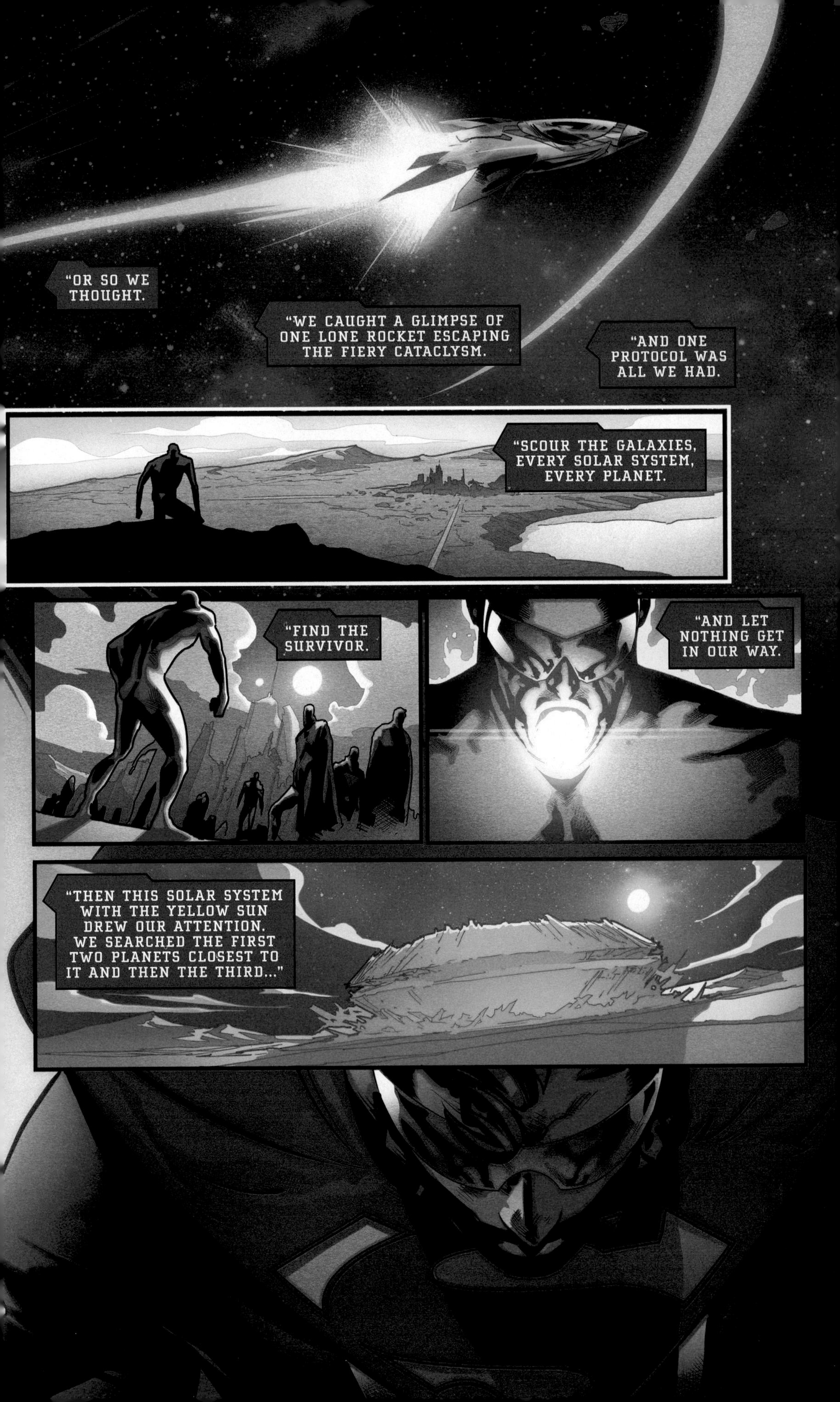
"OR SO WE THOUGHT.
"WE CAUGHT A GLIMPSE OF ONE LONE ROCKET ESCAPING THE FIERY CATACLYSM.
"AND ONE PROTOCOL WAS ALL WE HAD.
"SCOUR THE GALAXIES, EVERY SOLAR SYSTEM, EVERY PLANET.
"FIND THE SURVIVOR.
"AND LET NOTHING GET IN OUR WAY.
"THEN THIS SOLAR SYSTEM WITH THE YELLOW SUN DREW OUR ATTENTION. WE SEARCHED THE FIRST TWO PLANETS CLOSEST TO IT AND THEN THE THIRD..."

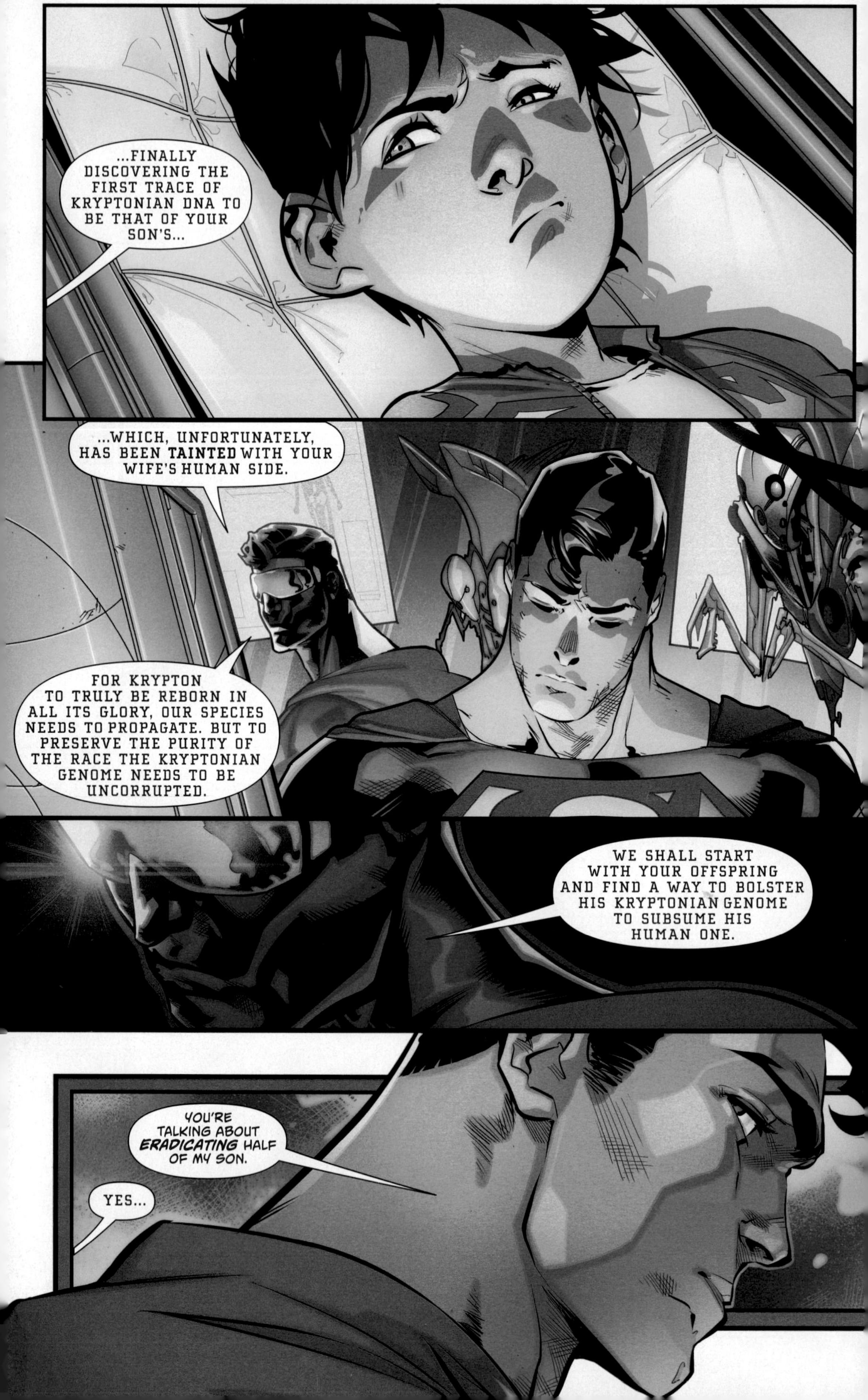
...FINALLY DISCOVERING THE FIRST TRACE OF KRYPTONIAN DNA TO BE THAT OF YOUR SON'S...
...WHICH, UNFORTUNATELY, HAS BEEN **TAINTED** WITH YOUR WIFE'S HUMAN SIDE.
FOR KRYPTON TO TRULY BE REBORN IN ALL ITS GLORY, OUR SPECIES NEEDS TO PROPAGATE. BUT TO PRESERVE THE PURITY OF THE RACE THE KRYPTONIAN GENOME NEEDS TO BE UNCORRUPTED.
WE SHALL START WITH YOUR OFFSPRING AND FIND A WAY TO BOLSTER HIS KRYPTONIAN GENOME TO SUBSUME HIS HUMAN ONE.
YOU'RE TALKING ABOUT ***ERADICATING*** HALF OF MY SON.
YES...

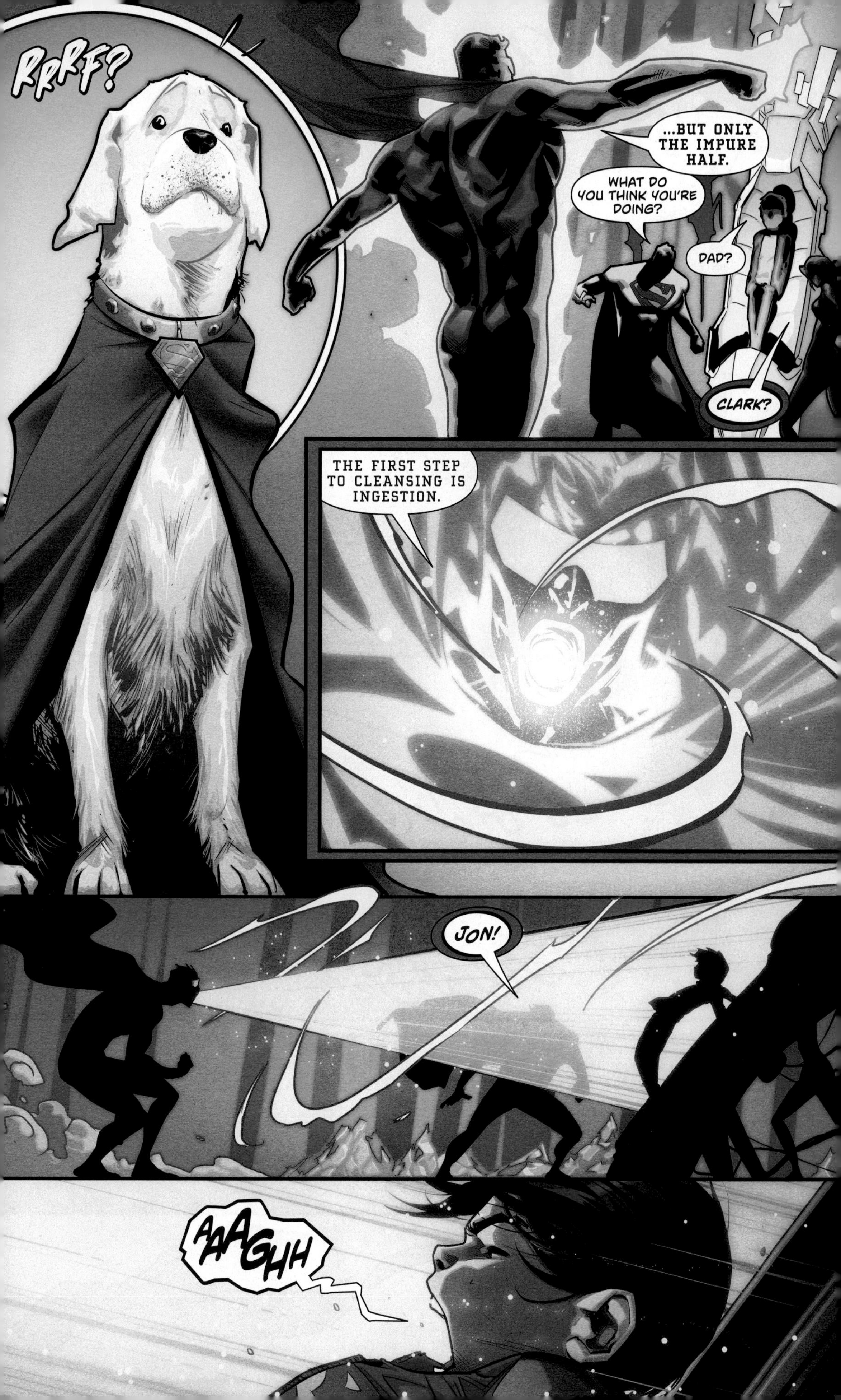
RRRF?
...BUT ONLY THE IMPURE HALF.
WHAT DO YOU THINK YOU'RE DOING?
DAD?
CLARK?
THE FIRST STEP TO CLEANSING IS INGESTION.
JON!
AAAGHH

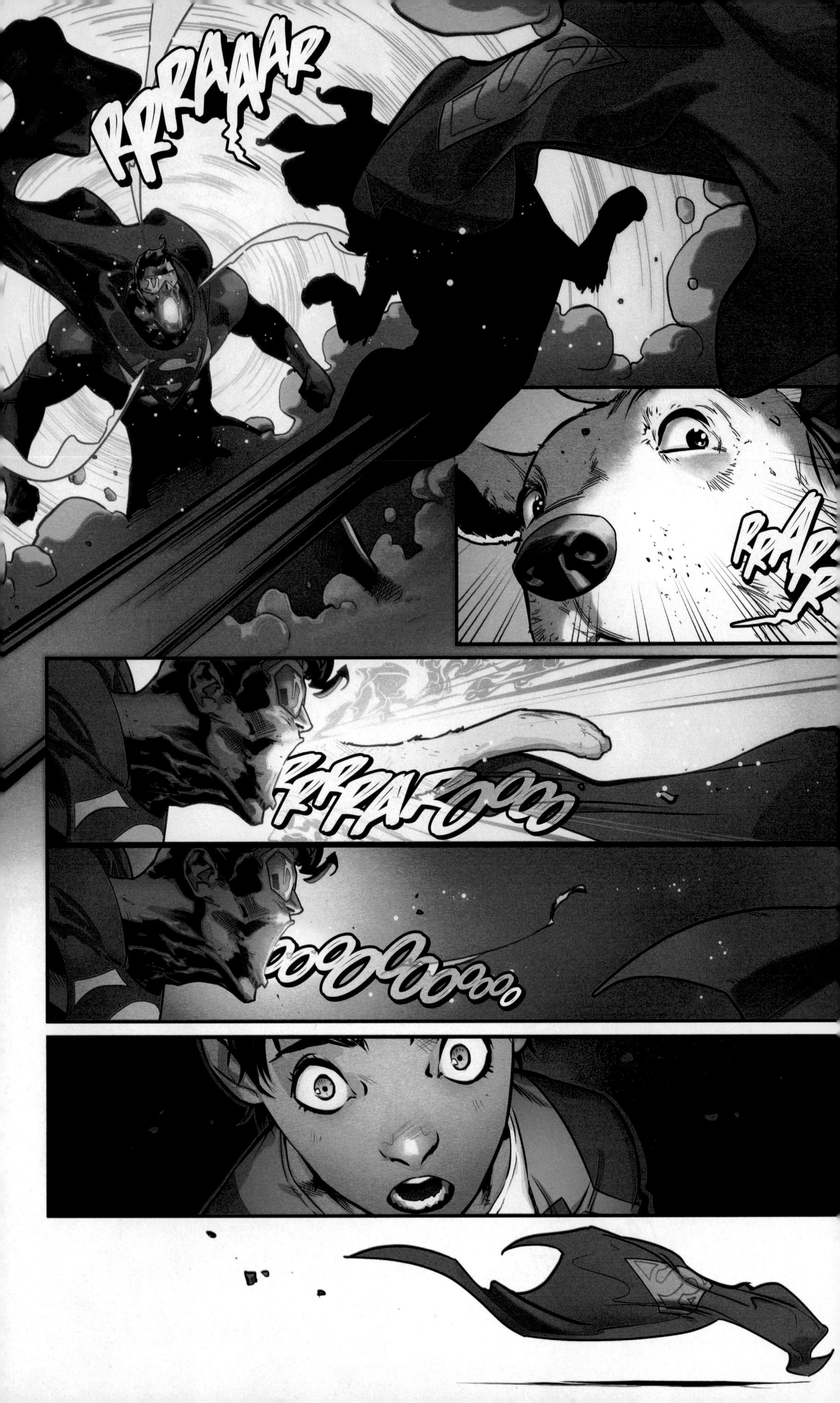
RRRAAAR
RRAAR
RRRAAROOOO
OOOOOOOooooo

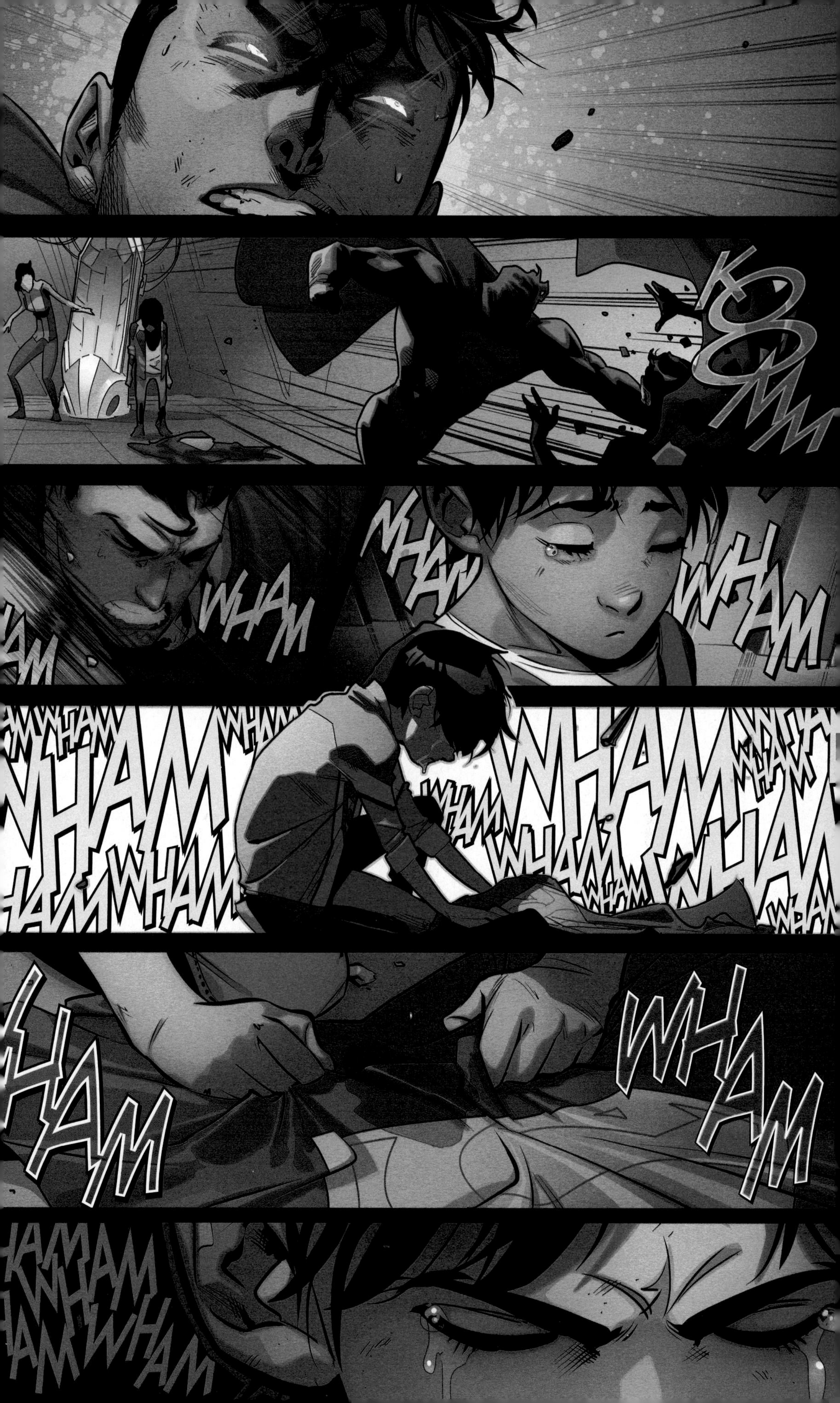
KOOMM
WHAM
WHAM
WHAM
WHAM
WHAM
WHAM
WHAM
WHAM
WHAM

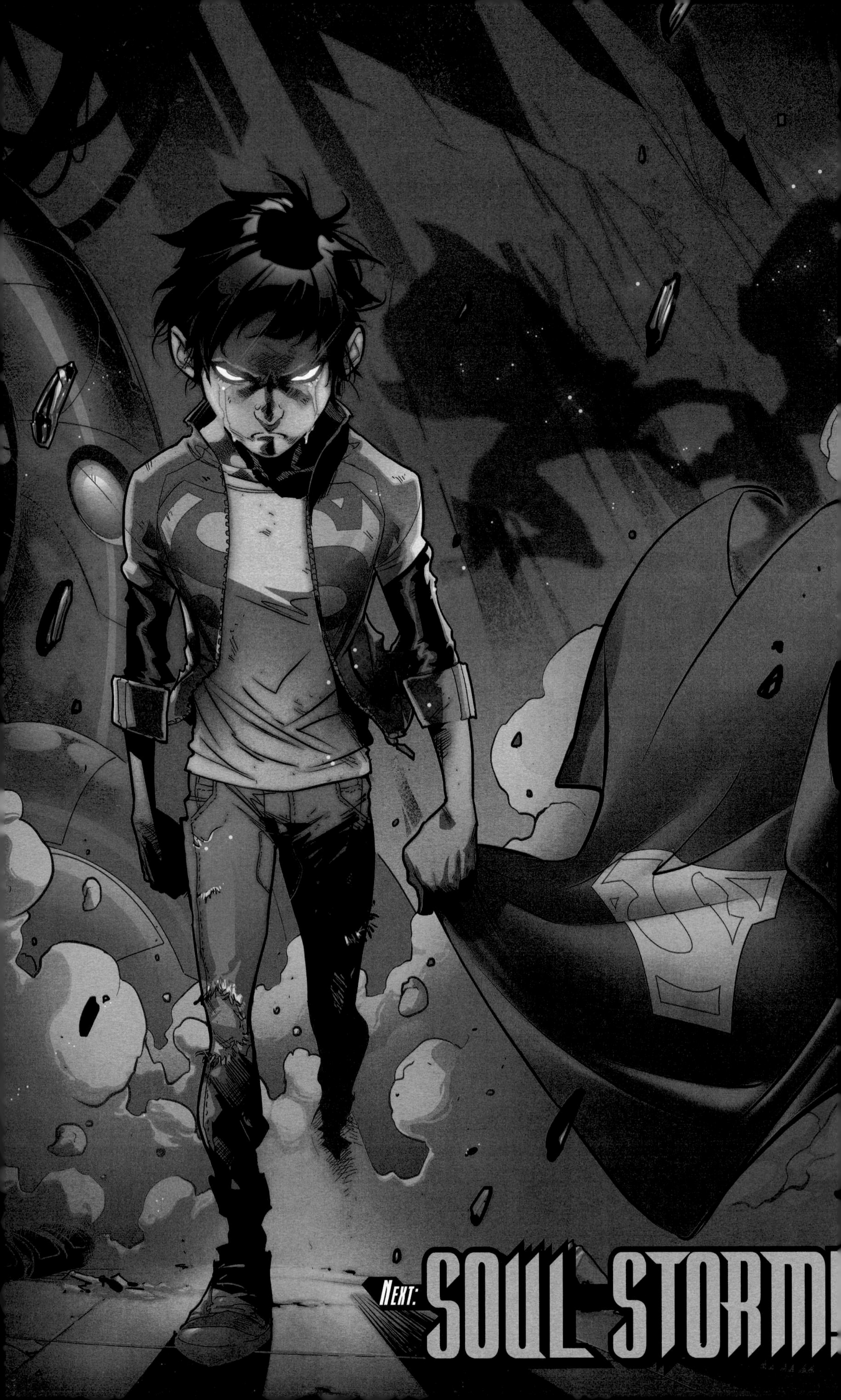
NEXT: SOUL STORM!

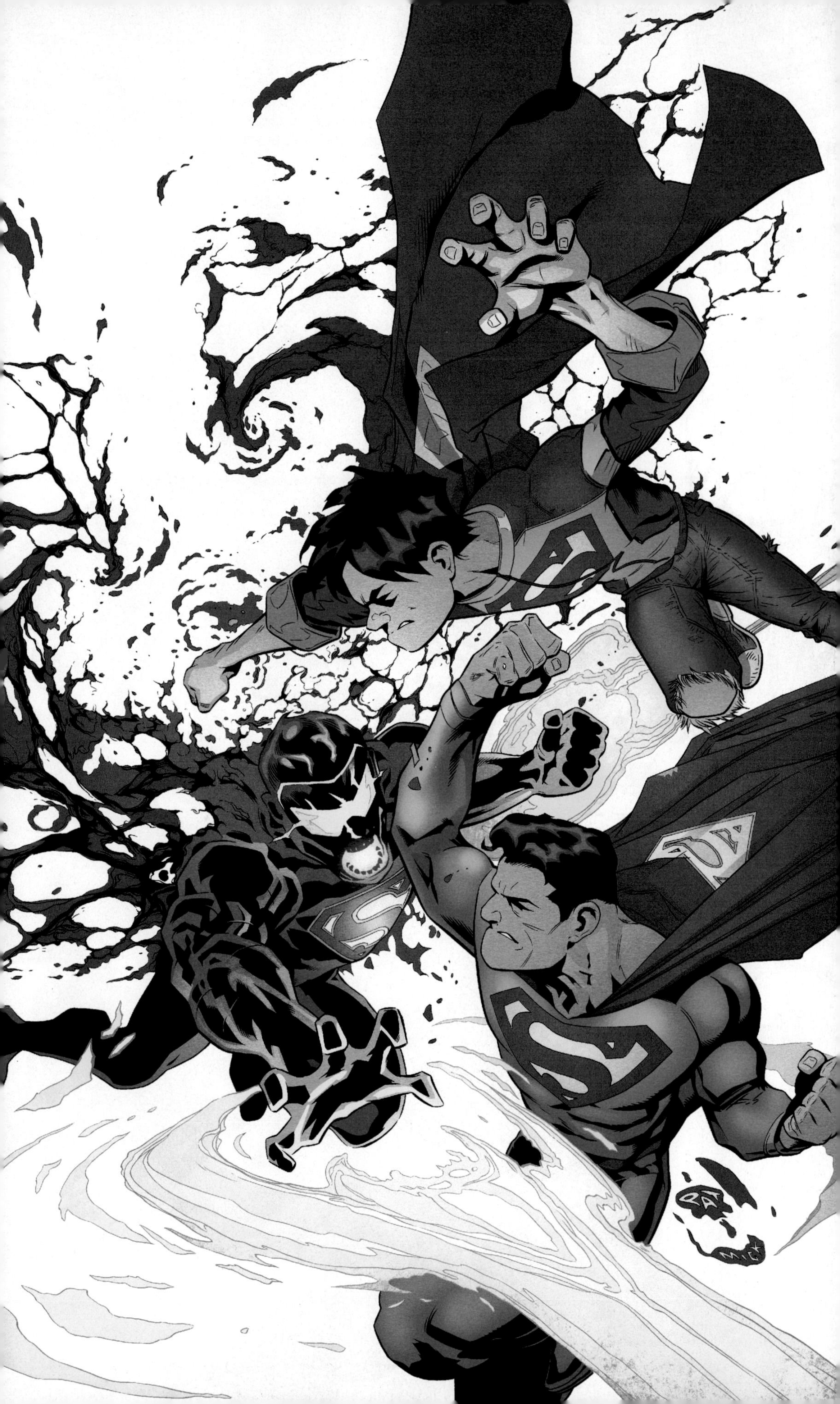

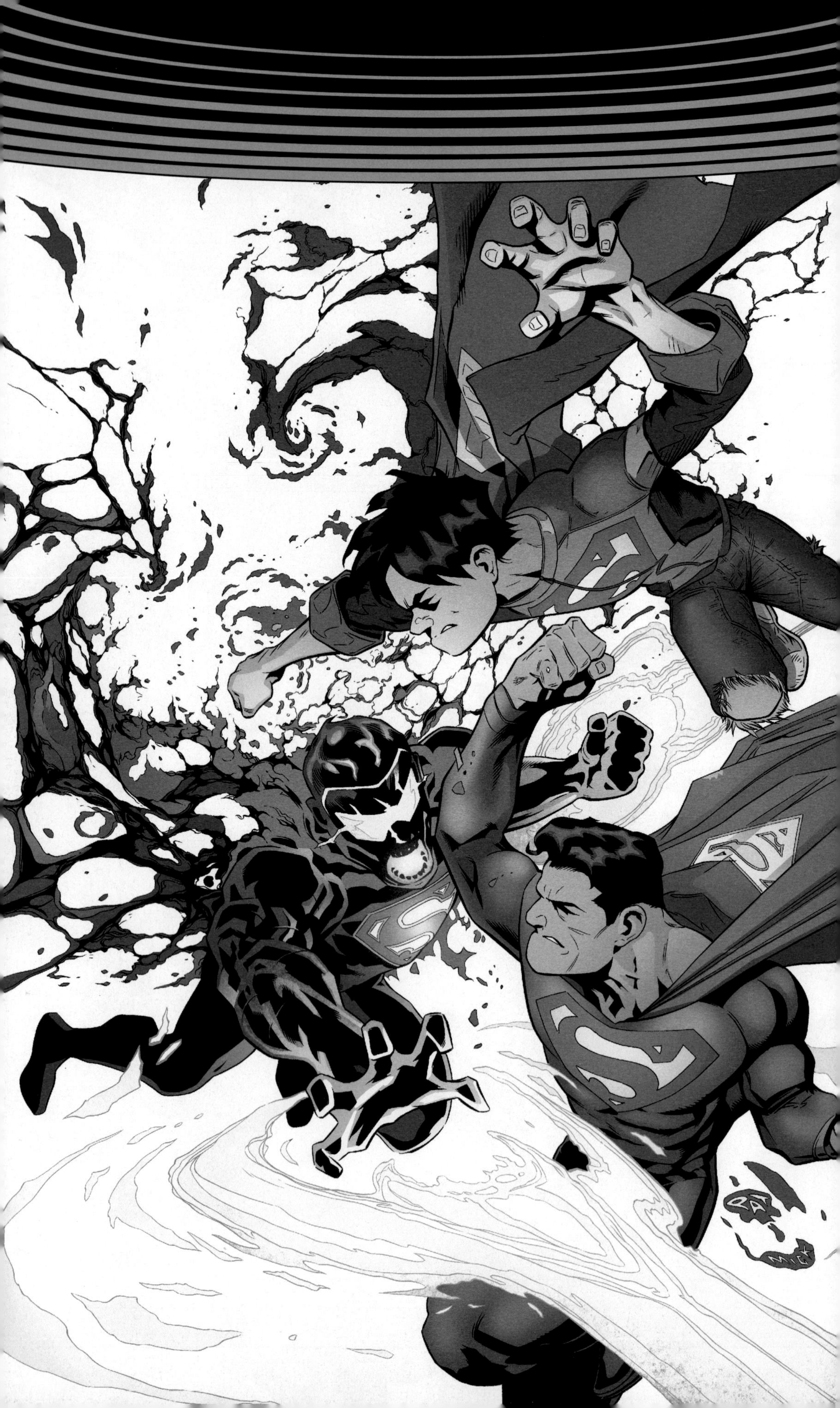

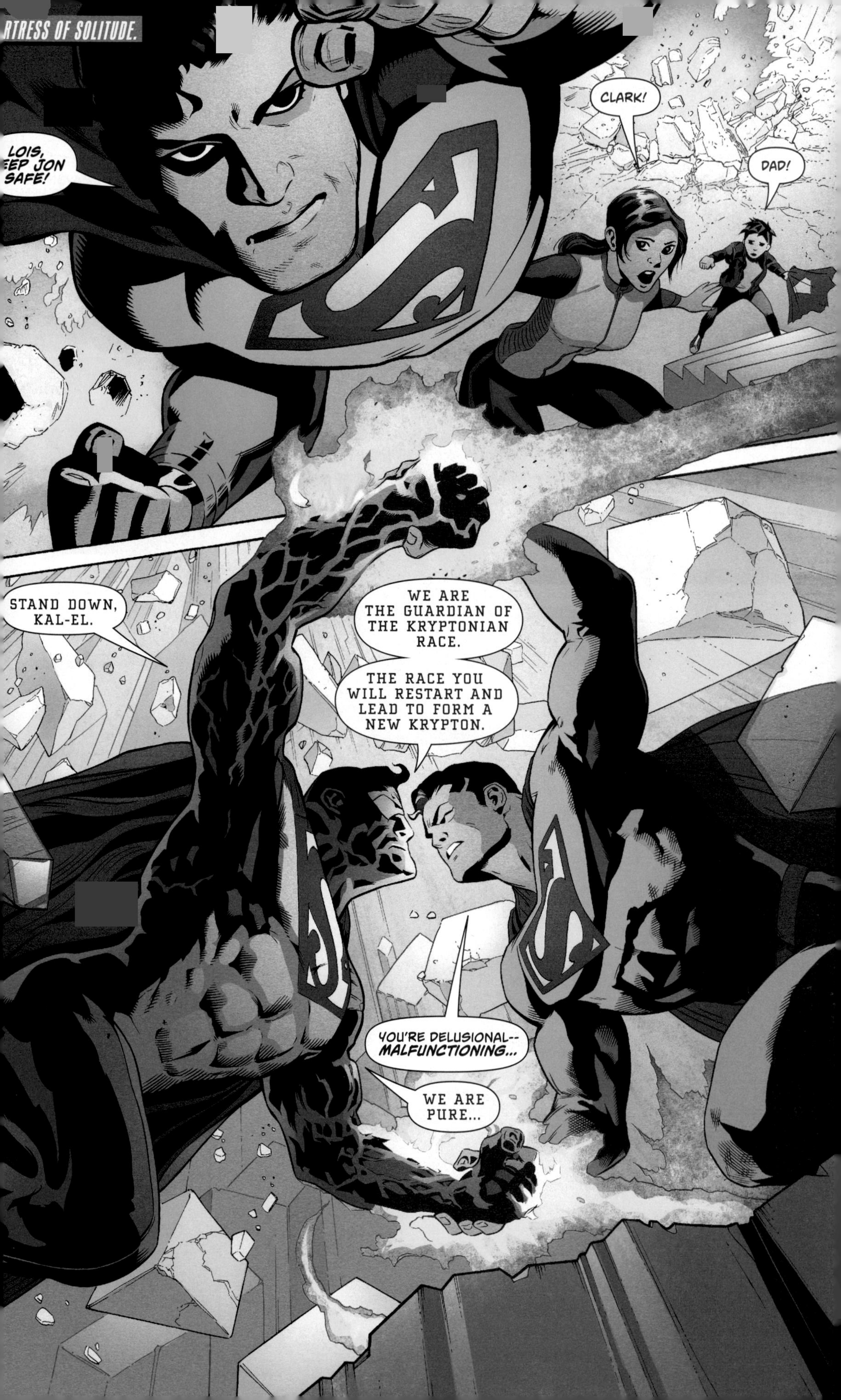
RTRESS OF SOLITUDE.
LOIS, EEP JON SAFE!
CLARK!
DAD!
STAND DOWN, KAL-EL.
WE ARE THE GUARDIAN OF THE KRYPTONIAN RACE.
THE RACE YOU WILL RESTART AND LEAD TO FORM A NEW KRYPTON.
YOU'RE DELUSIONAL-- **MALFUNCTIONING...**
WE ARE PURE...

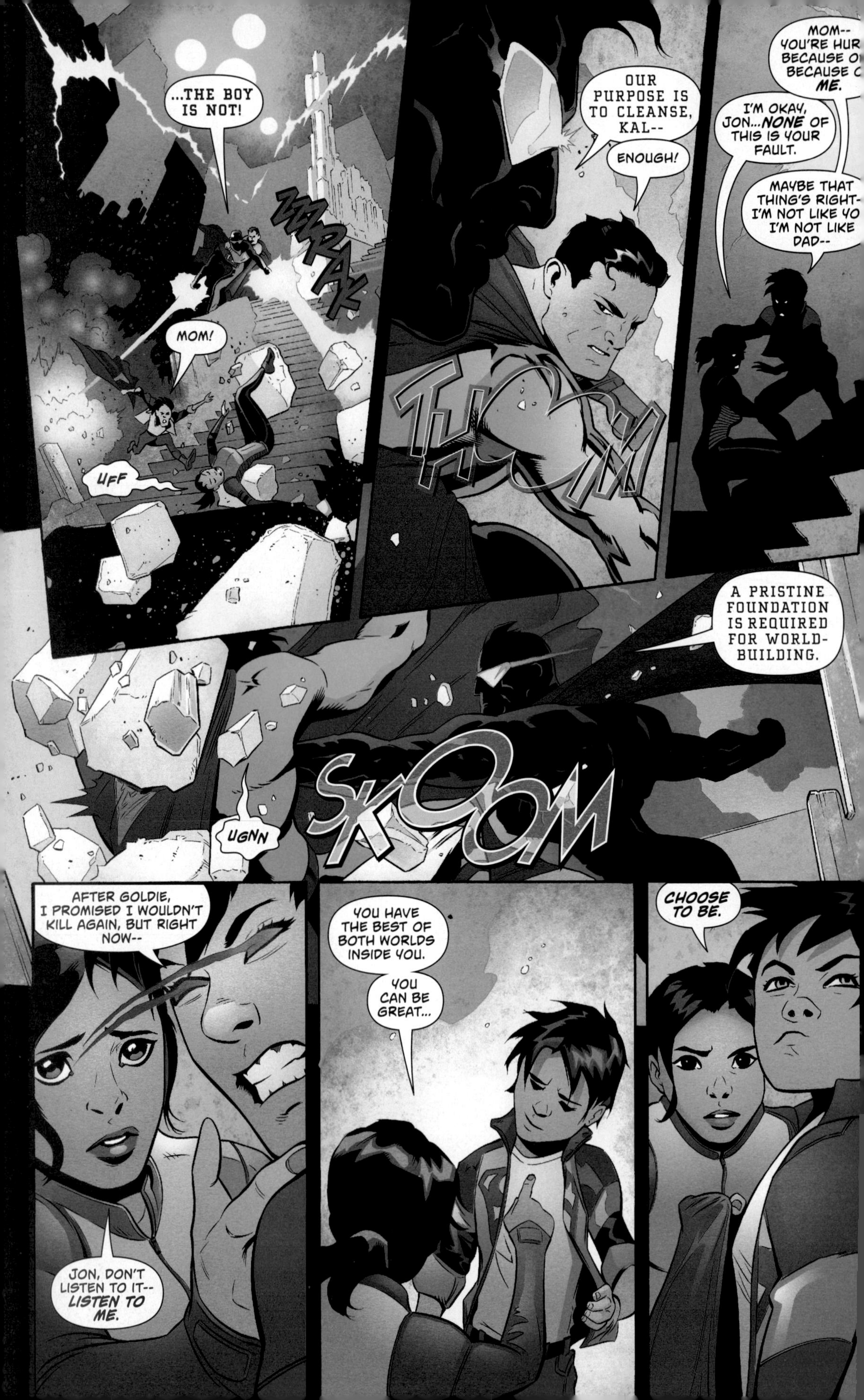

...THE BOY IS NOT!
ZZZRAK
MOM!
UFF
OUR PURPOSE IS TO CLEANSE, KAL--
ENOUGH!
THOOM
MOM-- YOU'RE HUR BECAUSE O BECAUSE O ME.
I'M OKAY, JON...NONE OF THIS IS YOUR FAULT.
MAYBE THAT THING'S RIGHT- I'M NOT LIKE YO I'M NOT LIKE DAD--
A PRISTINE FOUNDATION IS REQUIRED FOR WORLD-BUILDING.
SKOOM
UGNN
AFTER GOLDIE, I PROMISED I WOULDN'T KILL AGAIN, BUT RIGHT NOW--
JON, DON'T LISTEN TO IT-- LISTEN TO ME.
YOU HAVE THE BEST OF BOTH WORLDS INSIDE YOU.
YOU CAN BE GREAT...
CHOOSE TO BE.

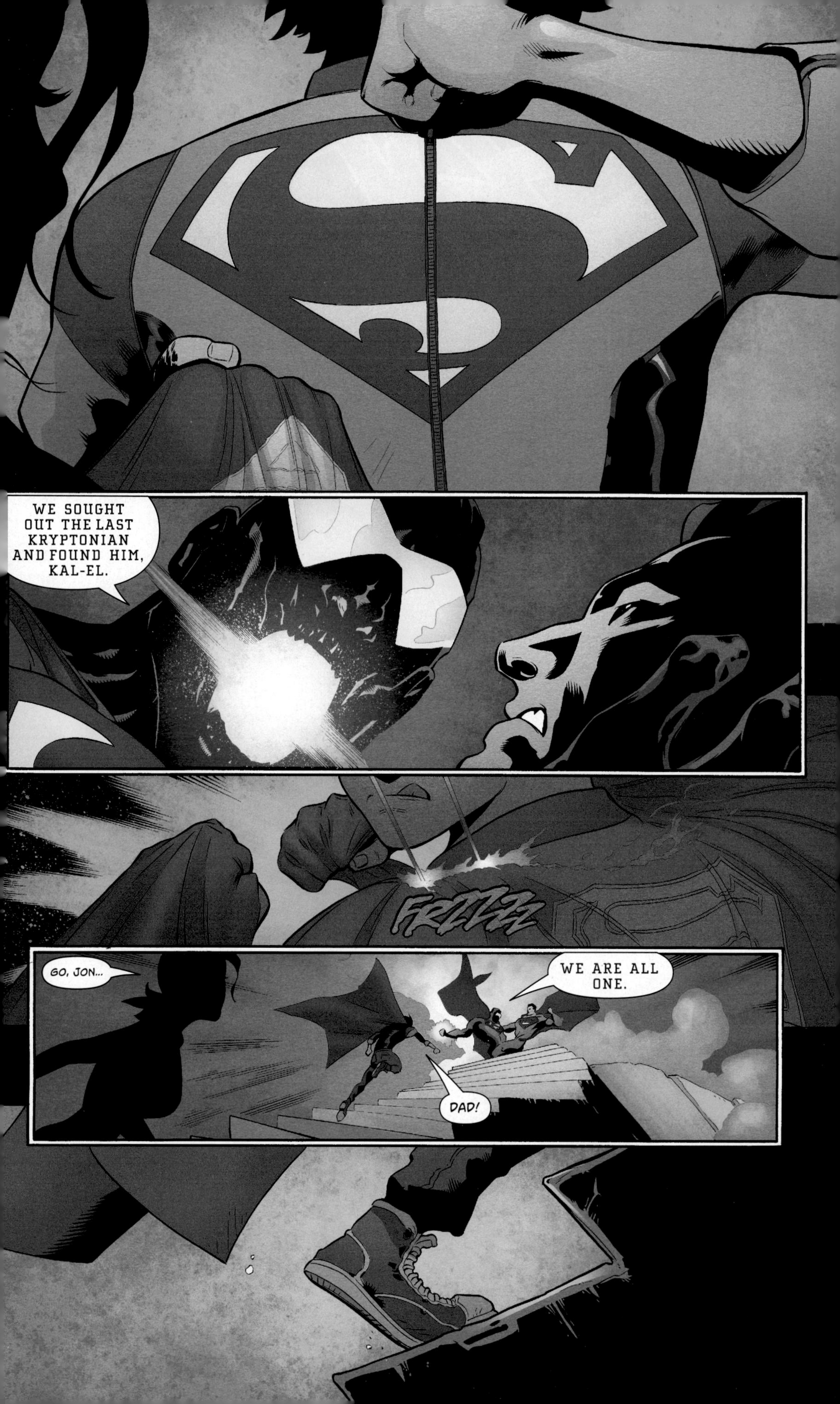
WE SOUGHT OUT THE LAST KRYPTONIAN AND FOUND HIM, KAL-EL.
FRZZZZ
GO, JON...
WE ARE ALL ONE.
DAD!

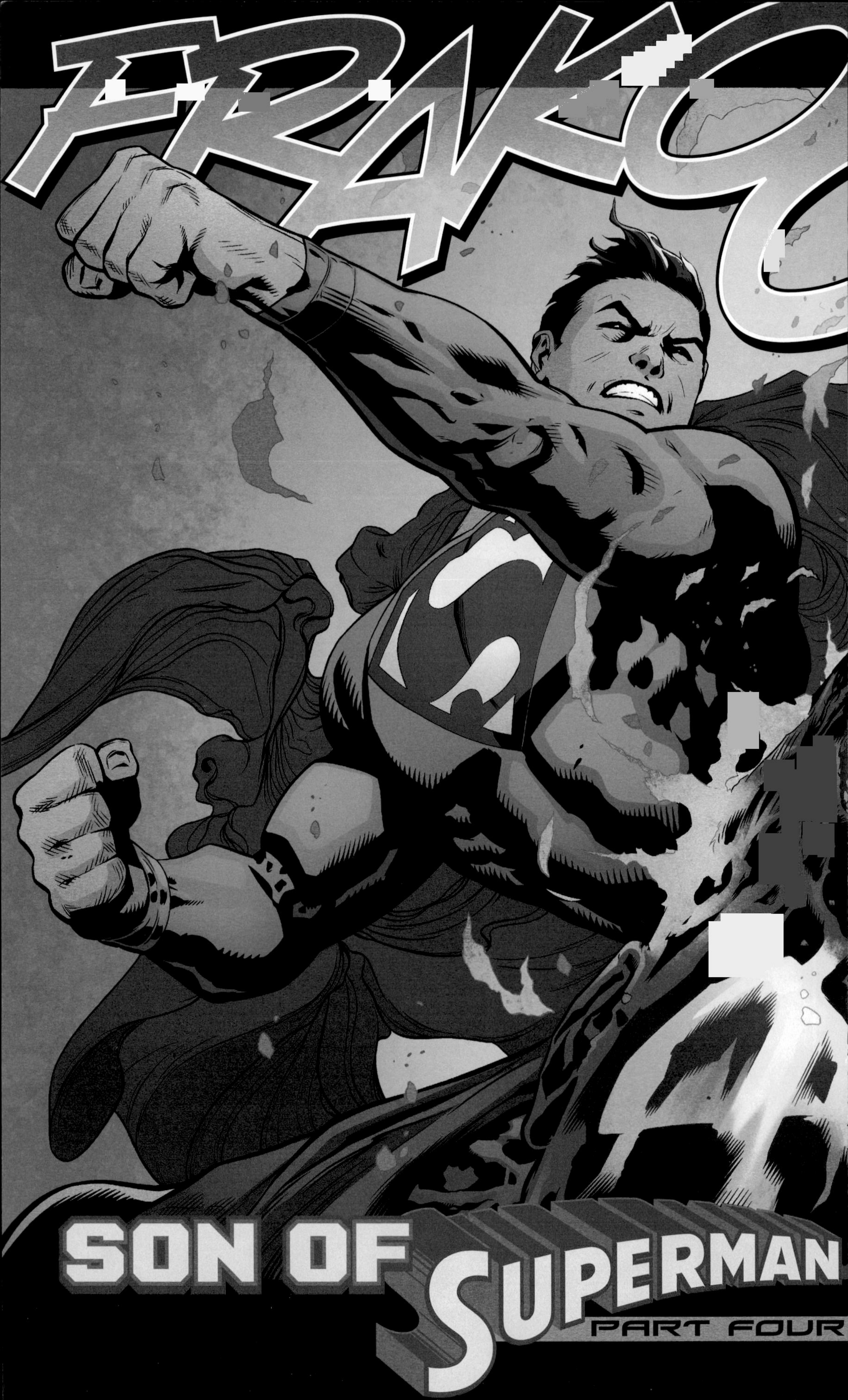
FRAKO
SON OF SUPERMAN
PART FOUR

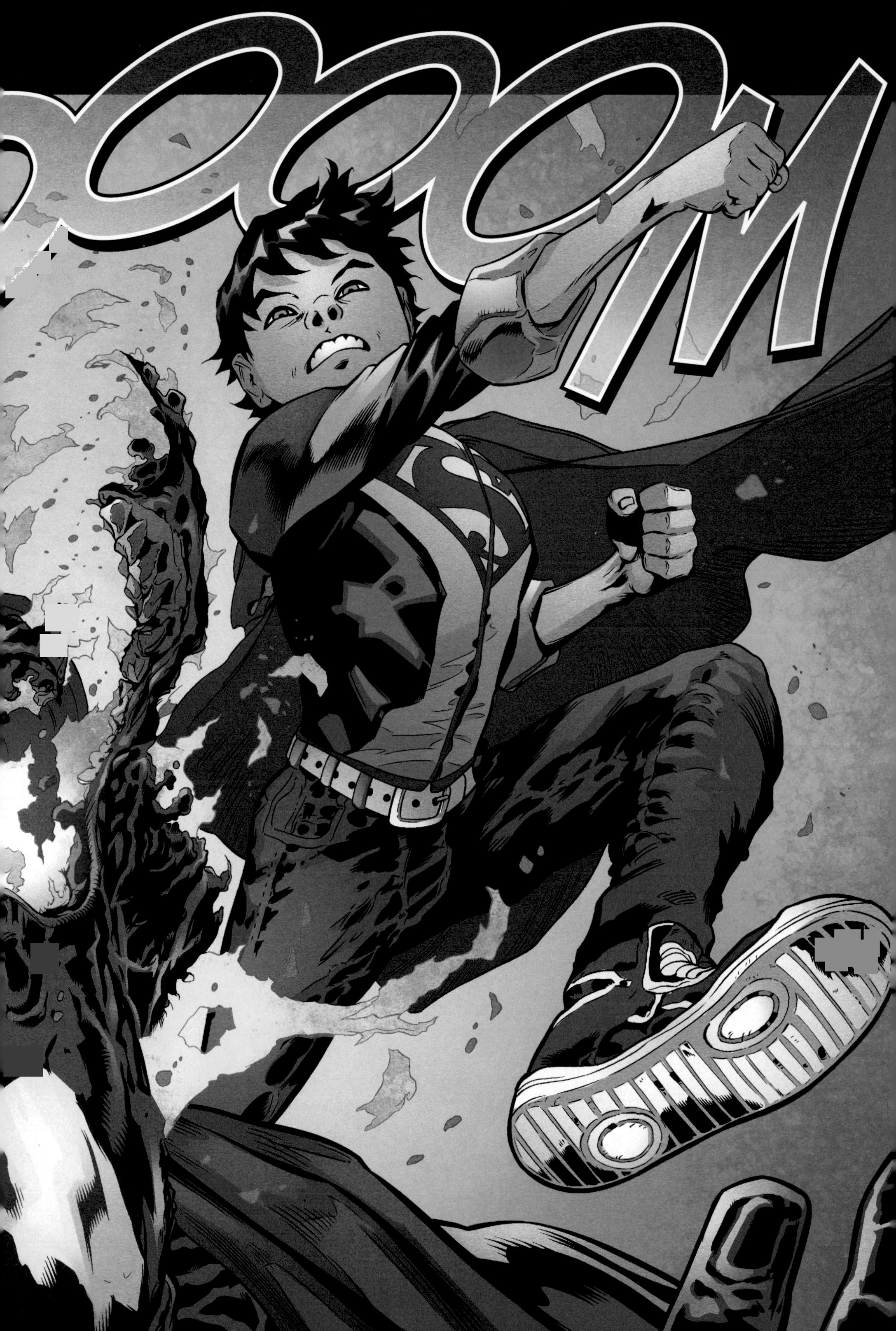
OOOM

PETER J. TOMASI & PATRICK GLEASON
story

PATRICK GLEASON
penciller

MICK GRAY
inker

JOHN KALISZ
colorist

ROB LEIGH
letterer

GLEASON, GRAY, KALISZ
cover

KENNETH ROCAFORT
variant cover

ANDREW MARINO
assistant editor

EDDIE BERGANZA
editor

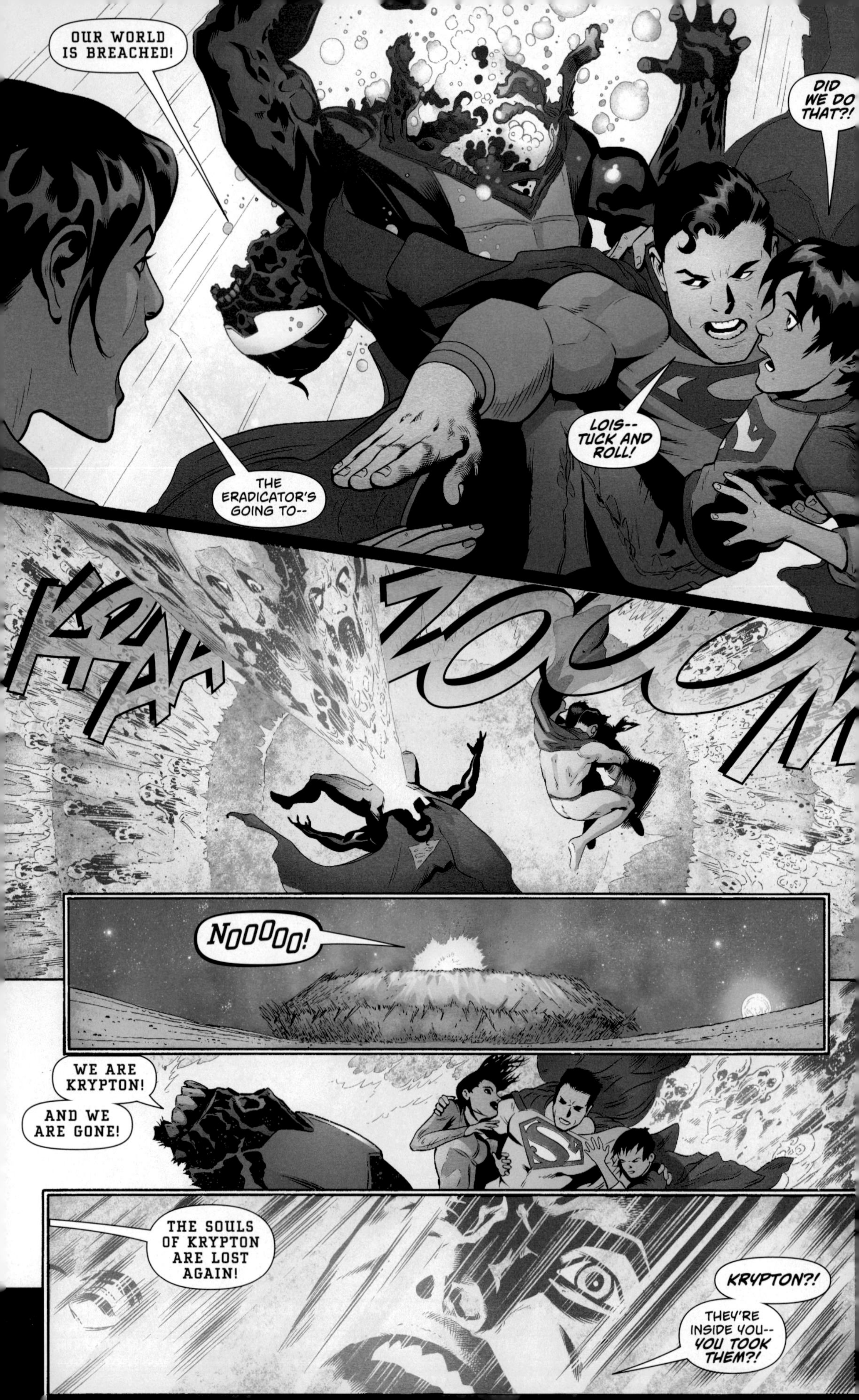
OUR WORLD IS BREACHED!
DID WE DO THAT?!
THE ERADICATOR'S GOING TO--
LOIS-- TUCK AND ROLL!
KRAKAZOOOM
NOOOOO!
WE ARE KRYPTON!
AND WE ARE GONE!
THE SOULS OF KRYPTON ARE LOST AGAIN!
KRYPTON?!
THEY'RE INSIDE YOU-- YOU TOOK THEM?!

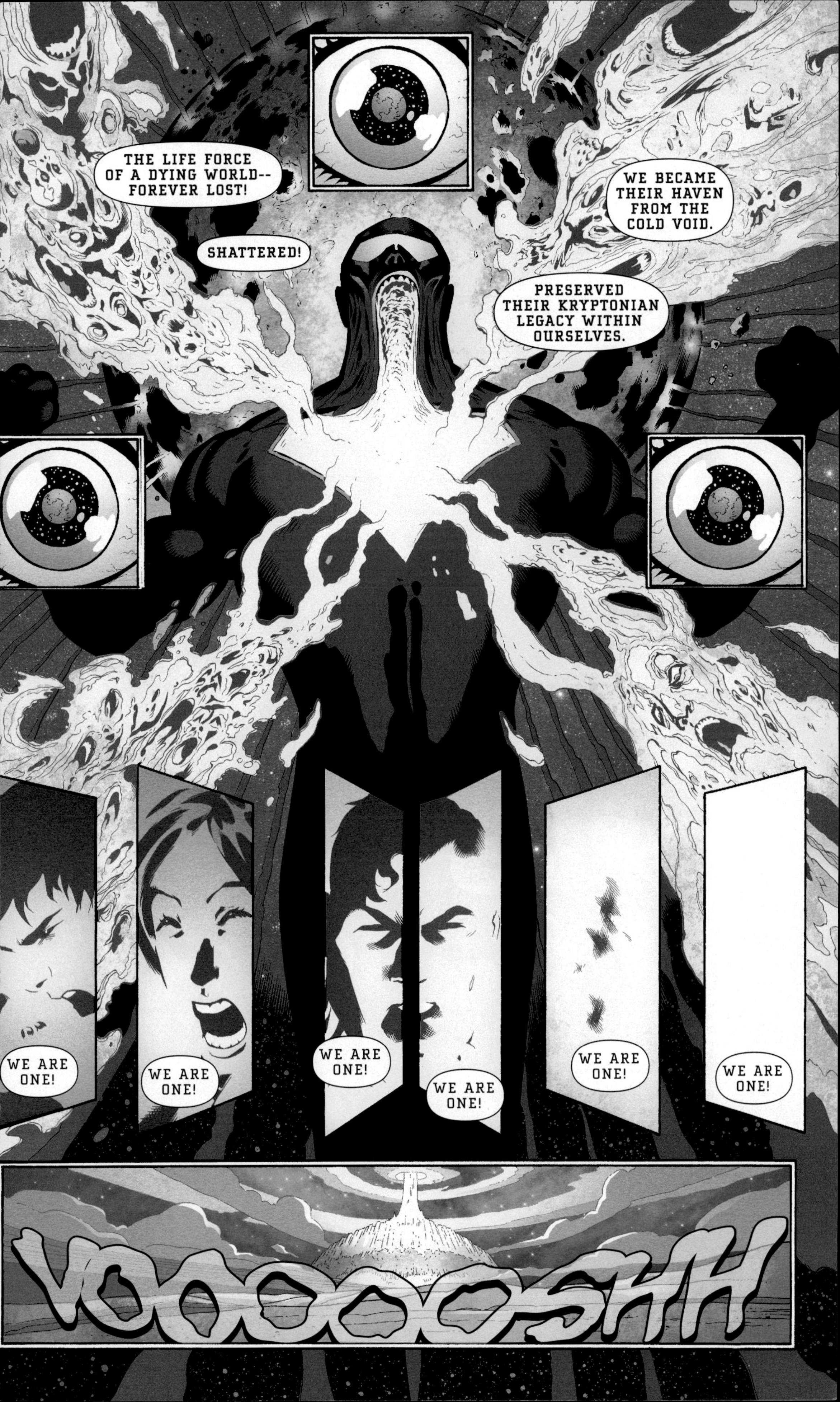

THE LIFE FORCE OF A DYING WORLD-- FOREVER LOST!
SHATTERED!
WE BECAME THEIR HAVEN FROM THE COLD VOID.
PRESERVED THEIR KRYPTONIAN LEGACY WITHIN OURSELVES.
WE ARE ONE!
WE ARE ONE!
WE ARE ONE!
WE ARE ONE!
WE ARE ONE!
WE ARE ONE!
VOOOOOOSHH

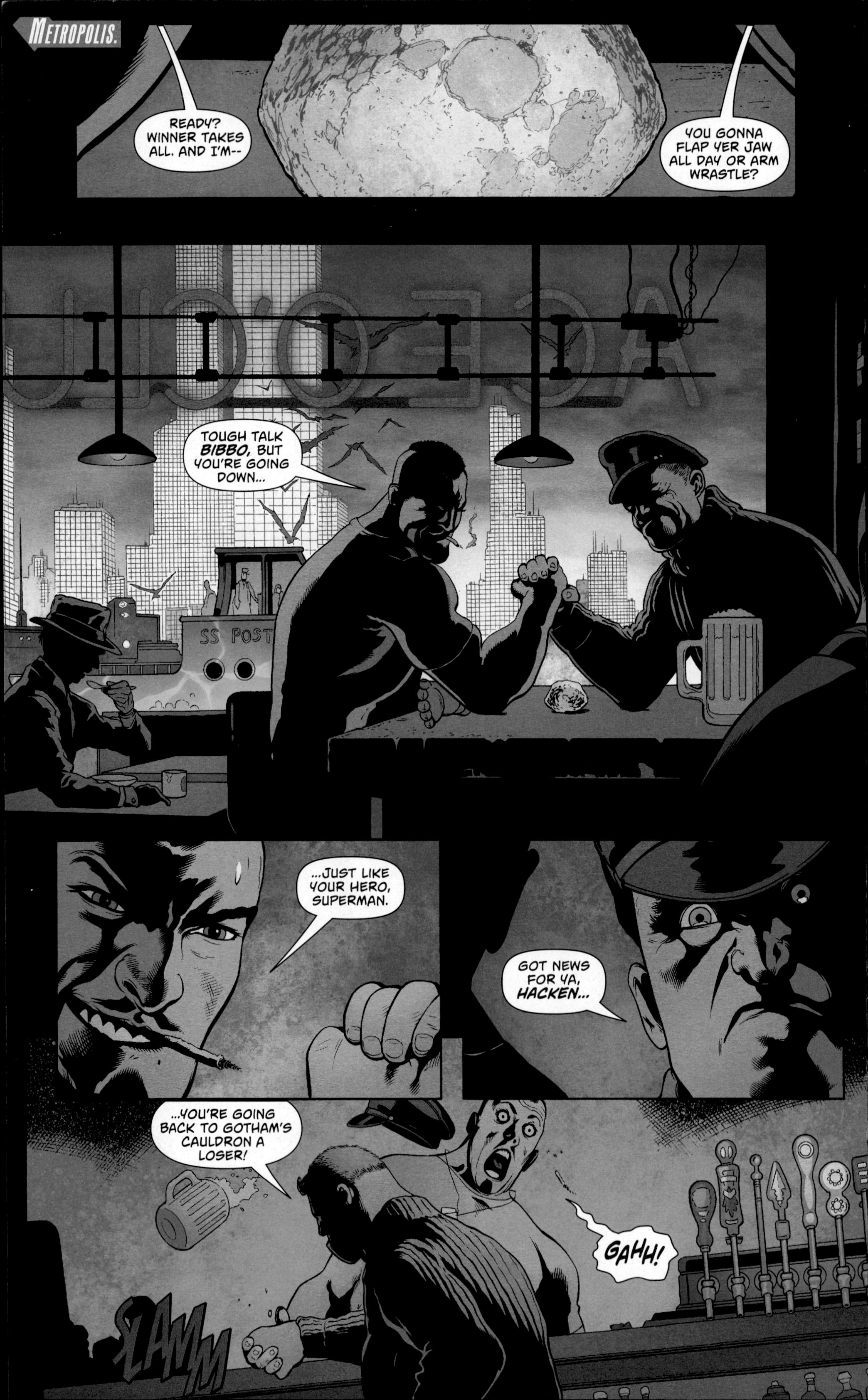
METROPOLIS.
READY? WINNER TAKES ALL. AND I'M--
YOU GONNA FLAP YER JAW ALL DAY OR ARM WRASTLE?
TOUGH TALK BIBBO, BUT YOU'RE GOING DOWN...
SS POST
...JUST LIKE YOUR HERO, SUPERMAN.
GOT NEWS FOR YA, HACKEN...
...YOU'RE GOING BACK TO GOTHAM'S CAULDRON A LOSER!
GAHH!
SLAMM

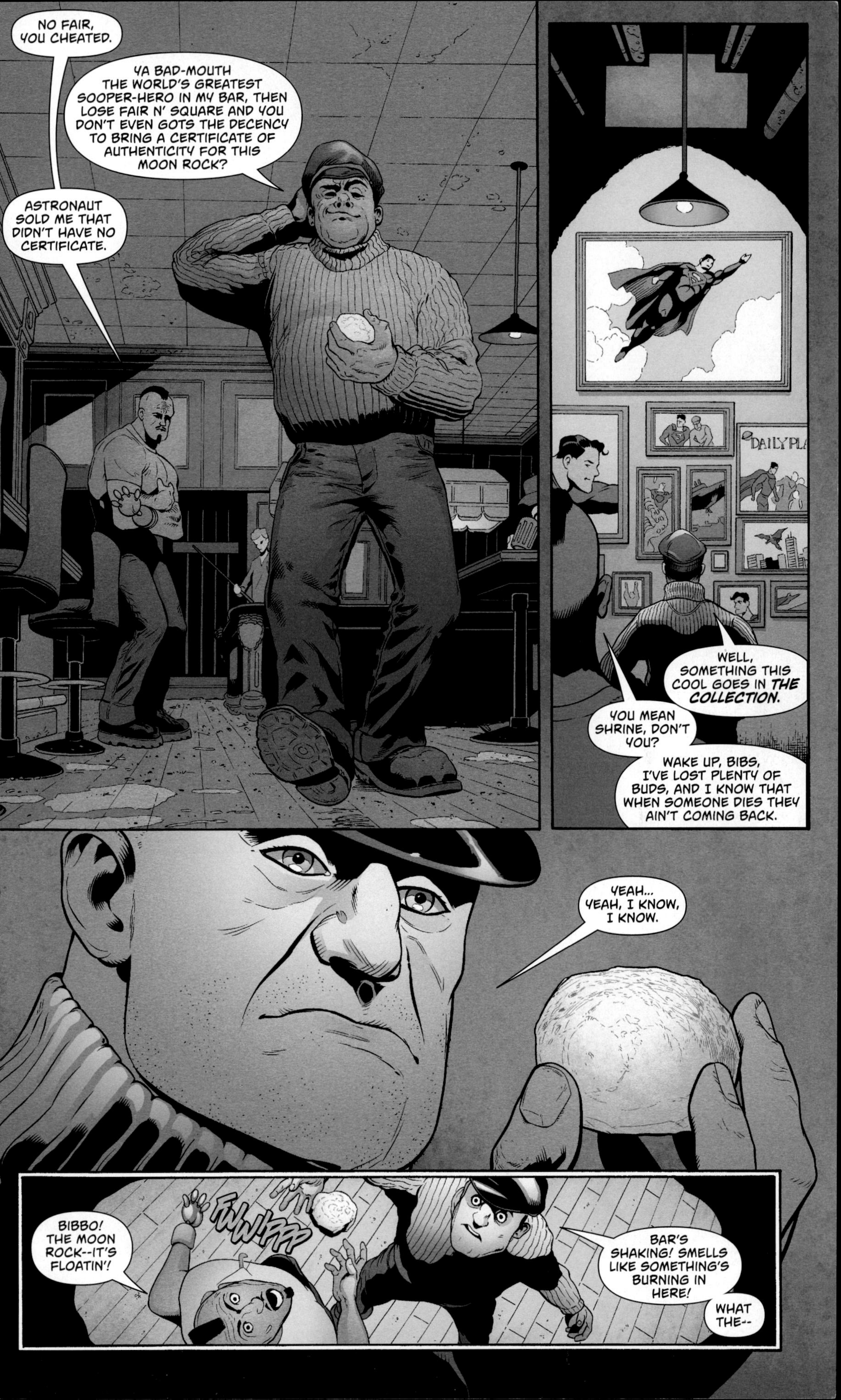
NO FAIR, YOU CHEATED.
YA BAD-MOUTH THE WORLD'S GREATEST SOOPER-HERO IN MY BAR, THEN LOSE FAIR N' SQUARE AND YOU DON'T EVEN GOTS THE DECENCY TO BRING A CERTIFICATE OF AUTHENTICITY FOR THIS MOON ROCK?
ASTRONAUT SOLD ME THAT DIDN'T HAVE NO CERTIFICATE.
DAILY PLA
WELL, SOMETHING THIS COOL GOES IN *THE COLLECTION*.
YOU MEAN SHRINE, DON'T YOU?
WAKE UP, BIBS, I'VE LOST PLENTY OF BUDS, AND I KNOW THAT WHEN SOMEONE DIES THEY AIN'T COMING BACK.
YEAH... YEAH, I KNOW, I KNOW.
FWWHIPPP
BIBBO! THE MOON ROCK--IT'S FLOATIN'!
BAR'S SHAKING! SMELLS LIKE SOMETHING'S BURNING IN HERE!
WHAT THE--

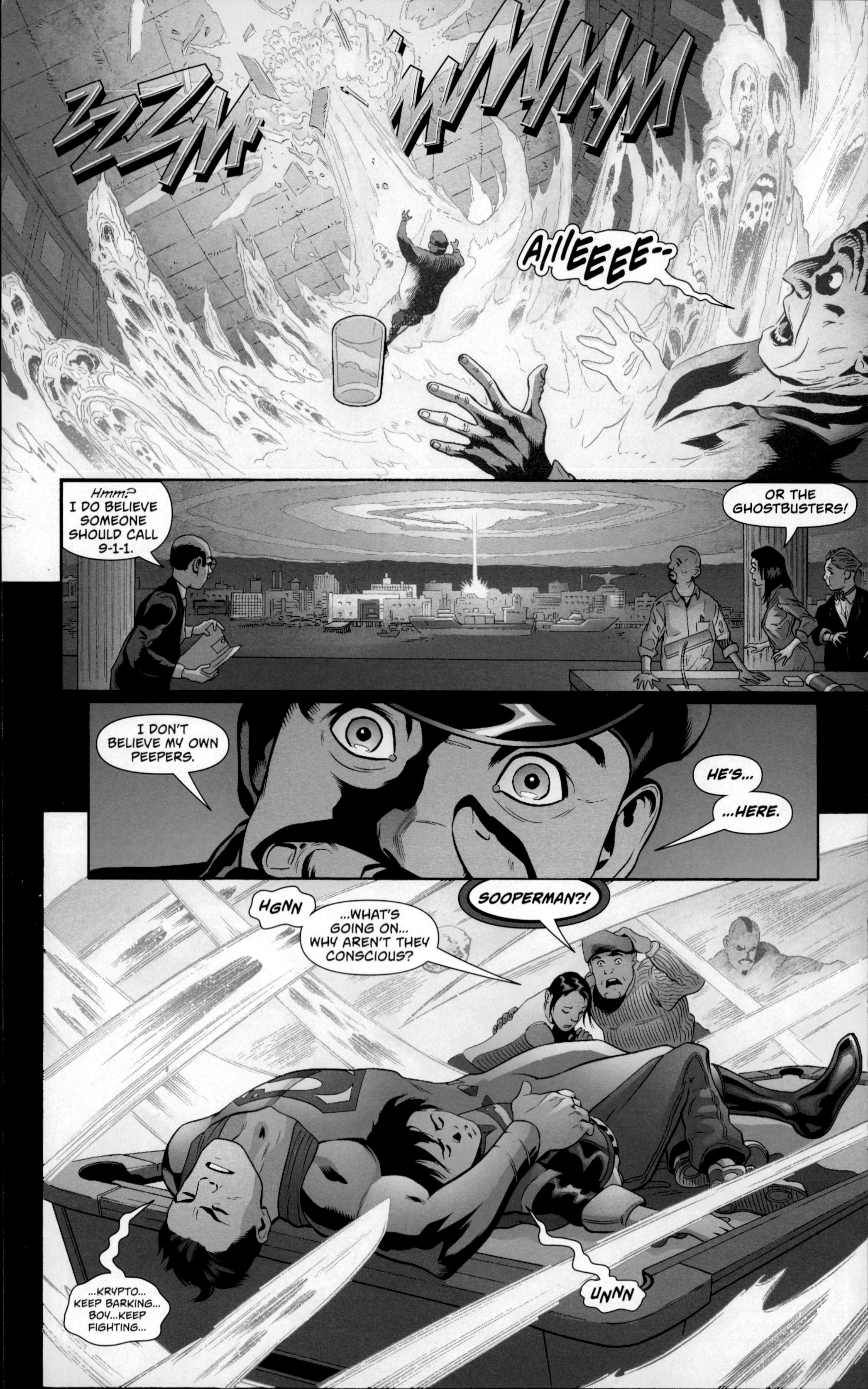
ZZZZWWWWWWWWWWW
AIIIEEEE--
Hmm? I DO BELIEVE SOMEONE SHOULD CALL 9-1-1.
OR THE GHOSTBUSTERS!
I DON'T BELIEVE MY OWN PEEPERS.
HE'S...
...HERE.
SOOPERMAN?!
HGNN
...WHAT'S GOING ON... WHY AREN'T THEY CONSCIOUS?
...KRYPTO... KEEP BARKING... BOY...KEEP FIGHTING...
UNNN

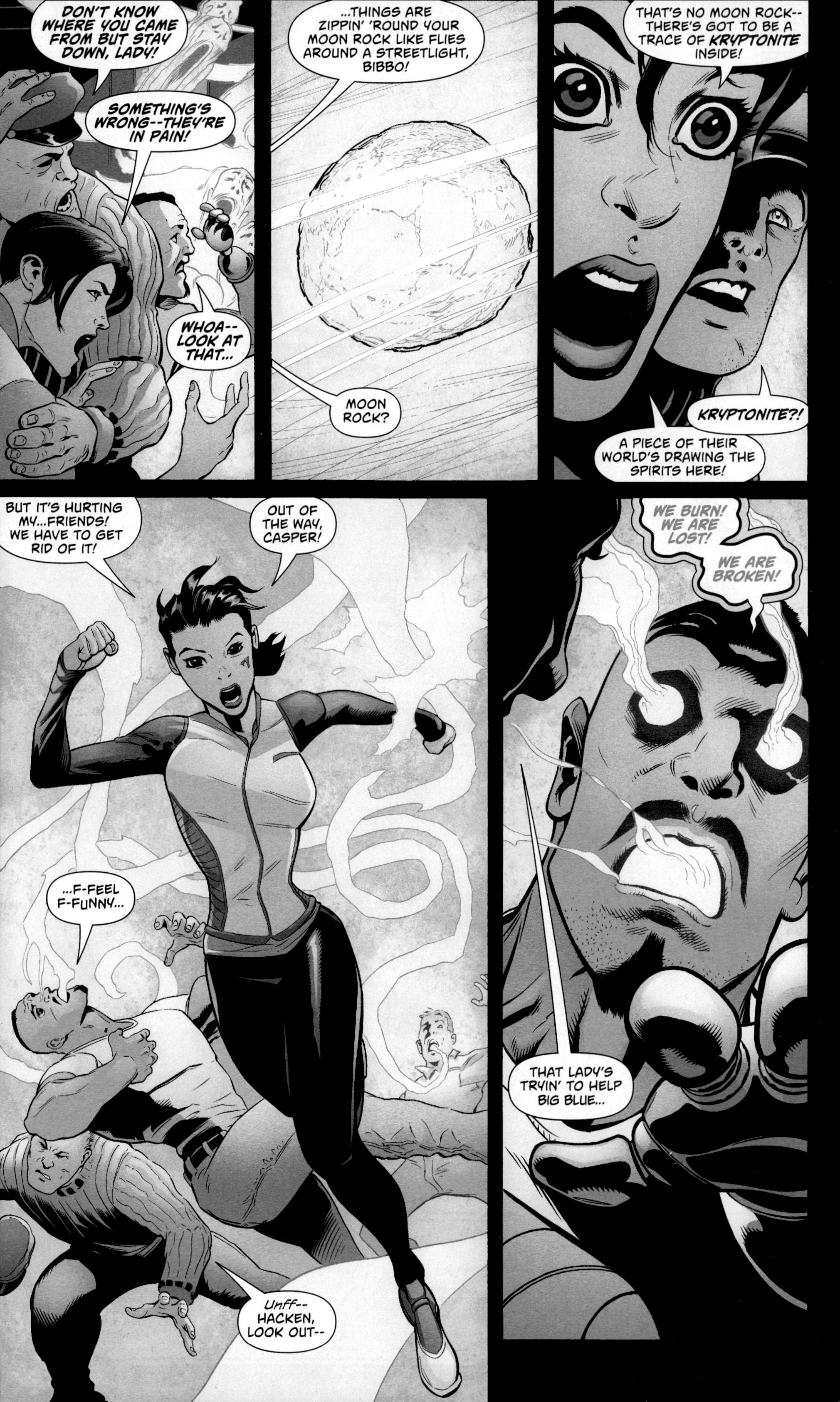
DON'T KNOW WHERE YOU CAME FROM BUT STAY DOWN, LADY!
SOMETHING'S WRONG--THEY'RE IN PAIN!
WHOA-- LOOK AT THAT...
...THINGS ARE ZIPPIN' 'ROUND YOUR MOON ROCK LIKE FLIES AROUND A STREETLIGHT, BIBBO!
MOON ROCK?
THAT'S NO MOON ROCK-- THERE'S GOT TO BE A TRACE OF KRYPTONITE INSIDE!
KRYPTONITE?!
A PIECE OF THEIR WORLD'S DRAWING THE SPIRITS HERE!
BUT IT'S HURTING MY...FRIENDS! WE HAVE TO GET RID OF IT!
OUT OF THE WAY, CASPER!
...F-FEEL F-FUNNY...
Unff-- HACKEN, LOOK OUT--
WE BURN! WE ARE LOST!
WE ARE BROKEN!
THAT LADY'S TRYIN' TO HELP BIG BLUE...

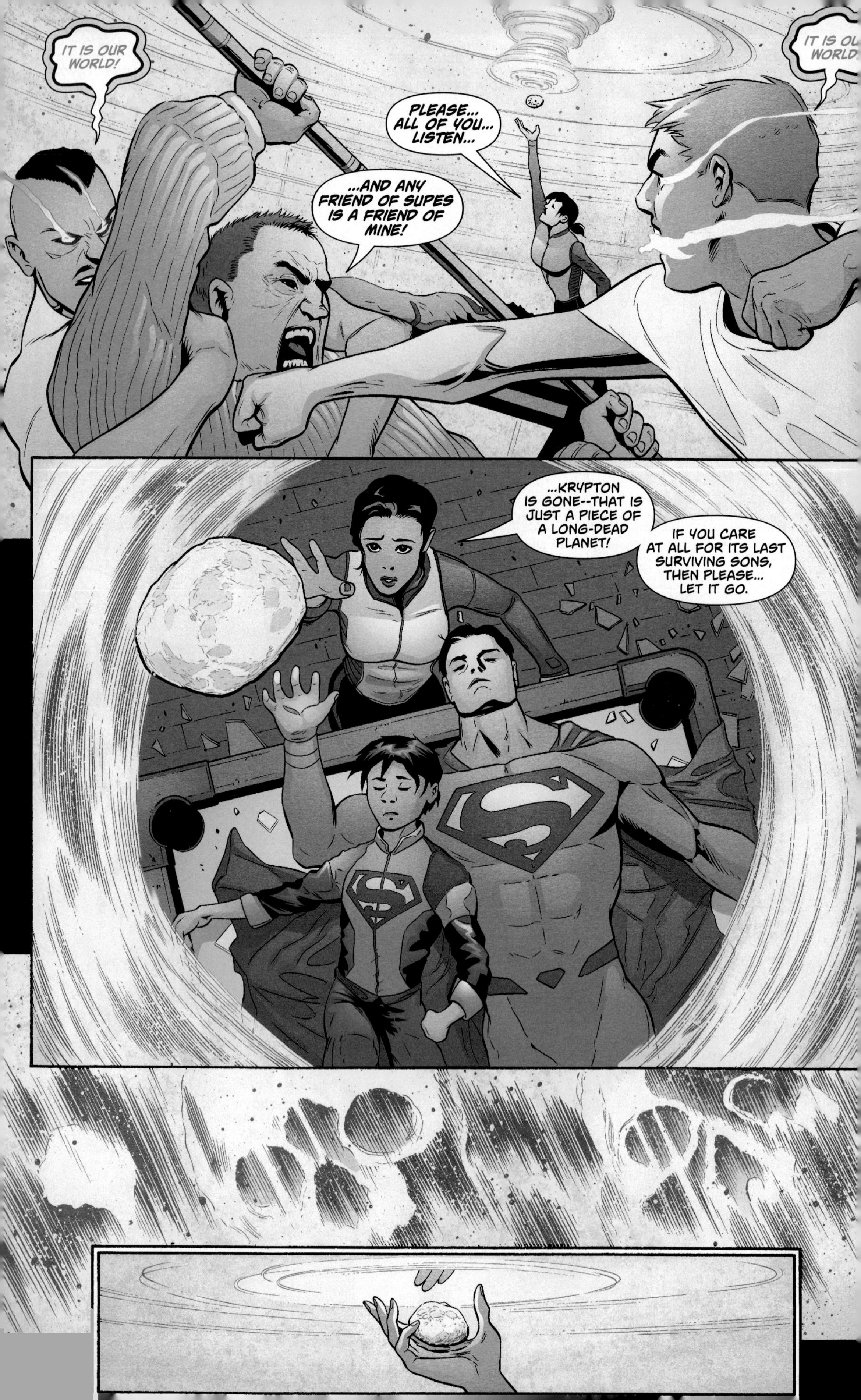
IT IS OUR WORLD!
IT IS OUR WORLD!
PLEASE... ALL OF YOU... LISTEN...
...AND ANY FRIEND OF SUPES IS A FRIEND OF MINE!
...KRYPTON IS GONE--THAT IS JUST A PIECE OF A LONG-DEAD PLANET!
IF YOU CARE AT ALL FOR ITS LAST SURVIVING SONS, THEN PLEASE... LET IT GO.

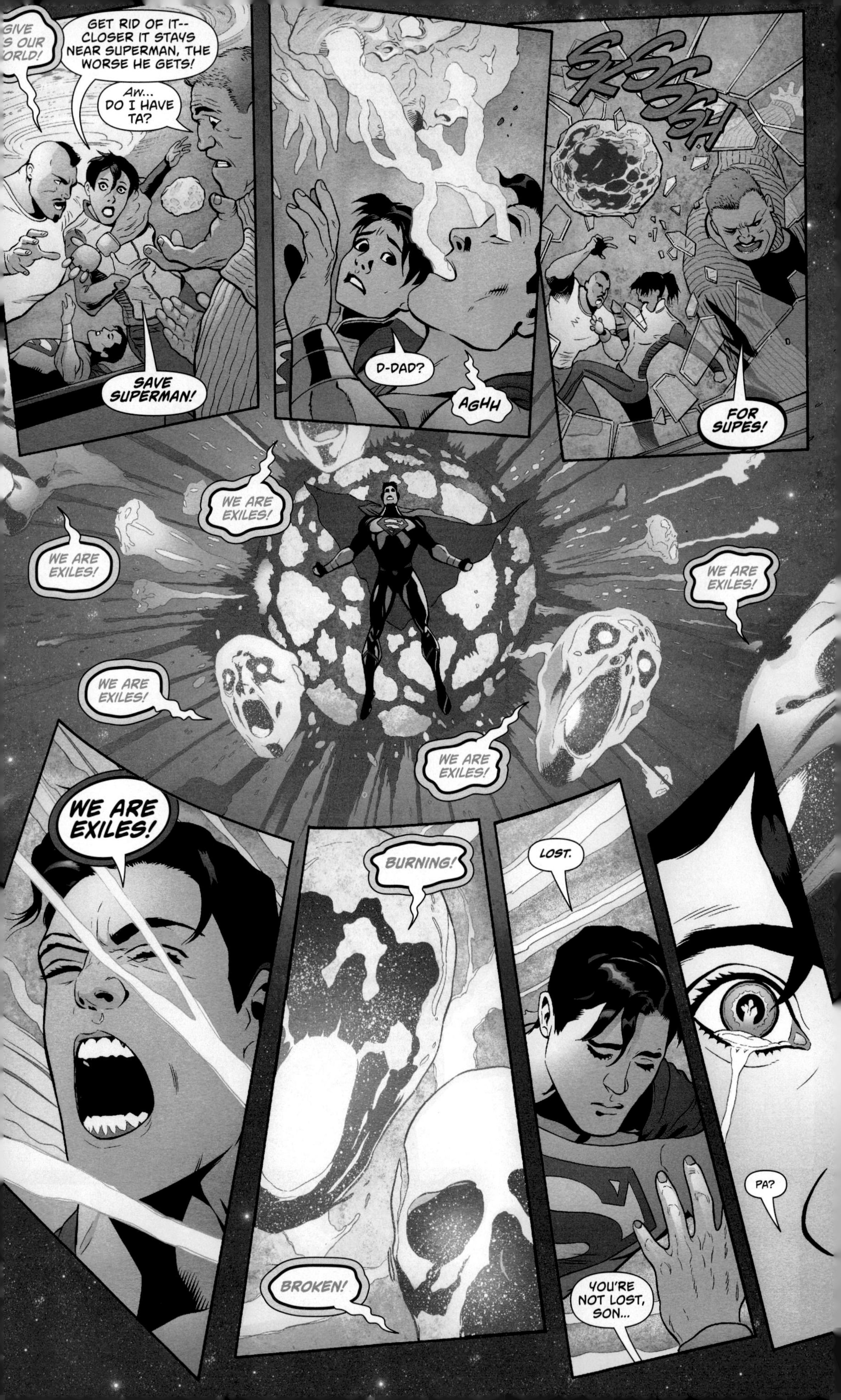
GIVE
S OUR
ORLD!
GET RID OF IT--
CLOSER IT STAYS
NEAR SUPERMAN, THE
WORSE HE GETS!
AW...
DO I HAVE
TA?
SAVE
SUPERMAN!
D-DAD?
AGHH
SKSSSSH
FOR
SUPES!
WE ARE
EXILES!
WE ARE
EXILES!
WE ARE
EXILES!
WE ARE
EXILES!
WE ARE
EXILES!
WE ARE
EXILES!
BURNING!
BROKEN!
LOST.
YOU'RE
NOT LOST,
SON...
PA?

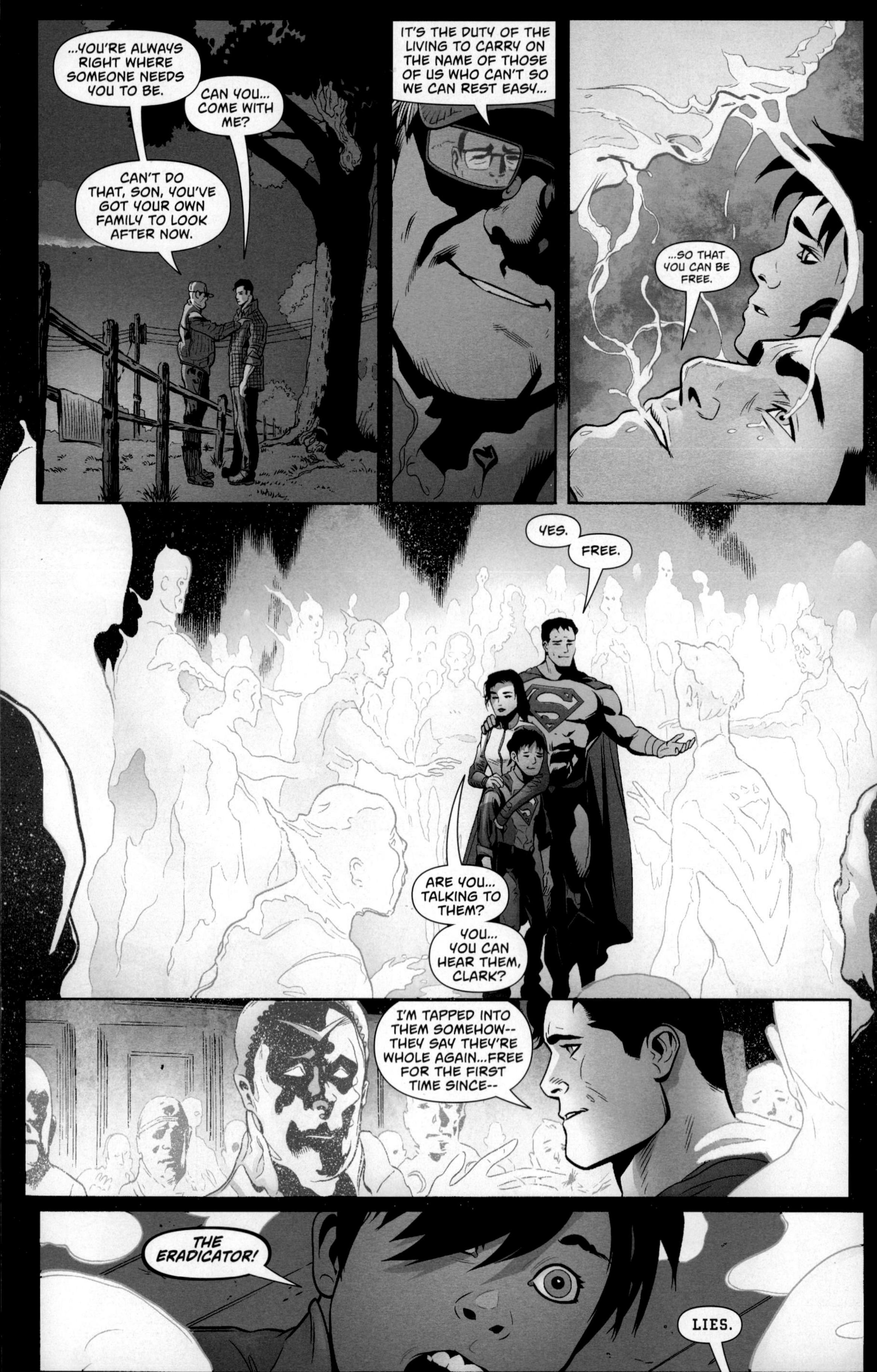
...YOU'RE ALWAYS RIGHT WHERE SOMEONE NEEDS YOU TO BE.
CAN YOU... COME WITH ME?
CAN'T DO THAT, SON, YOU'VE GOT YOUR OWN FAMILY TO LOOK AFTER NOW.
IT'S THE DUTY OF THE LIVING TO CARRY ON THE NAME OF THOSE OF US WHO CAN'T SO WE CAN REST EASY...
...SO THAT YOU CAN BE FREE.
YES.
FREE.
ARE YOU... TALKING TO THEM?
YOU... YOU CAN HEAR THEM, CLARK?
I'M TAPPED INTO THEM SOMEHOW-- THEY SAY THEY'RE WHOLE AGAIN...FREE FOR THE FIRST TIME SINCE--
THE ERADICATOR!
LIES.

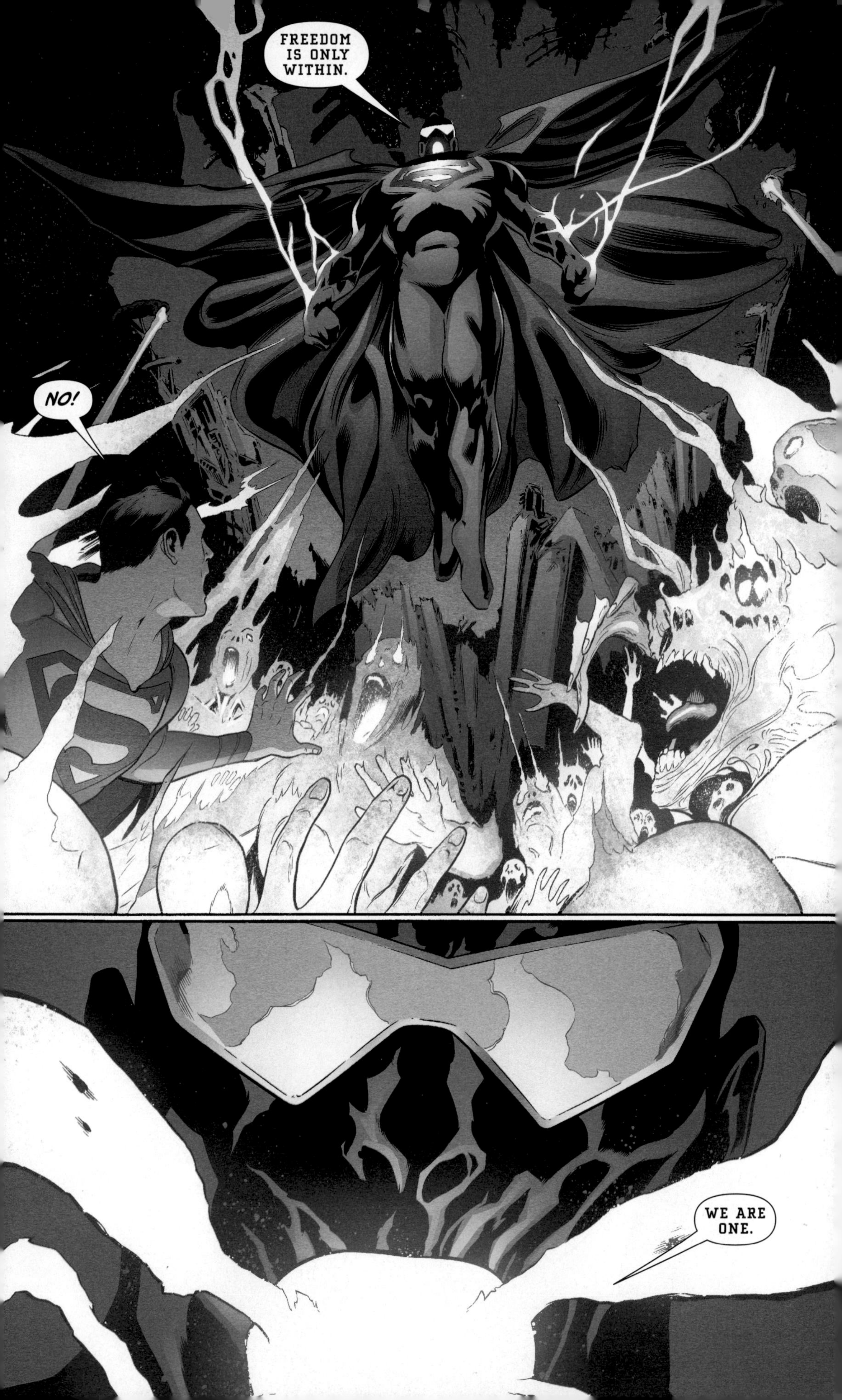

FREEDOM IS ONLY WITHIN.
NO!
WE ARE ONE.

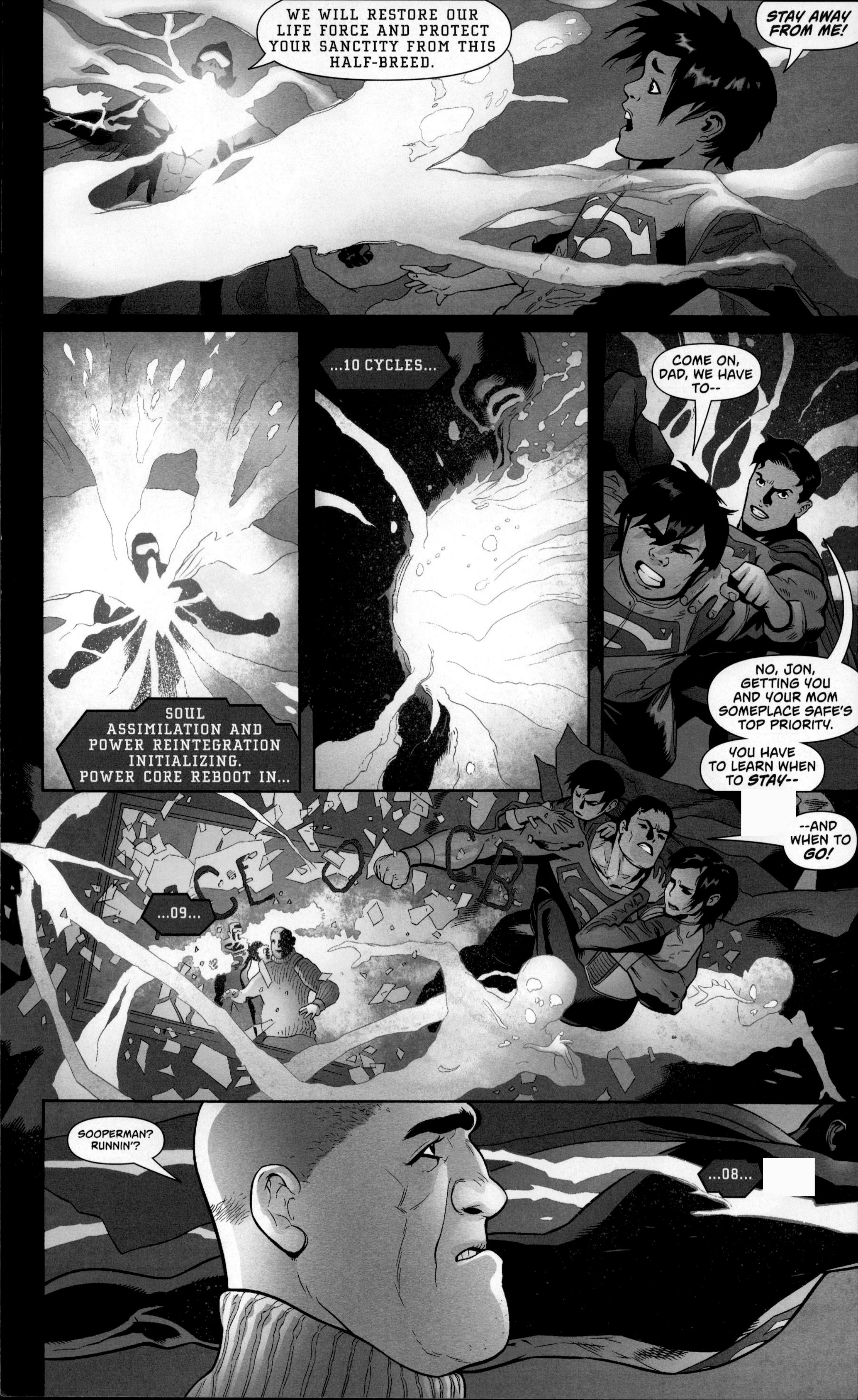
WE WILL RESTORE OUR LIFE FORCE AND PROTECT YOUR SANCTITY FROM THIS HALF-BREED.
STAY AWAY FROM ME!
SOUL ASSIMILATION AND POWER REINTEGRATION INITIALIZING. POWER CORE REBOOT IN...
...10 CYCLES...
COME ON, DAD, WE HAVE TO--
NO, JON, GETTING YOU AND YOUR MOM SOMEPLACE SAFE'S TOP PRIORITY.
YOU HAVE TO LEARN WHEN TO STAY--
--AND WHEN TO GO!
...09...
SOOPERMAN? RUNNIN'?
...08...

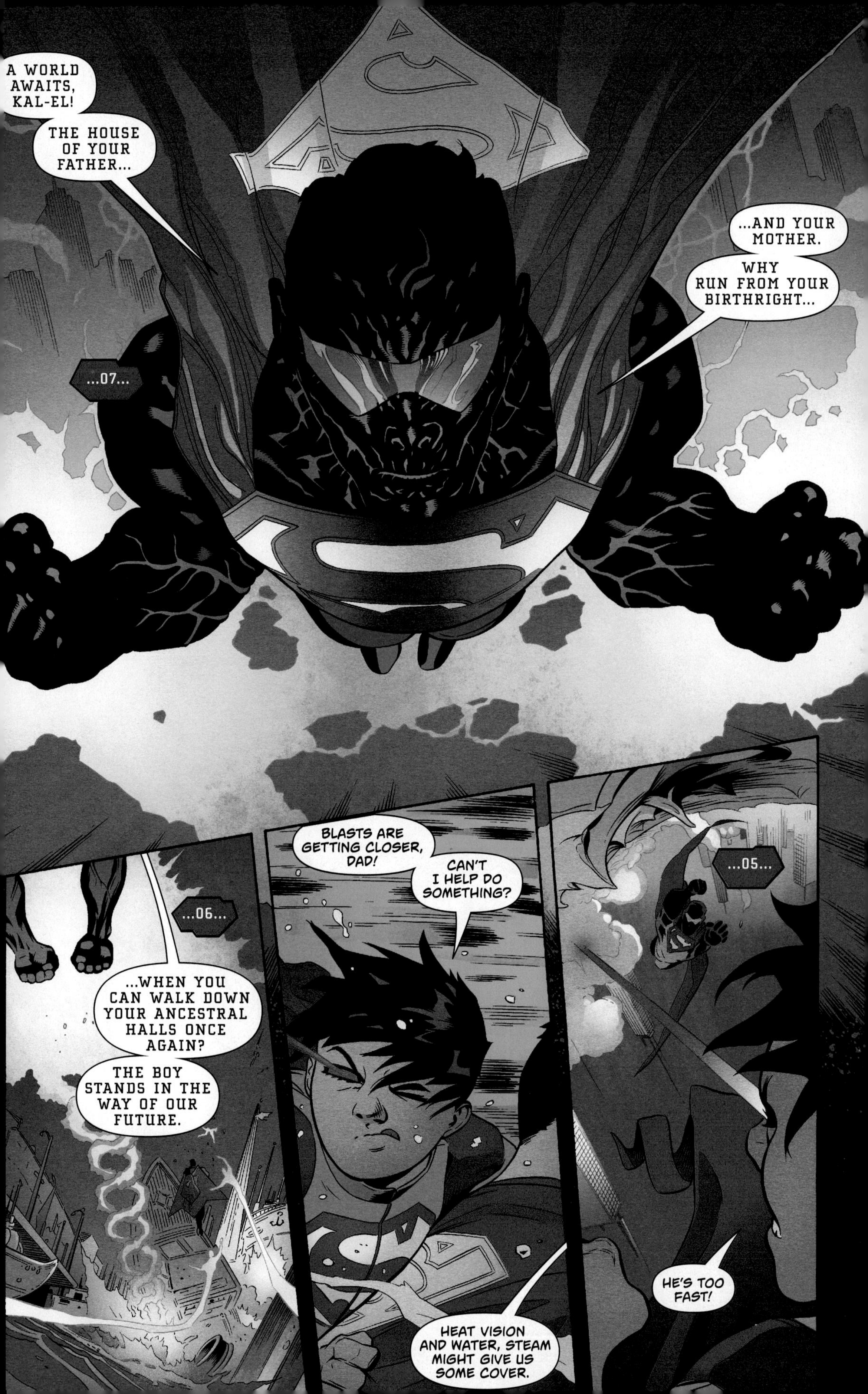

A WORLD AWAITS, KAL-EL!
THE HOUSE OF YOUR FATHER...
...AND YOUR MOTHER.
WHY RUN FROM YOUR BIRTHRIGHT...
...07...
...06...
...WHEN YOU CAN WALK DOWN YOUR ANCESTRAL HALLS ONCE AGAIN?
THE BOY STANDS IN THE WAY OF OUR FUTURE.
BLASTS ARE GETTING CLOSER, DAD!
CAN'T I HELP DO SOMETHING?
HEAT VISION AND WATER, STEAM MIGHT GIVE US SOME COVER.
...05...
HE'S TOO FAST!

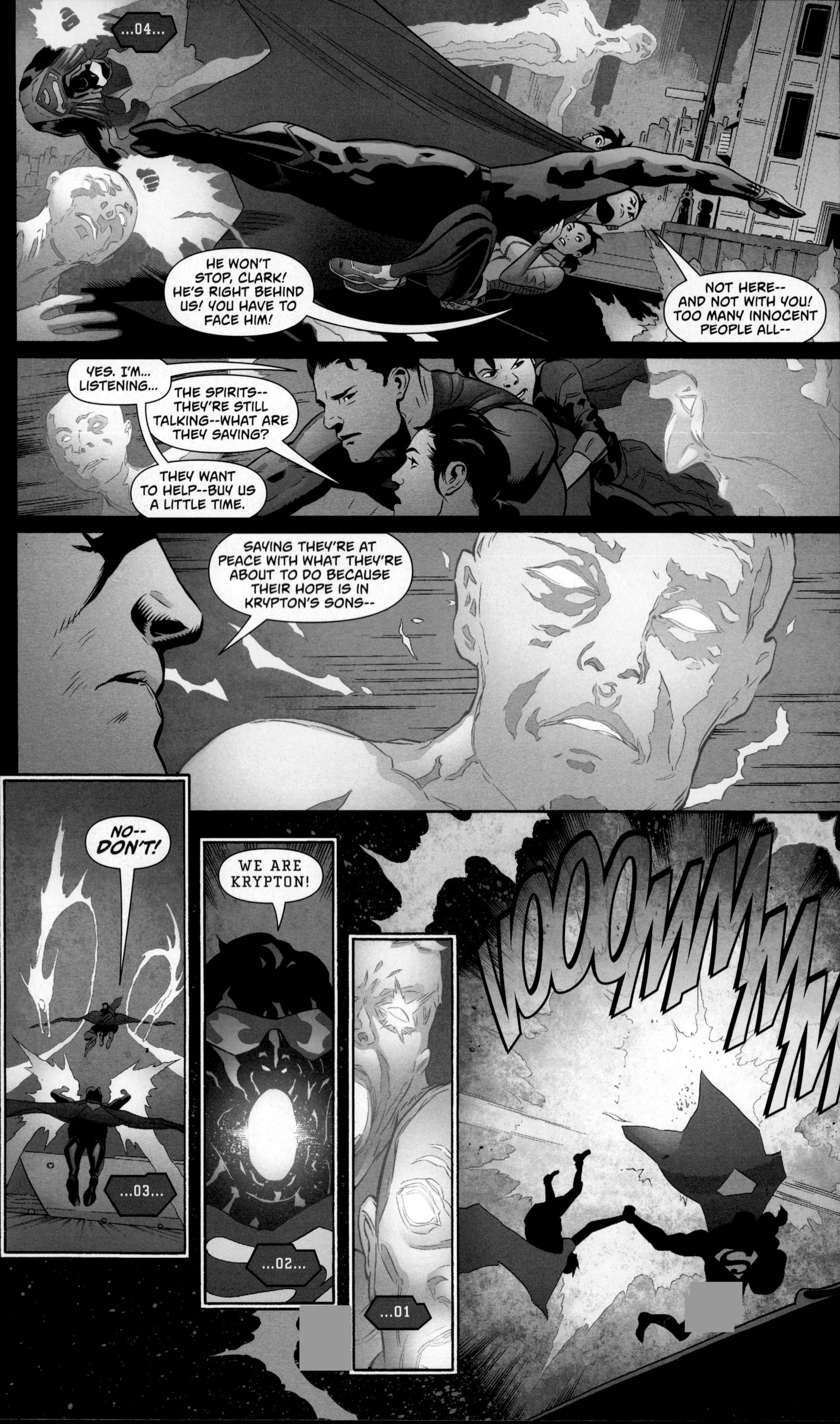
...04...
HE WON'T STOP, CLARK! HE'S RIGHT BEHIND US! YOU HAVE TO FACE HIM!
NOT HERE-- AND NOT WITH YOU! TOO MANY INNOCENT PEOPLE ALL--
THE SPIRITS-- THEY'RE STILL TALKING--WHAT ARE THEY SAYING?
YES. I'M... LISTENING...
THEY WANT TO HELP--BUY US A LITTLE TIME.
SAYING THEY'RE AT PEACE WITH WHAT THEY'RE ABOUT TO DO BECAUSE THEIR HOPE IS IN KRYPTON'S SONS--
NO-- DON'T!
...03...
WE ARE KRYPTON!
...02...
...01

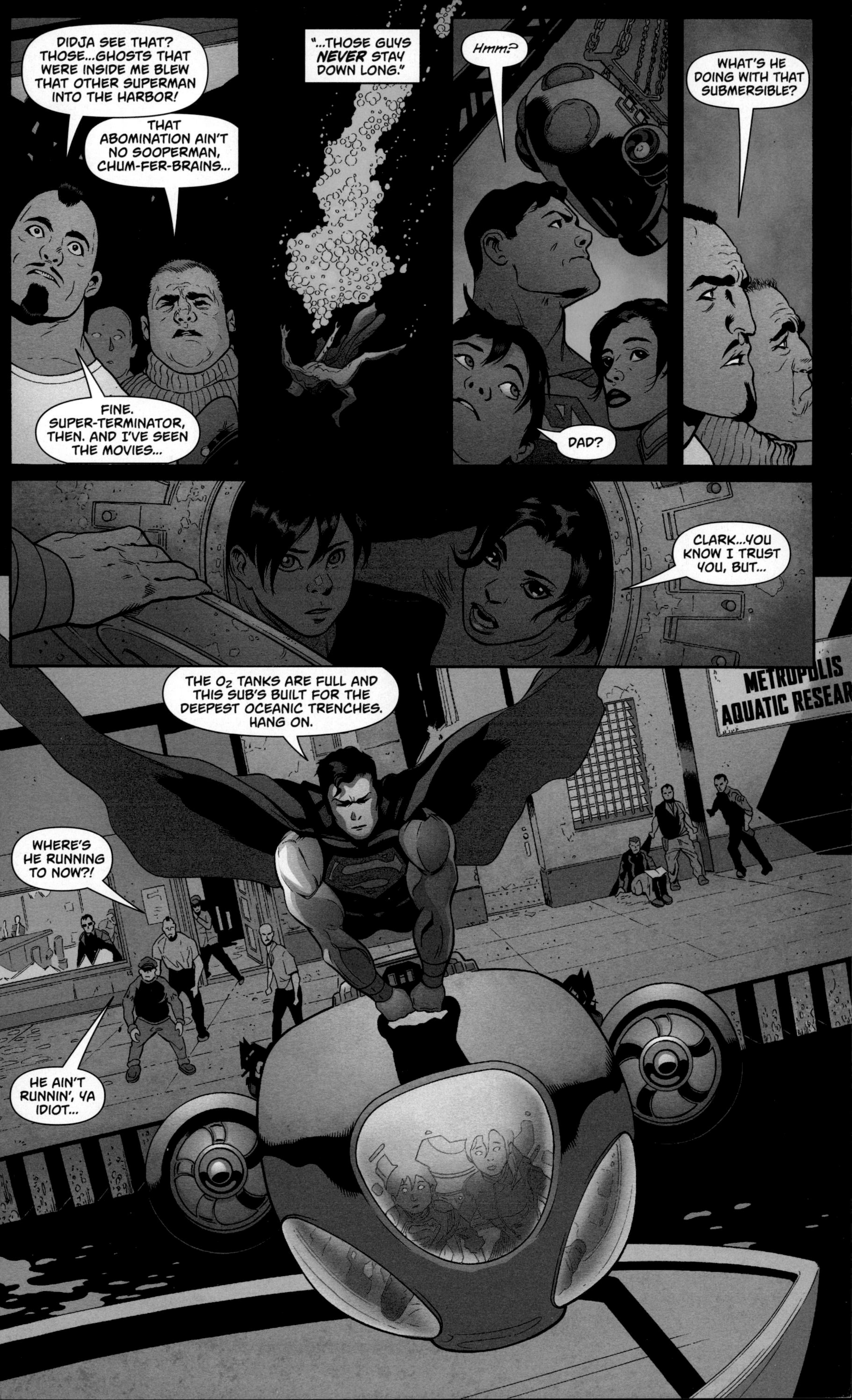

DIDJA SEE THAT? THOSE...GHOSTS THAT WERE INSIDE ME BLEW THAT OTHER SUPERMAN INTO THE HARBOR!
THAT ABOMINATION AIN'T NO SOOPERMAN, CHUM-FER-BRAINS...
FINE. SUPER-TERMINATOR, THEN. AND I'VE SEEN THE MOVIES...
"...THOSE GUYS NEVER STAY DOWN LONG."
Hmm?
DAD?
WHAT'S HE DOING WITH THAT SUBMERSIBLE?
CLARK...YOU KNOW I TRUST YOU, BUT...
THE O2 TANKS ARE FULL AND THIS SUB'S BUILT FOR THE DEEPEST OCEANIC TRENCHES. HANG ON.
METROPOLIS AQUATIC RESEAR
WHERE'S HE RUNNING TO NOW?!
HE AIN'T RUNNIN', YA IDIOT...

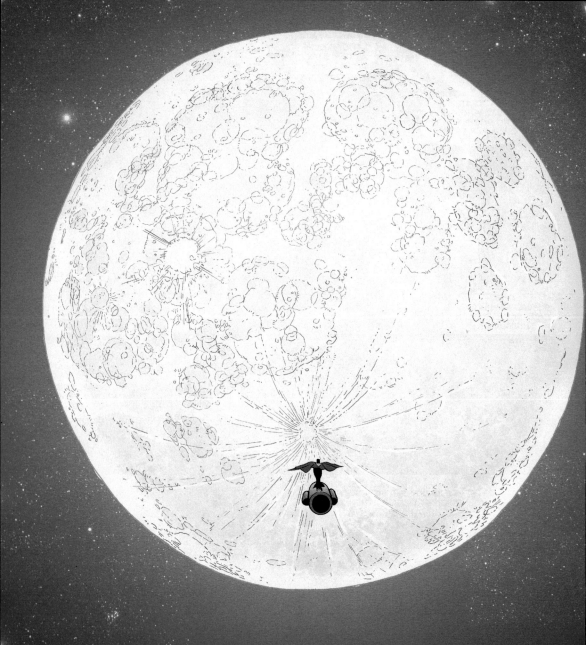

...THE MAN OF STEEL'S GOT A PLAN!

NEXT ISSUE: HELL MOON

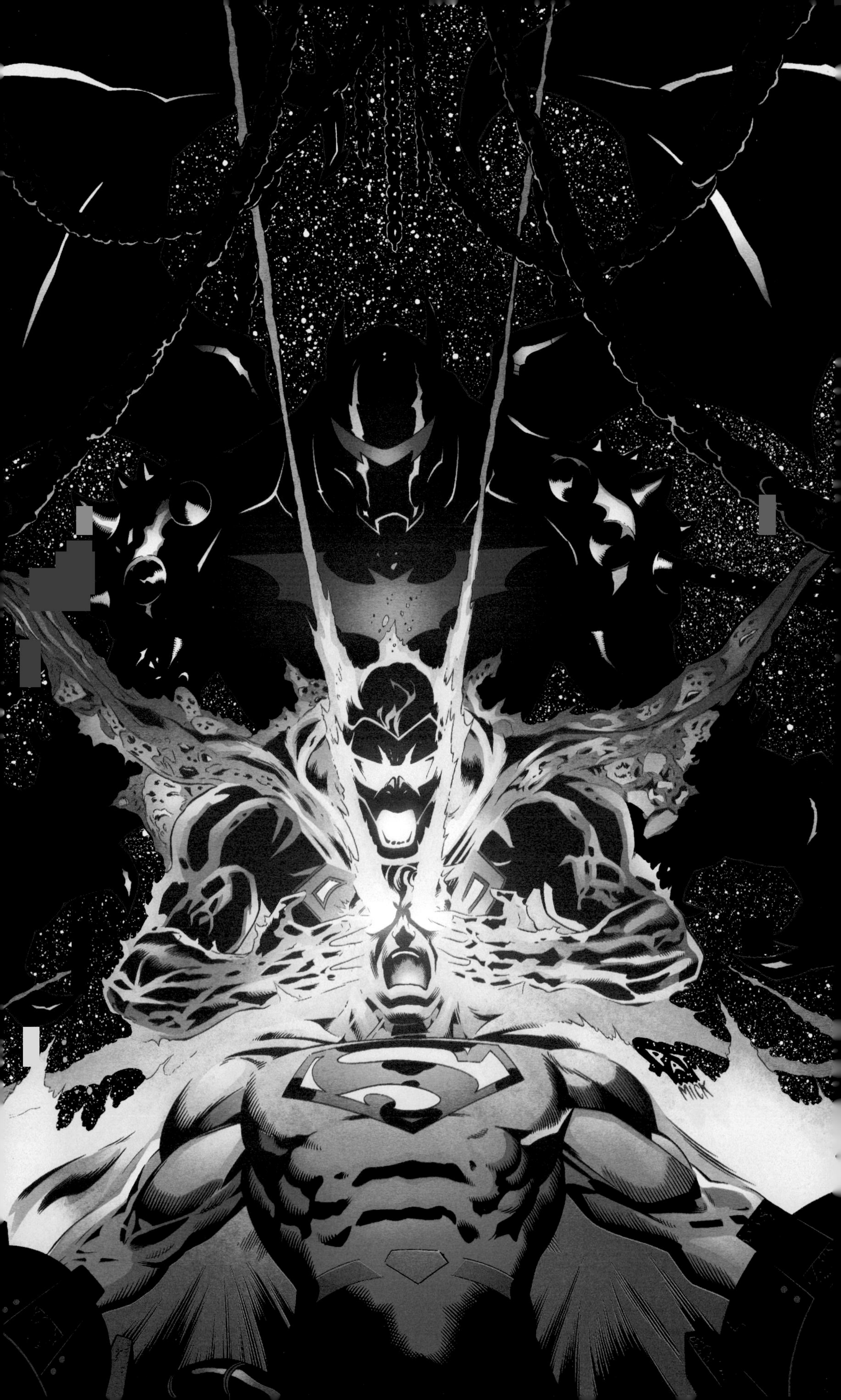

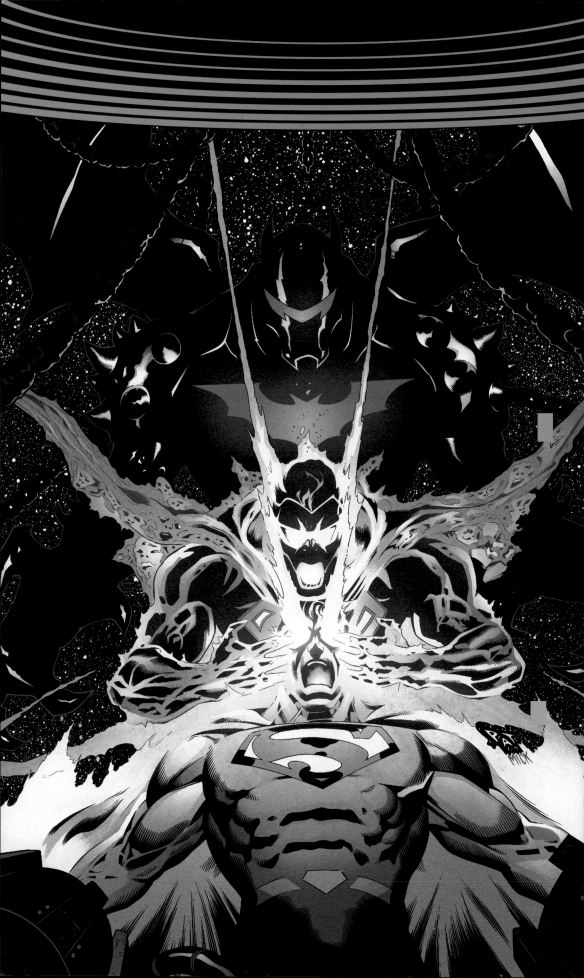

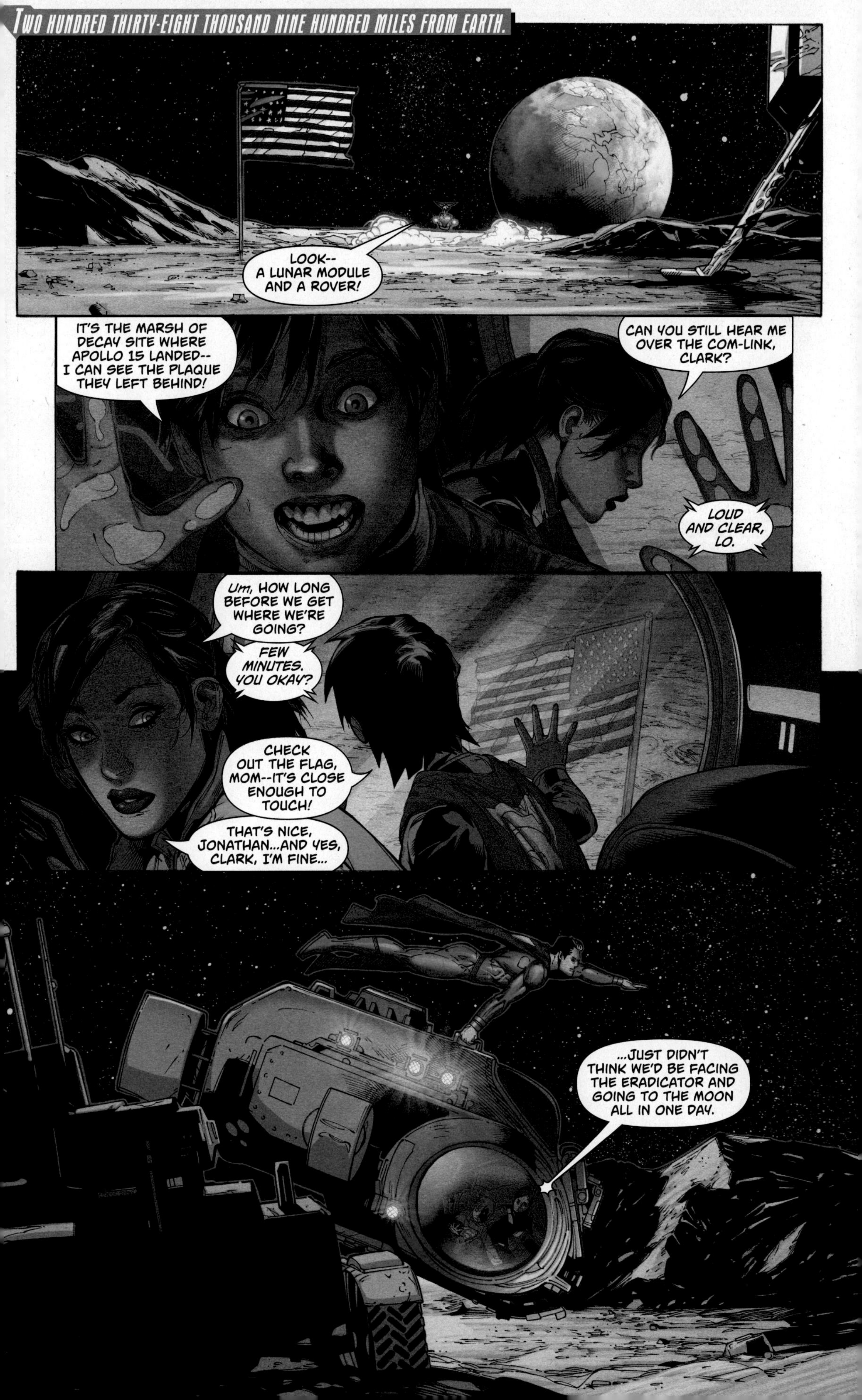

TWO HUNDRED THIRTY-EIGHT THOUSAND NINE HUNDRED MILES FROM EARTH.
LOOK-- A LUNAR MODULE AND A ROVER!
IT'S THE MARSH OF DECAY SITE WHERE APOLLO 15 LANDED-- I CAN SEE THE PLAQUE THEY LEFT BEHIND!
CAN YOU STILL HEAR ME OVER THE COM-LINK, CLARK?
LOUD AND CLEAR, LO.
Um, HOW LONG BEFORE WE GET WHERE WE'RE GOING?
FEW MINUTES. YOU OKAY?
CHECK OUT THE FLAG, MOM--IT'S CLOSE ENOUGH TO TOUCH!
THAT'S NICE, JONATHAN...AND YES, CLARK, I'M FINE...
...JUST DIDN'T THINK WE'D BE FACING THE ERADICATOR AND GOING TO THE MOON ALL IN ONE DAY.

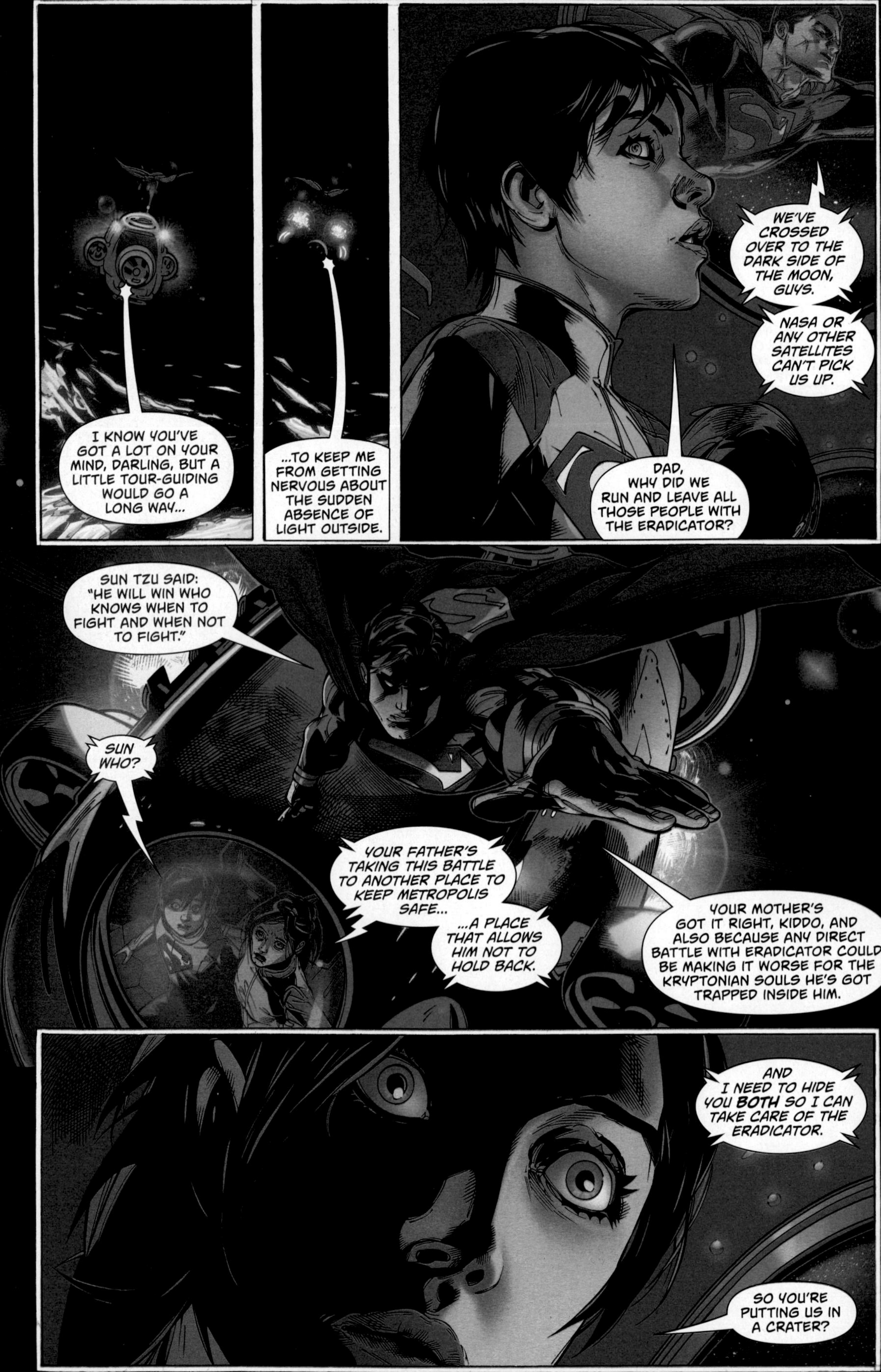
I KNOW YOU'VE GOT A LOT ON YOUR MIND, DARLING, BUT A LITTLE TOUR-GUIDING WOULD GO A LONG WAY...
...TO KEEP ME FROM GETTING NERVOUS ABOUT THE SUDDEN ABSENCE OF LIGHT OUTSIDE.
WE'VE CROSSED OVER TO THE DARK SIDE OF THE MOON, GUYS.
NASA OR ANY OTHER SATELLITES CAN'T PICK US UP.
DAD, WHY DID WE RUN AND LEAVE ALL THOSE PEOPLE WITH THE ERADICATOR?
SUN TZU SAID: "HE WILL WIN WHO KNOWS WHEN TO FIGHT AND WHEN NOT TO FIGHT."
SUN WHO?
YOUR FATHER'S TAKING THIS BATTLE TO ANOTHER PLACE TO KEEP METROPOLIS SAFE...
...A PLACE THAT ALLOWS HIM NOT TO HOLD BACK.
YOUR MOTHER'S GOT IT RIGHT, KIDDO, AND ALSO BECAUSE ANY DIRECT BATTLE WITH ERADICATOR COULD BE MAKING IT WORSE FOR THE KRYPTONIAN SOULS HE'S GOT TRAPPED INSIDE HIM.
AND I NEED TO HIDE YOU **BOTH** SO I CAN TAKE CARE OF THE ERADICATOR.
SO YOU'RE PUTTING US IN A CRATER?

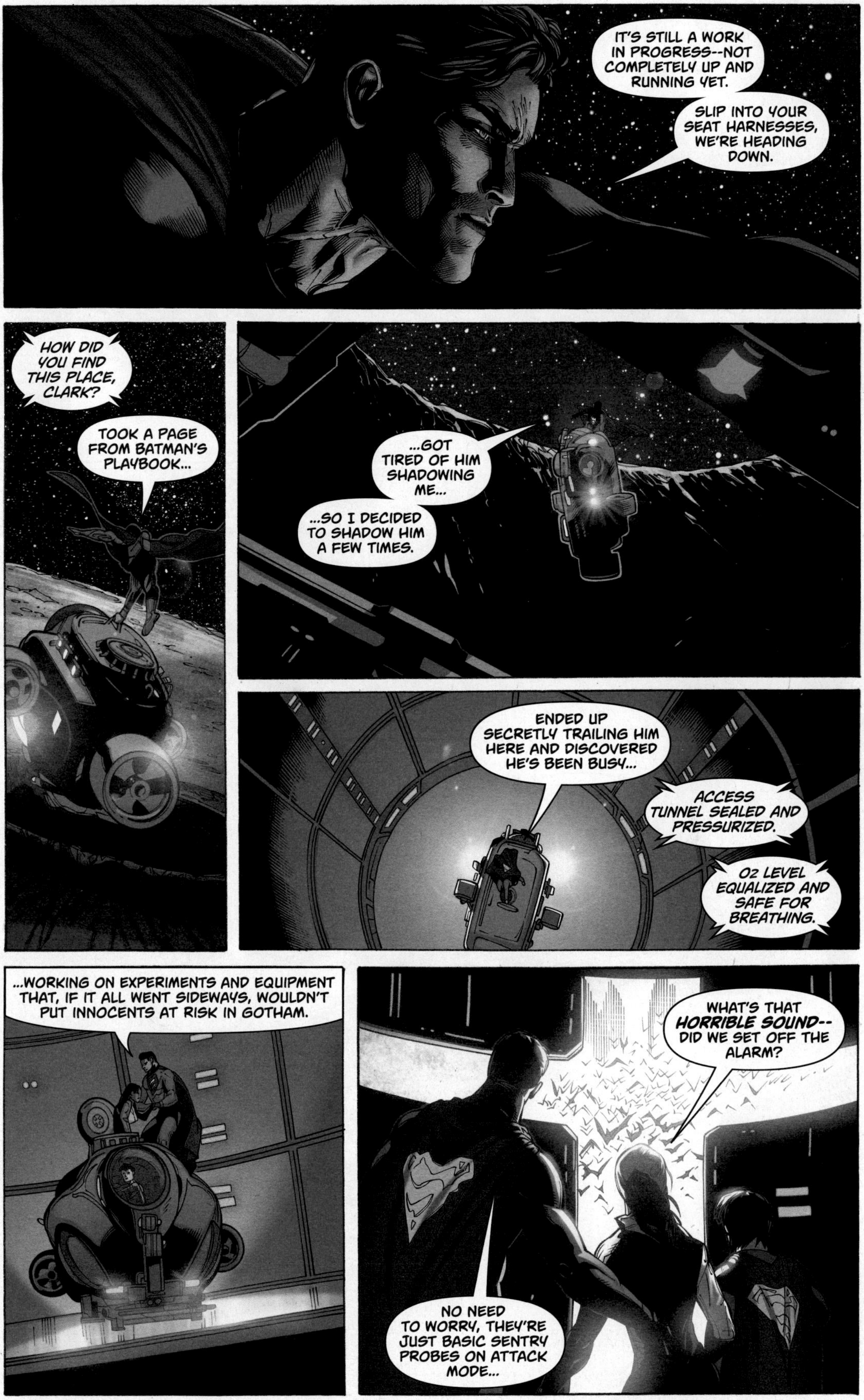
IT'S STILL A WORK IN PROGRESS--NOT COMPLETELY UP AND RUNNING YET.
SLIP INTO YOUR SEAT HARNESSES, WE'RE HEADING DOWN.
HOW DID YOU FIND THIS PLACE, CLARK?
TOOK A PAGE FROM BATMAN'S PLAYBOOK...
...GOT TIRED OF HIM SHADOWING ME...
...SO I DECIDED TO SHADOW HIM A FEW TIMES.
ENDED UP SECRETLY TRAILING HIM HERE AND DISCOVERED HE'S BEEN BUSY...
ACCESS TUNNEL SEALED AND PRESSURIZED.
O2 LEVEL EQUALIZED AND SAFE FOR BREATHING.
...WORKING ON EXPERIMENTS AND EQUIPMENT THAT, IF IT ALL WENT SIDEWAYS, WOULDN'T PUT INNOCENTS AT RISK IN GOTHAM.
WHAT'S THAT HORRIBLE SOUND-- DID WE SET OFF THE ALARM?
NO NEED TO WORRY, THEY'RE JUST BASIC SENTRY PROBES ON ATTACK MODE...

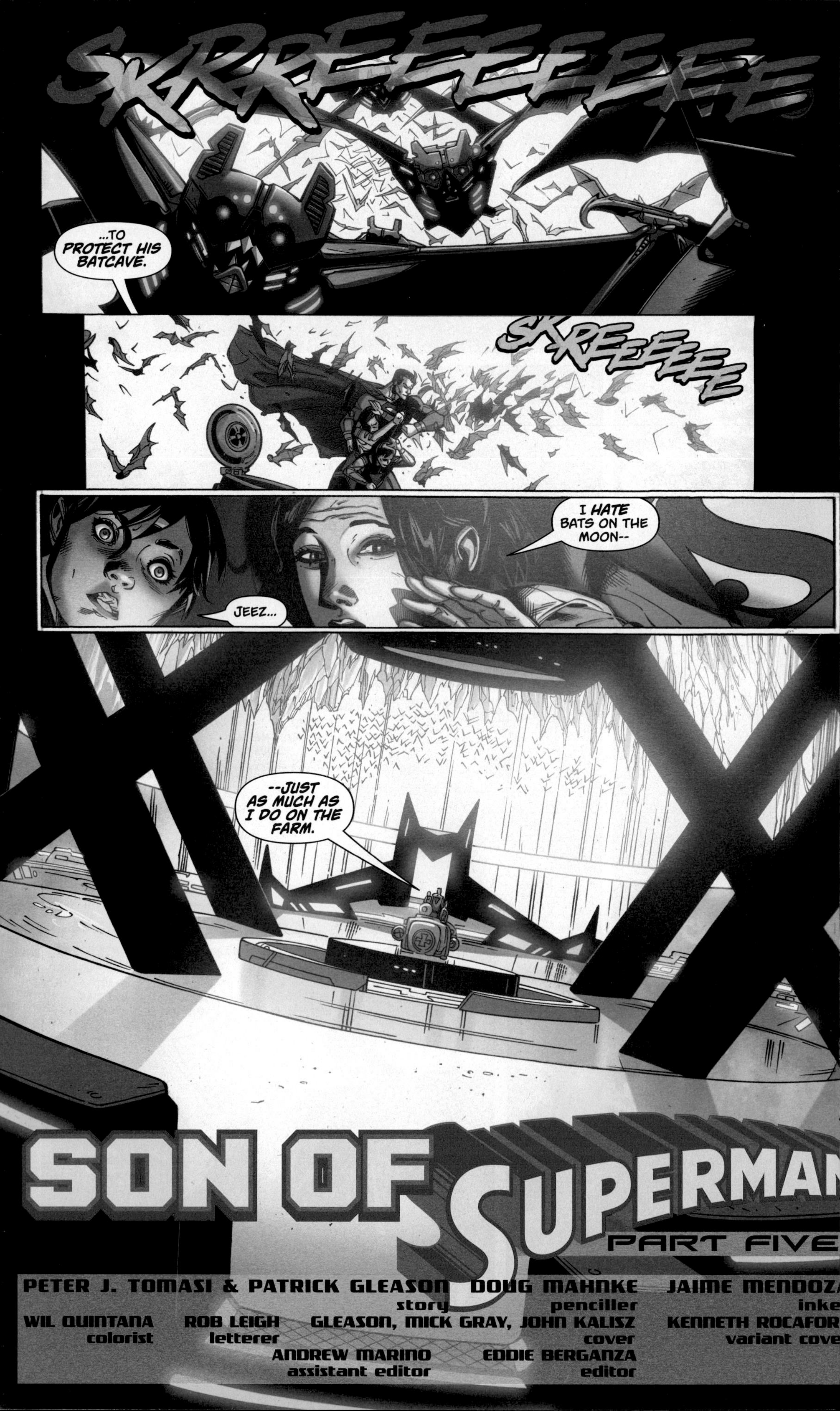
SKRREEEEEEEEE
...TO PROTECT HIS BATCAVE.
SKREEEEEEE
I HATE BATS ON THE MOON--
JEEZ...
--JUST AS MUCH AS I DO ON THE FARM.
SON OF SUPERMAN
PART FIVE
PETER J. TOMASI & PATRICK GLEASON story
DOUG MAHNKE penciller
JAIME MENDOZA inker
WIL QUINTANA colorist
ROB LEIGH letterer
GLEASON, MICK GRAY, JOHN KALISZ cover
KENNETH ROCAFORT variant cover
ANDREW MARINO assistant editor
EDDIE BERGANZA editor

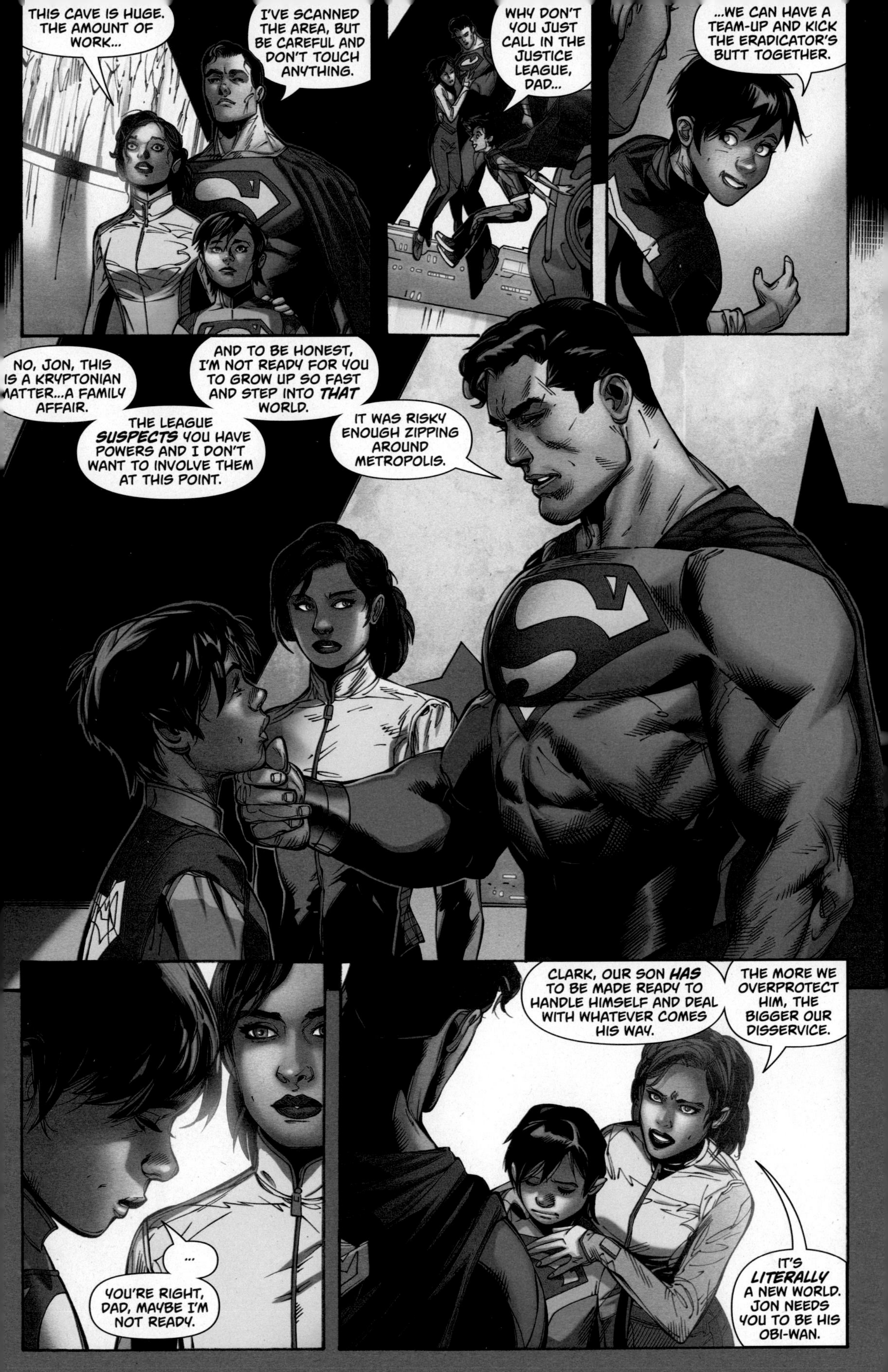
THIS CAVE IS HUGE. THE AMOUNT OF WORK...
I'VE SCANNED THE AREA, BUT BE CAREFUL AND DON'T TOUCH ANYTHING.
WHY DON'T YOU JUST CALL IN THE JUSTICE LEAGUE, DAD...
...WE CAN HAVE A TEAM-UP AND KICK THE ERADICATOR'S BUTT TOGETHER.
NO, JON, THIS IS A KRYPTONIAN MATTER...A FAMILY AFFAIR.
THE LEAGUE SUSPECTS YOU HAVE POWERS AND I DON'T WANT TO INVOLVE THEM AT THIS POINT.
AND TO BE HONEST, I'M NOT READY FOR YOU TO GROW UP SO FAST AND STEP INTO THAT WORLD.
IT WAS RISKY ENOUGH ZIPPING AROUND METROPOLIS.
...
YOU'RE RIGHT, DAD, MAYBE I'M NOT READY.
CLARK, OUR SON HAS TO BE MADE READY TO HANDLE HIMSELF AND DEAL WITH WHATEVER COMES HIS WAY.
THE MORE WE OVERPROTECT HIM, THE BIGGER OUR DISSERVICE.
IT'S LITERALLY A NEW WORLD. JON NEEDS YOU TO BE HIS OBI-WAN.

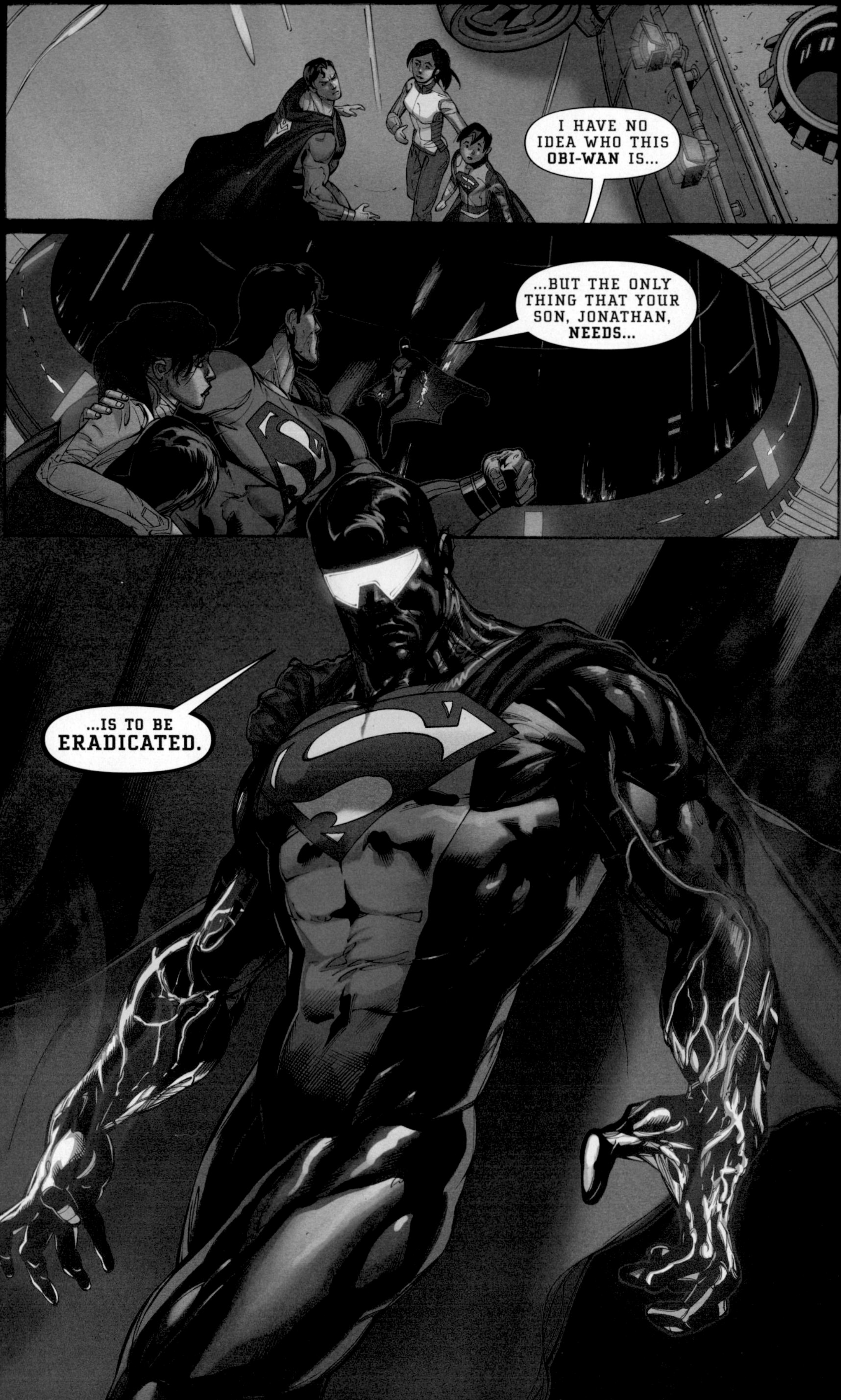
I HAVE NO IDEA WHO THIS OBI-WAN IS...
...BUT THE ONLY THING THAT YOUR SON, JONATHAN, NEEDS...
...IS TO BE ERADICATED.

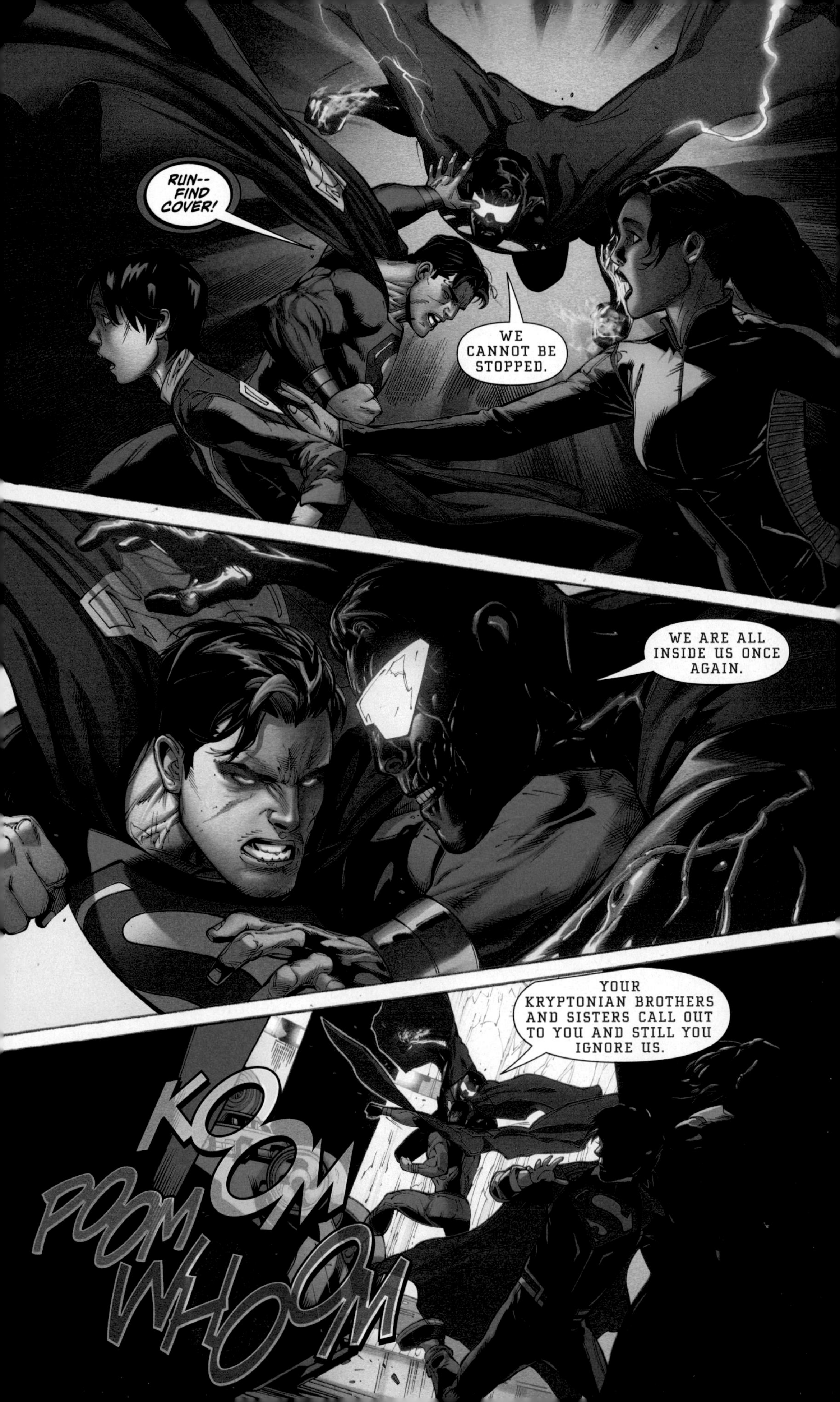

RUN--
FIND
COVER!
WE CANNOT BE STOPPED.
WE ARE ALL INSIDE US ONCE AGAIN.
YOUR KRYPTONIAN BROTHERS AND SISTERS CALL OUT TO YOU AND STILL YOU IGNORE US.
KOOM
POOM
WHOOM

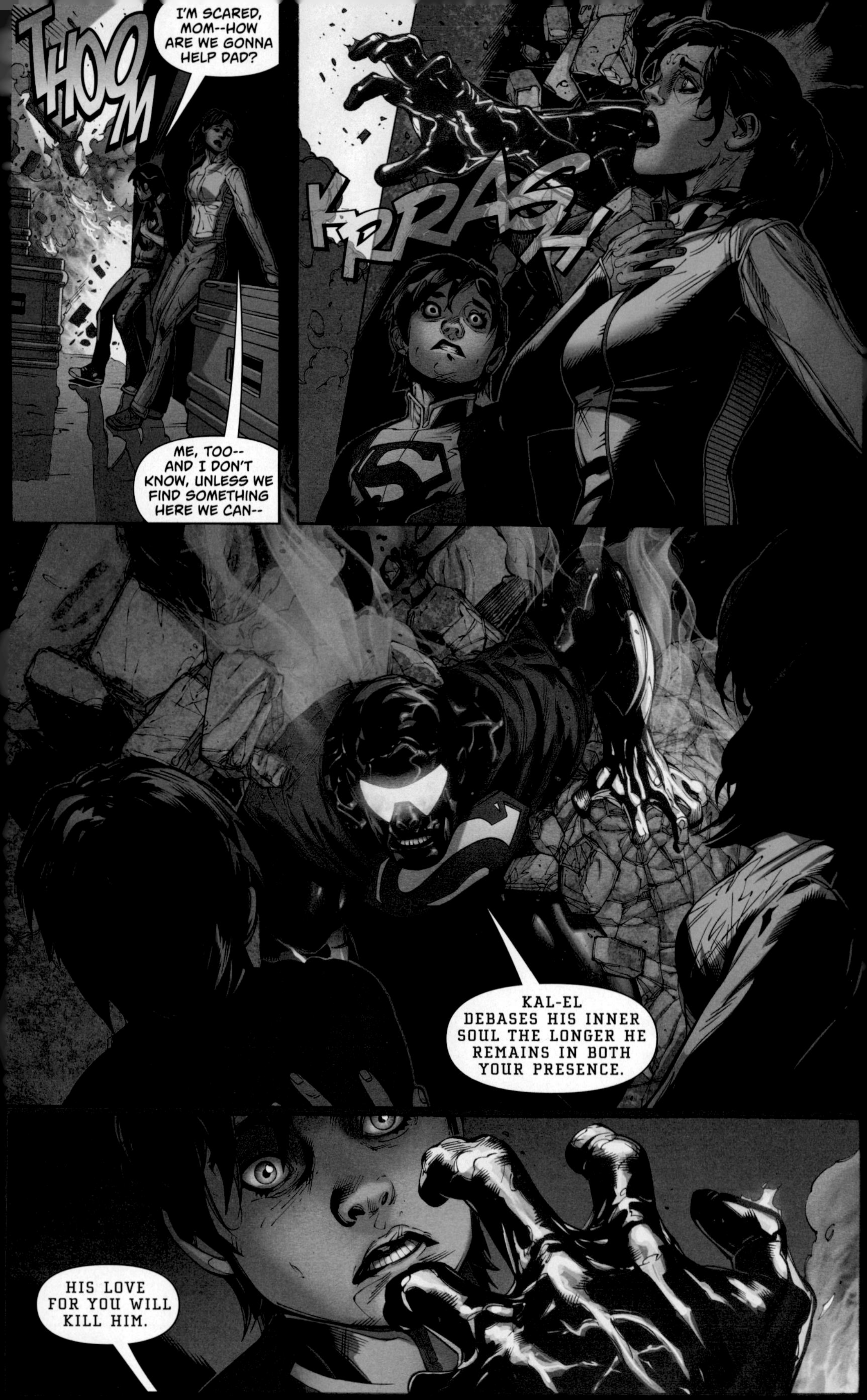
THOOM
I'M SCARED, MOM--HOW ARE WE GONNA HELP DAD?
ME, TOO-- AND I DON'T KNOW, UNLESS WE FIND SOMETHING HERE WE CAN--
KRASH
KAL-EL DEBASES HIS INNER SOUL THE LONGER HE REMAINS IN BOTH YOUR PRESENCE.
HIS LOVE FOR YOU WILL KILL HIM.

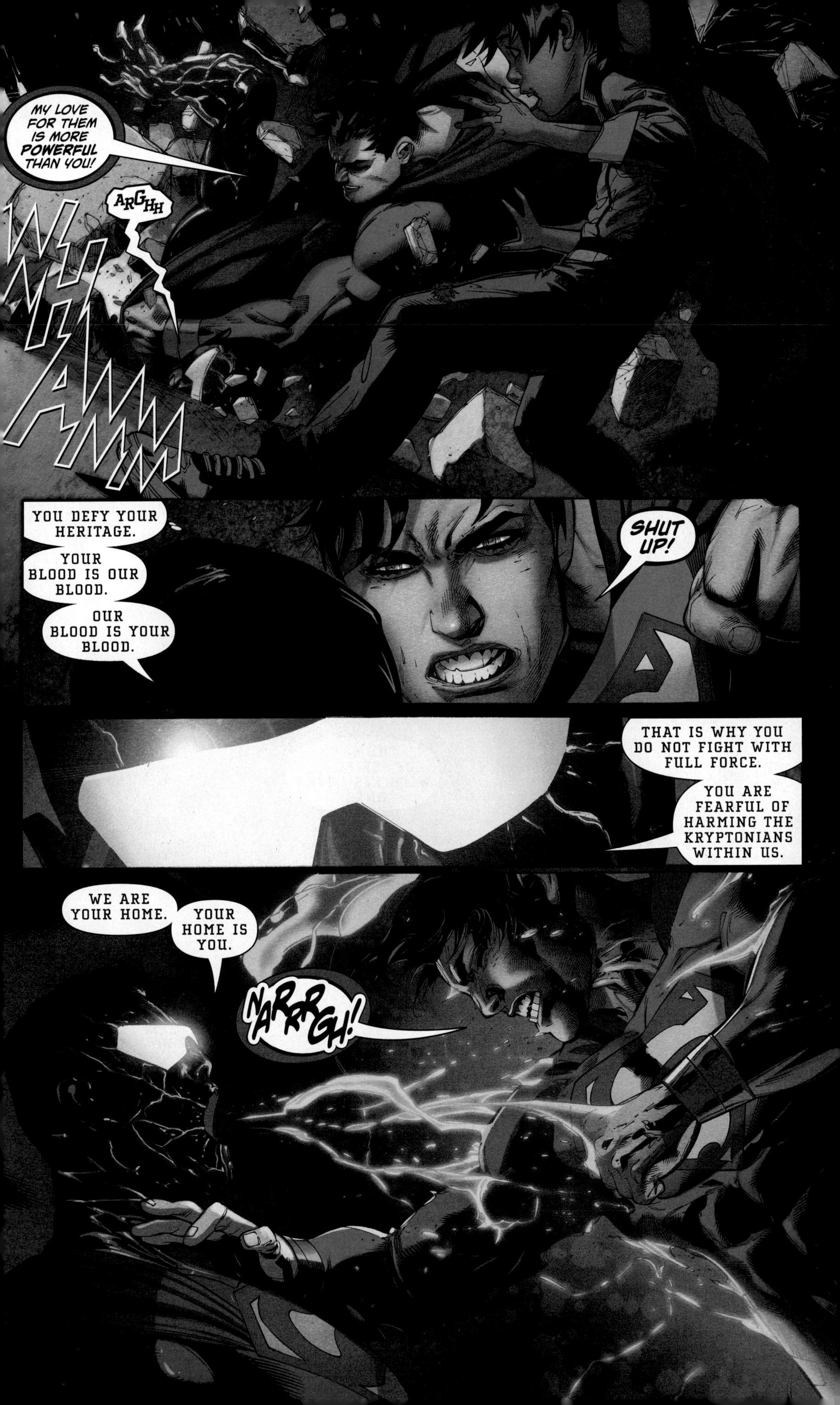
MY LOVE FOR THEM IS MORE POWERFUL THAN YOU!
ARGHH
WHAMM
YOU DEFY YOUR HERITAGE.
YOUR BLOOD IS OUR BLOOD.
OUR BLOOD IS YOUR BLOOD.
SHUT UP!
THAT IS WHY YOU DO NOT FIGHT WITH FULL FORCE.
YOU ARE FEARFUL OF HARMING THE KRYPTONIANS WITHIN US.
WE ARE YOUR HOME.
YOUR HOME IS YOU.
NARRRGH!

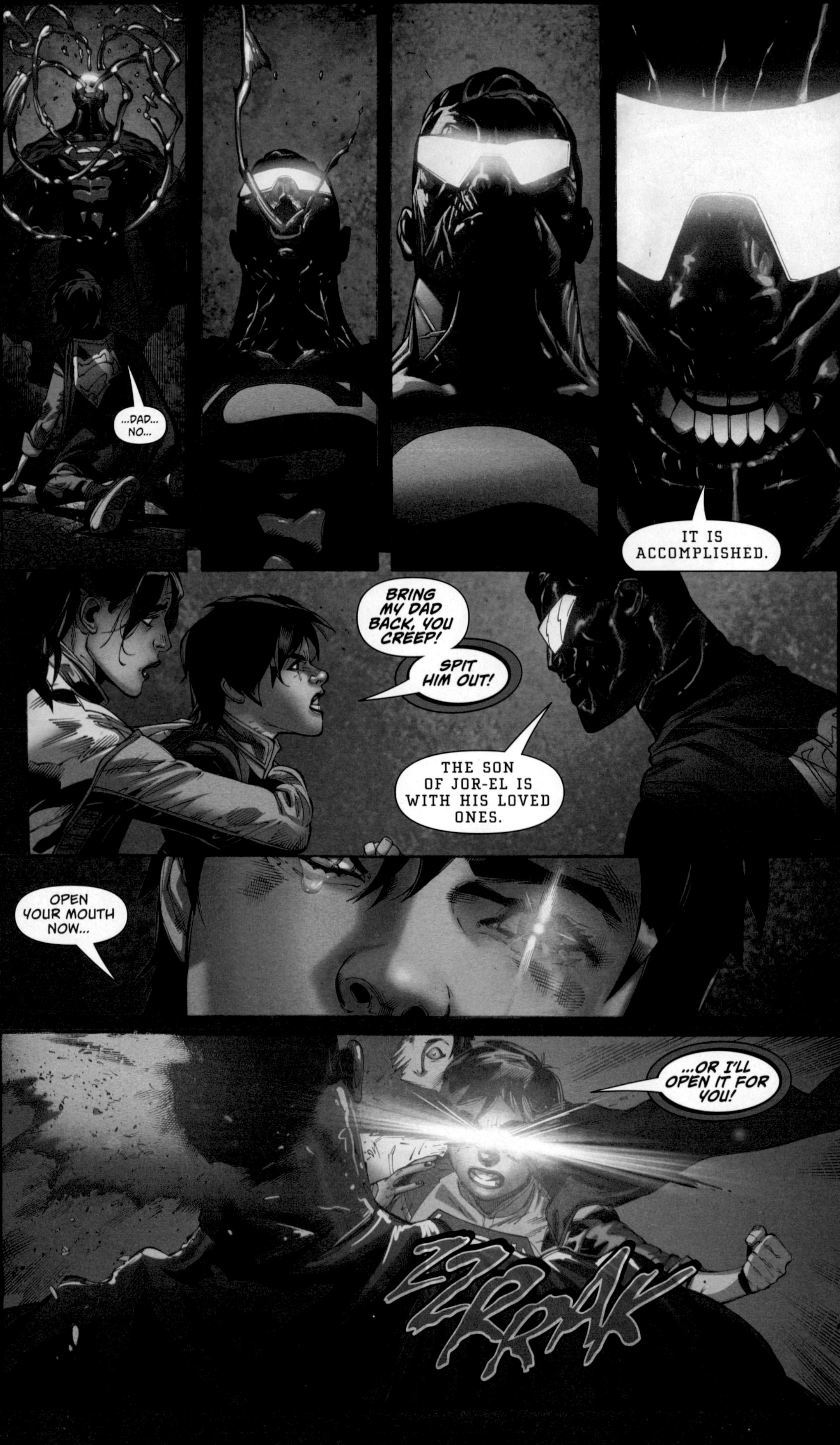
...DAD... NO...
IT IS ACCOMPLISHED.
BRING MY DAD BACK, YOU CREEP!
SPIT HIM OUT!
THE SON OF JOR-EL IS WITH HIS LOVED ONES.
OPEN YOUR MOUTH NOW...
...OR I'LL OPEN IT FOR YOU!
ZZRRAK

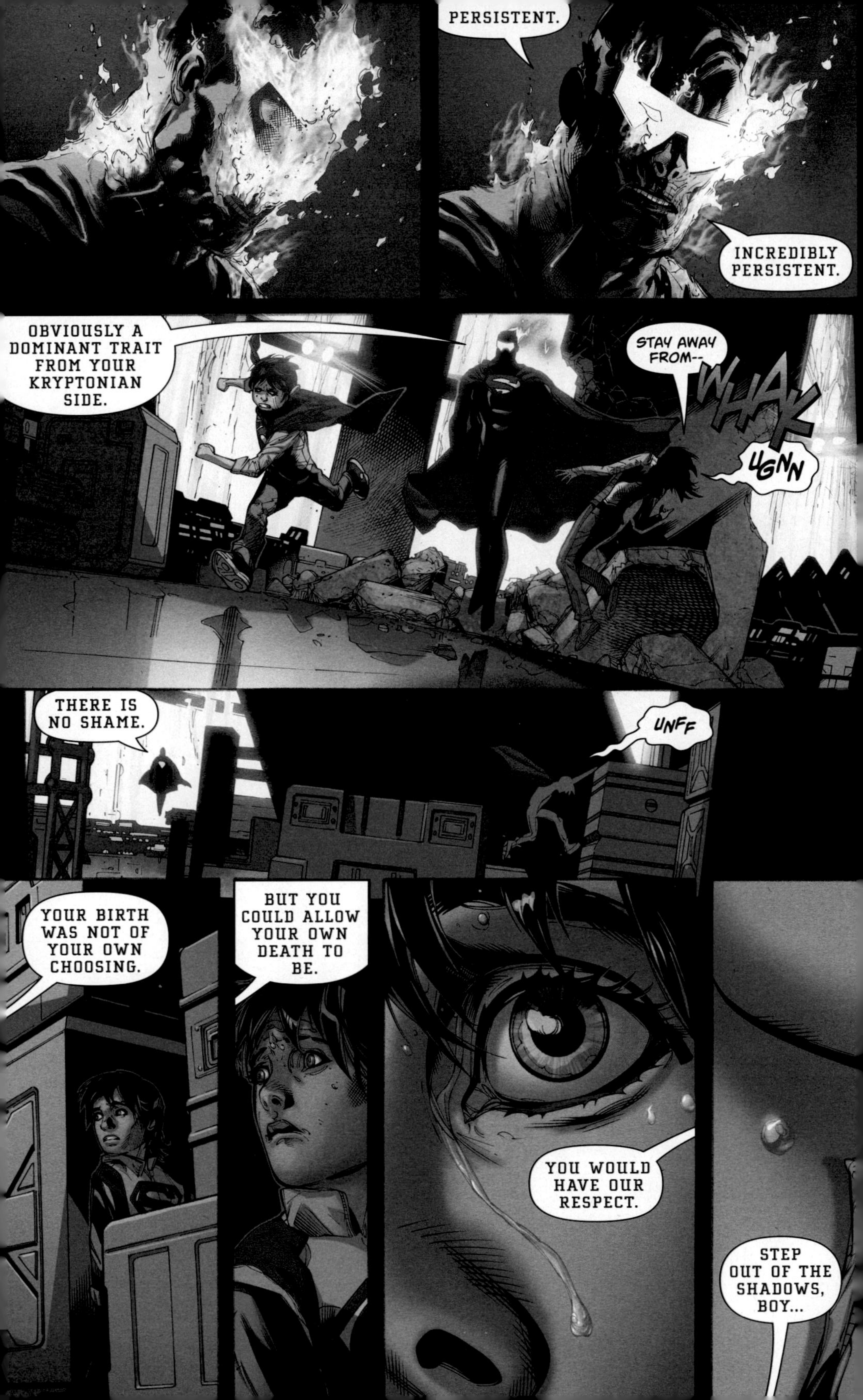
PERSISTENT.
INCREDIBLY PERSISTENT.
OBVIOUSLY A DOMINANT TRAIT FROM YOUR KRYPTONIAN SIDE.
STAY AWAY FROM--
WHAK
UGNN
THERE IS NO SHAME.
UNFF
YOUR BIRTH WAS NOT OF YOUR OWN CHOOSING.
BUT YOU COULD ALLOW YOUR OWN DEATH TO BE.
YOU WOULD HAVE OUR RESPECT.
STEP OUT OF THE SHADOWS, BOY...

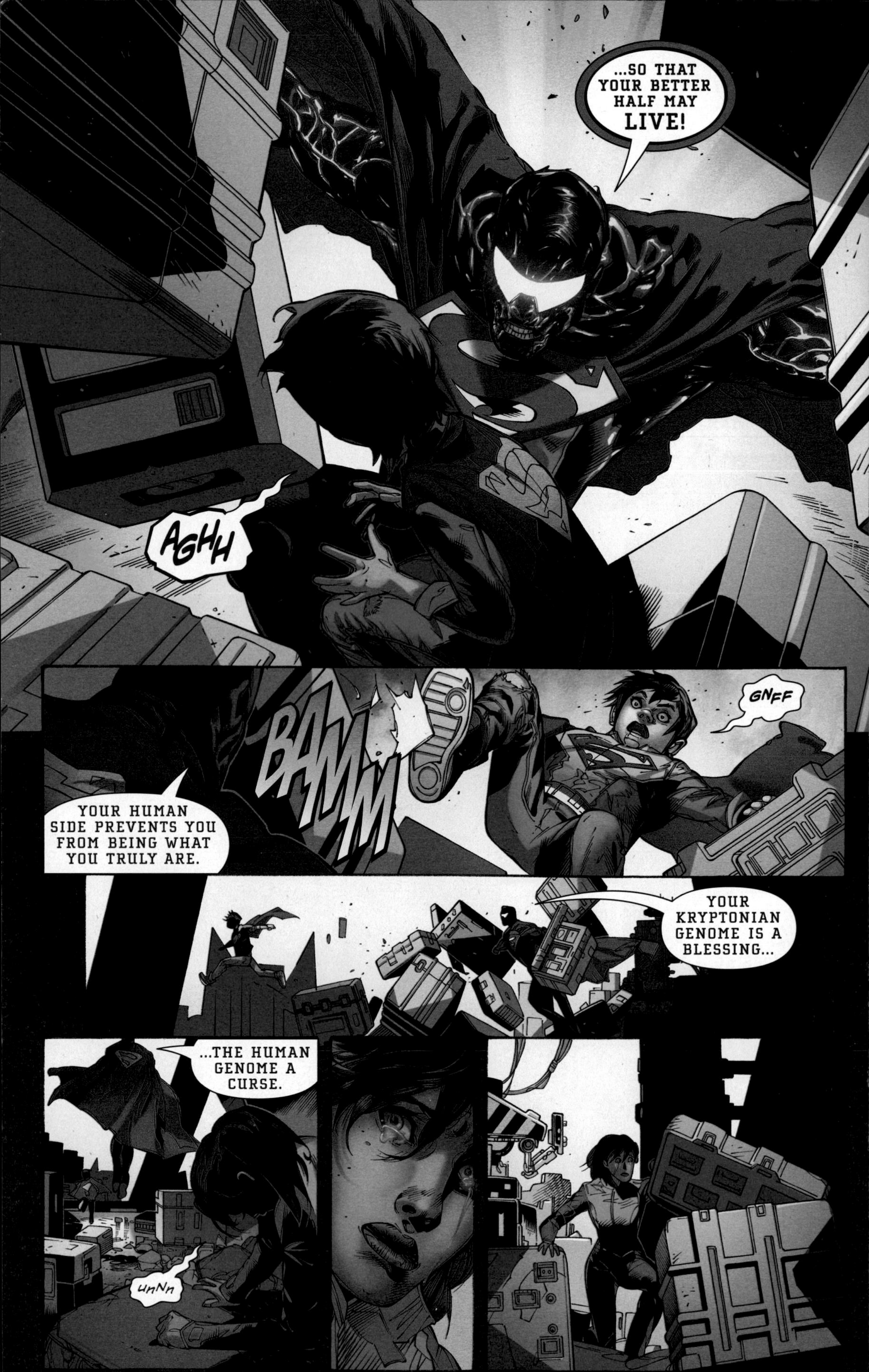
...SO THAT YOUR BETTER HALF MAY LIVE!
AGHH
BAMM
GNFF
YOUR HUMAN SIDE PREVENTS YOU FROM BEING WHAT YOU TRULY ARE.
YOUR KRYPTONIAN GENOME IS A BLESSING...
...THE HUMAN GENOME A CURSE.
unNn

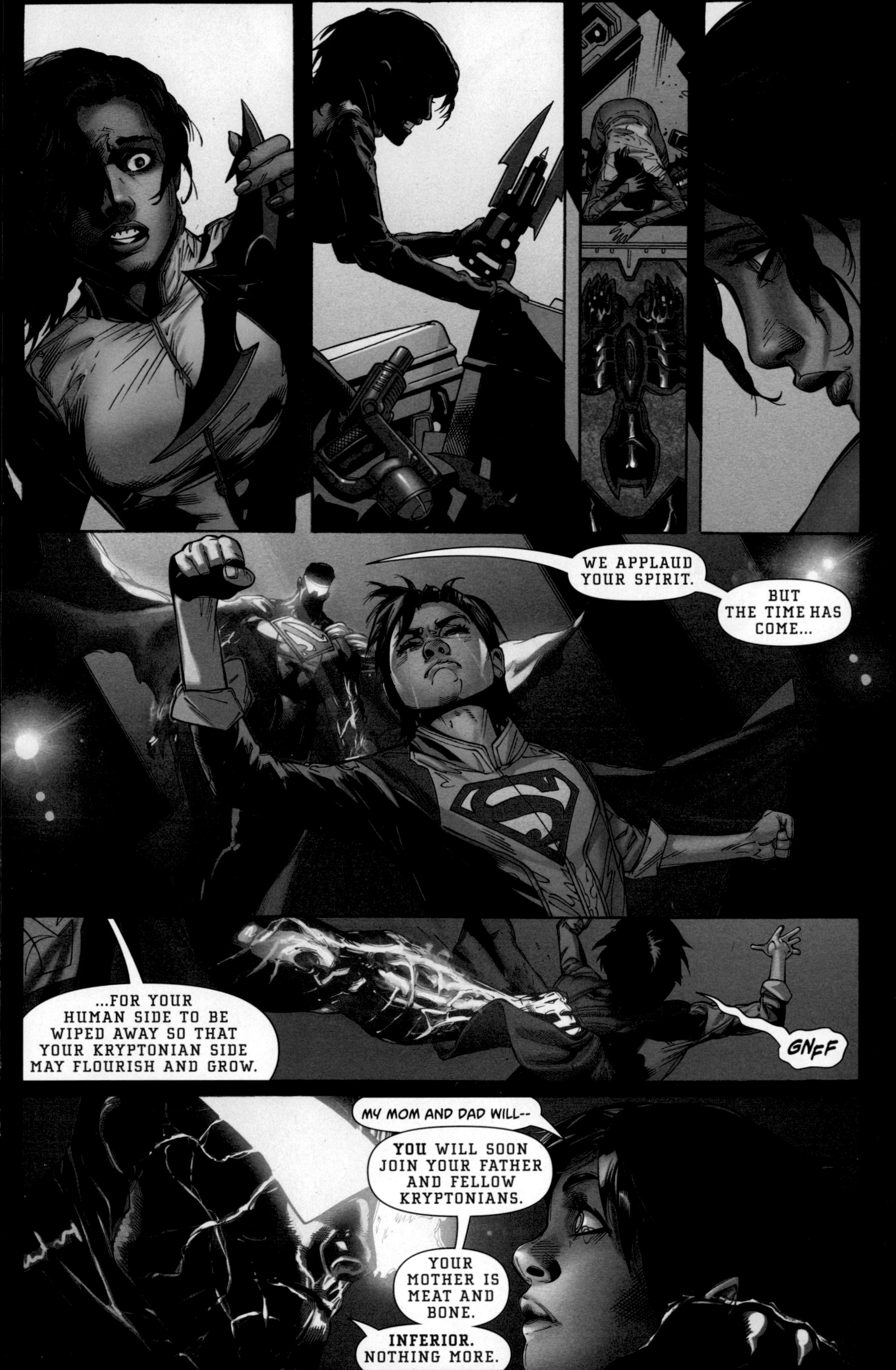

WE APPLAUD YOUR SPIRIT.
BUT THE TIME HAS COME...
...FOR YOUR HUMAN SIDE TO BE WIPED AWAY SO THAT YOUR KRYPTONIAN SIDE MAY FLOURISH AND GROW.
GNFF
MY MOM AND DAD WILL--
YOU WILL SOON JOIN YOUR FATHER AND FELLOW KRYPTONIANS.
YOUR MOTHER IS MEAT AND BONE.
INFERIOR. NOTHING MORE.

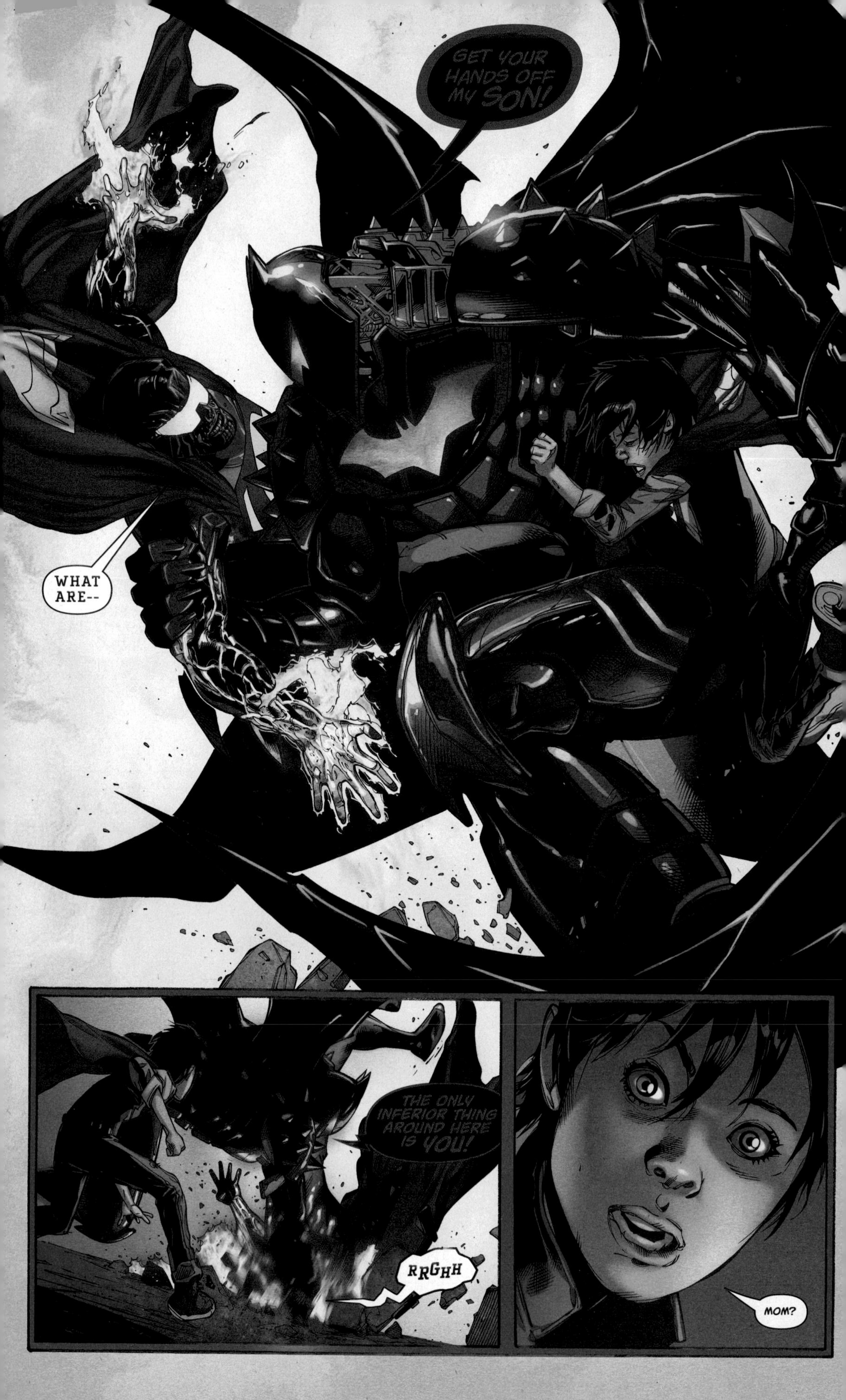
GET YOUR HANDS OFF MY SON!
WHAT ARE--
THE ONLY INFERIOR THING AROUND HERE IS YOU!
RRGHH
MOM?

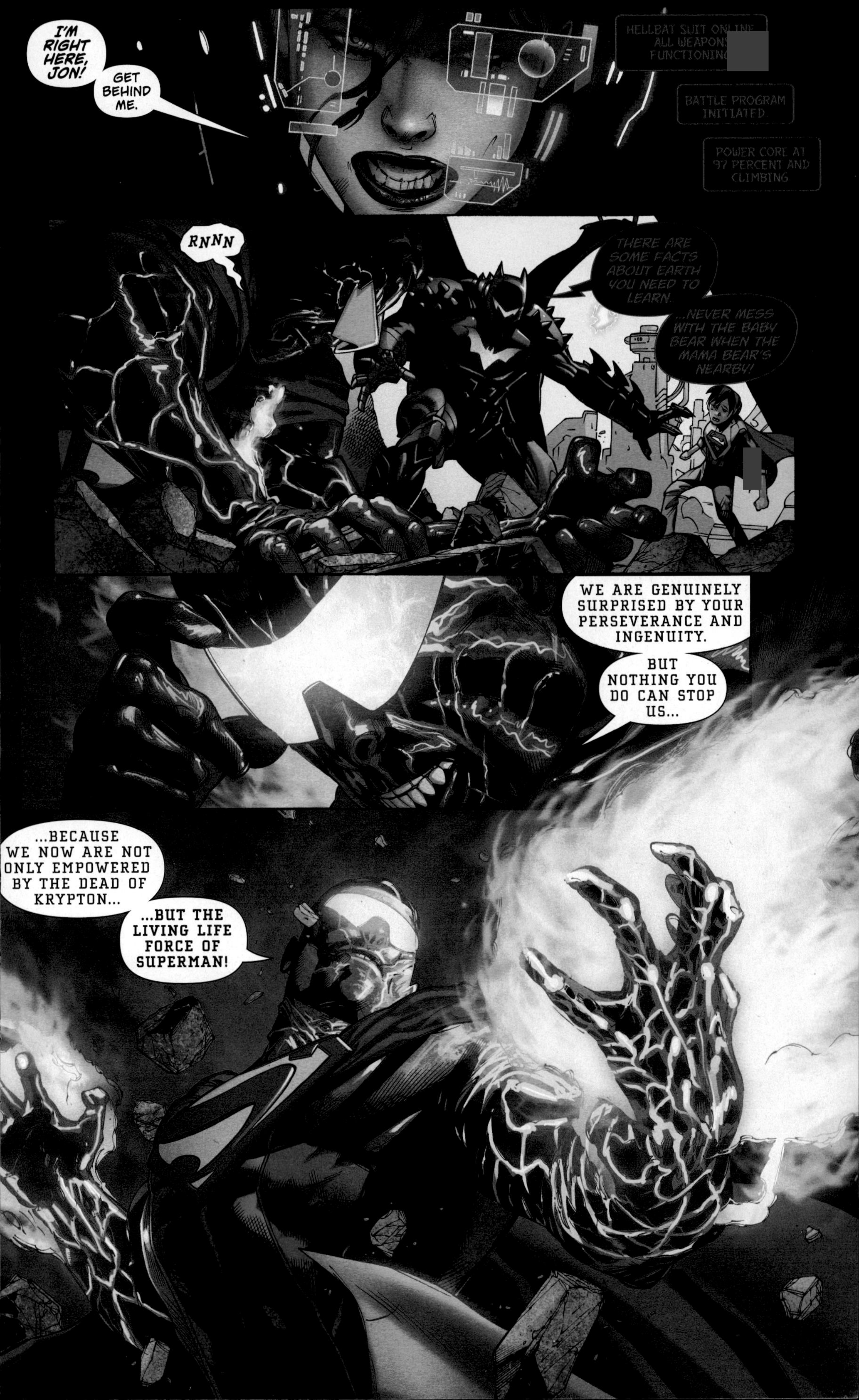

I'M RIGHT HERE, JON!
GET BEHIND ME.
HELLBAT SUIT ONLINE
ALL WEAPONS FUNCTIONING
BATTLE PROGRAM INITIATED
POWER CORE AT 97 PERCENT AND CLIMBING
RNNN
THERE ARE SOME FACTS ABOUT EARTH YOU NEED TO LEARN...
...NEVER MESS WITH THE BABY BEAR WHEN THE MAMA BEAR'S NEARBY!
WE ARE GENUINELY SURPRISED BY YOUR PERSEVERANCE AND INGENUITY.
BUT NOTHING YOU DO CAN STOP US...
...BECAUSE WE NOW ARE NOT ONLY EMPOWERED BY THE DEAD OF KRYPTON...
...BUT THE LIVING LIFE FORCE OF SUPERMAN!

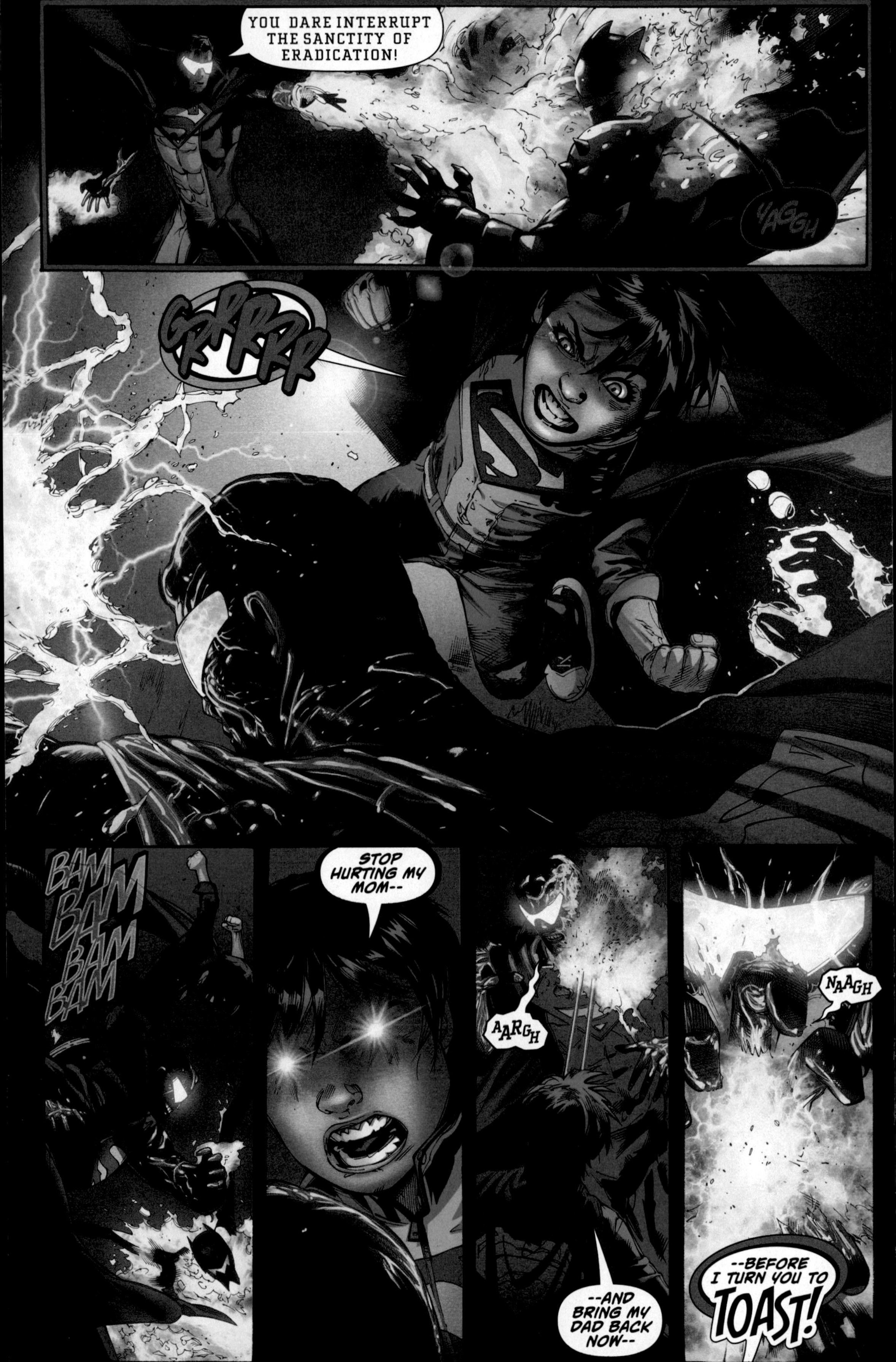
YOU DARE INTERRUPT THE SANCTITY OF ERADICATION!
YAGGH
GRRRRR
BAM BAM BAM BAM
STOP HURTING MY MOM--
AARGH
--AND BRING MY DAD BACK NOW--
NAAGH
--BEFORE I TURN YOU TO TOAST!

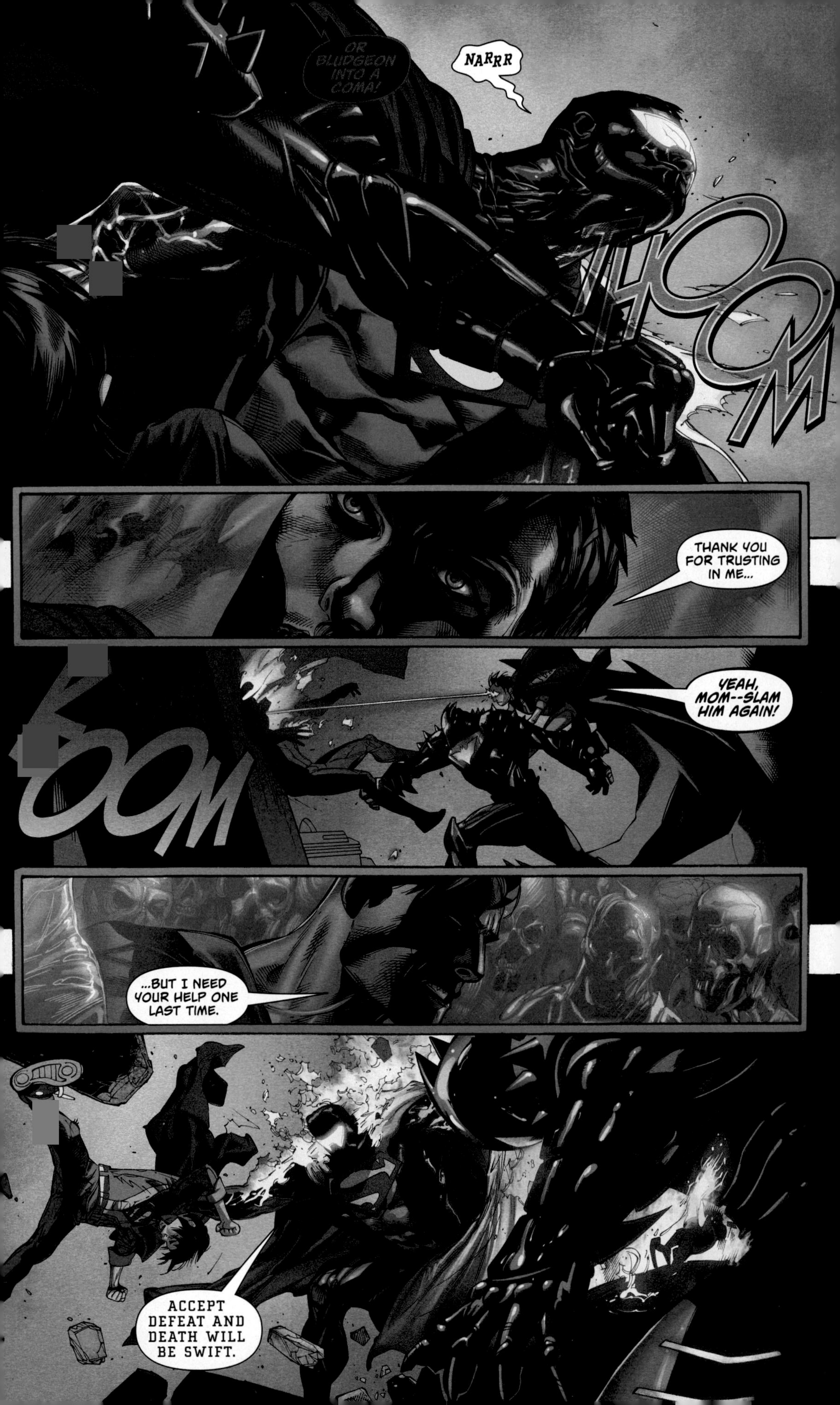

OR BLUDGEON INTO A COMA!
NARRR
THOOM
THANK YOU FOR TRUSTING IN ME...
KOOM
YEAH, MOM--SLAM HIM AGAIN!
...BUT I NEED YOUR HELP ONE LAST TIME.
ACCEPT DEFEAT AND DEATH WILL BE SWIFT.

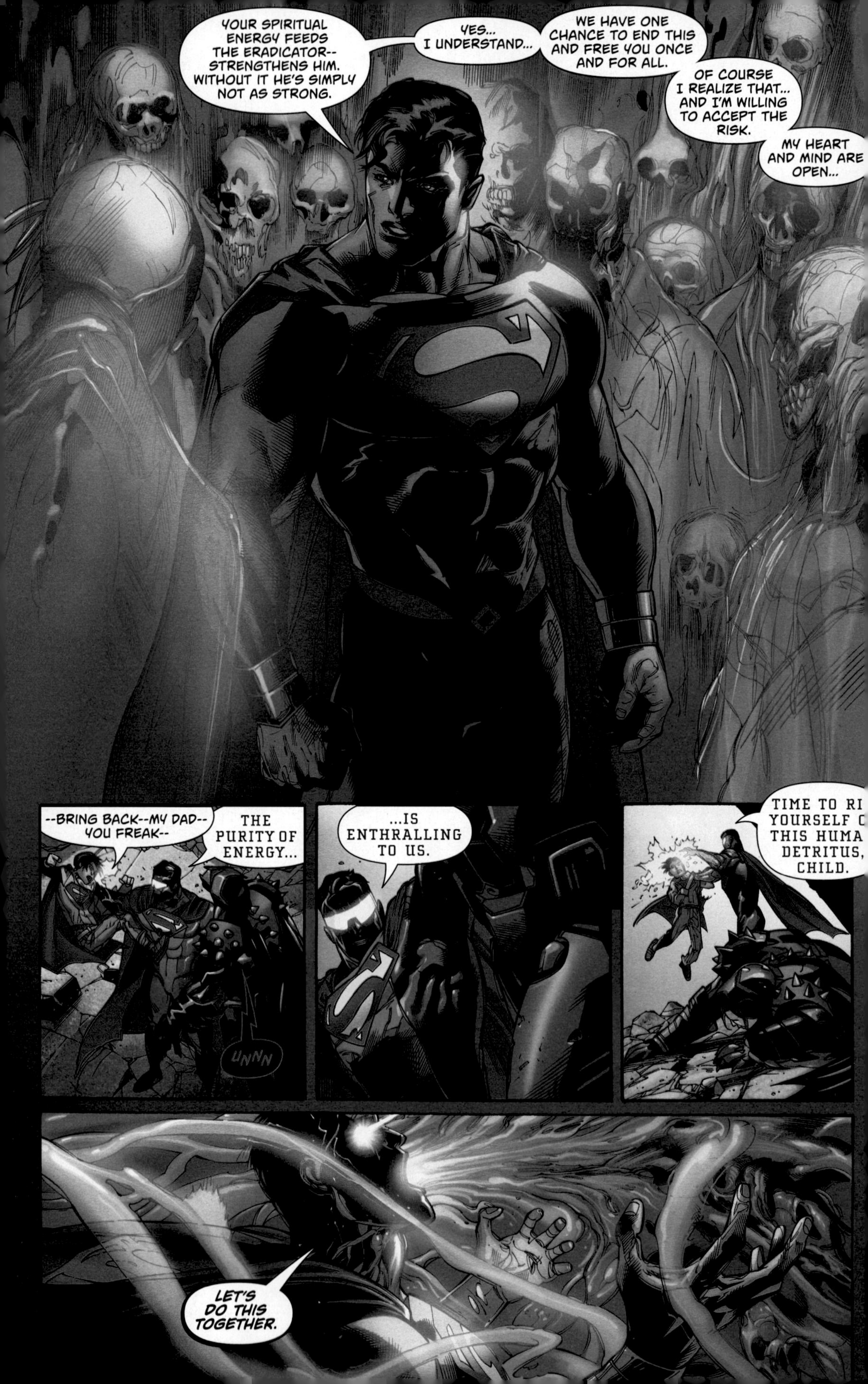
YOUR SPIRITUAL ENERGY FEEDS THE ERADICATOR-- STRENGTHENS HIM. WITHOUT IT HE'S SIMPLY NOT AS STRONG.
YES... I UNDERSTAND...
WE HAVE ONE CHANCE TO END THIS AND FREE YOU ONCE AND FOR ALL.
OF COURSE I REALIZE THAT... AND I'M WILLING TO ACCEPT THE RISK.
MY HEART AND MIND ARE OPEN...
--BRING BACK--MY DAD-- YOU FREAK--
THE PURITY OF ENERGY...
UNNN
...IS ENTHRALLING TO US.
TIME TO RI YOURSELF O THIS HUMA DETRITUS, CHILD.
LET'S DO THIS TOGETHER.

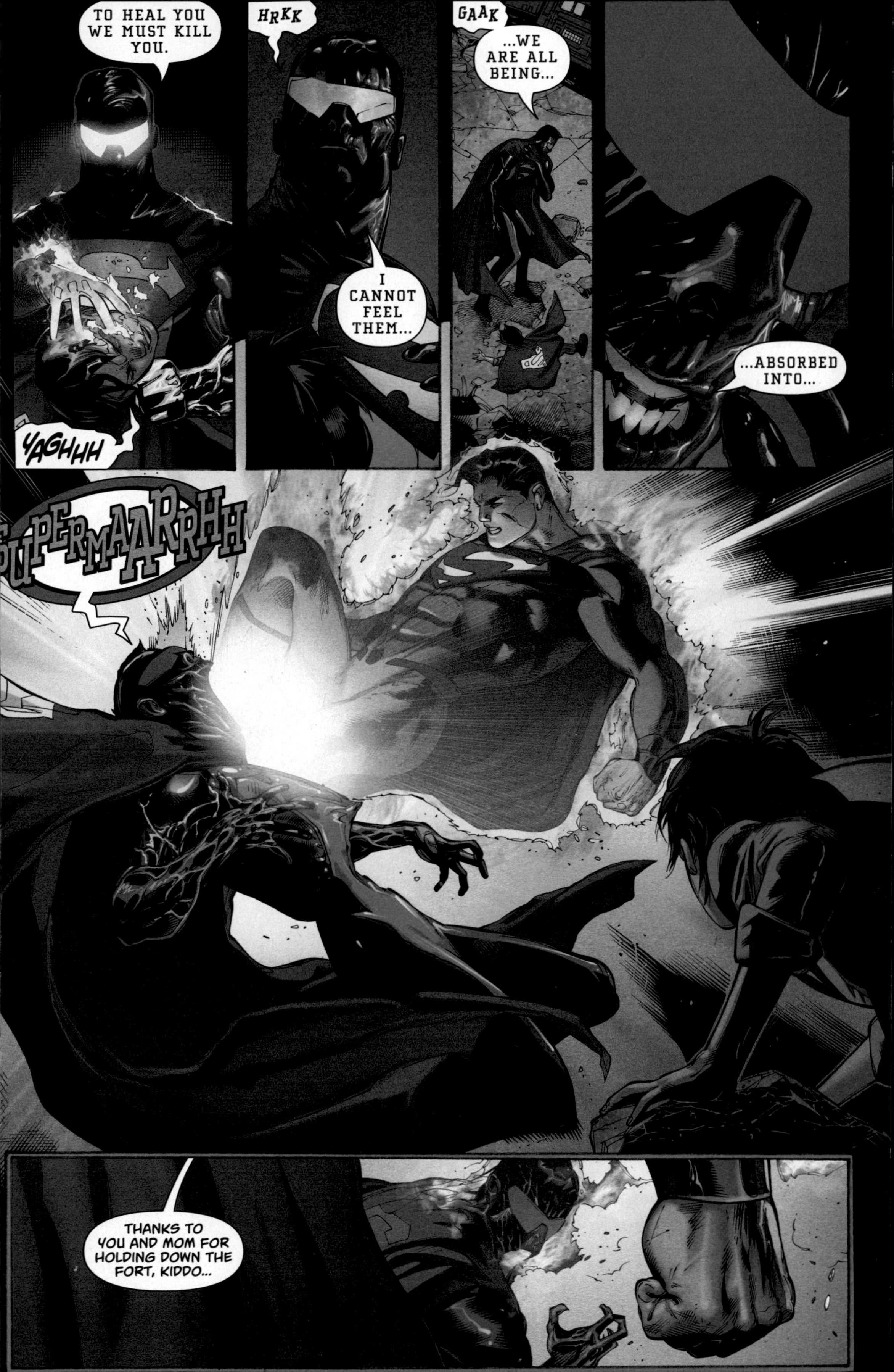
TO HEAL YOU WE MUST KILL YOU.
YAGHHH
HRKK
I CANNOT FEEL THEM...
GAAK
...WE ARE ALL BEING...
...ABSORBED INTO...
SUPERMAARRHH
THANKS TO YOU AND MOM FOR HOLDING DOWN THE FORT, KIDDO...

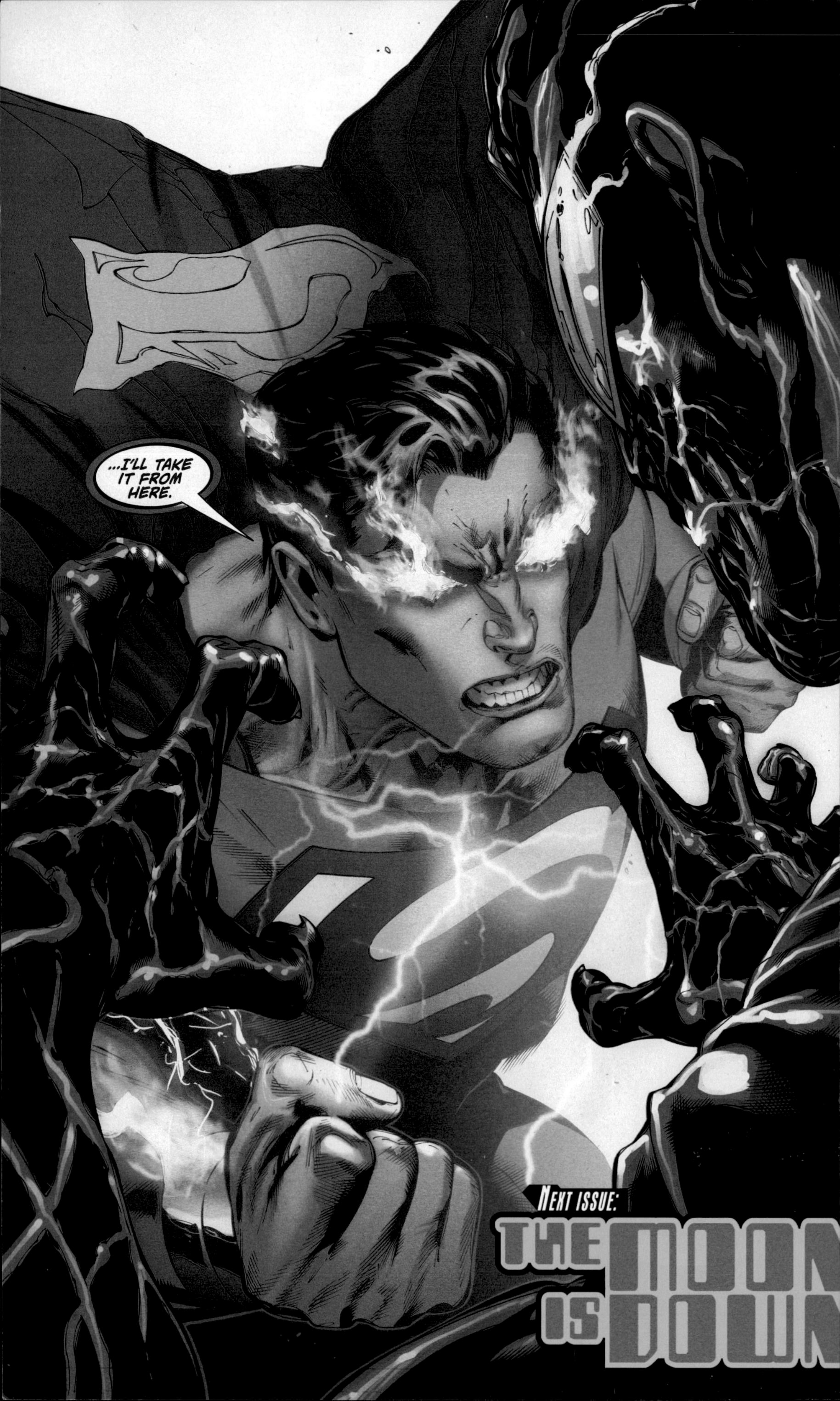

...I'LL TAKE IT FROM HERE.
NEXT ISSUE:
THE MOON IS DOWN

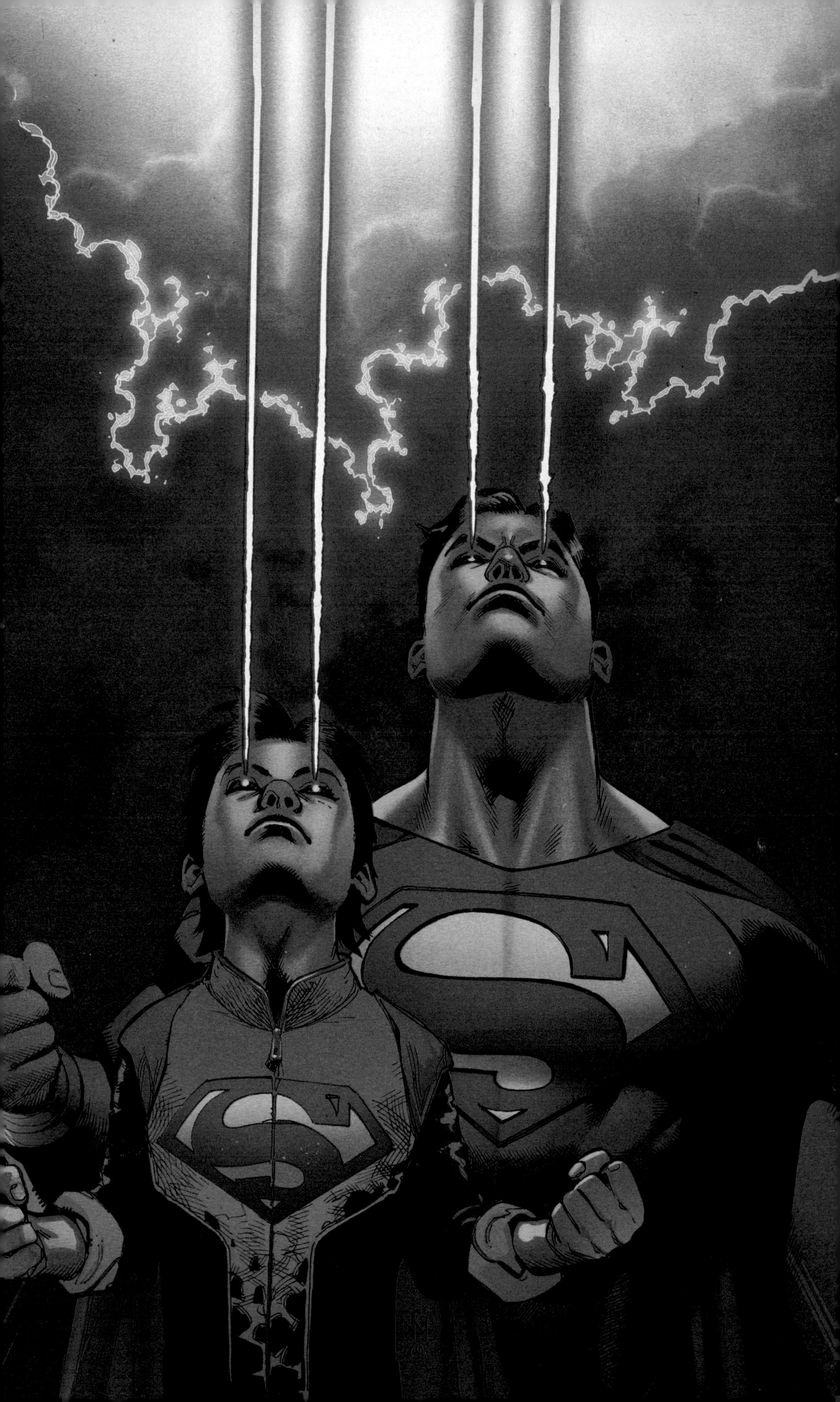

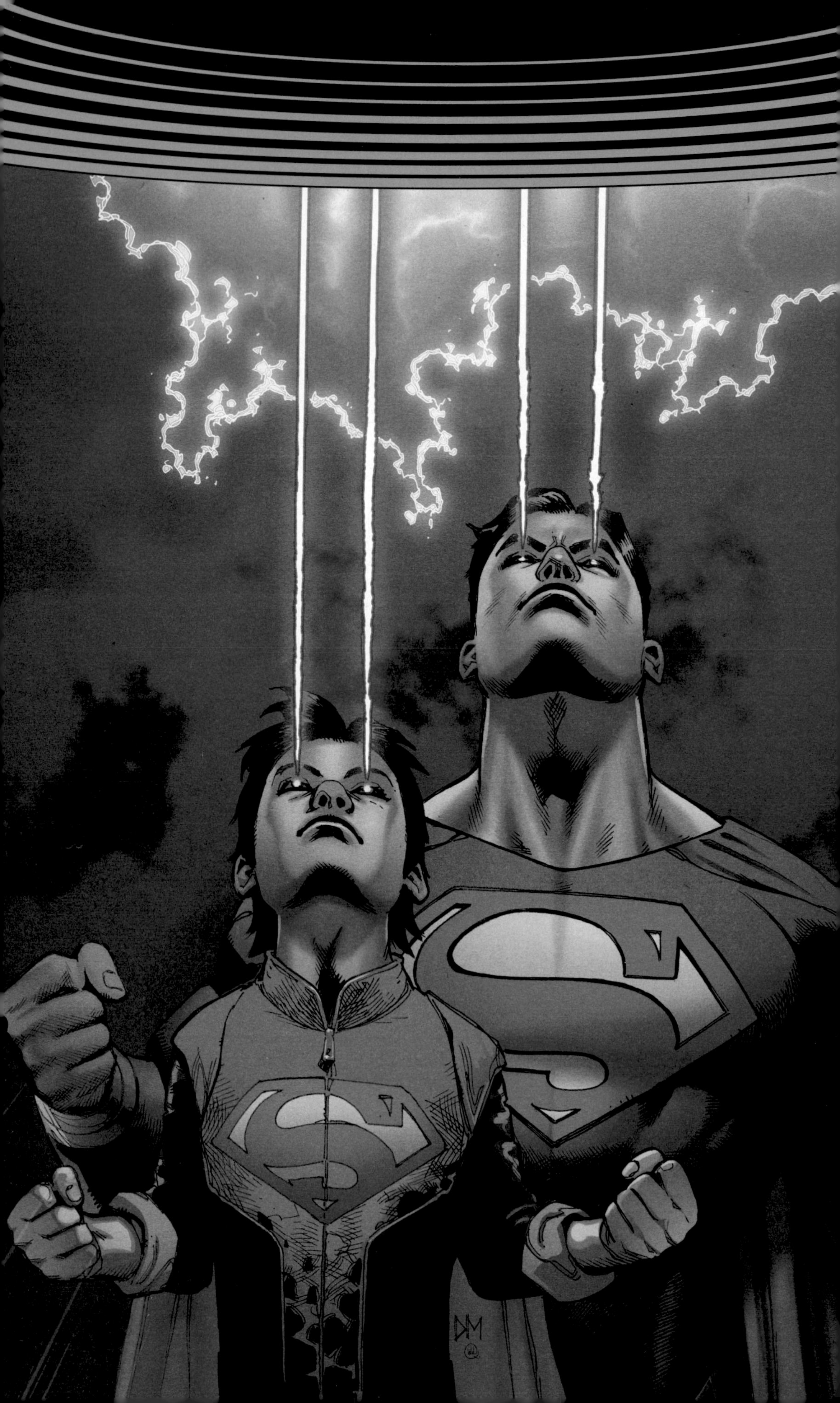

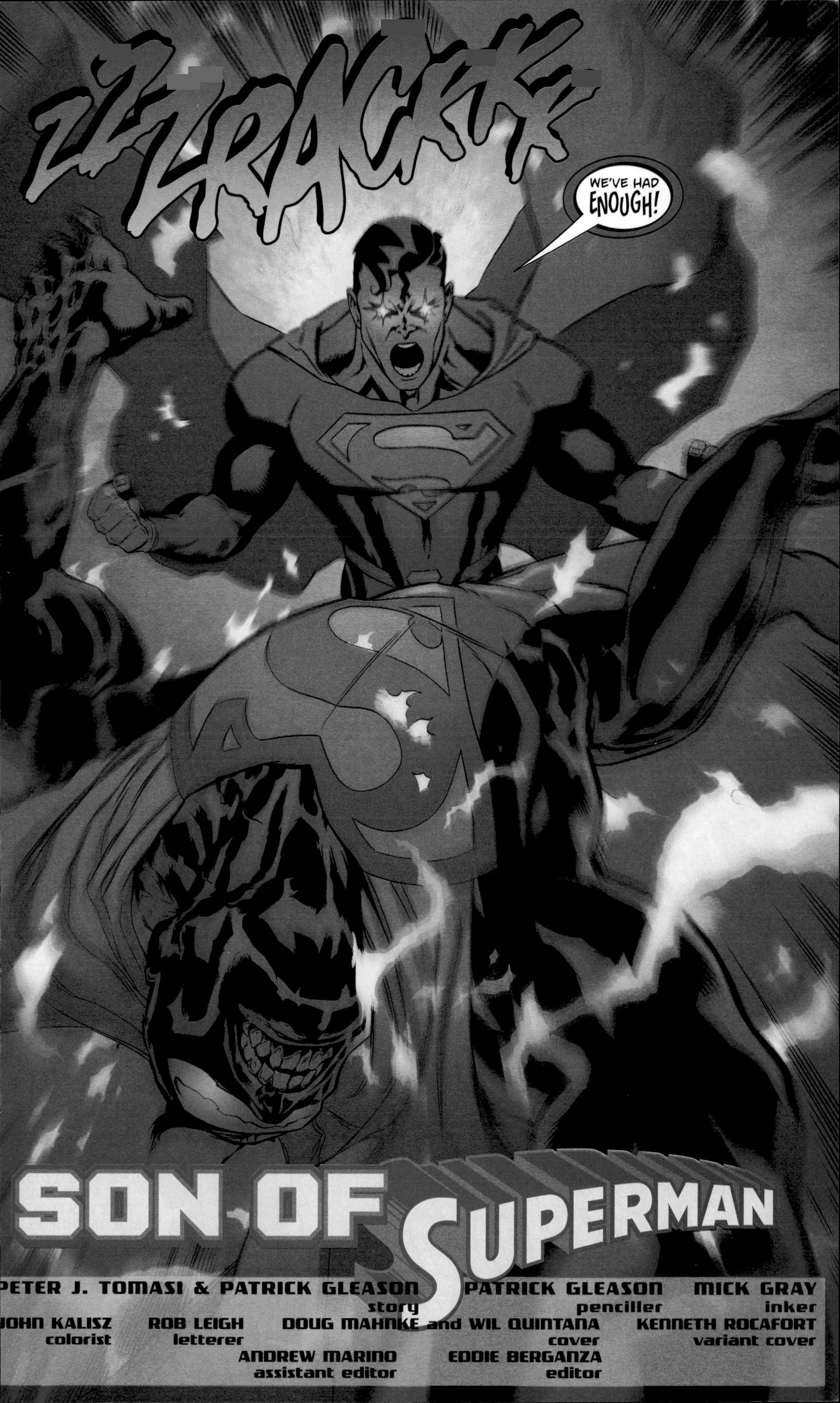
ZZRACKK
WE'VE HAD ENOUGH!
SON OF SUPERMAN
PETER J. TOMASI & PATRICK GLEASON story
PATRICK GLEASON penciller
MICK GRAY inker
JOHN KALISZ colorist
ROB LEIGH letterer
DOUG MAHNKE and WIL QUINTANA cover
KENNETH ROCAFORT variant cover
ANDREW MARINO assistant editor
EDDIE BERGANZA editor

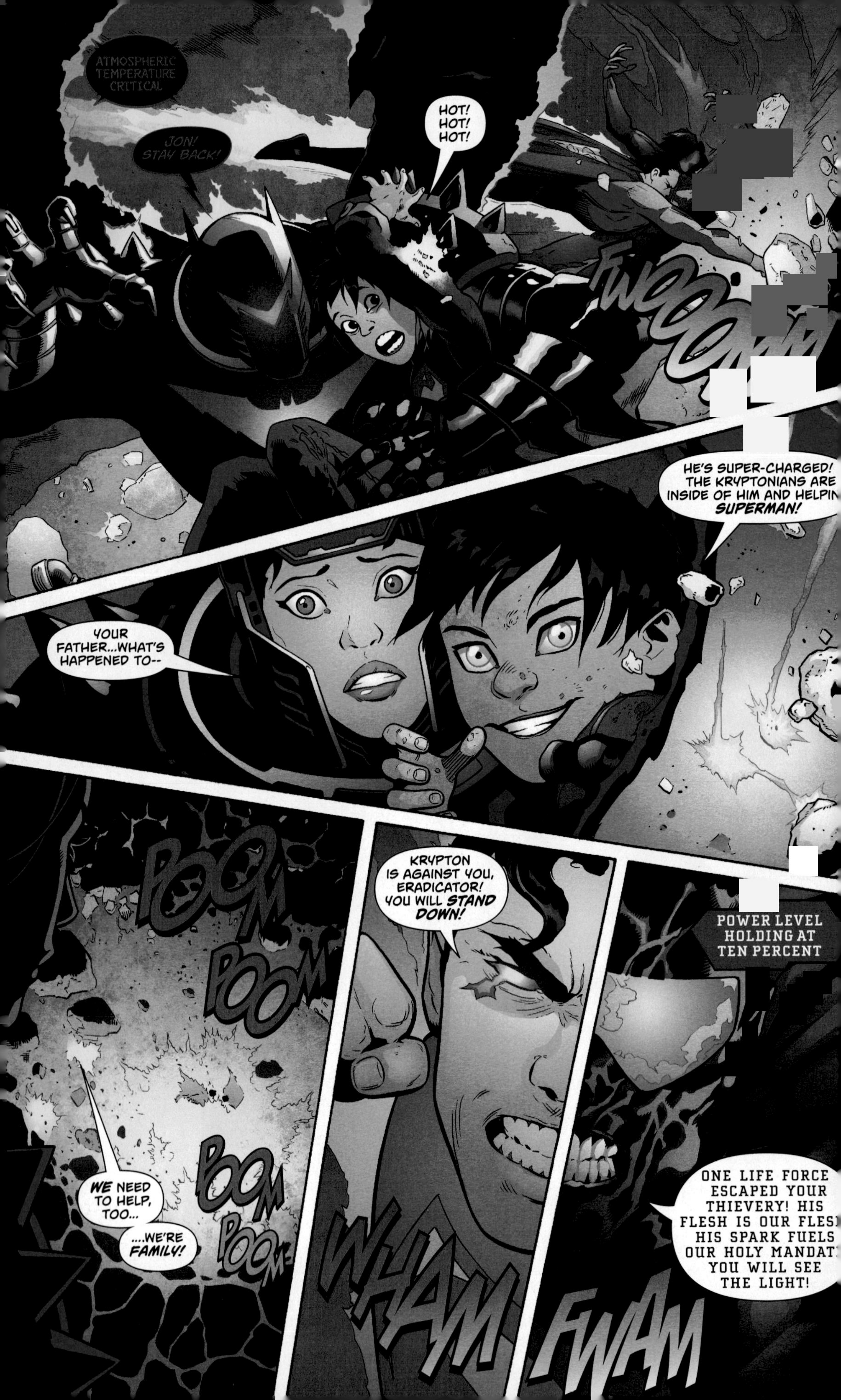
ATMOSPHERIC TEMPERATURE CRITICAL
JON! STAY BACK!
HOT! HOT! HOT!
HE'S SUPER-CHARGED! THE KRYPTONIANS ARE INSIDE OF HIM AND HELPIN SUPERMAN!
YOUR FATHER...WHAT'S HAPPENED TO--
POOM
POOM
WE NEED TO HELP, TOO...
....WE'RE FAMILY!
BOOM
POOM
KRYPTON IS AGAINST YOU, ERADICATOR! YOU WILL STAND DOWN!
WHAM
POWER LEVEL HOLDING AT TEN PERCENT
ONE LIFE FORCE ESCAPED YOUR THIEVERY! HIS FLESH IS OUR FLES HIS SPARK FUELS OUR HOLY MANDAT YOU WILL SEE THE LIGHT!
FWAM

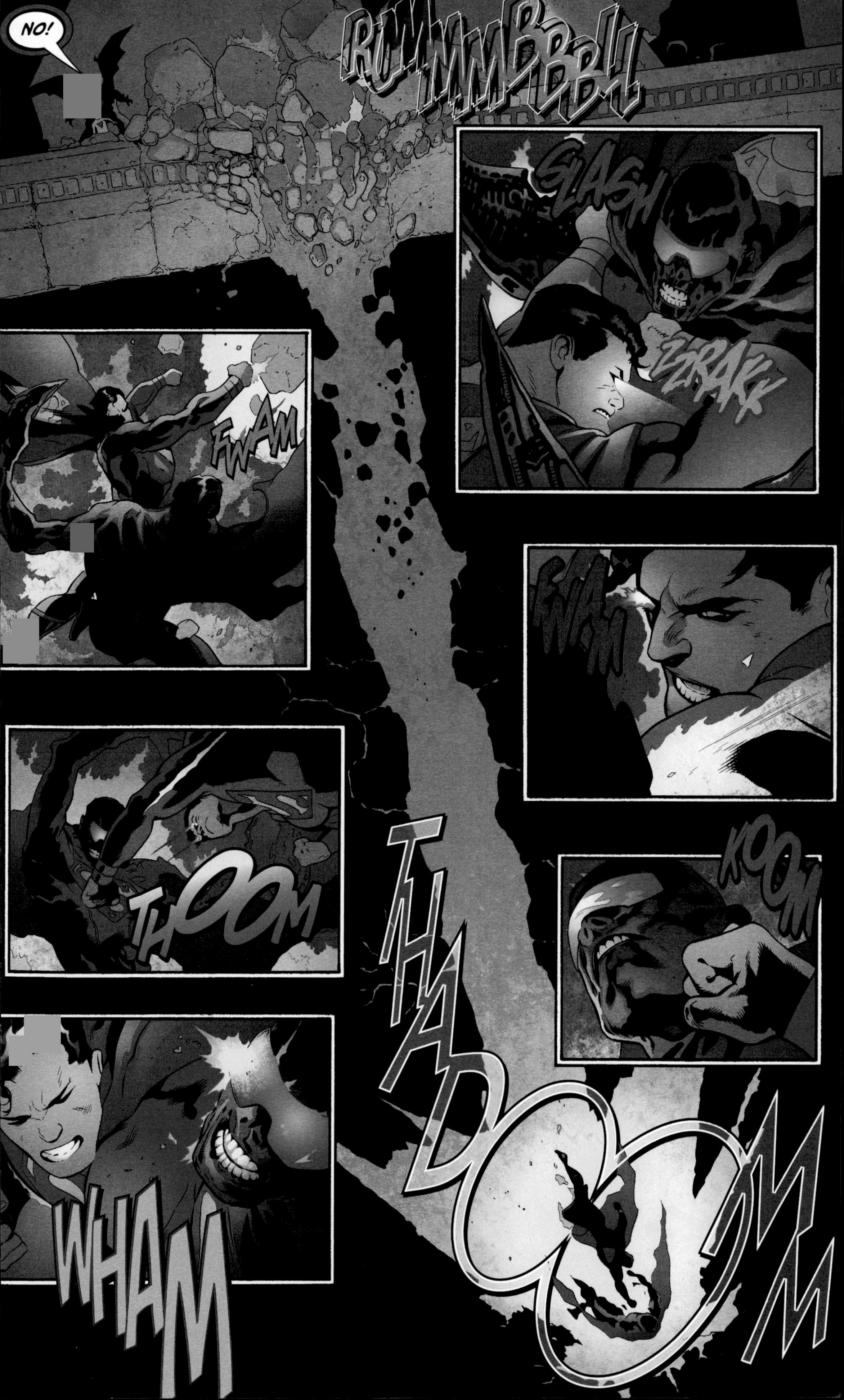
NO!
RUMMMBBBLL
SLASH
ZZRAKK
FWAM
THOOM
WHAM
FWAM
KOOM
THADOOMM

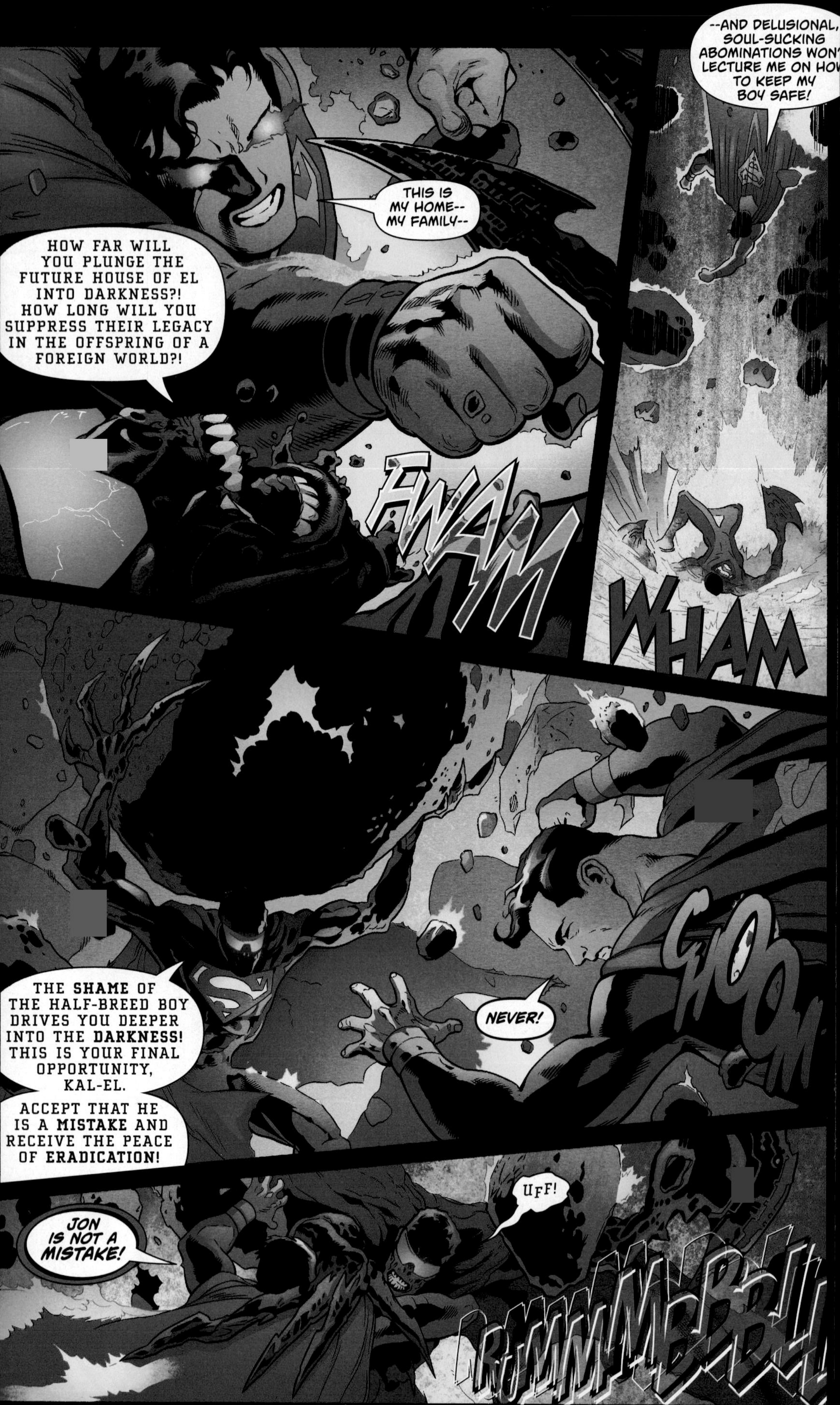

HOW FAR WILL YOU PLUNGE THE FUTURE HOUSE OF EL INTO DARKNESS?! HOW LONG WILL YOU SUPPRESS THEIR LEGACY IN THE OFFSPRING OF A FOREIGN WORLD?!
THIS IS MY HOME-- MY FAMILY--
FWAM
--AND DELUSIONAL, SOUL-SUCKING ABOMINATIONS WON' LECTURE ME ON HOW TO KEEP MY BOY SAFE!
WHAM
THE SHAME OF THE HALF-BREED BOY DRIVES YOU DEEPER INTO THE DARKNESS! THIS IS YOUR FINAL OPPORTUNITY, KAL-EL.
ACCEPT THAT HE IS A MISTAKE AND RECEIVE THE PEACE OF ERADICATION!
NEVER!
JON IS NOT A MISTAKE!
UFF!

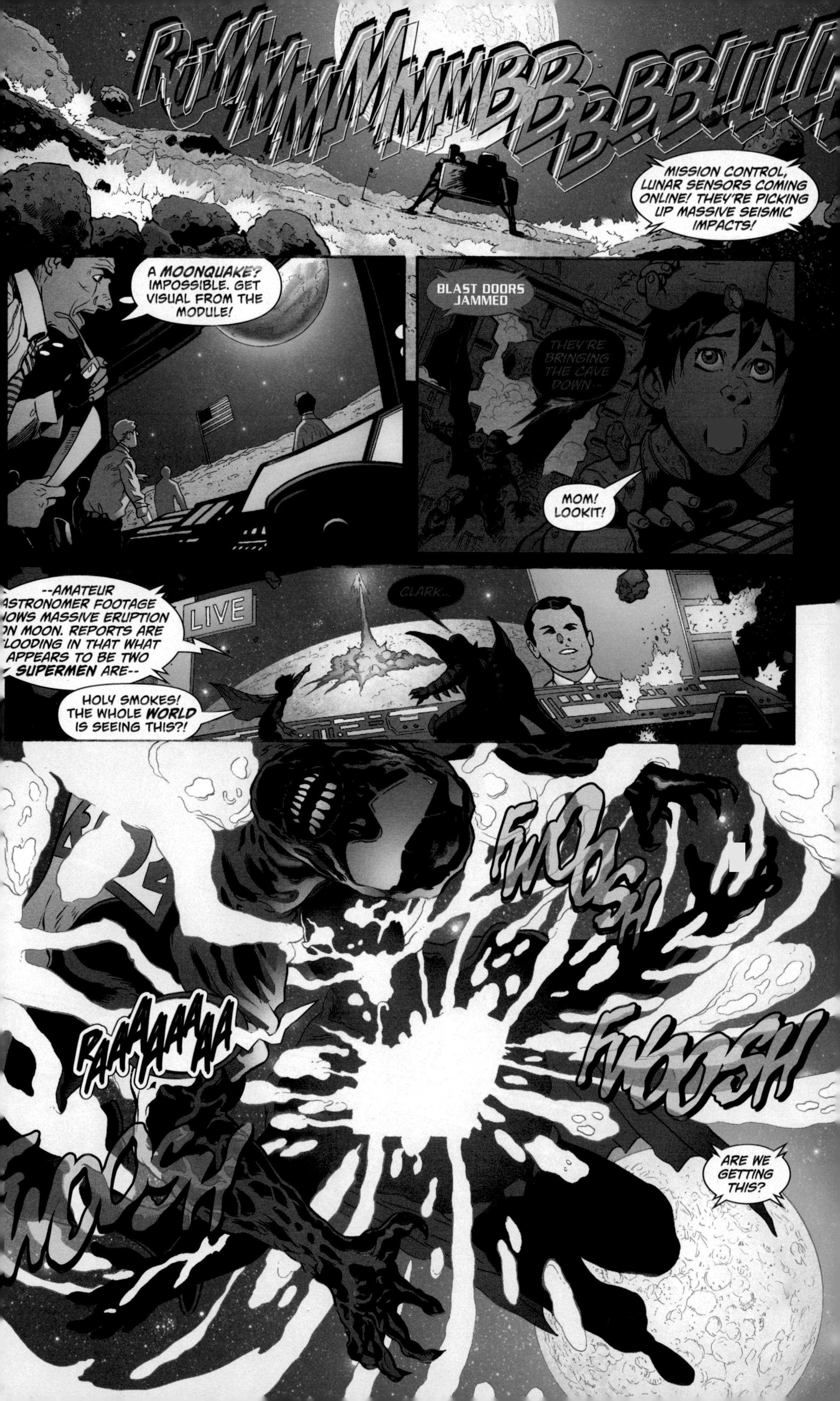
RUMMMMMMMBBBBBLLL
MISSION CONTROL, LUNAR SENSORS COMING ONLINE! THEY'RE PICKING UP MASSIVE SEISMIC IMPACTS!
A MOONQUAKE? IMPOSSIBLE. GET VISUAL FROM THE MODULE!
BLAST DOORS JAMMED
THEY'RE BRINGING THE CAVE DOWN--
MOM! LOOKIT!
--AMATEUR ASTRONOMER FOOTAGE HOWS MASSIVE ERUPTION ON MOON. REPORTS ARE LOODING IN THAT WHAT APPEARS TO BE TWO SUPERMEN ARE--
LIVE
CLARK...
HOLY SMOKES! THE WHOLE WORLD IS SEEING THIS?!
FWOOSH
RAAAAAAAA
FWOOSH
WOOSH
ARE WE GETTING THIS?

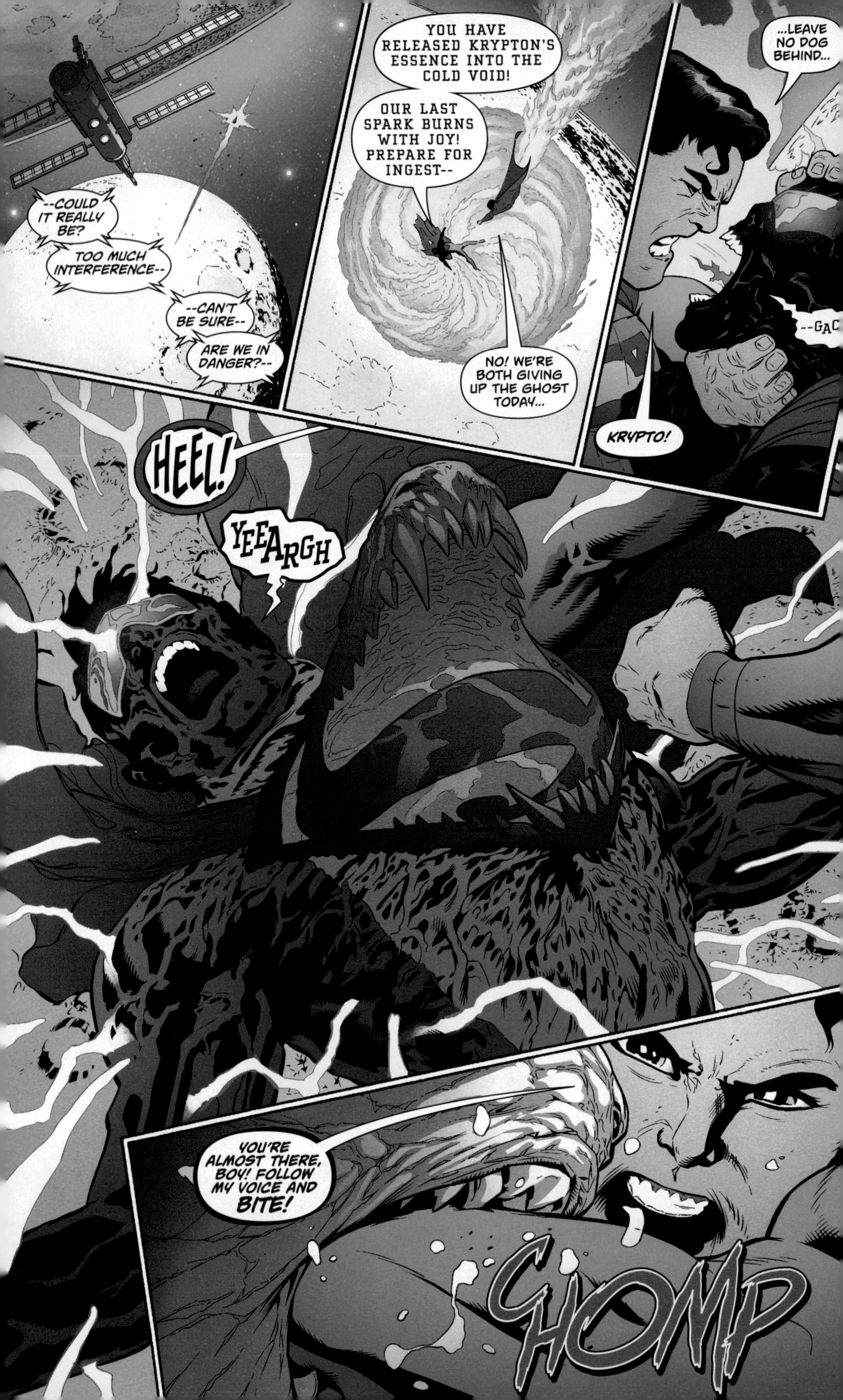
--COULD IT REALLY BE?
TOO MUCH INTERFERENCE--
--CAN'T BE SURE--
ARE WE IN DANGER?--
YOU HAVE RELEASED KRYPTON'S ESSENCE INTO THE COLD VOID!
OUR LAST SPARK BURNS WITH JOY! PREPARE FOR INGEST--
NO! WE'RE BOTH GIVING UP THE GHOST TODAY...
...LEAVE NO DOG BEHIND...
--GAC
KRYPTO!
HEEL!
YEEARGH
YOU'RE ALMOST THERE, BOY! FOLLOW MY VOICE AND BITE!
CHOMP

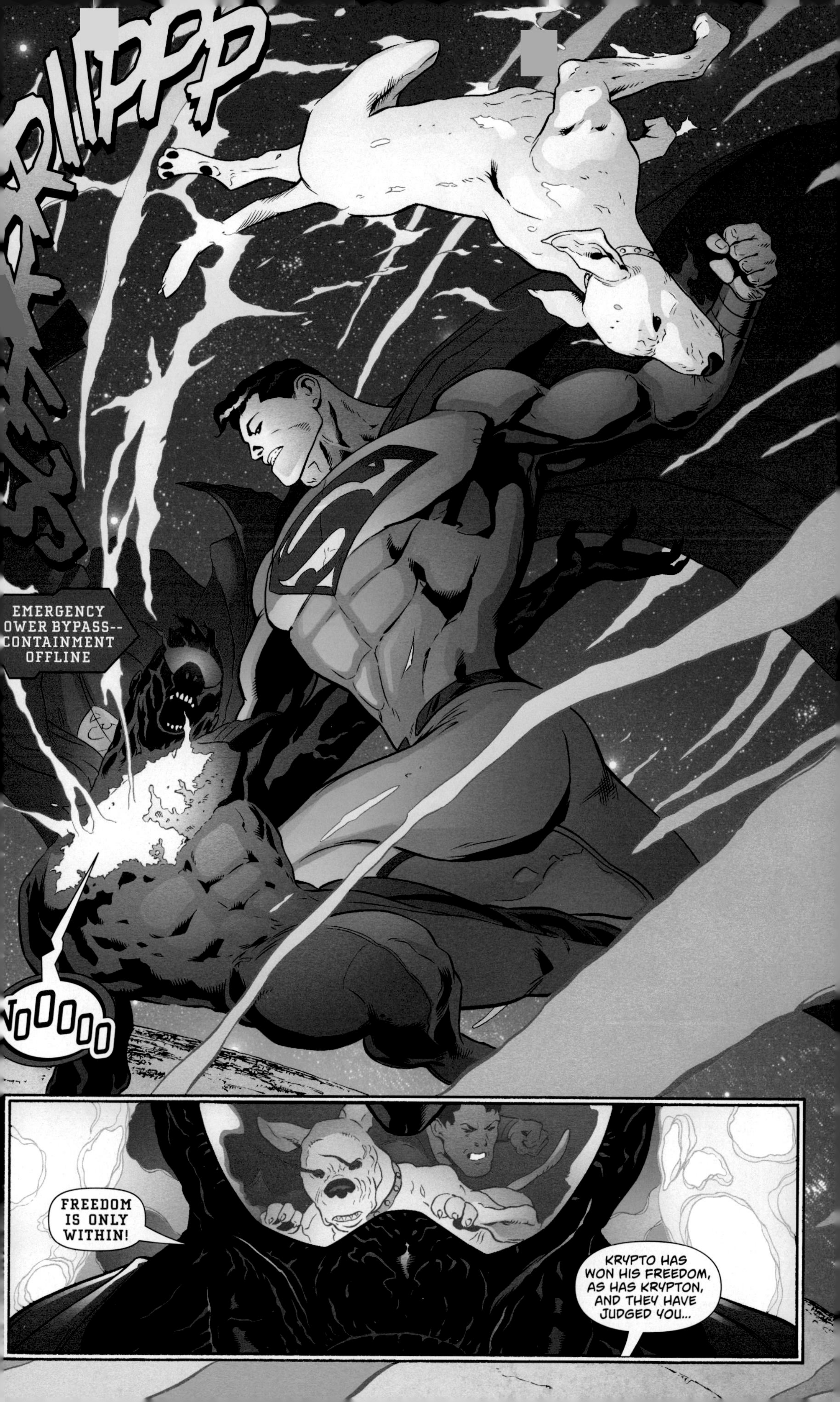

SCRIIIPPP
EMERGENCY
OWER BYPASS--
CONTAINMENT
OFFLINE
NOOOOO
FREEDOM
IS ONLY
WITHIN!
KRYPTO HAS
WON HIS FREEDOM,
AS HAS KRYPTON,
AND THEY HAVE
JUDGED YOU...

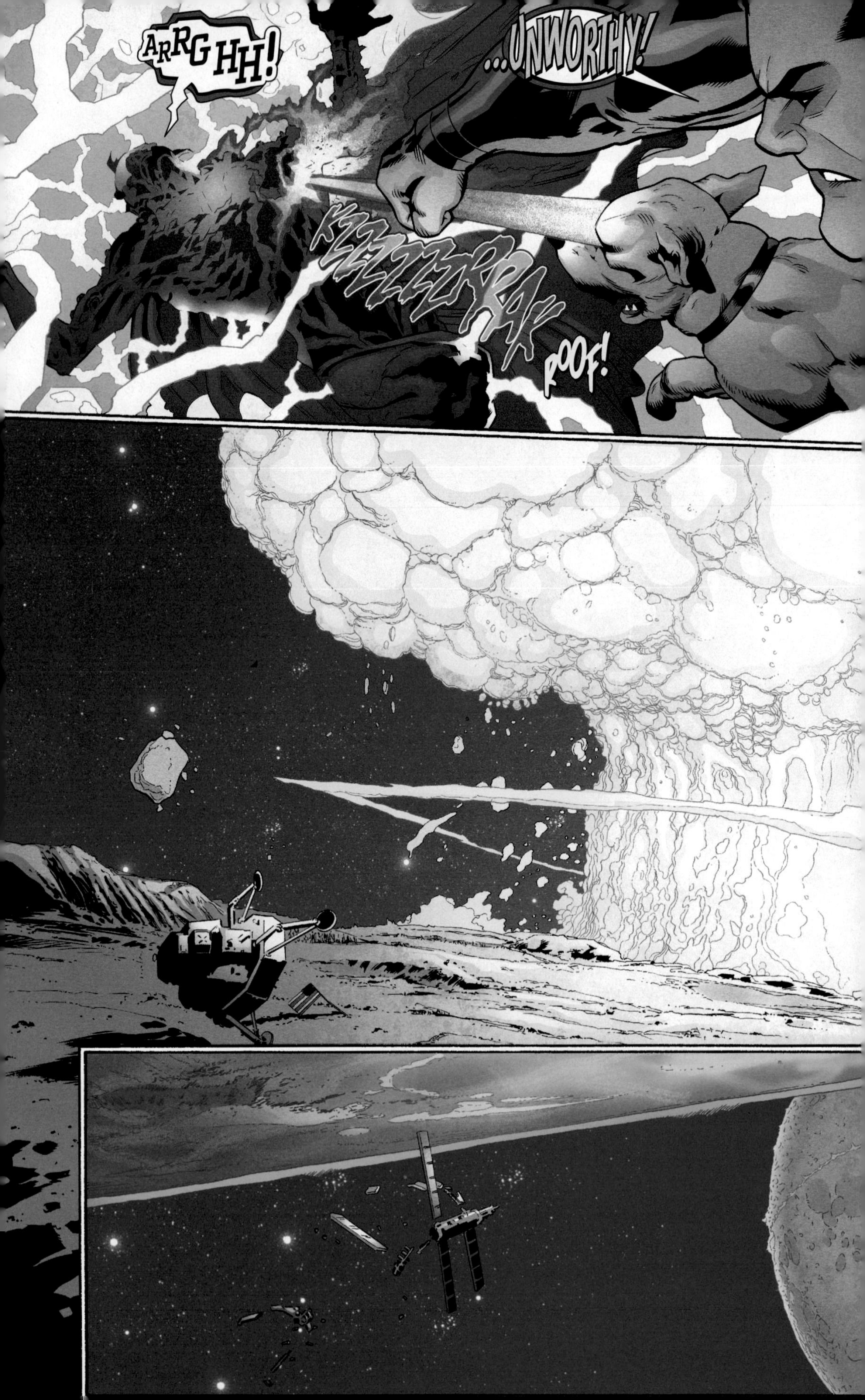
ARRGHH!
...UNWORTHY!
KZZZZZZRRAK
ROOF!

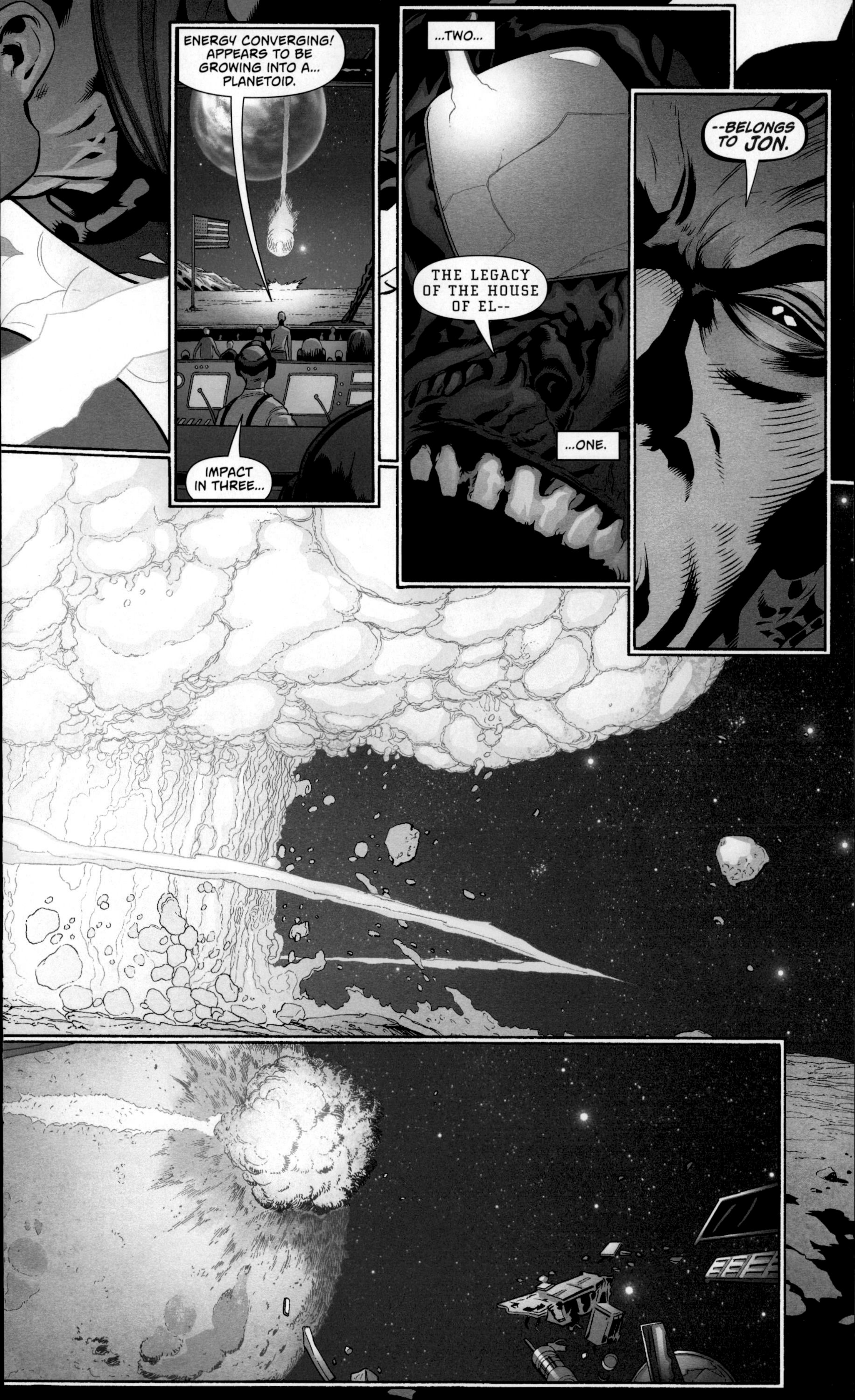
ENERGY CONVERGING! APPEARS TO BE GROWING INTO A... PLANETOID.
IMPACT IN THREE...
...TWO...
THE LEGACY OF THE HOUSE OF EL--
...ONE.
--BELONGS TO JON.

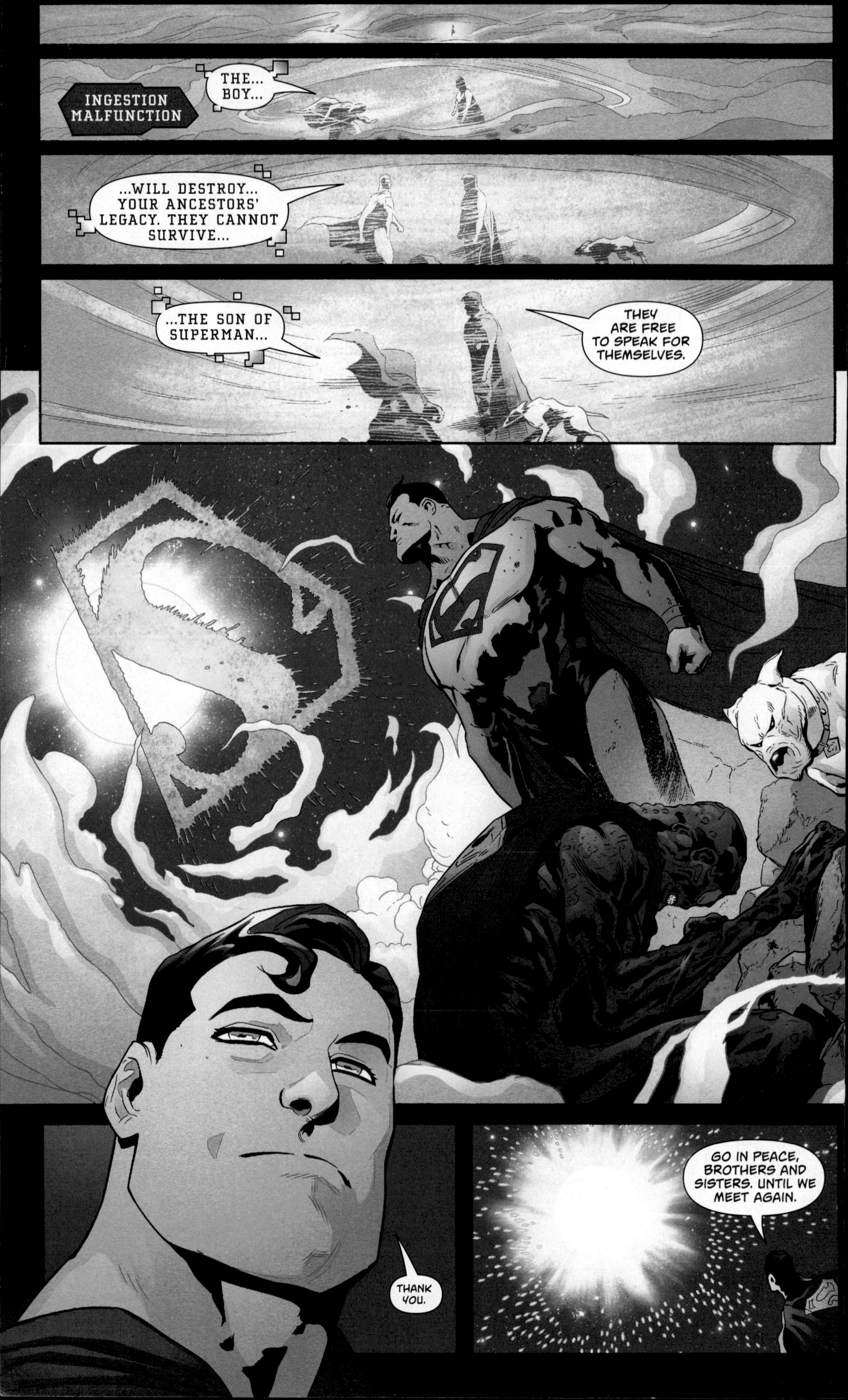
INGESTION MALFUNCTION
THE... BOY...
...WILL DESTROY... YOUR ANCESTORS' LEGACY. THEY CANNOT SURVIVE...
...THE SON OF SUPERMAN...
THEY ARE FREE TO SPEAK FOR THEMSELVES.
THANK YOU.
GO IN PEACE, BROTHERS AND SISTERS. UNTIL WE MEET AGAIN.

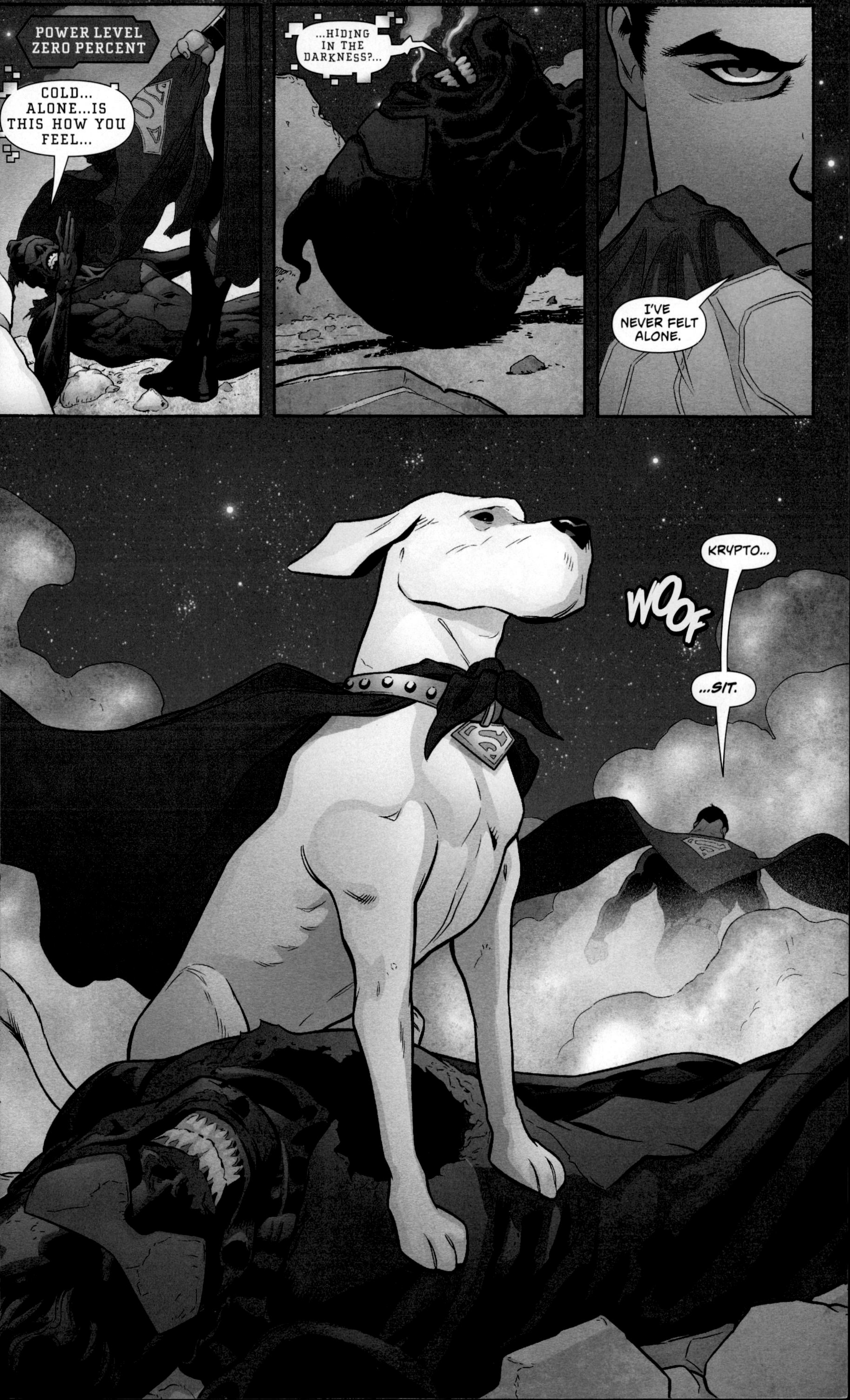
POWER LEVEL ZERO PERCENT
COLD... ALONE...IS THIS HOW YOU FEEL...
...HIDING IN THE DARKNESS?...
I'VE NEVER FELT ALONE.
WOOF
KRYPTO...
...SIT.

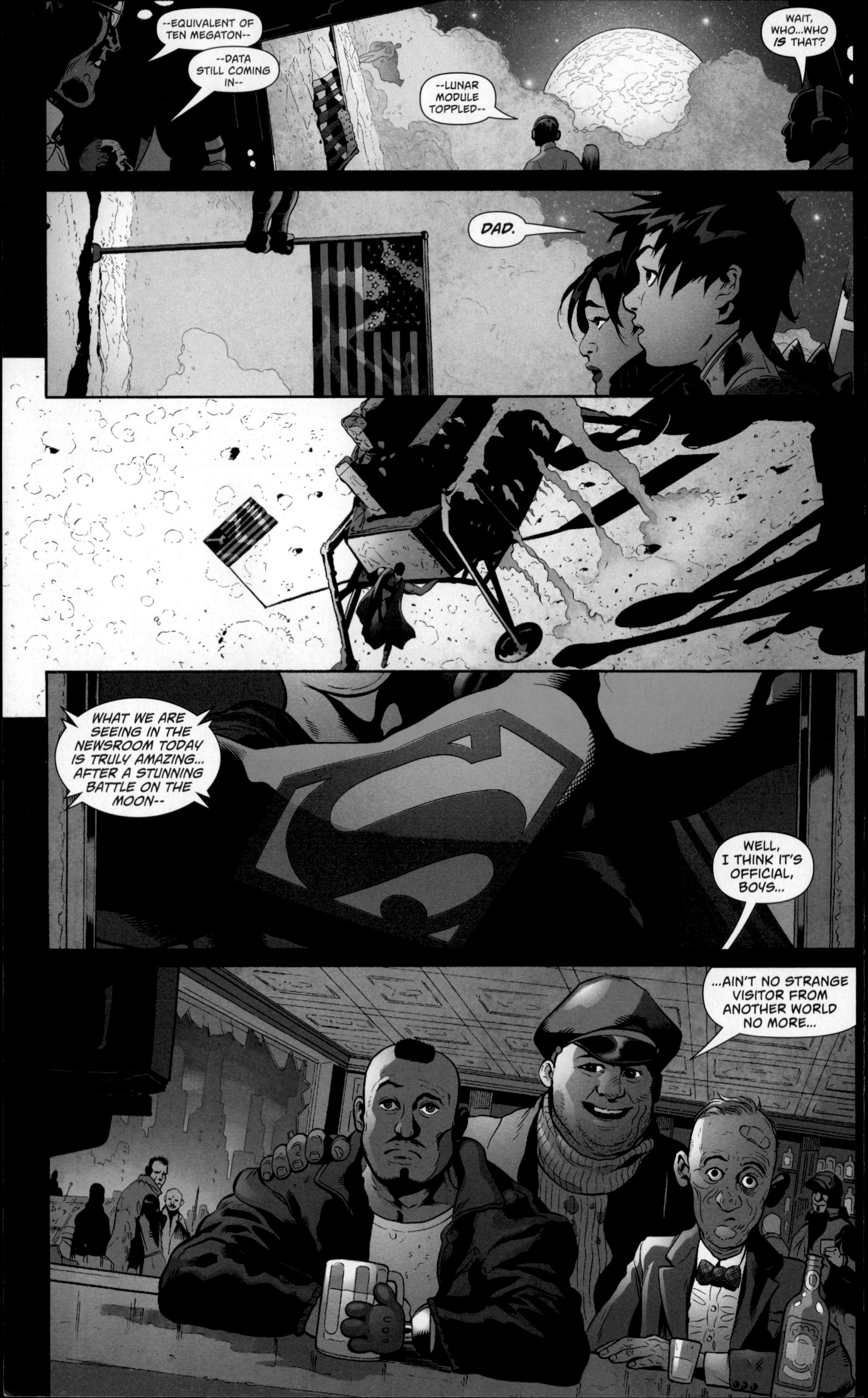
--EQUIVALENT OF TEN MEGATON--
--DATA STILL COMING IN--
--LUNAR MODULE TOPPLED--
WAIT, WHO...WHO IS THAT?
DAD.
WHAT WE ARE SEEING IN THE NEWSROOM TODAY IS TRULY AMAZING... AFTER A STUNNING BATTLE ON THE MOON--
WELL, I THINK IT'S OFFICIAL, BOYS...
...AIN'T NO STRANGE VISITOR FROM ANOTHER WORLD NO MORE...

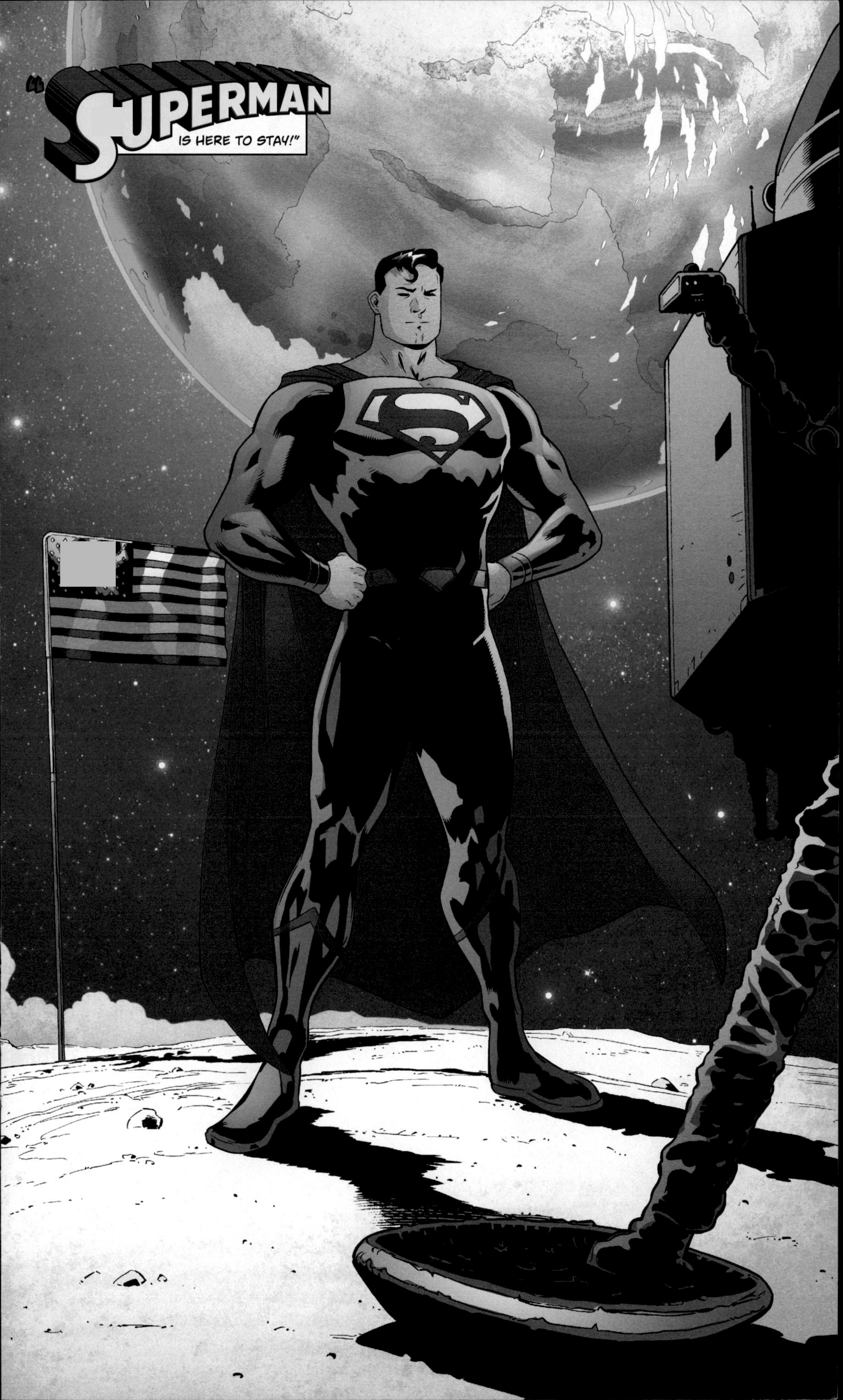
"SUPERMAN
IS HERE TO STAY!"

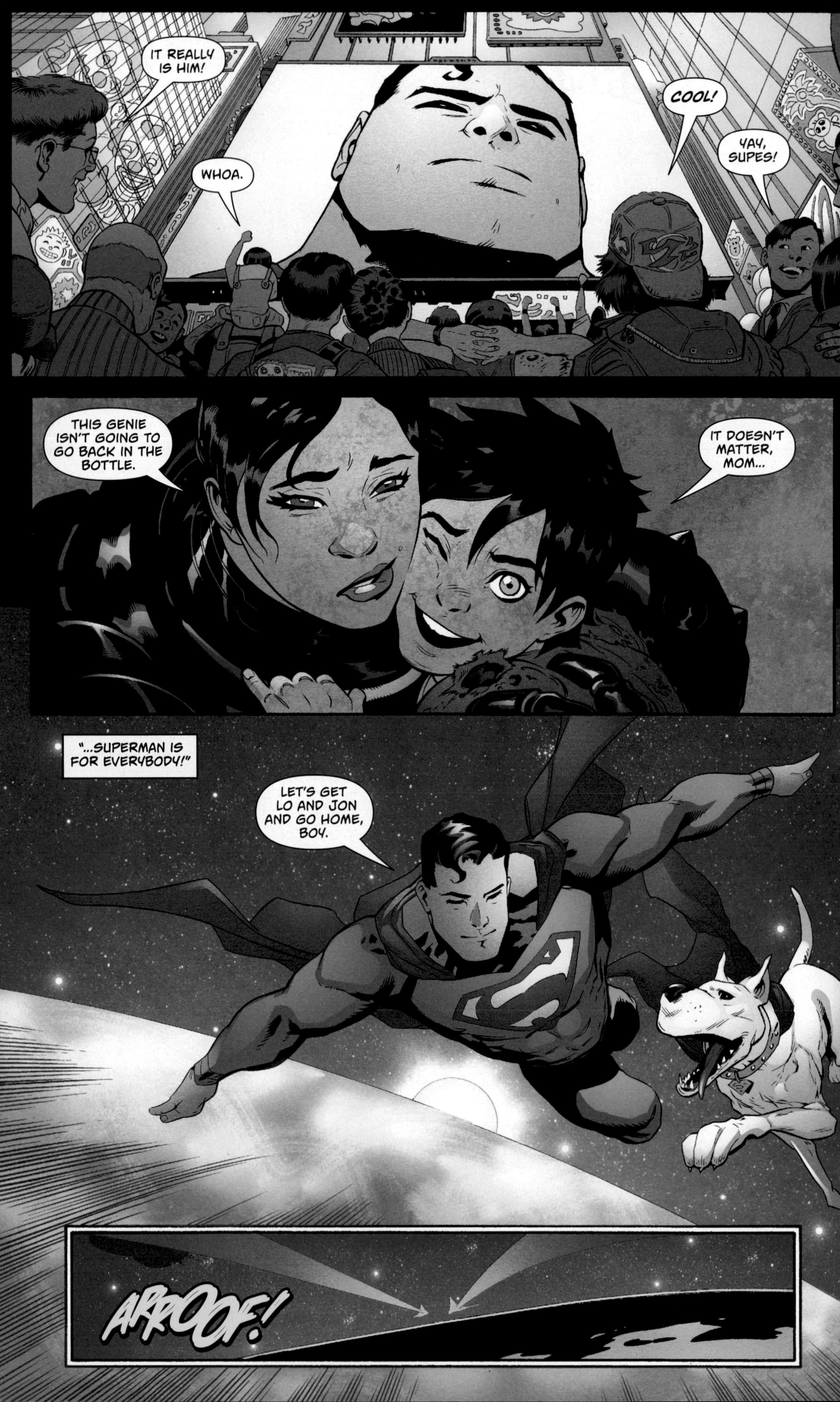

IT REALLY IS HIM!
WHOA.
COOL!
YAY, SUPES!
THIS GENIE ISN'T GOING TO GO BACK IN THE BOTTLE.
IT DOESN'T MATTER, MOM...
"...SUPERMAN IS FOR EVERYBODY!"
LET'S GET LO AND JON AND GO HOME, BOY.
ARROOF!

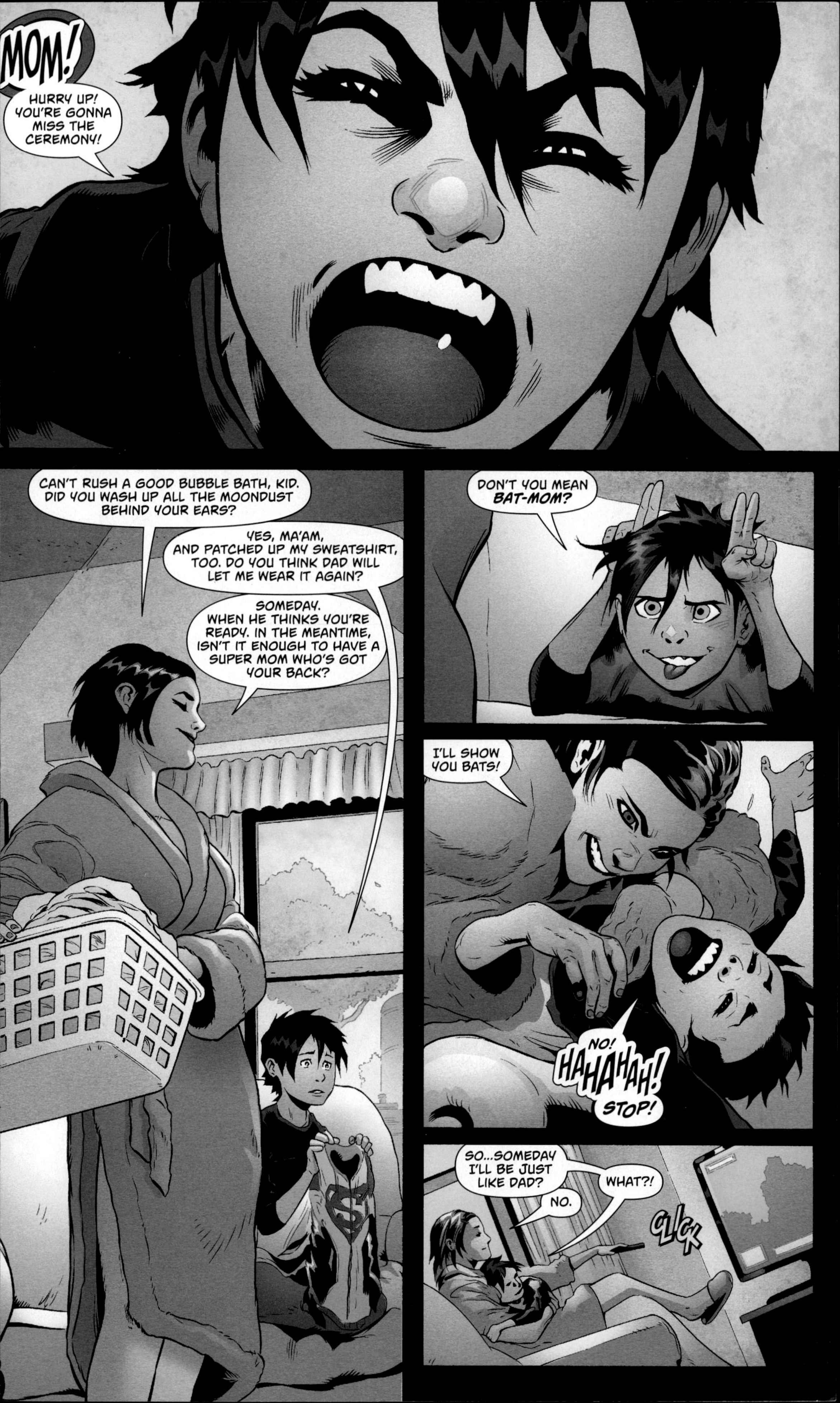
MOM!
HURRY UP! YOU'RE GONNA MISS THE CEREMONY!
CAN'T RUSH A GOOD BUBBLE BATH, KID. DID YOU WASH UP ALL THE MOONDUST BEHIND YOUR EARS?
YES, MA'AM, AND PATCHED UP MY SWEATSHIRT, TOO. DO YOU THINK DAD WILL LET ME WEAR IT AGAIN?
SOMEDAY. WHEN HE THINKS YOU'RE READY. IN THE MEANTIME, ISN'T IT ENOUGH TO HAVE A SUPER MOM WHO'S GOT YOUR BACK?
DON'T YOU MEAN BAT-MOM?
I'LL SHOW YOU BATS!
NO! HAHAHAH! STOP!
SO...SOMEDAY I'LL BE JUST LIKE DAD?
NO.
WHAT?!
CLICK

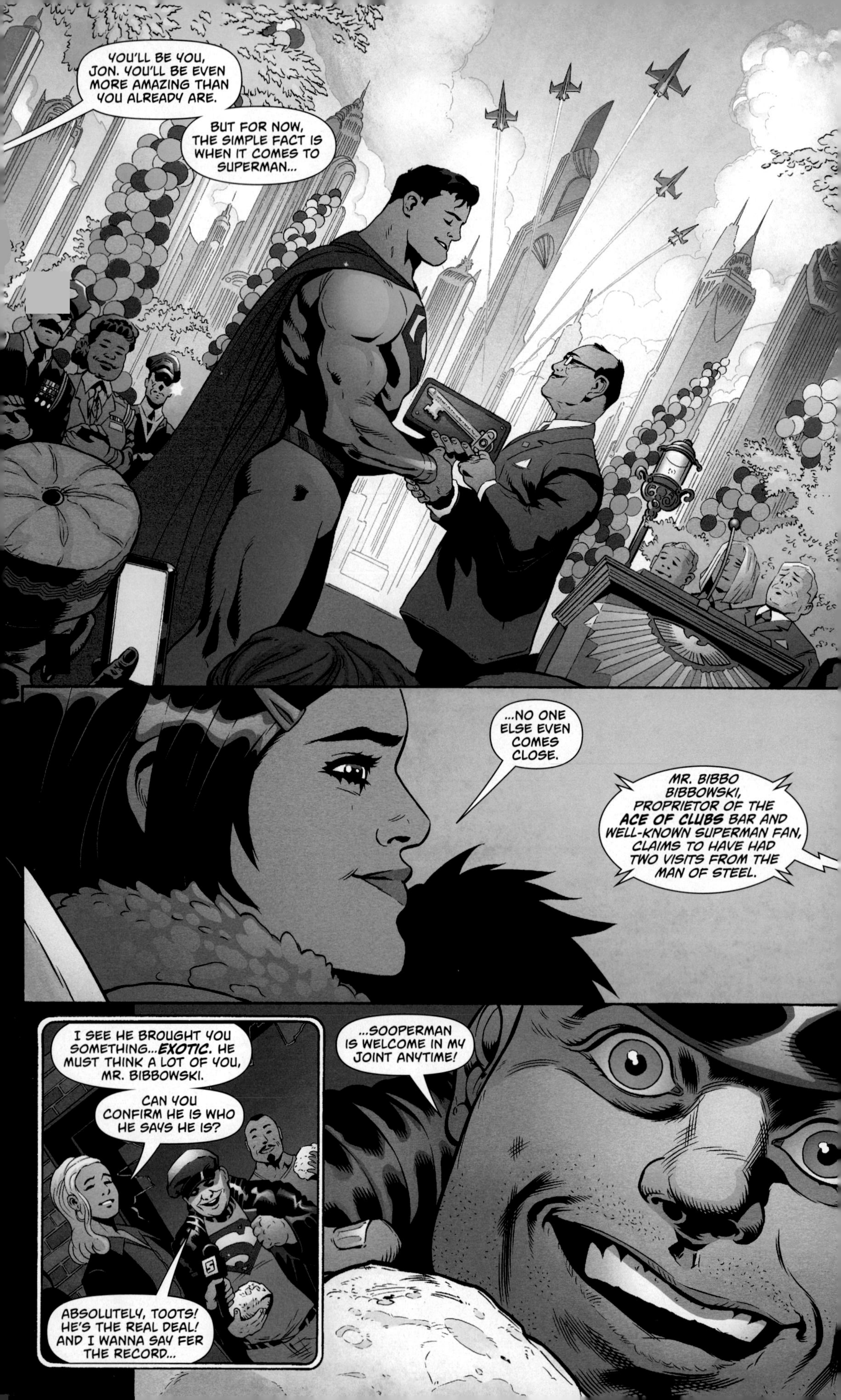

YOU'LL BE YOU, JON. YOU'LL BE EVEN MORE AMAZING THAN YOU ALREADY ARE.
BUT FOR NOW, THE SIMPLE FACT IS WHEN IT COMES TO SUPERMAN...
...NO ONE ELSE EVEN COMES CLOSE.
MR. BIBBO BIBBOWSKI, PROPRIETOR OF THE ACE OF CLUBS BAR AND WELL-KNOWN SUPERMAN FAN, CLAIMS TO HAVE HAD TWO VISITS FROM THE MAN OF STEEL.
I SEE HE BROUGHT YOU SOMETHING...EXOTIC. HE MUST THINK A LOT OF YOU, MR. BIBBOWSKI.
CAN YOU CONFIRM HE IS WHO HE SAYS HE IS?
ABSOLUTELY, TOOTS! HE'S THE REAL DEAL! AND I WANNA SAY FER THE RECORD...
...SOOPERMAN IS WELCOME IN MY JOINT ANYTIME!

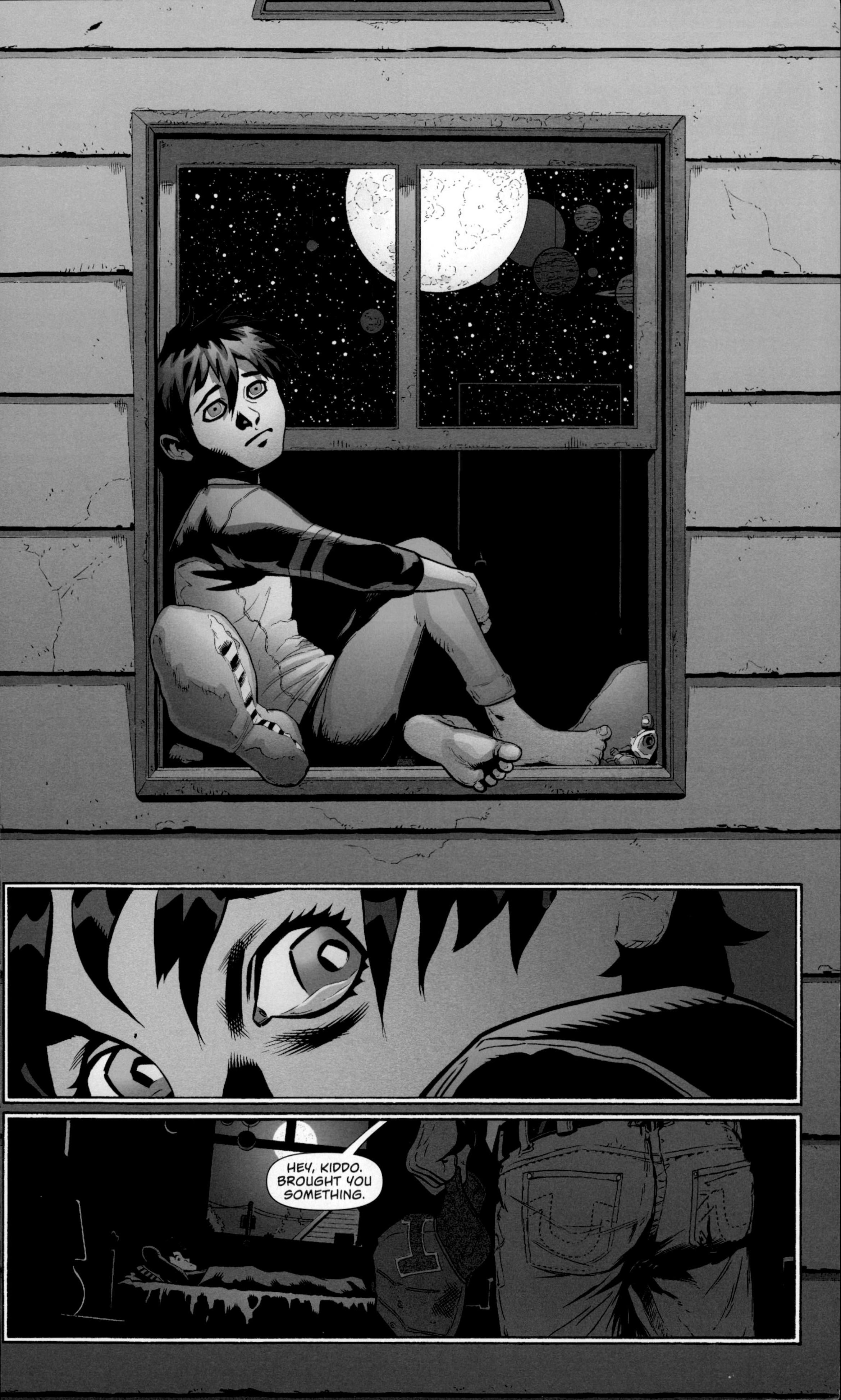
HEY, KIDDO. BROUGHT YOU SOMETHING.

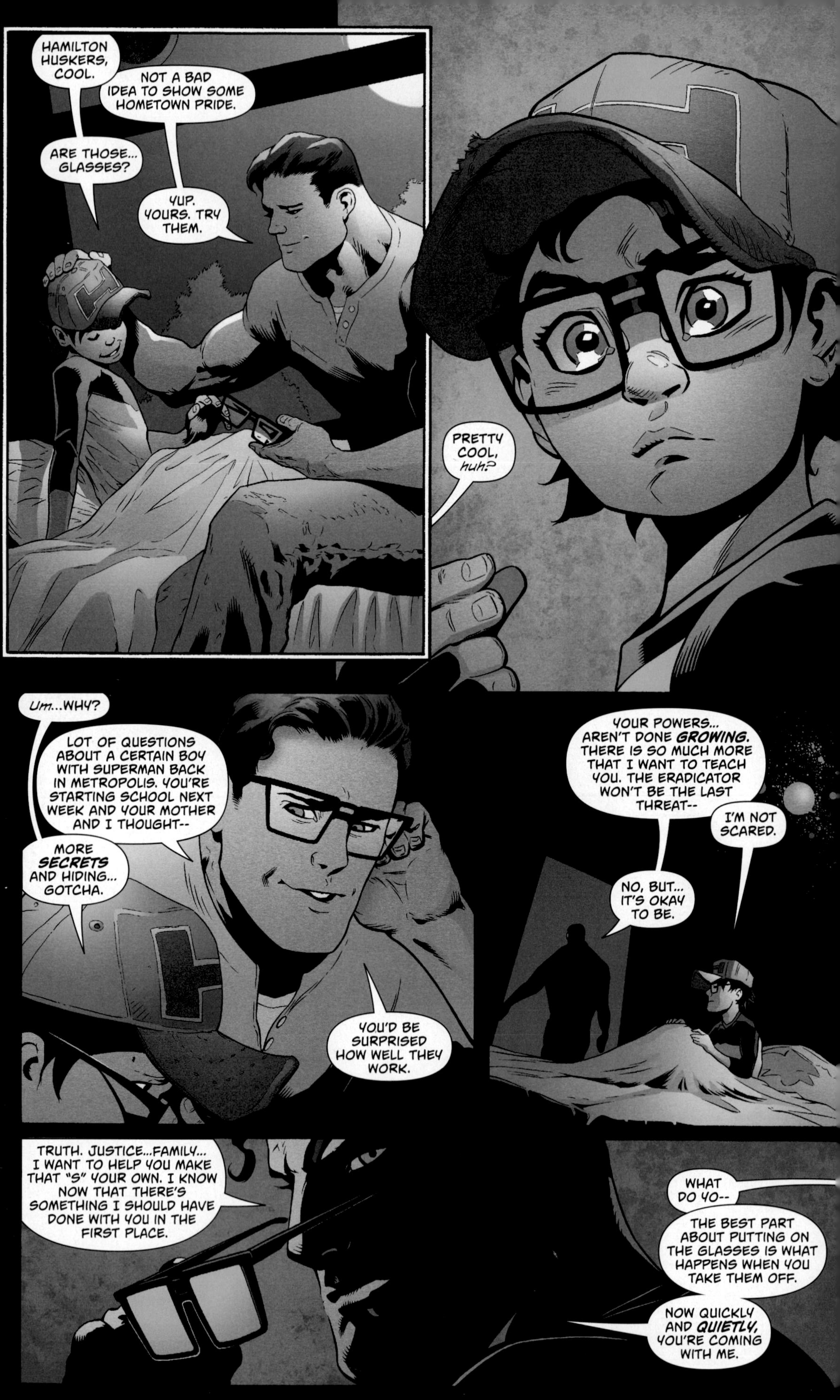
HAMILTON HUSKERS, COOL.
NOT A BAD IDEA TO SHOW SOME HOMETOWN PRIDE.
ARE THOSE... GLASSES?
YUP. YOURS. TRY THEM.
PRETTY COOL, *huh?*
Um...WHY?
LOT OF QUESTIONS ABOUT A CERTAIN BOY WITH SUPERMAN BACK IN METROPOLIS. YOU'RE STARTING SCHOOL NEXT WEEK AND YOUR MOTHER AND I THOUGHT--
MORE **SECRETS** AND HIDING... GOTCHA.
YOU'D BE SURPRISED HOW WELL THEY WORK.
YOUR POWERS... AREN'T DONE **GROWING**. THERE IS SO MUCH MORE THAT I WANT TO TEACH YOU. THE ERADICATOR WON'T BE THE LAST THREAT--
I'M NOT SCARED.
NO, BUT... IT'S OKAY TO BE.
TRUTH. JUSTICE...FAMILY... I WANT TO HELP YOU MAKE THAT "S" YOUR OWN. I KNOW NOW THAT THERE'S SOMETHING I SHOULD HAVE DONE WITH YOU IN THE FIRST PLACE.
WHAT DO YO--
THE BEST PART ABOUT PUTTING ON THE GLASSES IS WHAT HAPPENS WHEN YOU TAKE THEM OFF.
NOW QUICKLY AND ***QUIETLY,*** YOU'RE COMING WITH ME.

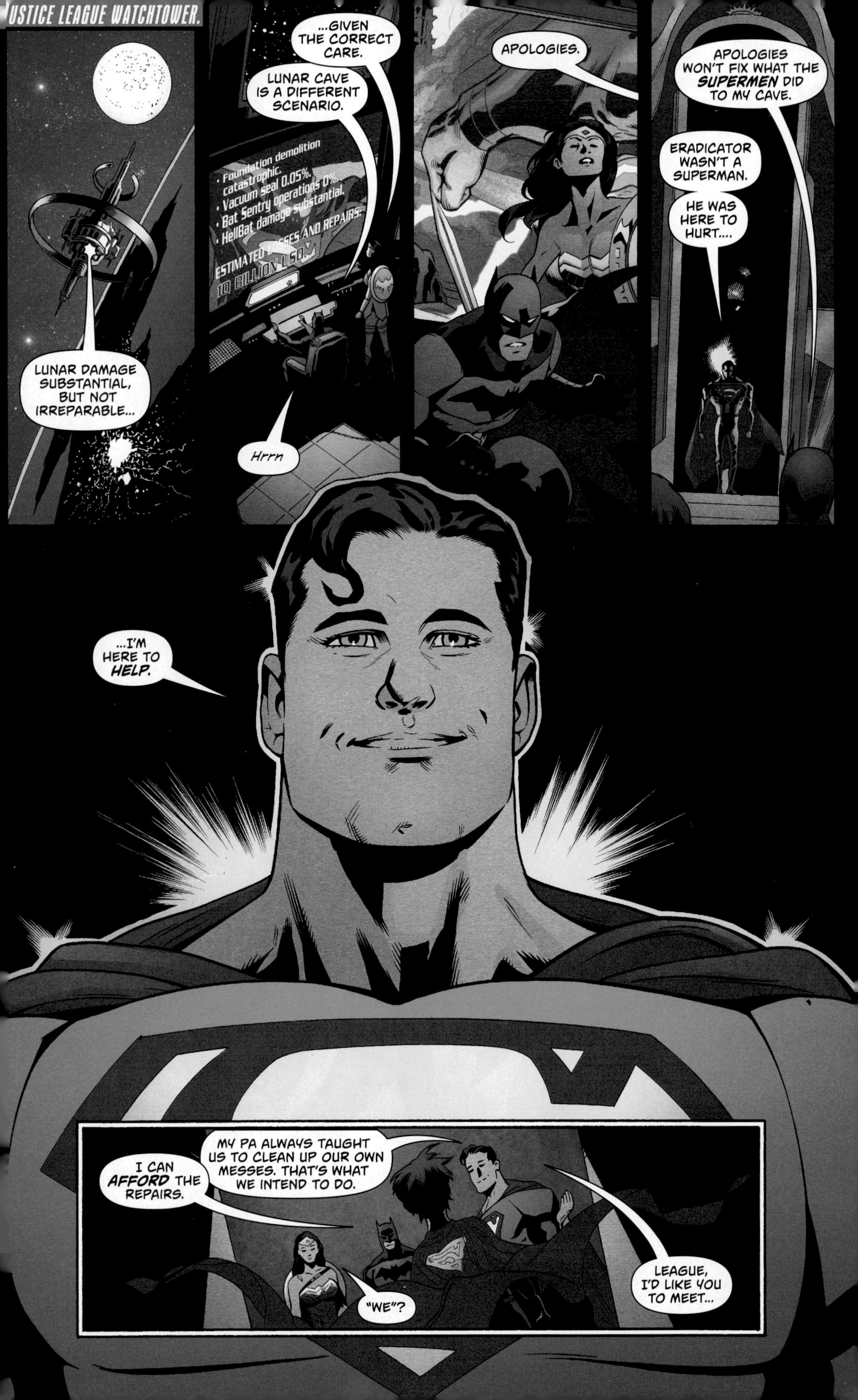
USTICE LEAGUE WATCHTOWER.
LUNAR DAMAGE SUBSTANTIAL, BUT NOT IRREPARABLE...
...GIVEN THE CORRECT CARE.
LUNAR CAVE IS A DIFFERENT SCENARIO.
• Foundation demolition catastrophic.
• Vacuum seal 0.05%.
• Bat Sentry operations 0%.
• HellBat damage substantial.
• ESTIMATED LOSSES AND REPAIRS:
10 BILLION USD.
Hrrn
APOLOGIES.
APOLOGIES WON'T FIX WHAT THE SUPERMEN DID TO MY CAVE.
ERADICATOR WASN'T A SUPERMAN.
HE WAS HERE TO HURT....
...I'M HERE TO HELP.
I CAN AFFORD THE REPAIRS.
MY PA ALWAYS TAUGHT US TO CLEAN UP OUR OWN MESSES. THAT'S WHAT WE INTEND TO DO.
"WE"?
LEAGUE, I'D LIKE YOU TO MEET...

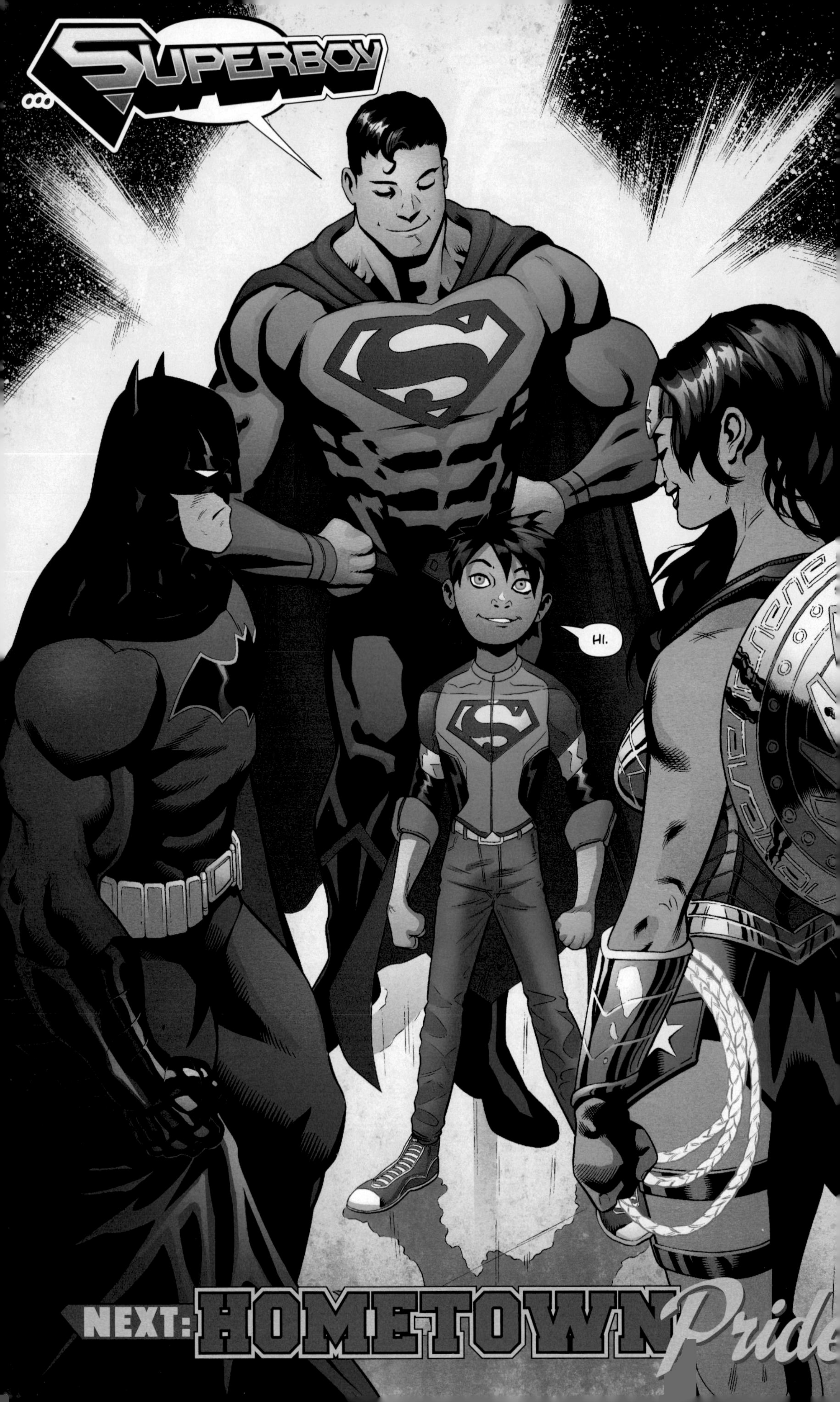
...SUPERBOY
HI.
NEXT: HOMETOWN Pride

Variant cover art for SUPERMAN: REBIRTH #1 by Andy Park

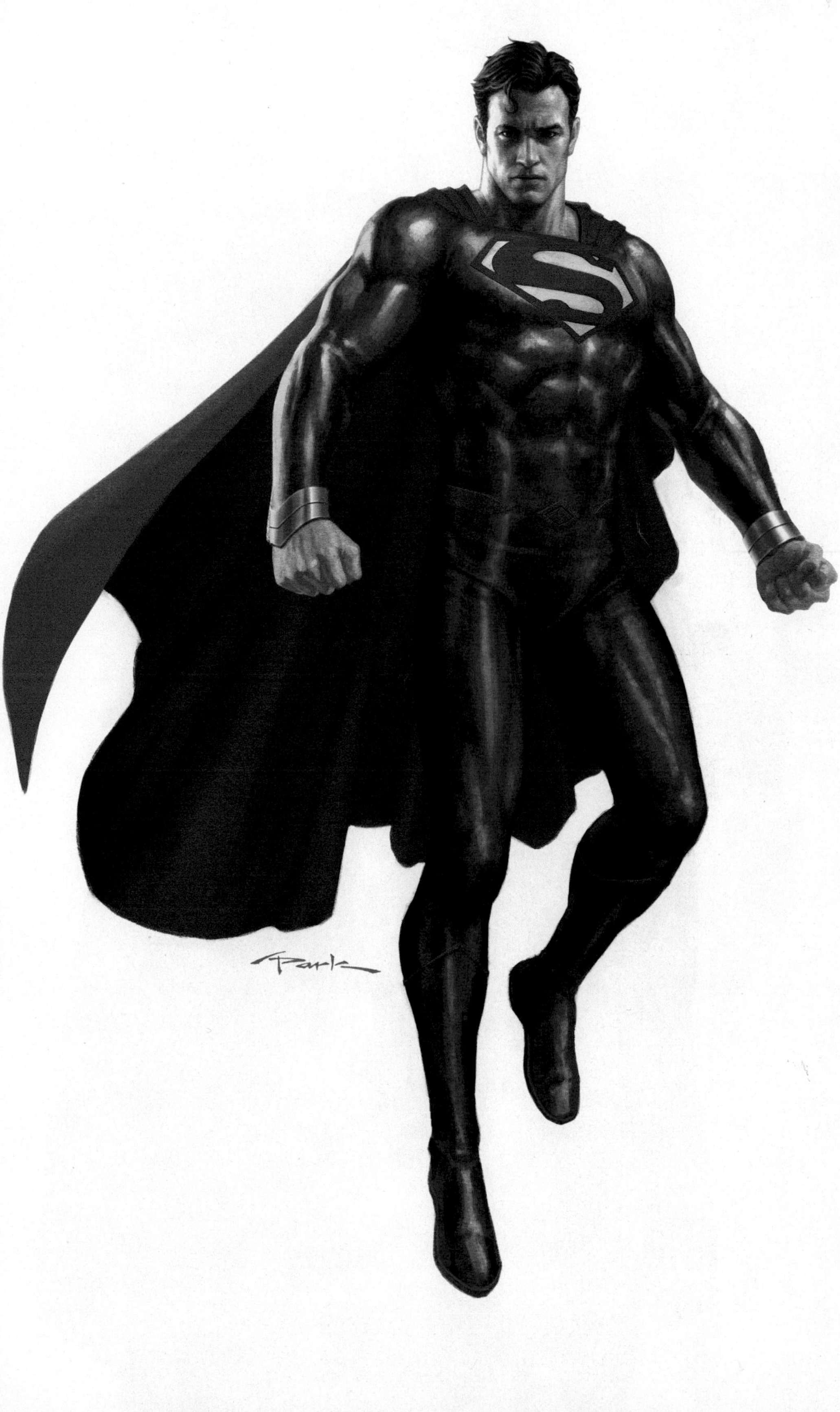
Park

Variant cover art for SUPERMAN #1 by Kenneth Rocafort

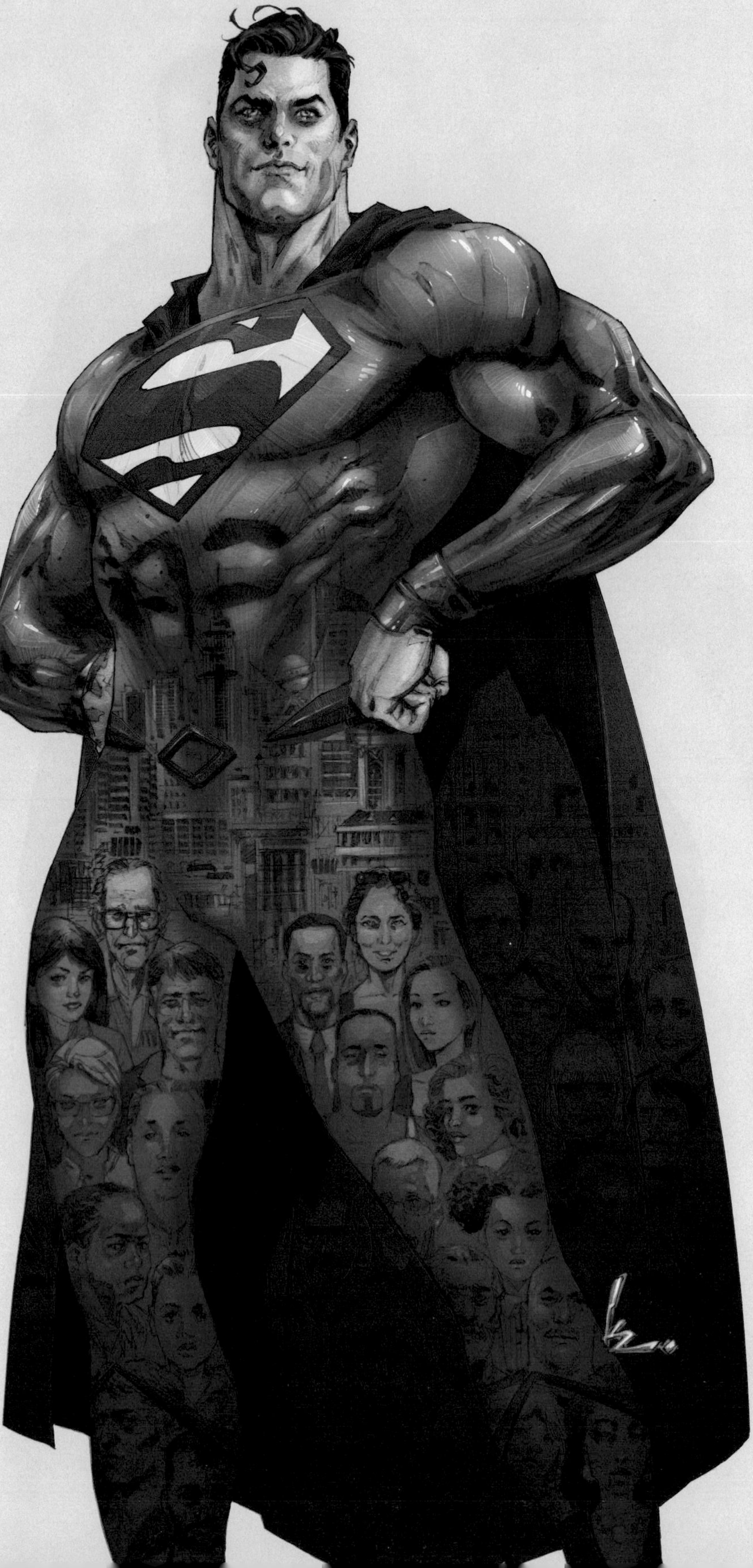

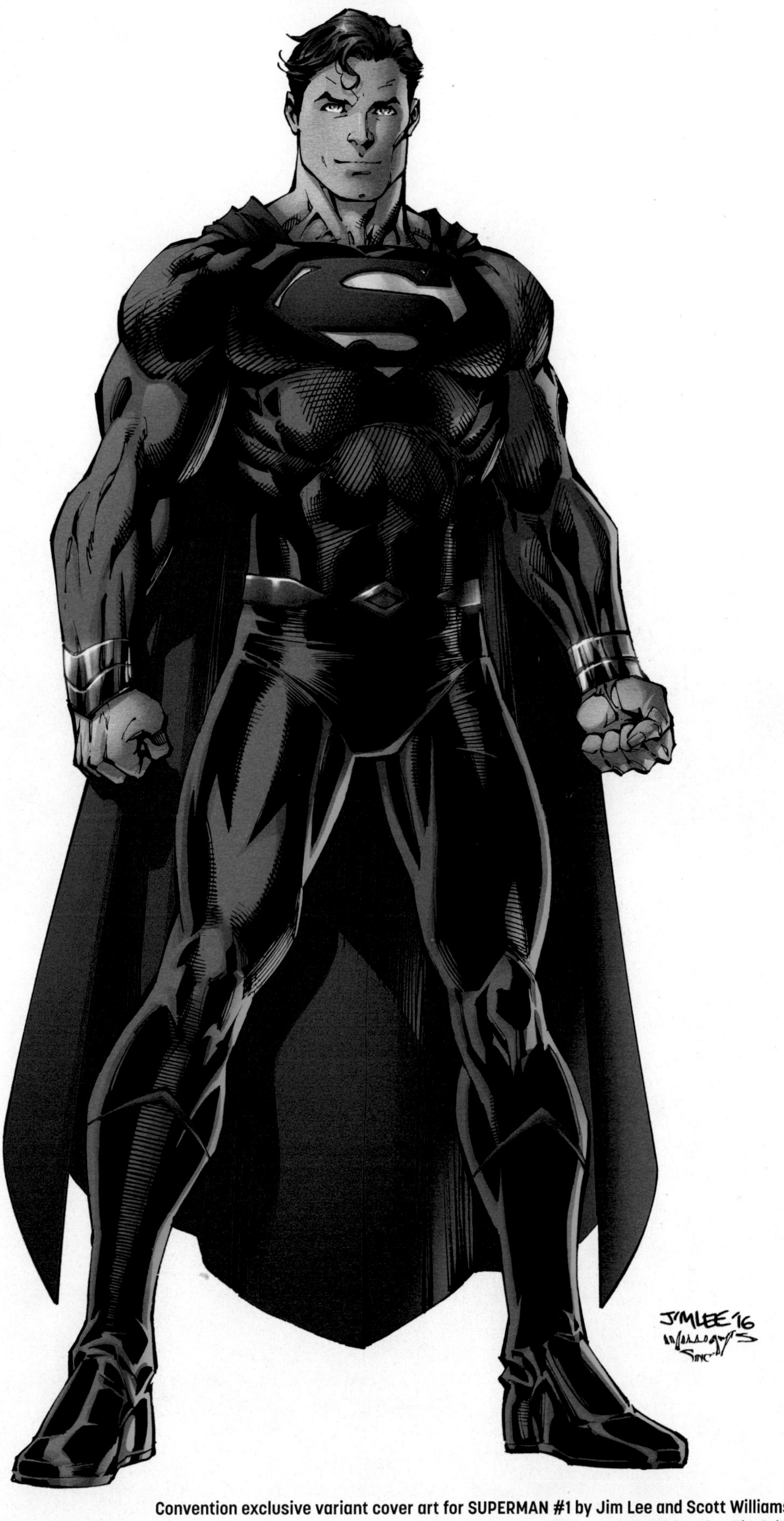
JIMLEE '16

Convention exclusive variant cover art for SUPERMAN #1 by Jim Lee and Scott Williams
(color by Alex Sinclair)

Variant cover art for SUPERMAN #2
by Kenneth Rocafort

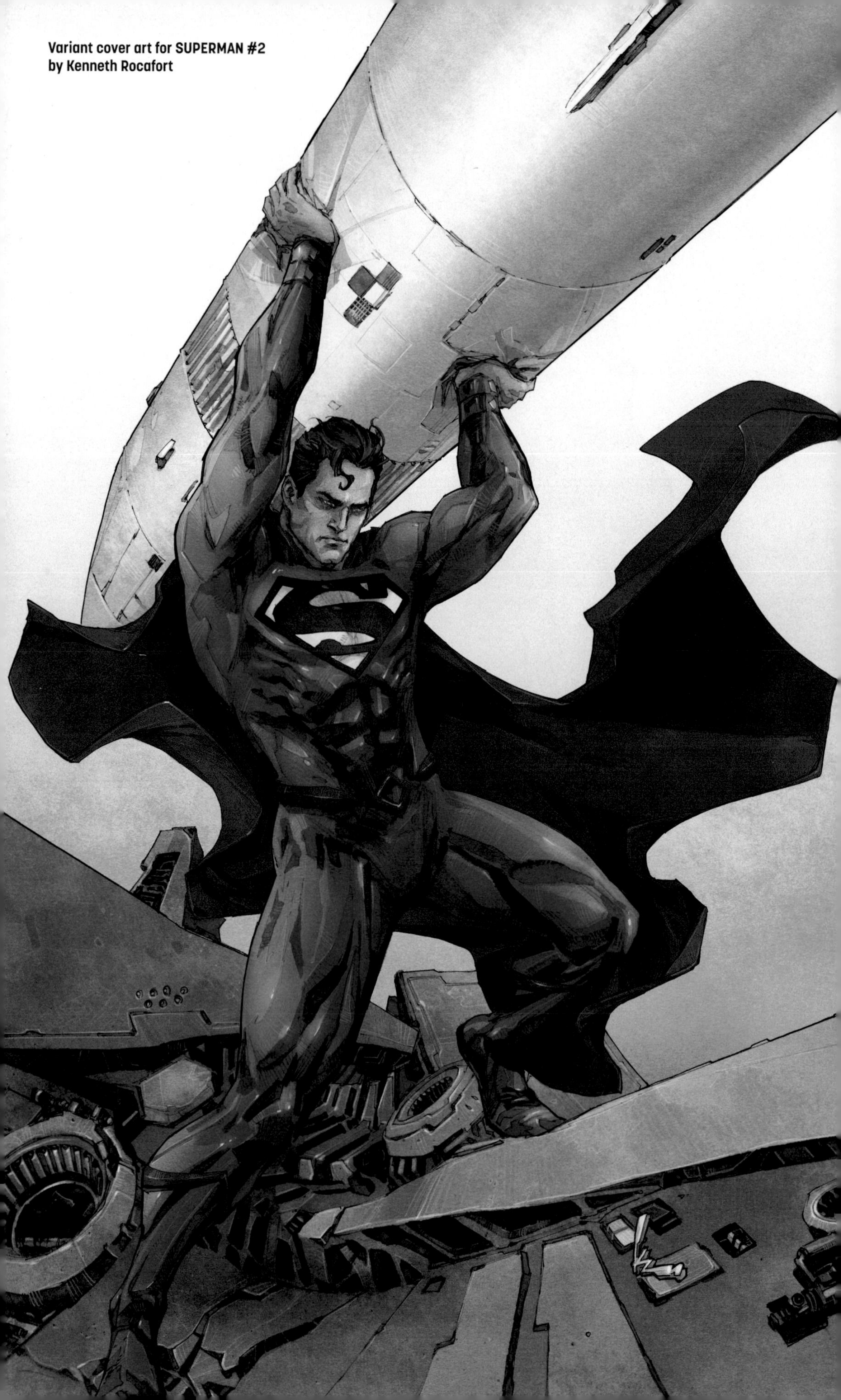

Variant cover art for SUPERMAN #3 by Kenneth Rocafort

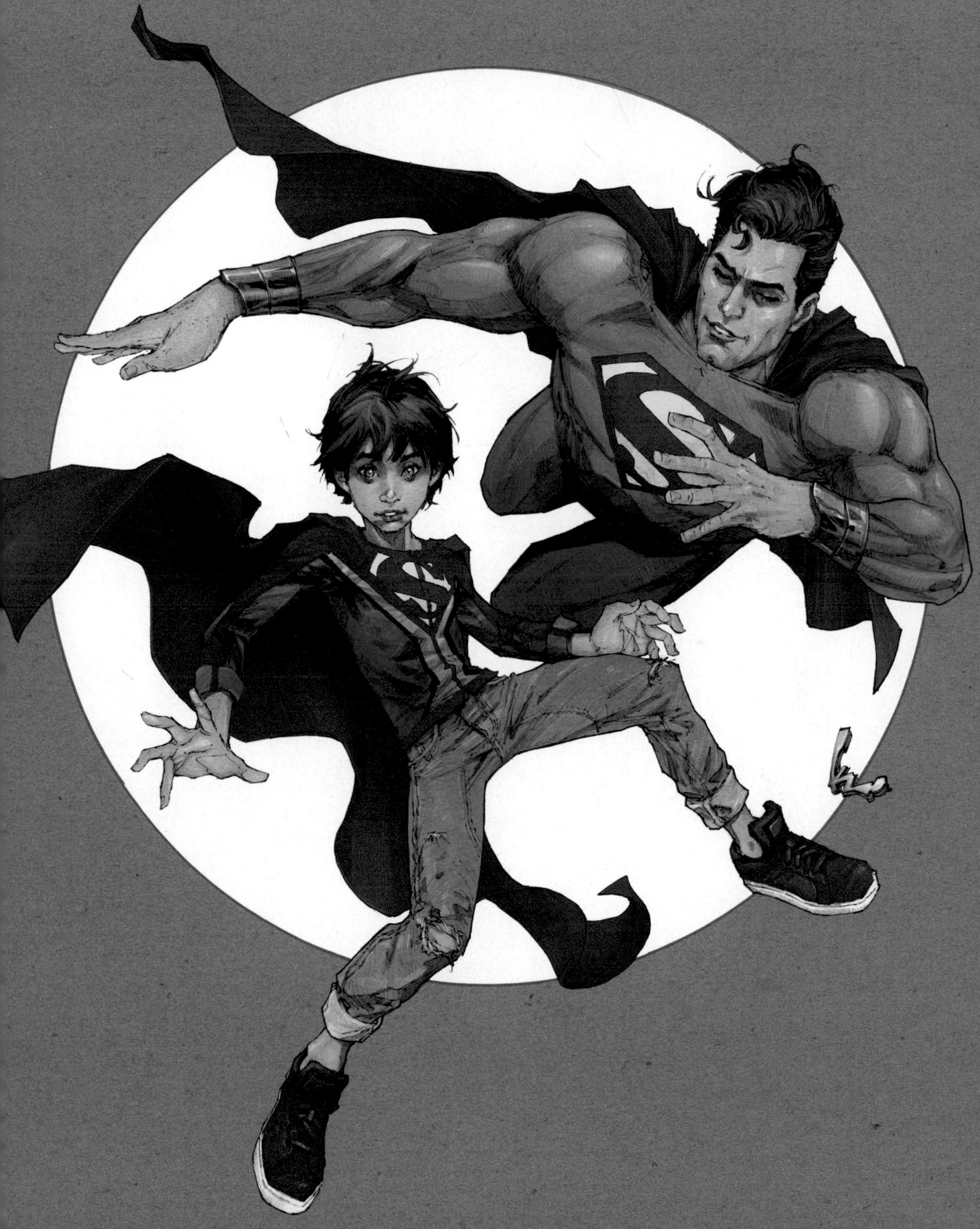

Variant cover art for SUPERMAN #4 by Kenneth Rocafort

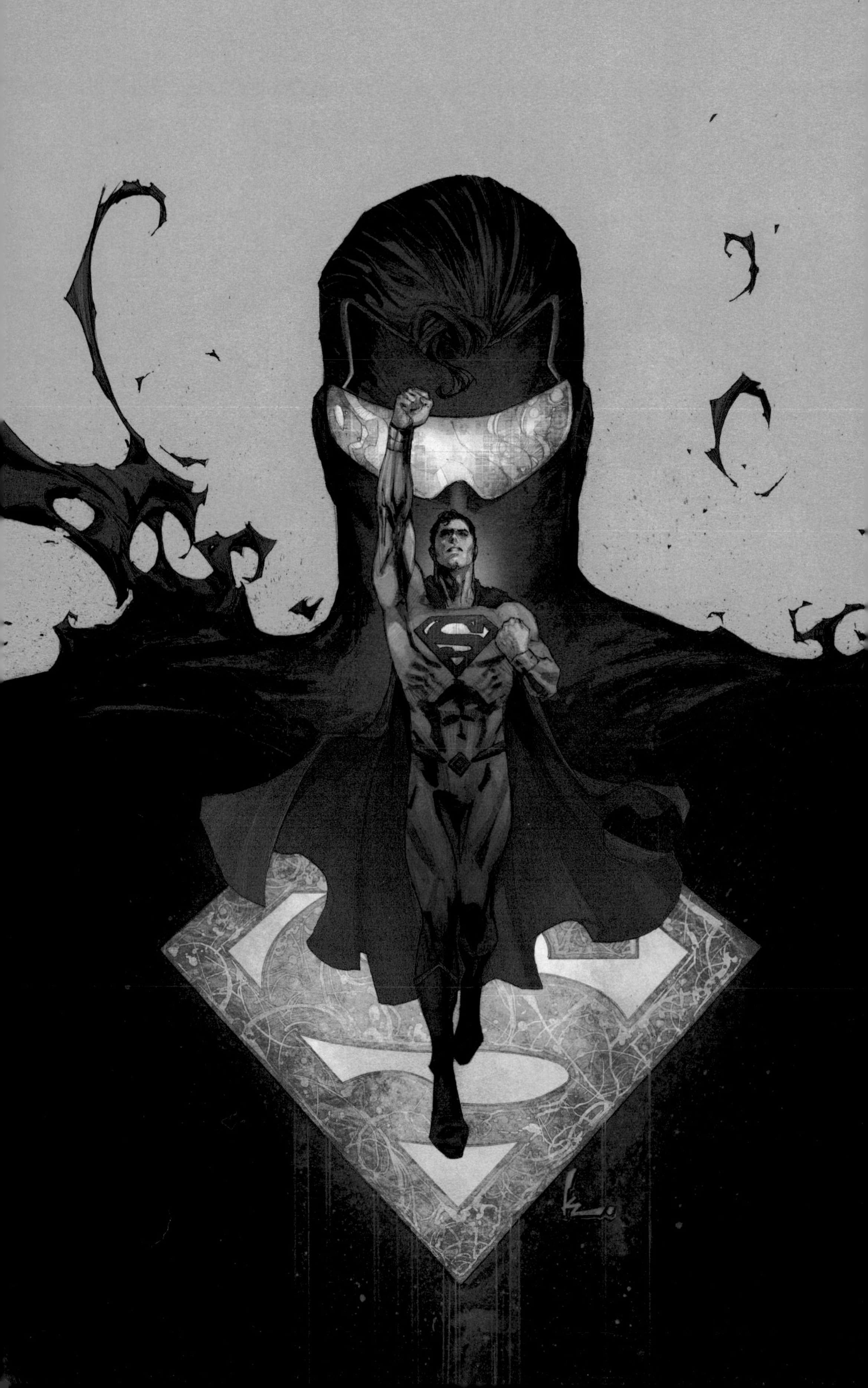

Variant cover art for SUPERMAN #5 by Kenneth Rocafort

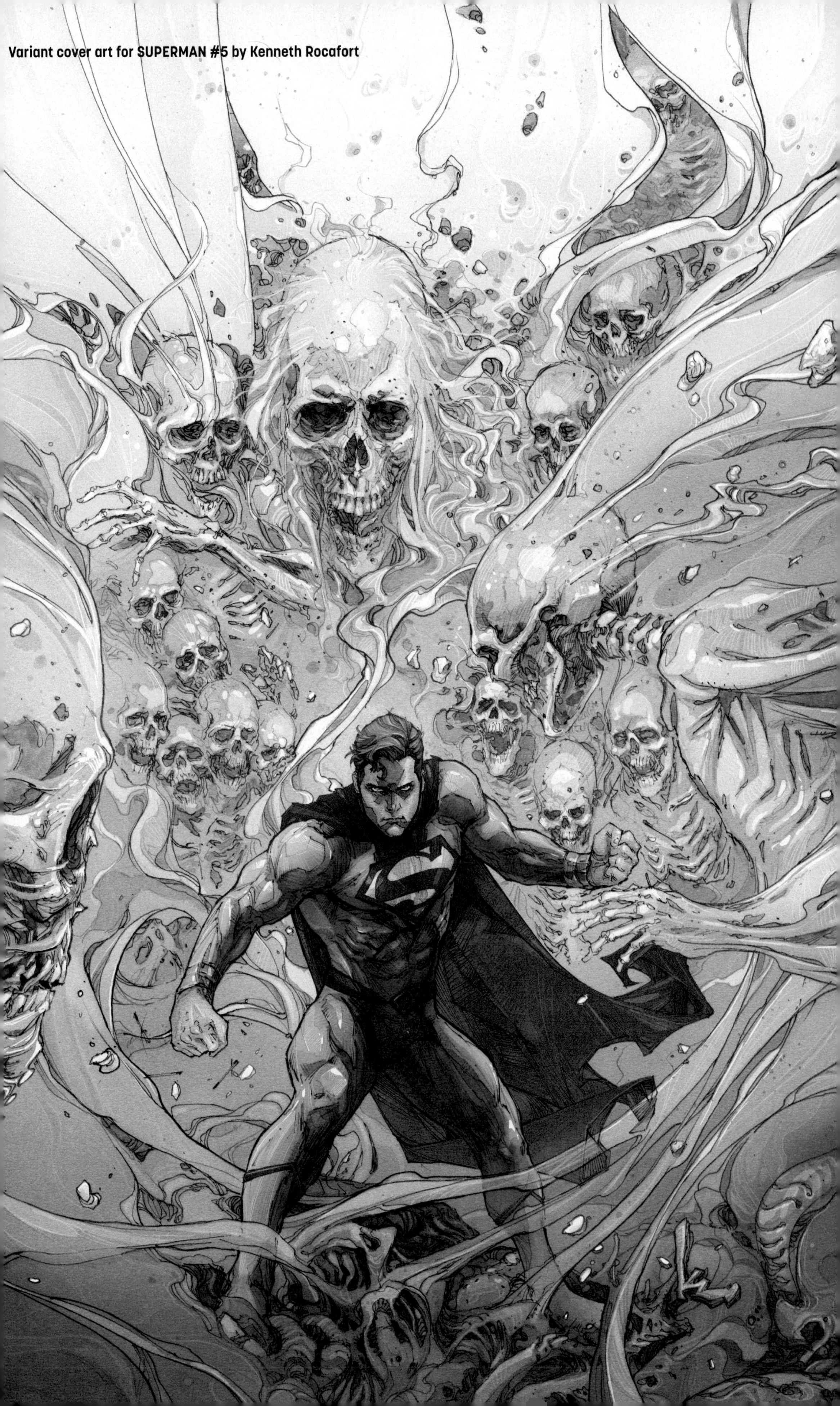

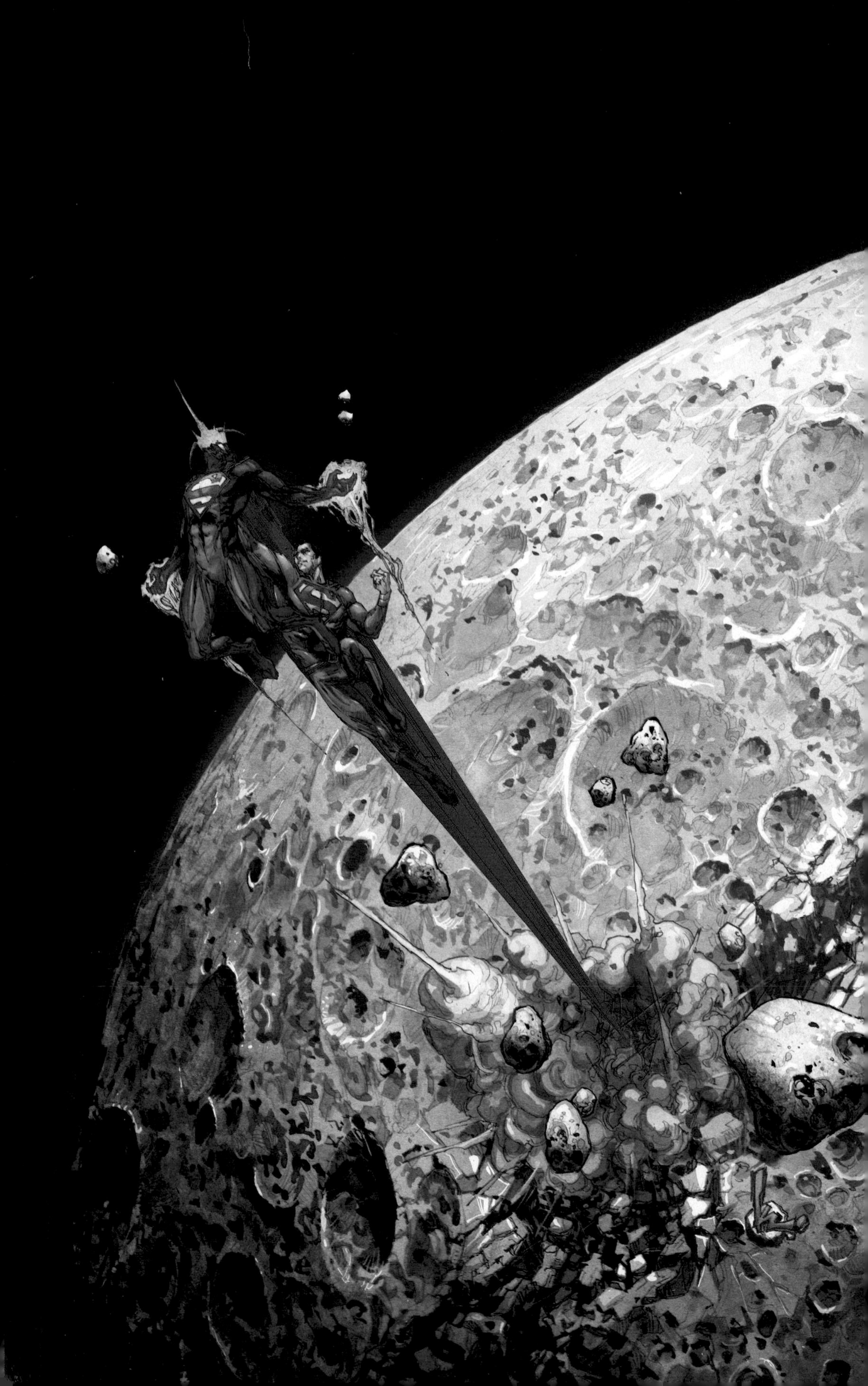

Variant cover art for SUPERMAN #6 by Kenneth Rocafort

SUPERMAN

SKETCHBOOK

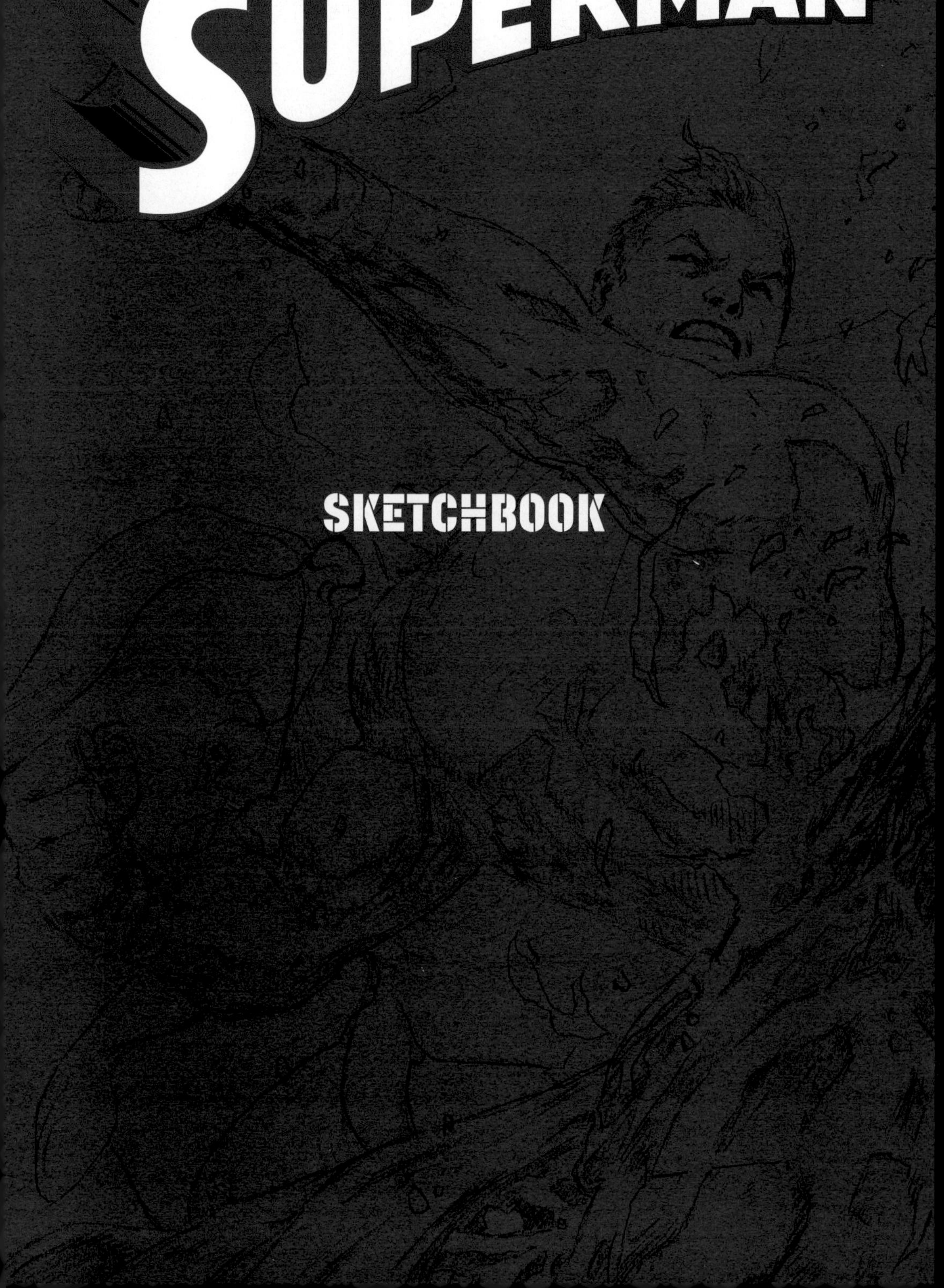

FATHER'S DAY

Script excerpts from **Peter J. Tomasi** and **Patrick Gleason**
and preliminary art from **Patrick Gleason**

SUPERMAN #1c

PAGES 2 and 3

Double page spread with main image across both pages and 5 panels across the bottom.

The Sun's just coming up. Clark, hands stuffed in his pockets, stands at the graves of Ma and Pa Kent in the Smallville Cemetery. If we can see it, there's a little less grass in the middle area between Ma and Pa's graves due to New 52 Clark being buried there.

No one's around. It's got a lonely feel but with the Sun coming up let's go for a new day feel too. Mid-Spring. There is a season, turn, turn, turn. Trees and grass are green signifying life and hope springs eternal. Clark should have a melancholy look on his face as everything that's happened has now led to this point in his life and his family's.

CLARK CAP: I'm Superman.

CLARK CAP: And I can do most anything.

CLARK CAP: Except of course raise the dead.

panel 2

Angle from behind Clark looking down at the graves where we now can see the slight difference in the shorter length of grass between Ma and Pa's stones.

CLARK CAP: But I'm glad I was able to help Lana honor your last wish and be buried here secretly between your folks instead of under that Metropolis behemoth.

panel 3

Clark now on one knee between the graves, ONE HAND FIRMLY on the grass.

CLARK CAP: Anyway...I'm here to say goodbye, Clark.

CLARK CAP: I know now you're not coming back.

CLARK CAP: Sleep well...brother.

panel 4

Angle on Clark pulling away his hand from the grass and LEAVING BEHIND A SUBTLE THIN BLUE OUTLINE OF ENERGY.

panel 5

Angle on Clark as he now stands but sees there's NO sign of the energy outline.

CLARK CAP: We both know what comes next – and that's keeping people safe...

CLARK CAP: ...with everything that's happened, I'm not sure I can do this the way I used to...the way we used to.

panel 6

Angle from behind the graves looking at Clark framed between them.
There's a resignation to his face, subtle, like a soldier getting on with it.

CLARK CAP: I think you'd be happy to know I put the black suit aside—we've been at half mast long enough.

CLARK CAP: The world needs to see again that there's a Superman looking out for them.

CLARK CAP: You may not be here in body, but you sure are in spirit.

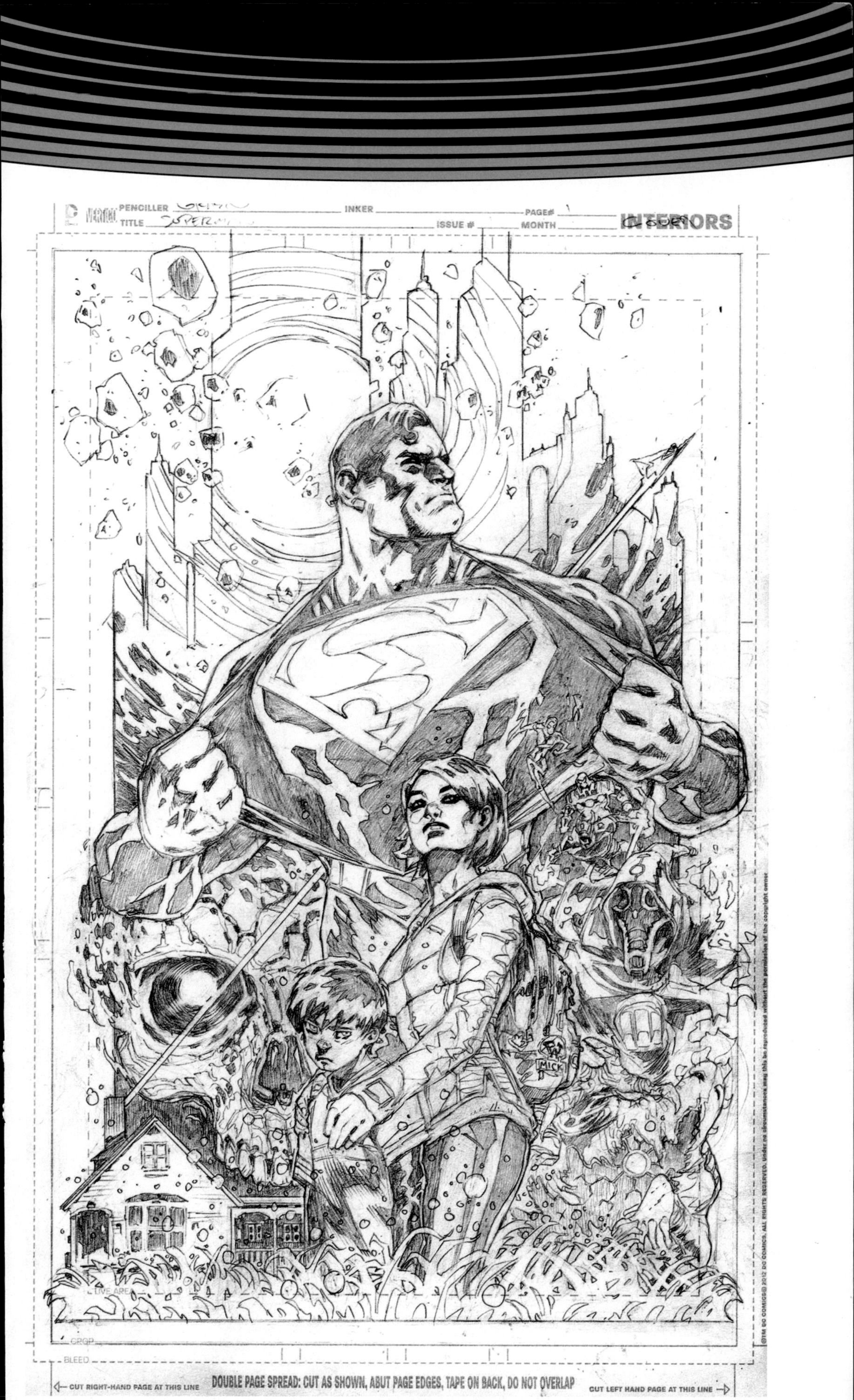

PENCILLER
INKER
PAGE#
TITLE
ISSUE #
MONTH
INTERIORS
MICK
LIVE AREA
CROP
BLEED
CUT RIGHT-HAND PAGE AT THIS LINE
DOUBLE PAGE SPREAD: CUT AS SHOWN, ABUT PAGE EDGES, TAPE ON BACK, DO NOT OVERLAP
CUT LEFT HAND PAGE AT THIS LINE

PAGE 8

panel 1

Angle close on JONATHAN KENT'S EYES. The reflection of flames in them. We're so close to his eyes they are all we see at the moment. We can't read any emotion just yet.

panel 2

Biggest on page. CLARK, a few feet off the ground, emerges quickly from the family barn that happens to be engulfed in fire thanks to a lightning strike we'll learn about. His flannel shirt and baseball cap are burning away to reveal the "S" symbol underneath as we see him holding and shielding a helpless BABY COLT.

panel 3

Angle close on Jonathan's full face, the glow of the fire reflecting off it.
We can see he looks calm and proud as he's watched his father save all the animals in the barn.

JON CAP: My dad is Superman.

panel 4

Angle on Jonathan in his pajamas as RANGER passes holding a chicken softly in his mouth and LOIS in a t-shirt and pajama bottoms stand several yards away, each of them holding the reins of a horse while also doing their best to keep the animals Clark's already saved close together. Establish a CAT that sticks close to Lois's feet.

LOIS: That's the last flannel shirt you're ever getting for Christmas, Clark.

PAGE 9

panel 1

Morning. Angle close on THE CAT clawing at the door, wanting to go out. Lois's hand is petting its back.

LOIS: Patience, Goldie. More than enough mice out there.

CAT: MEOWWMEOWW

panel 2

Angle on Lois opening the door to let the Cat out just as Jon, cereal bar in hand, goes leaping past raring to get started helping his dad fix the barn.

panel 3

Angle on Jon, hammer in hand, grabbing some nails, as he's now with Clark who is already at work starting to fix the barn, tossing the charred wood into a pile. We can see that about 50% was burnt. There's already wooden posts with wires encircling the previously saved animals outside as they wait for a new barn.

JON: Promise not to start without me?

CLARK: Promise to keep your powers holstered when I'm not around?

JON: Yessir.

SHORT
PONYTA

FABRIC
ACTIVE
WEAR

- TIGHT!
No Pack
On b.

SNEAKERS

CLARK: You got a deal. Now go fill the corn harvester. Ran out of gas yesterday.

panel 4

Angle on Jon now in the field far from the house and barn, he's tilting a ten gallon plastic gas can into the corn Harvester's tank hole. The field should be partially harvested.

panel 5

Closer, as we see LOIS'S CAT go bounding by Jon's feet chasing a mouse.

JON: Go get him, Goldie -- keep him out of mom's --

panel 6

Angle looking down at Jon as the SHADOW OF AN EAGLE falls across him as he looks up at us, concern on his face as he realizes...

JON: Oh no...

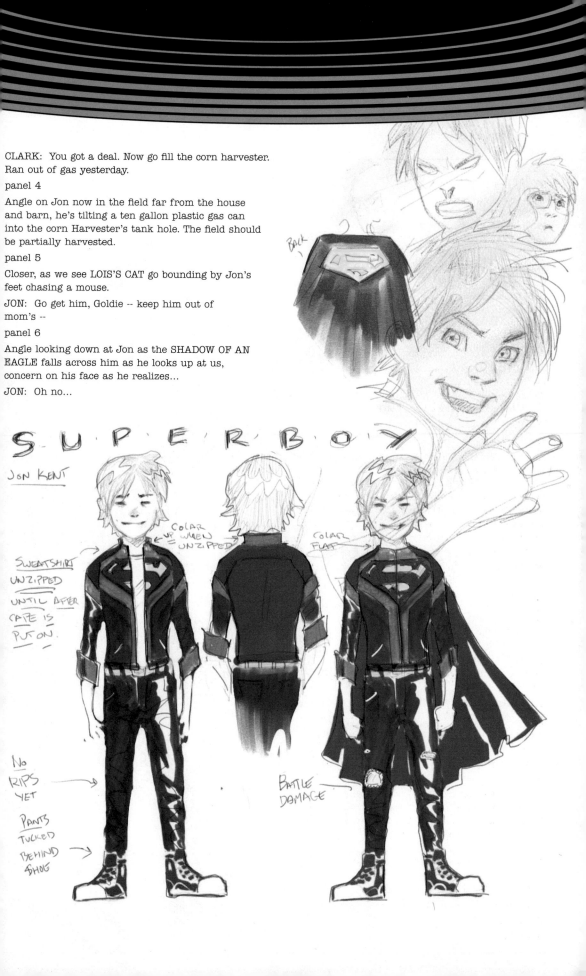

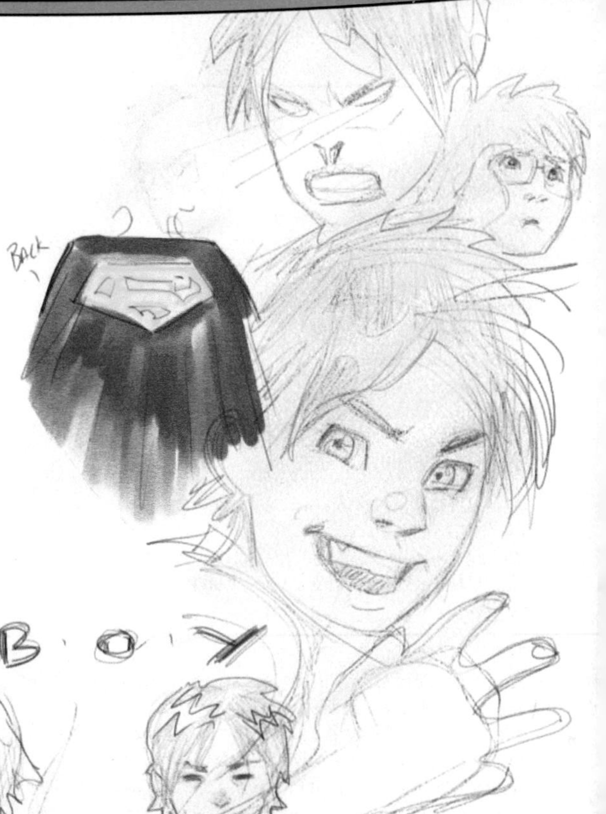
BACK

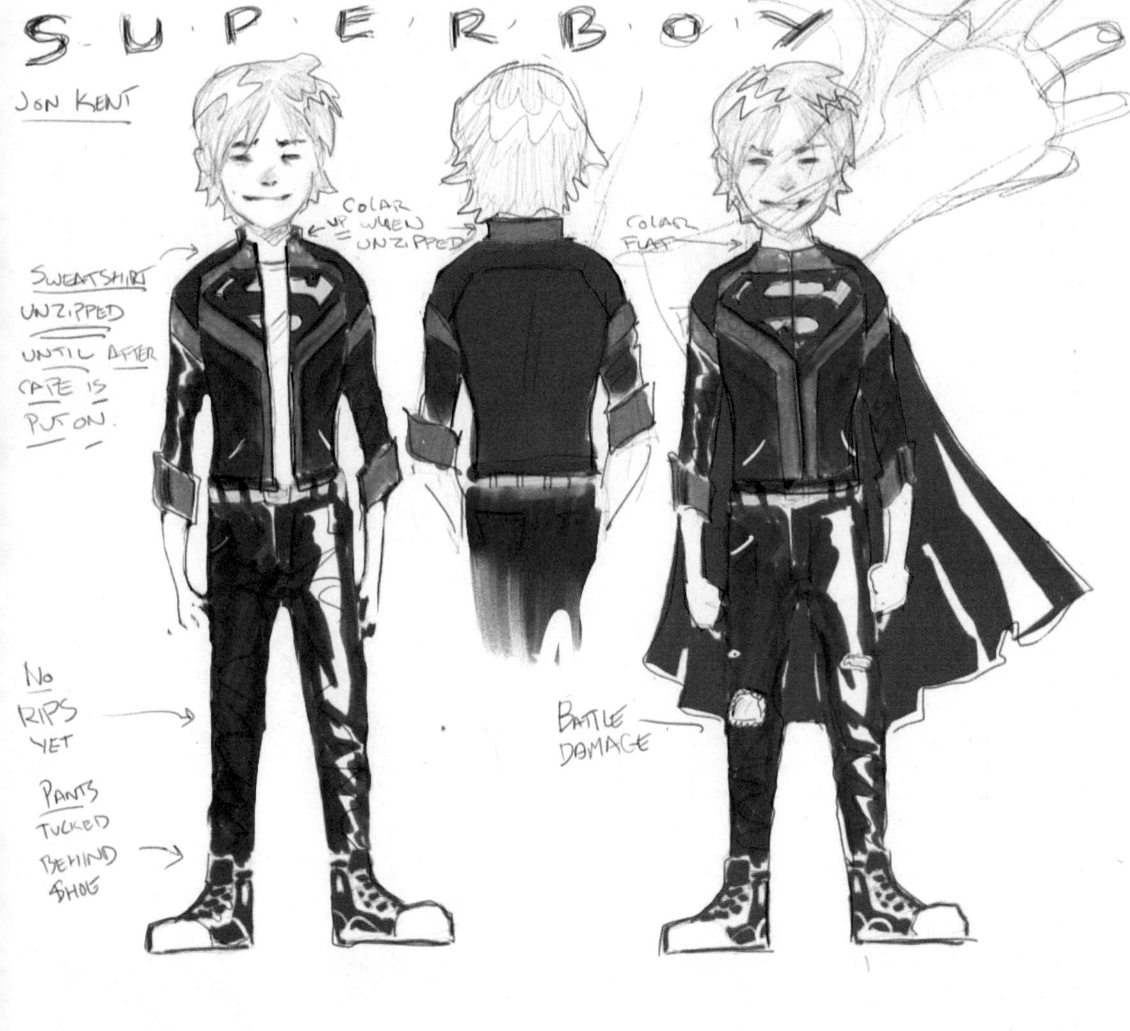
SUPERBOY
JON KENT
COLAR UP WHEN UNZIPPED
COLAR FLAT
SWEATSHIRT UNZIPPED UNTIL AFTER CAPE IS PUT ON.
NO RIPS YET
PANTS TUCKED BEHIND SHOE
BATTLE DAMAGE

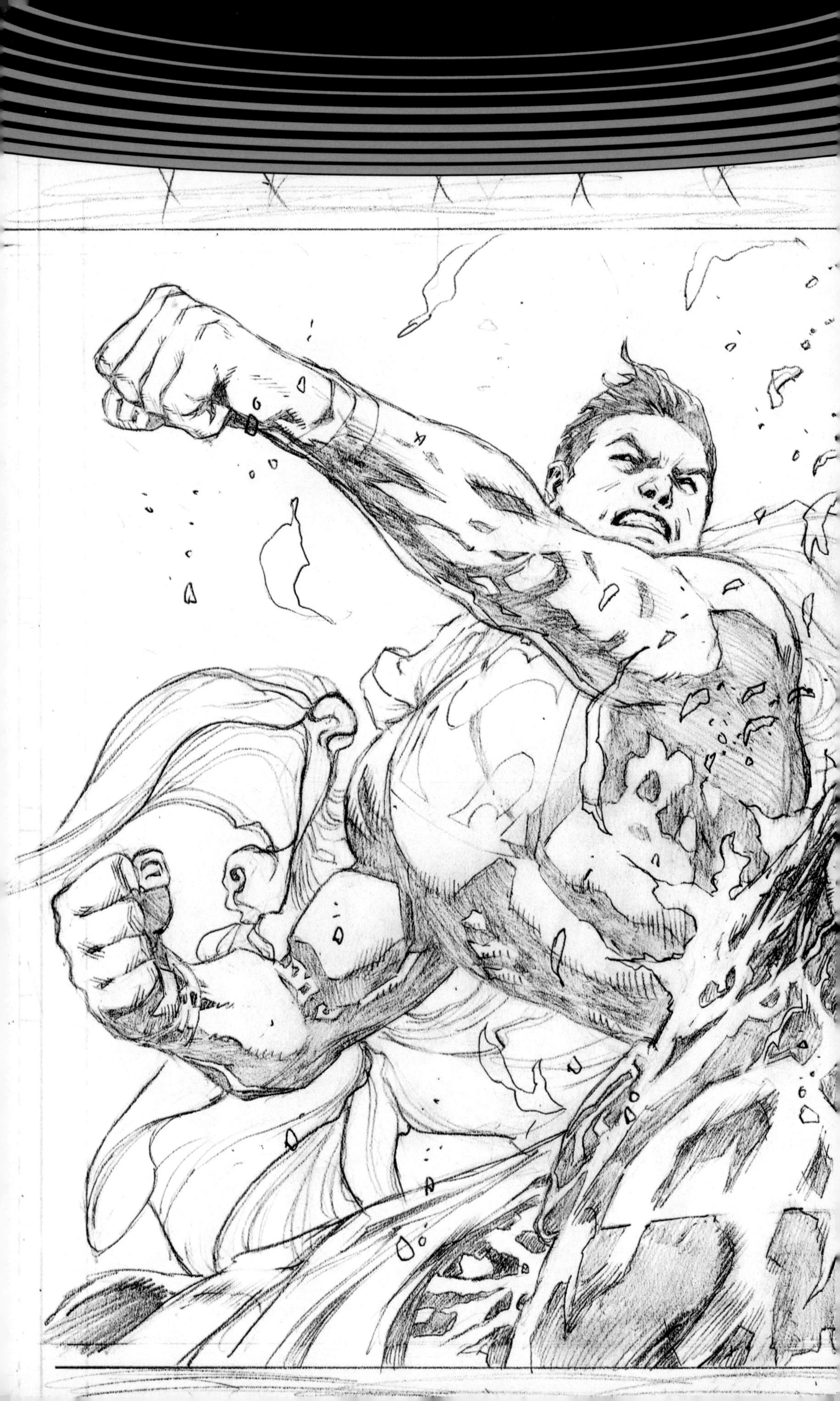

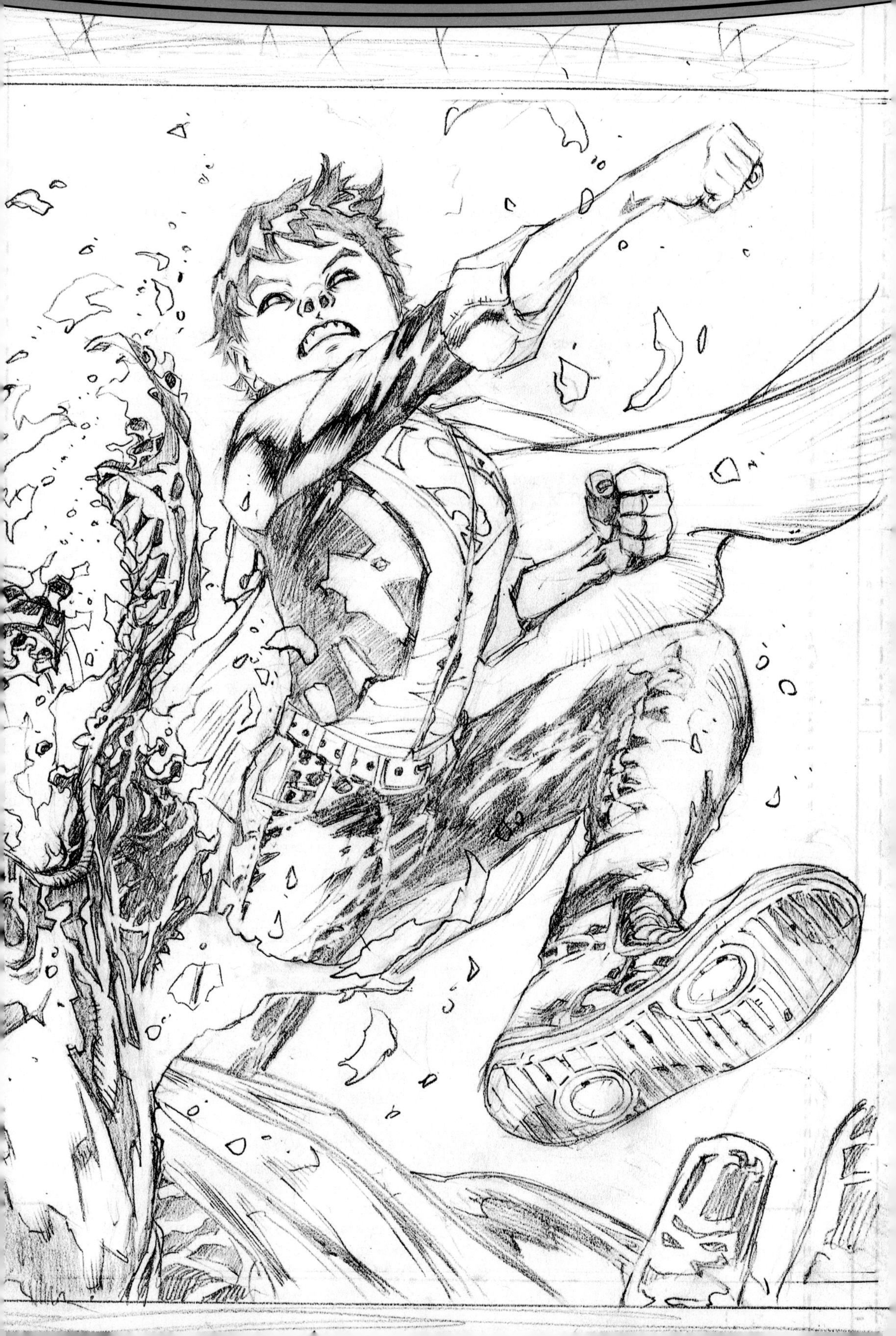

PAGE 13

panel 1

Angle on Lois escorting Kathy in as Jon closes the door not looking too thrilled about this surprise little visit. Clark is giving a wave from the table.

LOIS: Please, come in. My name's Lois, you met our tongue-tied son, Jonathan...and this is my husband, Clark.

CLARK: Hey there. And who do we have the pleasure?

KATHY: I'm Kathy Branden, my granddad bought the dairy farm across from you guys a few weeks ago.

panel 2

Angle on Kathy handing over the basket with the milk bottles to Lois as Jon gets that embarrassed young boy tone with his mother.

KATHY: He apologizes for not coming over, said he's got a lot to do to get things up and running but he wanted you to have these...

LOIS: We should have been the ones welcoming our new neighbors to the area. Please give him our thanks for the milk, this is just what a growing boy needs.

JON: Mom.

panel 3

Angle on Lois putting the milk in the fridge as Jon stands there uncomfortably looking at Kathy as Clark subtly watches as he eats.

LOIS: Oh, Kathy, on your way over did you catch sight of a goldish yellow cat prancing around and causing trouble?

panel 4

Angle on Kathy and Jon staring at each other. He's tense, ready for her to blurt out the whole thing with the Cat.

panel 5

Angle on Kathy as she starts to head for the door.

KATHY: No, but I could leave a saucer of my granddad's milk that may do the trick.

LOIS: We were hoping you could stay for dessert.

KATHY: Another time would be great -- lot of chores before bed.

panel 6

Lois and Jon are at door watching Kathy jog off into the night, Clark is still seated.

KATHY: Goodnight.

LOIS/CLARK: Night.

JON: Um, yeah, see ya.

PAGE 14

panel 1

Angle on them all now seated back at the table as they continue eating.

LOIS: Now that Kathy is one well-spoken young girl.

LOIS: You didn't say a word to her, Jonathan.

CLARK: He said four: Um, yeah, see, and ya.

panel 2

Angle on them eating now. Clark and Lois are relaxed, Jon is back to focusing on his food, but there's an emotional buildup evident on his face.

CLARK: Well, looks like two families have now made Branchbend, Minnesota their home.

LOIS: It'll be nice to have a neighbor someone your age, too, Jon.

panel 3

Angle on Jon as he looks at his parents, his emotion over the power discharge starting to get the best of him. Lois and Clark seem taken aback by this.

JON: What's so nice about it, huh? Everything we do is one big secret.

JON: I can't tell them who we really are, right -- that my mom writes books under a secret name and my dad is secretly a superhero and that I'm secretly half human and half Kryptonian?!?

panel 4

Angle on Lois and Clark, remaining calm but obviously upset at their son's words.

LOIS: We've been over all the reasons we have to do this, Jon, mainly to protect you.

CLARK: I thought we were clear about all the good we're able to do for this world and us as a family by maintaining our secret identities.

panel 5

Jon now standing, loses it. Lois and Clark are really taken aback by his sudden outburst.

JON: Don't use me as an excuse to be a buncha liars!

panel 6

Angle on Clark and Lois, emotional, as Clark points at Jon like all our dad's have.

CLARK: If you can't have a calm discussion, go upstairs to your room now!

panel 7 (OPTIONAL)

Angle with Lois and Clark in the foreground looking at each other with that "what was that?" parental stare as we see Jon in background with his back to us as he runs down the hall presumably to the stairs.

SILENT

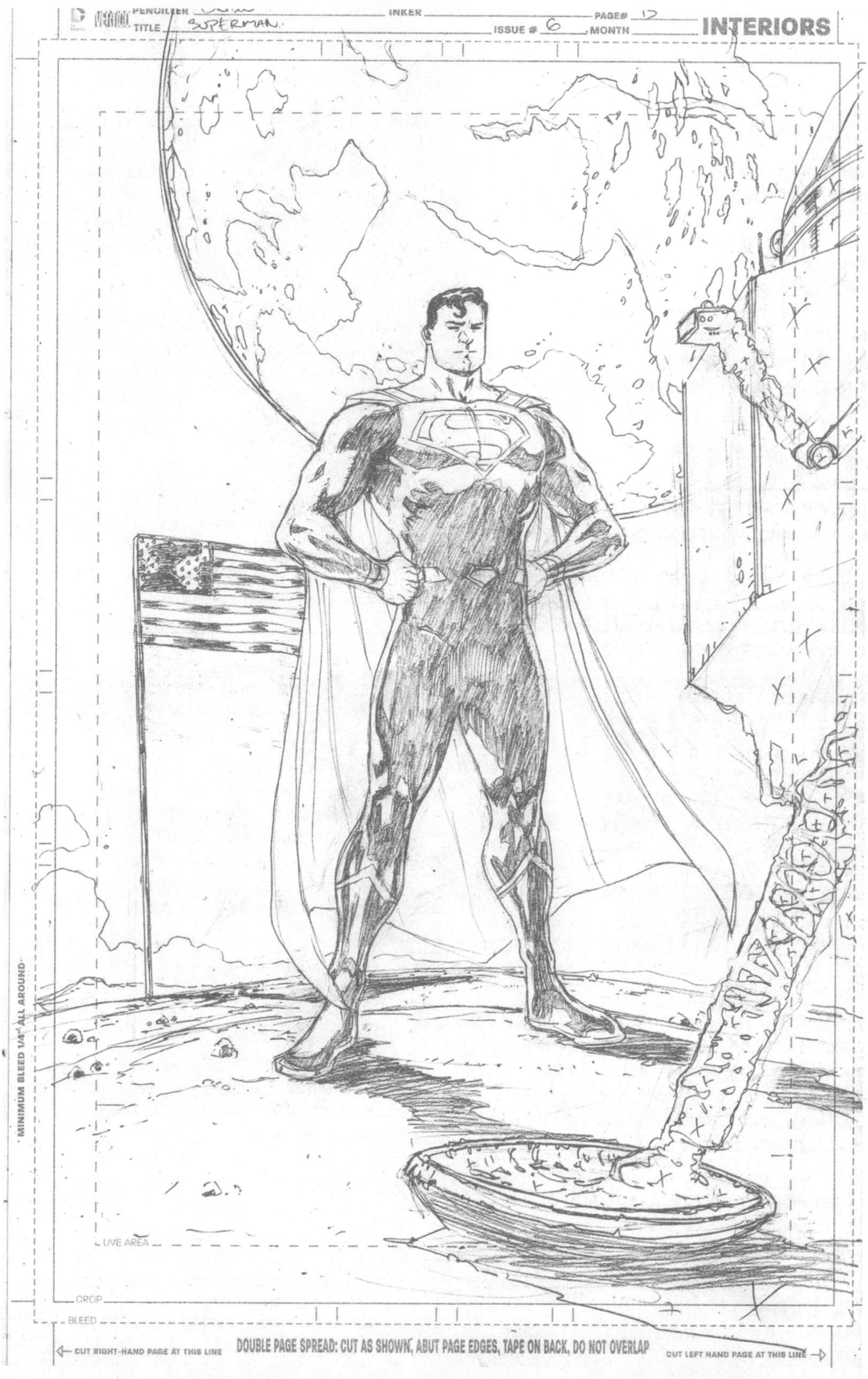

PENCILLER
INKER
PAGE# 12
INTERIORS
TITLE SUPERMAN
ISSUE # 6
MONTH
LIVE AREA
CROP
BLEED
MINIMUM BLEED 1/4" ALL AROUND
CUT RIGHT-HAND PAGE AT THIS LINE
DOUBLE PAGE SPREAD: CUT AS SHOWN, ABUT PAGE EDGES, TAPE ON BACK, DO NOT OVERLAP
CUT LEFT HAND PAGE AT THIS LINE

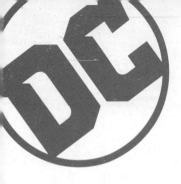

"Some really thrilling artwork that establishes incredible scope and danger."
–IGN

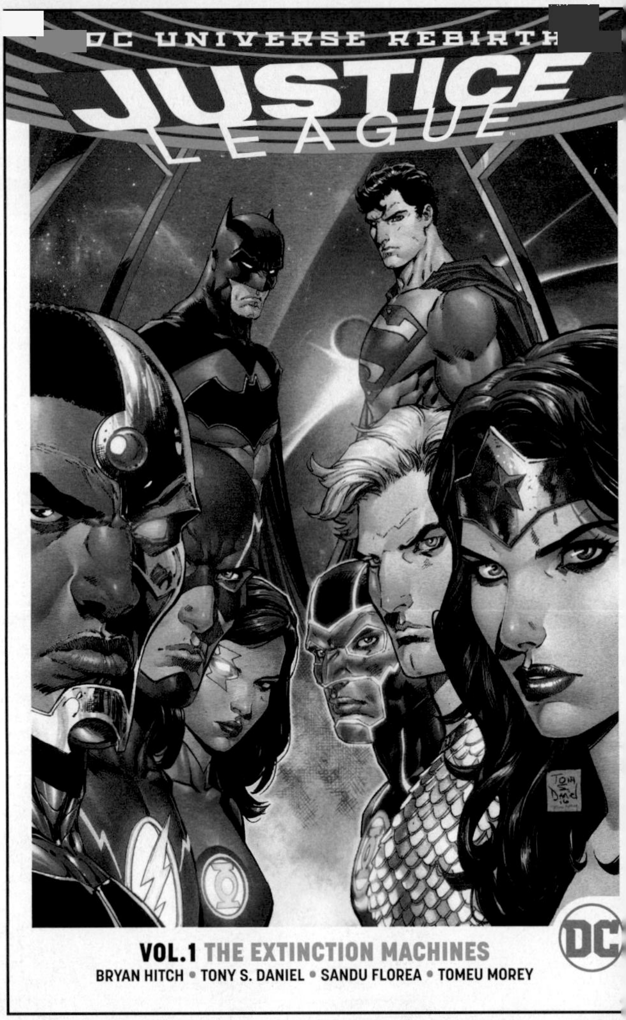
DC UNIVERSE REBIRTH
JUSTICE LEAGUE
VOL.1 THE EXTINCTION MACHINES
BRYAN HITCH • TONY S. DANIEL • SANDU FLOREA • TOMEU MOREY

DC UNIVERSE: REBIRTH

JUSTICE LEAGUE

VOL 1: The Extinction Machines

BRYAN HITCH
with TONY S. DANIEL

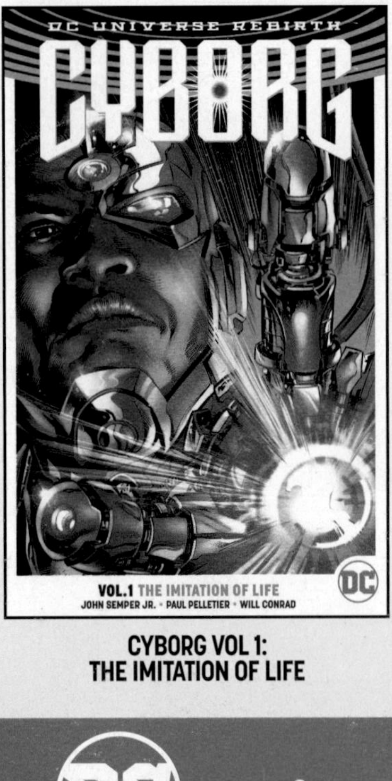
DC UNIVERSE REBIRTH
CYBORG
VOL.1 THE IMITATION OF LIFE
JOHN SEMPER JR. • PAUL PELLETIER • WILL CONRAD

CYBORG VOL 1: THE IMITATION OF LIFE

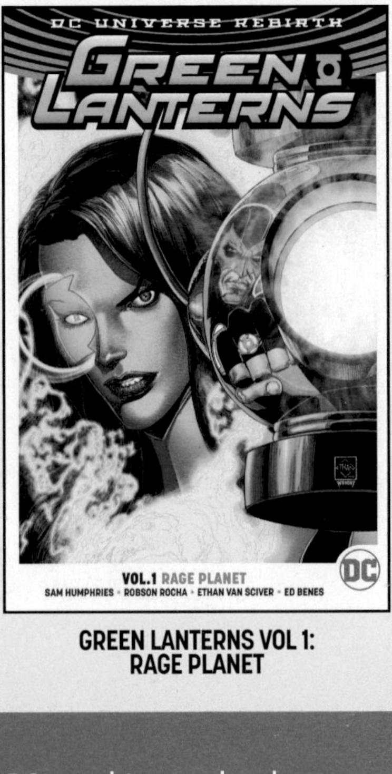
DC UNIVERSE REBIRTH
GREEN LANTERNS
VOL.1 RAGE PLANET
SAM HUMPHRIES • ROBSON ROCHA • ETHAN VAN SCIVER • ED BENES

GREEN LANTERNS VOL 1: RAGE PLANET

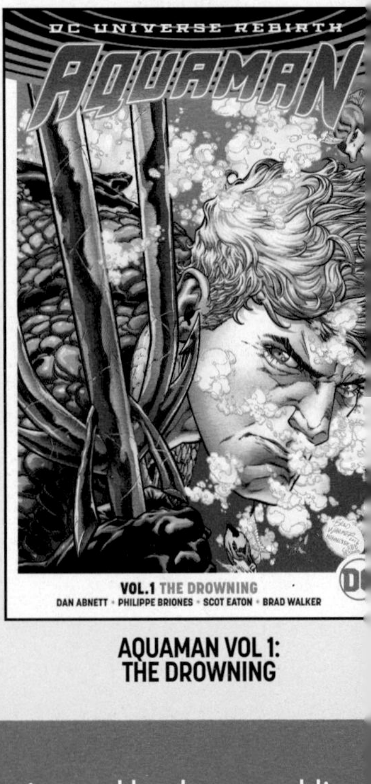
DC UNIVERSE REBIRTH
AQUAMAN
VOL.1 THE DROWNING
DAN ABNETT • PHILIPPE BRIONES • SCOT EATON • BRAD WALKER

AQUAMAN VOL 1: THE DROWNING

Get more DC graphic novels wherever comics and books are sold!